WEALTH
WITHOUT
RISK

How to Develop a Personal Fortune
Without Going out on a Limb

CHARLES J. GIVENS

SIMON AND SCHUSTER
New York London Toronto Sydney Tokyo

Simon and Schuster
Simon & Schuster Building
Rockefeller Center
1230 Avenue of the Americas
New York, New York 10020

SIMON AND SCHUSTER and colophon are registered trademarks of
Simon & Schuster Inc.

Designed by Irving Perkins Associates
Manufactured in the United States of America

12

Library of Congress Cataloging-in-Publication Data
Givens, Charles J.
Wealth without risk: how to develop a personal fortune without going out
on a limb / Charles J. Givens.
p.   cm.
1. Finance, Personal.   2. Investments.   I. Title.
HG179.G58   1988   88-23056
332.024—dc19   CIP
ISBN 0-671-61938-1

ACKNOWLEDGMENTS

This book was written on six continents including Antarctica. Adena, my fiancée, was always there with encouragement and patience.

Countless hours of typesetting and research over the two and one half years to completion were spent by Susan Mudgett, Veronica Byrd, Lisa Philpott, and Beth Webley.

Buddy and Jo Hewell, ATAP Financial Services, consultants to my organization, are responsible for the in-depth comparison studies of the annuities and life insurance rates. Buddy has also become the foremost authority on retirement plans and the new tax laws and his knowledge is reflected in Chapter 12.

Special thanks go to Fred Hills of Simon and Schuster for his initial recognition of the importance of this material and his patience while it was being organized.

To
Chuck and
Rob,
my sons,
and
Adena
My greatest supporters

CONTENTS

You will see all the elements of our se-
crets. The conclusion will be yours to
draw. We can help you learn it, but not to
accept it.

The sight, the knowledge, and the accep-
tance must be yours.

Ayn Rand,
Atlas Shrugged

Preface

MY STORY

Charles J. Givens

While I was still a young man my father died. Even after owning his own business for 15 years, he died absolutely broke. There wasn't even enough money to pay his own funeral expenses. I will never forget wondering how, in a great country like America, anyone could work so hard an entire lifetime and end up with nothing. With half-formed tears I promised myself that that would never happen to me. No matter how long or hard I had to search, how many books I had to read or how many people I had to ask, I was determined to find the answers. I wanted to be rich and nothing was about to stop me.

What I learned about money over the next fifteen years enabled me to build my personal and business fortune. The determination and single-mindedness paid off. If you read the financial articles in *USA Today*, *Newsweek*, *The Wall Street Journal*, *Success*, *Money*, or *Venture Magazine* you know the story. I feel fortunate to have been able to share my strategies through the great talk show hosts like Oprah Winfrey, Bryant Gumbel, Phil Donahue, Sally Jessy Raphael and Geraldo Rivera.

I have found that there is no downside to having a lot of money. Money is freedom and freedom is the ability to do whatever you want when you want to do it.

The path I followed in building my wealth was certainly not the easiest. Every possible mistake was made for one reason—no one was around to show me how.

At age 25, I was a millionaire for the first time through the creation of a Nashville music business conglomerate, Colony International. At 26, I was broke. No one had ever told me that I, and not my insurance agent, was responsible for being certain that I had enough of the right kind of insurance. My recording studio and office building burned to the ground and I never collected a dime.

During the next three years I moved from the bottom to the executive suites of Genesco, a major apparel conglomerate, by designing management computer systems in an era when computers were new and computer professionals almost nonexistent. The job gave me the leverage to use borrowed money to finance my way into almost a million dollars of stock market wealth. New companies, new issues, and new profits to borrow against. Then in 1968 the market turned. No one had ever told me that stocks can go down. Instead of continuing to follow my own instincts and common sense which had created the paper fortune, my emotions led me to a vested, fast-talking, stockbroker. "Here. You watch my money," I said, almost relieved. He must still be watching it because I never saw another cent. I traded my Cadillac for a mortgaged Volkswagen, sold my house to pay off the margin calls, left Corporate America and Nashville with a bankroll of $200 in my pocket.

My third fortune was made and lost through the creation of a luxurious yacht club. Cashing in a $3,000 insurance policy, I put a 60-day option on a million dollar estate previously owned by a Pittsburgh steel magnate on the banks of the Indian River in Florida. With no extra money and no income, the next few months were financed by a wallet full of credit cards.

The $50,000 required to close on the property was obtained only at the last possible minute. Everything seemed to be working. Plans to convert the estate to a yacht club were drawn up, and soon the club would be finished. No one, however, had pointed out that it was probably better to complete the docks before the club. The governor of the state of Florida signed a bill prohibiting dredging in the river until a five-year ecological study was finished. No docks—no boats; no boats —no yacht club. The trustee for the project neglected to make a mortgage payment and the third mortgage holder foreclosed. The balance sheet showed my net worth had jumped from the minus columns to $1,000,000 in one year. It was gone in one day. Three times in eight years I had created a million dollar fortune in less than 18 months starting with nothing. I knew how to make money, I just didn't seem to be able to keep it.

Beginning in 1971, through a combination of leveraged business and real estate investments, I managed to build and keep the fortune I now enjoy. In 1986, *Success Magazine* for the first time chose the 20 living Americans who they felt had started with the least chance, made the biggest mistakes along the way, and built the biggest fortunes. I felt very honored to be one of those 20. Why is that important to you? Because when it comes to money, yours or mine, I know what I'm talking about. If I tell you a strategy will work, you can bank on it. You can use these strategies to open financial doors never before available to you, to compress the time it takes to build your dreams. Most importantly, enjoy every moment of the journey as I have learned to do. That's what separates the real winners from the losers.

This book is simply a composite of the money strategies I have discovered over a lifetime of financial experience. You will find them both easy to understand and easy to apply.

Making financial decisions is like standing in a room full of doors, knowing that behind one is the financial reward you seek but behind the others are financial perils you seek to avoid. Without additional knowledge your alternatives are not appealing. Through trial and error you may make a choice detrimental to your wealth or you could refuse to choose at all as most do, letting fear create financial stagnation. An unseen third alternative is the one you have chosen through this book —making your financial decisions by knowing in advance what lies beyond each door, a form of X-ray vision that will connect predictable financial results to your choices. You cannot fail in a plan that allows you to choose results instead of only the processes or paths to be followed. That, my friend, is the power you now hold in your hand.

Without knowledge, personal and business financial decisions are made using an ounce of logic peppered with a pound of emotion. Money does not behave according to the rules of common sense. Instead, wealth building has its own set of principles—principles that work, work all the time and work for anyone. These principles, or money strategies, add to your wealth, compress time, and endow you with what most refer to as the Midas Touch.

I feel fortunate to have the financial success coupled with good people to run my businesses so that I can afford to devote most of my time to teaching my strategies. It was for that purpose that I created my nonprofit educational foundation in 1975. Today, it has grown into the Charles J. Givens Organization, with 150,000 members—families who depend on us for all their financial help and advice. It was only for that purpose that I have written this book. My money strategies are safe, practical, and they can be applied to every aspect of your financial life. Better yet, you don't have to be a financial wizard to put them to work for you.

To Your Success

Charles J. Givens

Part I

PERSONAL

FINANCE

STRATEGIES

Chapter 1

DEVELOPING YOUR FINANCIAL BLUEPRINT

I expect to spend the rest of my life in the future, so I want to be reasonably sure what kind of future it is going to be. That is my reason for planning.

Charles Kettering
Industrialist
1950

Objective: Turn dreams into realities.

There are three strategies we were never taught in school:

- How to run a successful marriage
- How to raise successful children
- How to build wealth successfully

The purpose of this book is to show you how to overcome the third of these educational gaps—how to build your wealth quickly and easily by making your financial decisions correctly and with confidence.

Everyone with self-earned wealth will tell you that money is not complicated. The confusing trade terms, buzz words, and complex explanations that are thrown around by investment counselors and financial people are not necessary. They just muddy the waters, and sometimes hide the fact that the so-called experts don't really know what they're talking about.

In the course of my life, I have discovered a success principle that

21

has enabled me to accumulate tens of millions of dollars while maintaining a constant state of happiness, emotional balance, and zest for life.

Strategy #1

ACHIEVE SUCCESS IN ANY AREA OF LIFE BY IDENTIFYING THE OPTIMUM STRATEGIES AND REPEATING THEM UNTIL THEY BECOME HABITS

Success with money, family, relatonships, health, and careers is the ability to reach your personal objectives in the shortest time, with the least effort and with the fewest mistakes. The goals you set for yourself and the strategies you choose become your blueprint or plan.

Strategies are like recipes: choose the right ingredients, mix them in the correct proportions, and you'll always produce the same predictable result: in this case, financial success. The success strategies for managing money and building wealth are called Money Strategies.

By learning to use Money Strategies as a part of your day-to-day life, financial frustration and failure will become a thing of the past. Why then, do so many people find it so difficult to accumulate wealth and, more importantly, to enjoy the journey? There are two reasons: not being clear about what they are after and not knowing the strategies for achieving it.

The starting point in any plan is where you are right now. Where you are is where you are. Your first objective is to accept yourself and your current status as an O.K. place to be without making excuses as to why you don't know more or aren't doing better. Excuses become the limiters that turn realistic dreams into idle wishes. Lack of action and the lack of a willingness to change are almost the only things in life that create frustration and depression.

When it comes to excuses for not taking financial control, I hear them again and again:

"I can't even balance my checkbook."   "I'm too young."

"I'm too old."   "I'm too tired."

"I'm too broke."   "I'm too dumb about money."

"I can't get my husband (or wife) to   "I'm too busy."

listen."   "I'm too scared."

"I don't want much."

Excuses do not produce results. You can find unlimited excuses for failure but no one ever makes an excuse for success.

Now figure out where you want to be—your goals in life—and write them down. Your written plan sets the tone, speed, and most importantly the direction for your life. If you've ever attended a rousing motivational lecture, you were probably struck by the spirit, humor, and drive, but walked out of the room thinking, "Now, what the hell am I supposed to do?" Enthusiasm, but NO DIRECTION.

Direction can turn the power of a light bulb into a laser beam. Lasers are nothing more than sharply focused light. Lasers have the power to cut through steel and destroy missiles in space. Same light as the light bulb—just focused and directed. Clearly establishing objectives and choosing your direction will turn the power of your mind into the laser beam it was meant to be, drawing to you the opportunities, people, knowledge you will need, allowing you to cut through the obstacles along your success path.

Power to accomplish also lies in knowing how to compress time—to do in one year what it takes everyone else ten years to accomplish. The strategies in this book are powerful time compressors.

Success also requires an understanding and use of the Momentum Principle.

Strategy #2

SUCCESS REQUIRES FIRST EXPENDING TEN UNITS OF EFFORT TO PRODUCE ONE UNIT OF RESULTS. YOUR MOMENTUM WILL THEN PRODUCE TEN UNITS OF RESULTS WITH EACH UNIT OF EFFORT.

Direction and control begin with a written plan spelled out in two parts. Part A lists "dreams"—what you are after both financially and personally. Part B lists your "strategies"—the specific financial and personal road map that will take you from where you are to where you want to be. By clearly defining your direction, and by adopting the correct money and attitude strategies for control, you will automatically establish the shortest possible route.

When I was 18, I sat down with a pad of paper and, without totally realizing what I was doing, wrote an action blueprint for my life. I called it my dreams list. The exercise will do the same for you, clearly defining at one time and in one place your goals, dreams, objectives, and even your fantasies. Choose a totally quiet spot where you will not be interrupted. At the top of the pad of paper write the following:

DREAMS LIST

If I had unlimited . . .

TIME
TALENT
MONEY
ABILITY
SELF-CONFIDENCE
SUPPORT FROM FAMILY

Here's what I'd do . . .

Relax and let the ideas pour from both your conscious and subconscious. Don't evaluate your potential for achieving each item you write. What you will write will excite you, motivate you, inspire you, make you laugh, and most of all, define desires and dreams that all too often are ready to surface but are held back by the complexities of daily living. Write it all down no matter how silly it seems, no matter what it costs. The ideas will come slowly at first, gaining speed as you leave behind the realities and limits in your life.

My first list was 181 dreams long, of which 170 have already become reality. Since that time I've added dozens of others, as you will probably find yourself doing.

All of us at any age have dreams, and the first step of turning dreams into reality is to get those dreams out in front of you where you can see and feel them.

Having taught my students this dreams list strategy for over 12 years, I have seen some truly wonderful things happen that might never have occurred otherwise.

A 66-year-old Ph.D. spent his birthday hang gliding with me off the huge sand dunes at Kitty Hawk, North Carolina.

A 14-year-old boy started his own successful business.

A 45-year-old, recently separated housewife with no previous sense of adventure, rappelled straight down a 200-foot cliff, then rode a zip line 60 feet in the air, 300 yards across a valley at 40 miles per hour hanging from only wrist straps, resulting in more self-confidence in two days than she had achieved in her entire lifetime.

Through the dreams list strategy a 35-year-old mother swam and played with dolphins at Kings Dominion Park in Virginia, a dream she had had since she was a child.

A 28-year-old European immigrant, who barely spoke English, built a $5,000,000 fortune in five years starting with a $6.00 an hour job. I will never forget the tears of joy in his eyes as he sat in my office in Orlando telling me the story of his success and the part my strategies had played in his life.

Once you have made your list with no limits, choose those objectives which are the most important to you. Some will be individual objectives, others will include and require the support of your family. Encourage your spouse and children, if you have them, to create their own lists.

After you define your dreams, the things you want to do, places you want to go, what you want to be and accomplish, the next logical step is to build your roadmap—your strategies list. The rest of the chapters will show you all of the safe alternatives for creating the wealth to live out your dreams.

Chapter 2

BECOMING YOUR OWN FINANCIAL EXPERT

The easiest job I have ever tackled is that of making money.
It is, in fact, almost as easy as losing it.

H. L. Mencken
Writer
1922

Objective: Take control of your financial future.

The two most important words in managing money and building wealth are "take control." No one will ever watch your money or your financial future as well as you—no broker, financial planner, or insurance agent. Control begins with your written plan and is exercised through your choice of money strategies. The correct strategies turn wealth building, like walking, into a series of small, easy-to-accomplish steps.

Unless you were fortunate enough to be left a million dollars by a rich uncle, you must begin by learning to transform your income into wealth. There are only three types of money strategies needed to transform income into wealth, but you must use all three—none is optional. Omitting any one from your plan would have the same effect as removing a leg from a three-legged stool.

PERSONAL FINANCE STRATEGIES

Personal Finance Strategies are those day-to-day personal and family decisions you make unrelated to your job, taxes, or investments. Personal Finance Strategies enable you to save money as you spend it. The objective of Personal Finance Strategies is to increase your

26

spendable income each year by thousands by getting rid of financial waste.

Personal Finance Strategies will:

A. Cut the cost of your life insurance by 80%.
B. Cut your automobile, mortgage, and homeowners insurance premiums by 50%.
C. Reduce your lifetime mortgage payments by 50%.
D. Cut your MasterCard and VISA interest 40%.
E. Turn your home equity or insurance policy cash values into income or wealth.
F. Restore your credit in 60 days.
G. Get your kids through college free.

TAX-REDUCING STRATEGIES

Income taxes are the biggest expense you'll encounter in life, bigger than the mortgage on your home or the cost of getting your kids through college. You can never build any real wealth without first getting your tax life under control.

One third of all the wealth you will or won't accumulate is dependent on whether you have a good tax plan. My experience in working with over 100,000 families during the past 14 years indicates most families are paying twice as much in income taxes as necessary. Why? Lack of a good tax-reducing plan. Your objective is to pay no more than 5% of your income in taxes.

The biggest taxpayer in American history was Elvis Presley. I remember from my days in the Nashville music business how Elvis prided himself on the massive amount of taxes he paid. He had no tax plan, no tax shelters, and got little or no tax advice. He was also in a unique position. He couldn't outspend his income; money literally came in faster than he could get rid of it. After the excessive income and estate taxes were paid, and because of pitiful planning, Elvis's estate was incredibly small, the government got it all.

You, on the other hand, are probably having no difficulty in outspending your income and, if so, a good tax plan will begin to plug the dike. Every dollar you save in taxes is one dollar added to your tax-free wealth. Under the new tax laws, $1,000 of additional tax deductions will save you approximately $300 in taxes.

There are two steps in reducing your taxes:

A. Make money you spend tax deductible as you spend it.

There are 75 strategies that will turn your personal expenses into tax deductions; you can make your vacation, education, automobile, videotape recorder, money you give to children, club memberships, interest on loans and entertainment tax deductible. A good tax plan will make up to 60% of your income deductible as you spend it.

B. Use the power of retirement plans and investment tax shelters.

Tax-free compounding is one secret to financial success. Retirement plans and tax shelters give you the power of tax-free compounding.

POWERFUL INVESTMENT STRATEGIES

Investing money and saving money are not at all the same strategies. Savers are those that earn less than 10% per year and do little more than make financial institutions wealthy. Successful investing, on the other hand, requires knowledge and not risk to accomplish the following three-pronged objective: to earn 20% per year safely, with no commissions, and no taxes.

How can you safely earn 20% a year in a world that expects only 7% from banks and bonds? By using any of what I consider the ten best investment opportunities in America—those that you won't find advertised in the financial pages or sold through brokers and financial partners. All are uncovered in Part III, Powerful Investment Strategies:

1. Asset Management Accounts.	Chapter 22
2. No-Load Mutual Fund Families.	Chapter 24*
3. Mutual Fund Margin Accounts.	Chapter 25
4. Self-Directed IRA and Keogh Accounts.	Chapters 12* and 26*
5. 401(k) and 403(b) Employer Retirement Plans.	Chapter 12*
6. Tax-sheltered Mutual Funds—Self-Directed Annuities.	Chapter 27*
7. Discounted Mortgages.	Chapter 28
8. Tax Lien Certificates and Liened Property Sales.	Chapter 29
9. Reinvested Home Equity.	Chapter 6
10. Your Own Home.	Chapter 6

* Requires use of the *Money Movement Strategy* (Chapter 23)

Paying unnecessary fees and commissions on your investments is like throwing $20 bills into the fireplace to heat your home. You'll get the job done but the method is extremely ineffective. You cannot be splitting your money with everyone else and expect to have much left for yourself. By learning to work directly with financial institutions, you can eliminate the middleman, the commissioned salesman, and keep 100% of your money working for you. On October 19, 1987, the stock market and most investors' stock portfolios dropped by 20%. The one-day drop shocked the world and crowded other news items from the headlines. Yet every day millions of investors turn over billions of dollars to investment salesmen, and experience a one-day drop in their investment capital of 8%. Although no headlines are made, paying commissions is the same kind of investment loss.

To start your Wealth Without Risk program you need only income. It doesn't matter whether you have $1.00 or $100,000 in your investment plan. Making big money does not take big money, only knowledge and a little time.

It might surprise you to know that the average couple in America earns $35,000 per year and lives paycheck-to-paycheck with little hope of breaking the cycle. Here is a chart that shows you where the money goes.

WHERE THE MONEY GOES*

(Average Family Income $35,000)

Household Expenses

Food	3,000	
Clothes	600	
Utilities	1,800	
Household	2,500	**Household**
Car	400	**$9,000**
Gifts	500	
Pets	200	
	9,000	

* From USA Today study and Charles J. Givens Organization Study

Insurance

Car	1,000	
Life	1,000	
Children	300	
Health	600	**Insurance**
Disability	300	**$4,200**
Credit Life	250	
Mortgage	500	
Homeowners	250	
	4,200	

Taxes

Federal	3,000	
State Income	1,000	**Taxes**
Social Security	2,500	**$6,500**
	6,500	

Payments

Mortgage	8,000	
Car Loan	3,600	**Payments**
Credit Cards	1,200	**$13,800**
Personal Loans	1,000	
	13,800	

For Self

Fun	500	**Self**
Vacation	1,000	**$1,500**
	1,500	

No Savings
No IRA
No Investments

TOTAL
$35,000

Now here is a chart showing where the money goes before and *after* Money Strategies are used.

USING THE CHARLES J. GIVENS
PERSONAL FINANCE AND TAX STRATEGIES

Family Income—$35,000

	Before	After	Difference
Insurance	$4,200	$1,120	$3,080
Taxes	$6,500	$3,900	$2,600
Credit Cards	$1,200	$ 700	$ 500
TOTAL	$11,900	$5,720	$6,180

New money for investments, fun, vacations:
$6,180

After applying just the Personal Finance and Tax Strategies the couple now has $6,180 extra tax-free dollars to spend and invest—each year. Same income, but a new lifestyle and outlook for the future. You will save thousands each year in all of these areas by using the Personal Finance and Tax Strategies. Coupled with powerful investment strategies, you will automatically and systematically achieve your objective: Wealth Without Risk.

Chapter 3

CASUALTY INSURANCE— CUTTING YOUR PREMIUMS 50%

"By promoting insurance on the basis of what people think about uncertainty, instead of what they would be correct in thinking, by exploiting the fallacy that one buys insurance to collect for a loss instead of showing that the purpose of insurance is to avoid uncertainty, we have invited a plague of problems upon the insurance industry."

Henry K. Duke
Letter to *Harvard Business Review*
1955

Objective: Save 50% of your premiums on automobile, homeowners, mortgage, disability, liability, and rental car insurance.

Casualty insurance covers most everything life insurance doesn't cover. There are a dozen types of casualty insurance policies and coverages salesmen will try to sell you. Half no one needs yet everyone buys, the other half, everyone needs but few know how to buy. This chapter will clear up the mystery of what you need, what to avoid, and how to save thousands of dollars per year in the process. Have your current automobile, homeowners and other policies in front of you and make notes on the items you wish to change as you learn the correct strategies.

AUTOMOBILE INSURANCE

Auto insurance laws were enacted to protect innocent victims of accidents from serious financial loss. Most states require that registered car owners have insurance. Automobile insurance is one of your biggest expenses, yet you'll find you can cut your premiums 30% to 50% with these strategies. There are eight different automobile coverages you must understand: Bodily injury liability, Property damage liability, Umbrella liability, Comprehensive, Collision, Medical payments, No-fault insurance, and Uninsured motorists coverage.

LIABILITY INSURANCE

The liability portion of your policy covers your legal liability for damage you do to other people or their property. There are three types of liability coverage available on your policy.

Bodily Injury Liability

Covers injury to people in other cars, pedestrians, and passengers in the policyholder's car. The policyholder and family members are also covered while driving someone else's car, including rental cars. Bodily injury liability covers legal defense and any damages up to the limits stated in the policy, whether determined by negotiation or a jury. There are two limits you choose on a policy; the maximum the insurance company will pay each person injured and the maximum the company will pay per accident. Most states require that you carry at least $10,000/$20,000 limits, meaning $10,000 per person and $20,000 per accident.

Strategy #3

CARRY ENOUGH BODILY INJURY LIABILITY INSURANCE TO COVER YOUR NET ASSETS PLUS ALL POTENTIAL LEGAL FEES.

How much liability protection should you carry? Enough per person to cover the net value of your assets, plus an extra one third for attorney's fees. If you rent your home and are living paycheck-to-paycheck with few assets, the minimum protection is probably enough. If you have $100,000 equity in your home, $50,000 of personal assets and money in retirement plans, you will want to carry $250,000/$500,000, or even up to $1,000,000. (See Umbrella Liability Insurance—Strategy #5)

Property Damage Liability

Property damage liability covers damage to someone else's car or property caused by the policyholder's car. Family members and others driving with permission are also covered. Limits should be at least $50,000 because of the current high cost of automobiles and the possibility of multiple car damage. The limit applies per accident.

Strategy #4
CARRY A MINIMUM OF $50,000 PROPERTY DAMAGE LIABILITY COVERAGE, OR A MAXIMUM OF $100,000.

Umbrella Liability

Most everyone these days is concerned about personal liability and the possibility of being sued rightly or wrongly. The more assets you accumulate the more important personal liability protection becomes. The two potential mistakes are being underinsured and overpaying for the liability insurance you do have.

Strategy #5
BUY $1,000,000 OF UMBRELLA LIABILITY COVERAGE FOR UNDER $150 PER YEAR.

Liability insurance is part of every automobile and homeowners policy. Instead of raising the limits on both automobile and homeowners policies and paying double premiums, you can buy an inexpensive supplemental umbrella liability policy that covers all personal liabilities. You can buy $1,000,000 of protection with an umbrella policy for only $100 to $150 per year covering the same potential liability losses included in both your homeowners and automobile policies. You must ask for umbrella liability insurance by name. Since the commissions are so small, your insurance agent may neglect to mention it.

Before selling you the umbrella liability supplement, most companies require you to:

1. Carry a minimum required limit on your homeowners and automobile policies, usually $100,000/$300,000.
2. Place both your automobile and homeowners policy with the company issuing the umbrella policy.

COMPREHENSIVE AND COLLISION INSURANCE

Comprehensive

Comprehensive insurance pays for losses due to theft, damage from fire, glass breakage, falling objects, explosions, etc. The deductible ranges from $50 to $500.

Collision

Collision insurance covers damage to your car in the event of a collision with another vehicle or object no matter who is at fault. Your insurance company will seek reimbursement from the other driver's insurer if you are not at fault, and then reimburse you for the deductible. Deductibles usually range from $100 to $1,000.

Strategy #6

WHEN VALUE OF YOUR CAR DROPS BELOW $1500 DROP THE COLLISION AND COMPREHENSIVE COVERAGE.

Remember, if your car is damaged, you can't collect more than the car is worth no matter how much in premiums you've been paying. When your car is older and not worth much, it no longer pays to carry comprehensive and collision coverage at all. Thieves don't tend to steal old cars; the penalty is no greater for stealing a new car. When you look at the amount of premiums you pay plus the high deductible, it doesn't make sense to carry comprehensive and collision insurance on older, less expensive cars.

Strategy #7

DROP DUPLICATE COVERAGES LIKE MEDICAL PAYMENTS, NO-FAULT (PIP) INSURANCE, AND UNINSURED MOTORISTS COVERAGE (UMC).

Medical Payments

Medical payments coverage pays for medical expenses caused by a car accident to your family members, or another person riding in your automobile. You and family members are already covered under your hospitalization policy, and others riding in your car are covered by the liability portion of your policy or by their own hospitalization policy. Typical premiums for this coverage are $40 per year for $5,000 of insurance. You cannot collect twice for the same medical expenses, so if you have hospitalization insurance, medical payments coverage is a complete waste of your money.

No-Fault Insurance (Personal Injury Protection)

No-fault insurance is based on state laws that are supposed to lower the cost of automobile insurance by allowing an injured party to collect without litigation. No-fault laws allow you to recover losses from your own insurance company even if someone else is at fault, but require you to give up your right to sue. These laws vary by state, but the common features include:

- reimbursement for medical expenses,
- reimbursement for lost income,
- compensation for death, permanent injury, or disfigurement, and
- reimbursement for property damage.

No-fault is more duplicate or unnecessary coverage, and should not be taken unless required by state law. Medical expenses are covered under your hospitalization plan, and property damage is covered under the collision portion of your policy.

Uninsured Motorists Coverage (UMC)

If you take the UMC, you and your family members are covered by your own insurance company for bodily injury caused by an uninsured motorist or hit-and-run driver. UMC also pays if your medical bills are in excess of the other driver's liability limits.

Notice that the liability portion of your insurance policy covers only injury you do to others; the uninsured motorists coverage is for injury others do to you. UMC is just a high-priced combination life insurance and hospitalization plan and thus is a complete waste of money. If you have other hospitalization and medical coverage, you cannot collect the medical benefits twice even though you paid both premiums.

Here is a section from a State Farm policy:

No Duplication of Benefits—no insured shall recover twice for the same expense or loss under this or similar vehicle insurance or self insurance.

STRATEGIES FOR INSURANCE DEDUCTIBLES

Strategy #8
RAISE THE DEDUCTIBLES ON YOUR AUTOMOBILE AND HOMEOWNERS POLICY TO $500 OR MORE.

The deductible is the amount you agree to pay before the insurance company has to kick in. Most policyholders opt for the lowest possible deductible—usually $100—on automobile comprehensive and collision coverage, and the same on homeowners' policies. Lower deductibles may make you feel good, but they do you no good. Each year, less than 10% of all automobiles and homes will be involved in accidents or losses, and only half of those policyholders will have to pay any deductible. Choose the deductible with which you feel most comfortable, $500 or even $1,000. As your assets and income increase, increase your deductibles accordingly. Increasing your auto insurance deductible to $500 will reduce your comprehensive and collision premiums as much as 30%. Increasing the deductible to $1,000 will cut those premiums up to 60%.

The following two strategies will show you why low deductibles don't make sense.

Strategy #9
NEVER FILE AN INSURANCE CLAIM FOR UNDER $500.

Smart policyholders don't file small claims. The insurance company will raise your premiums next year by as much as 25%, or worse yet, cancel the policy. Save your insurance claims only for the big losses.

Strategy #10
NEVER PAY OUT MORE IN PREMIUMS THAN YOU CAN COLLECT IN DAMAGES.

You pay so much extra for lower deductibles that, over the years, you could not collect in damages half of what you're paying in premiums. Lower deductibles waste dollars. Remember, insurance is not free. Collecting on a claim from an insurance company is not a gift. The insurance company's cost of processing even the smallest claim is over $400 just for the administrative expenses and paperwork, and these costs are added to the premiums you pay for lower deductibles.

Strategy #11
SUBSTITUTE A FREE CREDIT CARD FOR EXPENSIVE LOW INSURANCE DEDUCTIBLES.

For some the concern is, "What if I am responsible for a deductible or can't collect from the other driver, and don't have the extra money to fix my car?"

Your best "no cost" insurance is a no-annual-fee MasterCard or VISA which is never used for purposes other than emergencies or unusual one-time expenses. With a $1,000 to $2,000 limit, you have the cash available, but unlike premiums, the credit card costs you nothing unless you use it. (See Chapter 6 for credit cards with no yearly fees.)

HOW YOUR AUTOMOBILE INSURANCE PREMIUMS ARE DETERMINED

In addition to how much and what kind of coverage you choose, there are five factors relating to where you live, how you drive, and what kind of car you own that also affect the premiums you pay.

RATING TERRITORIES

Rates are higher in cities where population density and traffic congestion are higher, and lower in rural areas.

The company's accident experience in your area also determines your rates. Rates from company to company for the same city can vary as much as 100% because of different accident ratios for different companies.

DRIVER CLASSIFICATION

Includes age, sex, and marital status.

Those over 25, women, and married people have fewer accidents and the lowest rates. Males under 25 who are unmarried and the principal drivers of a car have the greatest chance of accidents and, therefore, the highest rates.

DRIVING RECORD

Those responsible for accidents or who have been convicted of driving violations tend to have a greater chance for future accidents, and therefore, pay higher premiums.

USE OF CAR

Those who drive to and from work have a greater chance for accidents than those who use a car for pleasure only. Premium categories are usually:

1. No commuting—Lowest premium
2. Less than ten miles to work—Higher premium
3. More than ten miles to work—Highest premium

TYPE OF CAR

Expensive cars cost more to repair and, therefore, cost more to insure. Using the damageability rating charts that follow, you can determine in advance whether the insurance premiums are worth the pleasure derived from driving certain types of cars.

Strategy #12
CHECK INSURANCE RATES ON AN AUTOMOBILE BEFORE YOU BUY IT.

Because some cars are more expensive to replace or repair, insurance companies assign code numbers (1–21) to each model. The higher the code number, the more expensive your car and the more expensive your collision and comprehensive premiums will be.

The damageability rating is initially assigned from the sticker price and then raised or lowered depending on the average cost of parts and repairs on that particular model.

For example, if a model type is initially rated a 7, its sticker price is between $6,501 and $8,000 (see Automobile Insurance Sticker Price Code Number chart). The rating is then upgraded by +1 or more if the car is more expensive to repair than other cars costing the same amount, or lowered by −1 or more if the car is less expensive to repair. This means that while the car's sticker price is $6,501–$8,000, its damageability factor may make its cost of repair like that of a car that initially costs $8,001–$10,000.

These damageability ratings will give you an idea of the difference in comprehensive and collision premiums you will pay for a car you are buying. The insurance could cost more or less than you bargained for, and is a factor in determining which car you can afford to drive.

AUTOMOBILE INSURANCE
STICKER PRICE CODE NUMBERS
(used in Auto Damageability Chart)

Code Number	$ Sticker Price
1	0– 1,600
2	1,601– 2,100
3	2,101– 2,750
4	2,751– 3,700
5	3,701– 5,000
6	5,001– 6,500
7	6,501– 8,000
8	8,001–10,000
10 *	10,001–12,500
11	12,501–15,000
12	15,001–17,000
13	17,001–20,000
14	20,001–24,000
15	24,001–28,000
16	28,001–33,000
17	33,001–39,000
18	39,001–46,000
19	46,001–55,000
20	55,001–65,000
21	Above 65,000

* Note: There is no code 9 in the rating system

AUTOMOBILE DAMAGEABILITY RATING CHART

American Motors

Eagle
Sedan	7 – 2
Wagon	7 – 2

Eagle Limited
Wagon	7 – 2

Audi

4000S Sedan	13 + 2

Audi Coupe
Sedan	14 + 2

5000S
Sedan	13 + 1
Wagon	14 + 1

Quattro
Coupe	17
Sedan	14 + 2

BMW

318i Sedan	14 + 2

Buick

Skyhawk Custom
Coupe	7
Sedan	6 – 1
Wagon	7 – 1

Skyhawk Limited
Coupe	8
Sedan	7 – 1
Wagon	7 – 1

Skyhawk T-Type
Coupe	8

Skyhawk Custom
Coupe	7 – 1
Sedan	6 – 2

Skyhawk Limited
Coupe	7 – 1
Sedan	6 – 2

Skylark T-Type
Coupe	8 – 1

Century Custom
Coupe	8
Sedan	8 – 1
Wagon	8 – 1

Century Limited
Coupe	10
Sedan	8 – 1
Estate	
Wagon	8 – 1

Century T-Type
Coupe	10
Sedan	8 – 1

Regal
Coupe	10
Sedan	6 – 3

Regal Limited
Coupe	10
Sedan	6 – 3

Regal T-Type
Coupe	10

LeSabre Custom
Coupe	10
Sedan	7 – 2

LeSabre Limited
Coupe	8 – 1
Sedan	7 – 2

Electra Limited
Coupe	10 – 1
Sedan	10 – 1

Electra Park Avenue
Coupe	10 – 1
Sedan	11 – 1

Electra Estate
Wagon	11 – 1

Riviera Luxury
Coupe	12
Conv	15

Riviera T-Type
Coupe	12

Cadillac

Camarron
Sedan	10 – 1

Deville
Coupe	13
Sedan	12 – 1

Eldorado
Coupe	14
Conv	16
Seville Sedan	14

Fleetwood Brougham
Coupe	
Sedan	14
Limo	15 – 1
Formal	
Limo	15 – 1

Chevrolet

Chevette Hchbk	6

Chevette CS
Hchbk	6

Cavalier
Coupe	7
HB Cpe	7
Sedan	6 – 1
Wagon	6 – 1

Cavalier CS
Sedan	6 – 1
Wagon	6 – 1

Citation II
Coupe	6 – 1
Hchbk	6 – 1
Hchbk	5 – 2

Camaro Sport
Coupe	12 + 2

Camaro Berlinetta
Coupe	13 + 1

Celebrity
Coupe	8
Sedan	7 – 1
Wagon	7 – 1

Monte Carlo
Spt	
Coupe	8
Impala Sedan	6 – 2

Caprice Coupe
Caprice Coupe	10
Sedan	8 – 1
Wagon	8 – 1

AUTOMOBILE DAMAGEABILITY RATING CHART

Corvette
Spt
Coupe — 17 + 3
Blazer S-10 — 10 + 1
Blazer — 11 + 1
Suburban — 10
Sportvan — 7 − 2
El Camino
Pickup — 8
S-10 Pickup — 7

Chrysler

LeBaron
Sedan — 8 − 1
Conv — 8 − 1
Sedan — 7 − 1
E-Class Sedan — 8 − 1
Town & Country
Wagon — 8 − 1
New Yorker
Sedan — 10 − 1
Executive Sedan — 13
Fifth Avenue
Sedan — 8 − 2
Laser Hchbk — 8
Laser XE Hchbk — 10

Dodge

Charger Hchbk — 8 + 1
Charger 2.2
Hchbk — 8 + 1
Shelby Charger
Hchbk — 10 + 1
Omni Hchbk — 6
Omni SE Hchbk — 6
Aries
Sedan — 7
Sedan — 5 − 2
Aries Custom
Wagon — 6 − 2

Aries Special Edition
Sedan — 8
Sedan — 6 − 2
Wagon — 6 − 2
600 Sedan — 8
Conv — 10
Sedan — 6 − 2
600ES Sedan — 8 − 1
Diplomat Salon
Sedan — 7 − 1
Daytona Hchbk — 8
Daytona Turbo
Hchbk — 10
Ram Charger — 11 + 1
Ram Wagon — 10
Rampage
Pickup — 7
Rampage Sport — 7
Ram 50
Cust
Pickup — 7 + 1
Roy.
Pickup — 8 + 1

Ford

EXP
Hchbk — 8 + 1
Spt
Coupe — 10 + 1
Escort
Hchbk — 6
Hchbk — 6 − 1
Escort L
Hchbk — 7
Hchbk — 6 − 1
Wagon — 6 − 1
Escort GL
Hchbk — 7
Hchbk — 6 − 1
Wagon — 6 − 1
Escort LX
Hchbk — 7 − 1
Wagon — 7 − 1

Escort GT
Hchbk — 8
Mustang
Sedan — 8 + 1
Hchbk — 10 + 1
Mustang LX
Conv — 12 + 1
Tempo L
Sedan — 7
Sedan — 6 − 1
Tempo GL
Sedan — 7
Sedan — 6 − 1
Tempo GLX
Sedan — 8
Sedan — 7 − 1
LTD
Sedan — 7 − 1
Wagon — 7 − 1
LTD Crown Victoria
Sedan — 8 − 1
Sedan — 7 − 2
Wagon — 7 − 2
LTD Country Squire
Wagon — 7 − 2
Thunderbird
Coupe — 12 + 1
Bronco II — 11 + 1
Club Wagon
E-150 — 8 + 1
E-250 — 8 − 1
E-350 — 8 − 1
Econoline
E-150 — 8
E-250 — 8
E-350 — 8
Ranger Pickup — 6

AUTOMOBILE DAMAGEABILITY RATING CHART

GMC	
Jimmy S-15	10 + 1
Jimmy	11 + 1
Suburban	10
Rally	7 − 1
Caballero	
Pickup	8
S15	7

Honda	
Civic CRX	
Spt	
Coupe	7 + 1
Civic	
Sedan	7
Wagon	7
Civic 1.3 Hchbk	6
Civic 1.5 Hchbk	7
Accord	
Hchbk	8
Sedan	8
Accord LX	
Hchbk	8
Sedan	10
Prelude Coupe	11 + 1

Isuzu	
I-Mark	
Coupe	8 + 1
Sedan	7
Impulse	
HB Cpe	11 + 1

Jaguar	
XJ6 Sedan	16
XJ6-VDP Sedan	17

Jeep	
CJ-7	10
Scrambler	8 + 1
Cherokee	
Wagon	10
Cherokee Pioneer	
Wagon	10

Cherokee Chief	
Wagon	10
Wagoneer	
Wagon	11
Wagoneer	
Limited	13
Grand	
Wagoneer	13
Pickup	10

Lincoln/Continental	
Town Car	12 − 1
Sedan	13 − 1
Mark VII Coupe	14

Mercedes-Benz	
190 Sedan	13 − 1
300	
Coupe	17
Sedan	15 − 1
Wagon	16 − 1
380	
Coupe	20 + 2
Sedan	17 − 1
500	
Coupe	21 + 1
Sedan	19

Mercury	
Lynx	
Hchbk	6
Hchbk	6 − 1
Lynx L	
Hchbk	7
Hchbk	6 − 1
Lynx GS	
Hchbk	7
Hchbk	6 − 1
Wagon	6 − 1
Lynx LTS	
Hchbk	7 − 1
Lynx RS Hchbk	8
Capri Hchbk	11 + 2

Topaz GS	
Sedan	8
Sedan	7 − 1
Topaz LS	
Sedan	8
Sedan	7 − 1
Marquis	
Sedan	7 − 1
Wagon	8 − 1
Grand Marquis	
Sedan	10 − 1
Sedan	8 − 2
Colony	
Park	
Wagon	8 − 2
Cougar	
Sedan	11 + 1
XR-7 Cpe	12 + 1

Mitsubishi	
Cordia Hchbk	8 + 1
Tredia Sedan	7
Starion Hchbk	13 + 2
Pickup	6
Montero Utility	8

Nissan	
Sentra	
Sedan	7 + 1
Sedan	8 + 1
HB Cpe	
XE	8 + 1
Wagon	8 + 1
Pulsar NX Cpe	10 + 1
Stanza Hchbk	8
Sedan	8
300 ZX	
Spt	
Coupe	14 + 2
Coupe	
2 + 2	14 + 1

AUTOMOBILE DAMAGEABILITY RATING CHART

Maxima			**Custom Cruiser**			**Sunbird 2000**	
Sedan	10		Wagon	7 − 2		Coupe	7
Wagon	11		**98 Regency**			Hchbk	7
Pickup	7 + 1		Coupe	11		Sedan	6 − 1
King Cab	10 + 1		Sedan	10 − 1		Wagon	6 − 1
Oldsmobile			**98 Regency Brougham**			**Sunbird 2000 LE**	
Firenza			Sedan	11 − 1		Coupe	7
Coupe	7		**Toronado Brougham**			Sedan	7 − 1
Sedan	6 − 1		Coupe	11 − 1		Wagon	7 − 1
Cruiser	7 − 1					Conv	10
Firenza Brougham			*Peugeot*			**Sunbird 2000 SE**	
Coupe	8		**505 GL**			Coupe	8
Sedan	7 − 1		Sedan	7 − 2		Hchbk	8
Cruiser	7 − 1		Wagon	8 − 2		Sedan	7 − 1
Omega			**505S**			**Phoenix**	
Coupe	7 − 1		Sedan	10 − 2		Coupe	7
Sedan	6 − 2		Wagon	10 − 2		Hchbk	6 − 1
Omega Brougham			**604 Sedan**	13 − 1		**Phoenix LE**	
Coupe	7 − 1					Coupe	8
Sedan	6 − 2		*Plymouth*			Hchbk	7 − 1
Cutlass Ciera LS			**Turismo Hchbk**	8 + 1		**Phoenix SE**	
Coupe	8		**Turismo 2.2**			Coupe	8
Sedan	7 − 2		Hchbk	8 + 1		**Firebird Coupe**	12 + 3
Cruiser	7 − 2		**Horizon Hchbk**	6		**Firebird Trans Am**	
Cutlass Ciera Brougham			**Horizon SE**			Coupe	13 + 3
Coupe	10		Hchbk	6		**Firebird SE**	
Sedan	7 − 2		**Reliant**			Coupe	13 + 3
Cutlass Supreme			Sedan	7		**Pontiac 6000**	
Coupe	10		Sedan	5 − 2		Coupe	8
Sedan	7 − 2		**Reliant Custom**			Sedan	7 − 1
Cutlass Supreme			Wagon	6 − 2		Wagon	8 − 1
Brougham			**Reliant Special Edition**			**Pontiac 6000 LE**	
Coupe	10		Sedan	8		Coupe	10
Sedan	7 − 2		Sedan	6 − 2		Sedan	8 − 1
Cutlass Calais			Wagon	6 − 2		Wagon	8 − 1
Coupe	10		**Grand Fury Salon**			**Pontiac 6000 STE**	
Delta 88 Royale			Sedan	7 − 1		Sedan	10 − 1
Coupe	8 − 1		*Pontiac*			**Grand Prix**	
Sedan	7 − 2		**Pontiac 1000**			Coupe	10
Delta 88 Royale Brougham			Hchbk	7 + 1		**Grand Prix LE**	
Coupe	8 − 1					Coupe	10
Sedan	7 − 2					**Grand Prix Brougham**	
						Coupe	10

AUTOMOBILE DAMAGEABILITY RATING CHART

Bonneville			*Saab*			Celica	
Sedan	7 − 2		900			Spt Cpe	
Bonneville LE			Hchbk	12 + 2		ST	11 + 2
Sedan	7 − 2		Sedan	11 + 1		Spt Cpe	
Bonneville Brougham			900S			GT	11 + 2
Sedan	7 − 2		Hchbk	13 + 2		Lftbk GT	11 + 2
Parisienne			Sedan	12 + 1		Celica Supra	
Sedan	8 − 1		900 Turbo			Spt	
Wagon	8 − 1		Hchbk	14 + 2		Coupe	13 + 1
Parisienne Brougham			Sedan	14 + 1		Camry	
Sedan	8 − 1		*Subaru*			Sedan	8
Fiero						Lftbk	8
Coupe	10 + 1		Standard Hchbk	8 + 2		Cressida	
Spt			DL			Sedan	10 − 1
Coupe	10 + 1		Hchbk	8 + 2		Wagon	10 − 1
Fiero SE			Hdtp	10 + 2		Land Cruiser	
Spt			Sedan	8 + 1		Wagon	12 + 1
Coupe	11 + 1		Wagon	8 + 1		Van	8
Porsche			GL			Pickup	7 + 1
911			Hchbk	10 + 2		*Volkswagen*	
Coupe	17 + 1		Hdtp	10 + 2		Rabbit L Hchbk	7
Targe/			Sedan	8 + 1		Rabbit GL	
Conv	18 + 1		Wagon	10 + 1		Hchbk	8
928S Coupe	19 + 1		Brat GL Pickup	7		Rabbit GTI	
944 Coupe	17 + 3		*Toyota*			Hchbk	8
Renault			Starlet Lftbk	7 + 1		Rabbit Conv	10
Alliance Sedan	7		Tercel			Jetta Sedan	10 + 1
Alliance L			Lftbk	7 + 1		Quantum GL	
Sedan	7		Lftbk	8 + 1		Sedan	10 − 1
Alliance DL			Wagon	8 + 1		Wagon	10 − 1
Sedan	8		Corolla			Scirocco Coupe	13 + 3
Alliance Ltd			Spt Coupe	10 + 1		Vanagon	11 − 1
Sedan	8		Lftbk			*Volvo*	
Encore Lftbk	6		Lftbk	8 + 1		240	
Encore S Lftbk	7		Sedan	8 + 1		Sedan	10
Encore LS Lftbk	7					Sedan	8 − 1
Encore GS Lftbk	8					Wagon	10 − 1
						760 Sedan	13 − 1

45

STRATEGIES TO CUT YOUR AUTO INSURANCE PREMIUMS

Strategy #13

SHOP AROUND TO SAVE 25% ON AUTO INSURANCE PREMIUMS.

Automobile insurance companies set premiums based on the amount of claims paid in each area. Auto insurance rates vary as much as 100% from company to company. According to an independent study, fewer than one in four drivers will get more than one quote before buying auto insurance. When your policy is up for renewal, get several quotes. Shop around. You will be amazed at the differences in prices.

Some of the companies that seem to have lower rates in many areas are Geico, USAA, State Farm, Travelers, and Liberty Mutual. Many agents, to make shopping more difficult, will not quote over the phone, but don't let that stop you. Let your wheels do the walking.

Strategy #14

DON'T TAKE EXTRA COVERAGES SUCH AS TOWING, CAR RENTAL, AND AUDIO EQUIPMENT.

The premiums for extras on an auto policy cost you more money that you could ever collect. Towing and car rental costs between $20 and $80 extra per car per year, and yet, only a small percentage of policy-holders will ever file a claim on either. The high premiums charged to insure a few hundred dollars of audio equipment also make a poor investment. However, do insure your car phone or audio equipment worth over $1,000, which is more expensive and highly visible.

Strategy #15
DETERMINE HOW MUCH AN ACCIDENT OR A TICKET WILL RAISE YOUR PREMIUMS.

You'll be shocked at the different practices auto insurance companies have affecting policyholders who get ticketed or are involved in an accident. Some will raise your rates 25% after only one occurrence, others will cancel your insurance altogether. Choose a company that won't brand you a loser just because of one bad experience.

Strategy #16
ASK FOR THE FIVE BASIC AUTOMOBILE INSURANCE DISCOUNTS.

There are five discounts offered by auto insurance companies to those who fall into special groups. When buying auto insurance be certain to ask; the agent may not bring them up.

Discount	Amount Saved
1. Multi-car—more than one automobile insured by the same company.	5–20%
2. Driver training—take a state certified course.	5–15%
3. Good driver	5–20%
4. Anti-theft equipment—alarm or systems that disengage the ignition	5–20%
5. Senior citizen	5–20%

If you ask for all of the discounts to which you are entitled, your premiums may drop another 20% or more. It pays to ask.

REDESIGNING YOUR AUTOMOBILE INSURANCE POLICY

Use the form that follows to redesign your automobile policy for lower premiums. Part 1 gives you a synopsis of the coverages you need and don't need. Part 2 will help you analyze and redesign your auto policy. On this form, list the liability limits and coverages you have on each automobile that you now own along with any changes you wish to make using these insurance strategies. If you have more than two automobiles, make a copy of the sheet. Contact your insurance agent and make all of the changes, noting the changes in your premiums.

Also use copies of the form when getting auto insurance quotes. Many automobile premiums are stated on policies as six month premiums. If you pay every six months you must double the premiums shown to obtain the yearly figures.

In some states, unnecessary coverages are unfortunately required. Check your state rules through your insurance agent.

REDESIGNING YOUR AUTOMOBILE INSURANCE POLICY
PART 1:

Coverages You Need

Liability
  Bodily Injury   Pays for damage to other people.
  Property Damage   Pays for damage to other people's property.
Comprehensive   Pays for damage to your car by fire, theft, or anything but collision.

Collision   Pays for damage to your car by collision with another car or object.

Coverages You Don't Need

No-Fault (PIP)   Pays your medical and funeral expenses and work loss.

Medical Payments   Pays your medical and funeral expenses.
Uninsured Motorists   Pays your medical and funeral expenses caused by a noninsured or underinsured driver.
Emergency Road Service   Pays for towing.
Car Rental Expense   Pays for a rental car if yours is damaged.
Death/Dismemberment   Pays for death or certain injuries.
Specialty Coverage   Pays for audio equipment, glass breakage, etc.

REDESIGNING YOUR AUTOMOBILE INSURANCE POLICY
PART 2

Coverages to Reorganize

Coverage	Current Limits	Desired Limits	Current Premiums	New Premiums	Notes
Bodily Injury Liability					Check for all possible discounts
Property Damage Liability					
Umbrella Liability					Optional for those needing high limits
Comprehensive Deductible					At least $500
Collision Deductible					At least $500

Coverages to Drop

No-Fault				-0-	
Medical Payments				-0-	
Uninsured Motorists (PIP)				-0-	
Emergency Road Service				-0-	
Car Rental Expense				-0-	
Death/ Dismemberment				-0-	
Specialty Coverage				-0-	
Other				-0-	
					AMOUNT SAVED:
TOTAL PREMIUMS			$	$	$

RENTAL CAR INSURANCE STRATEGIES

Strategy #17

DECLINE ALL EXTRA INSURANCE COVERAGES WHEN YOU RENT A CAR.

Another great insurance scheme has been created by the rental car companies. By advertising low daily or weekly rates, and adding on big unnecessary insurance premiums, the rental car companies create huge profits from the confusion and fear of customers. The four add-on optional rental car insurance premiums are: collision damage waiver (CDW), personal accident insurance (PAI), personal effects coverage (PEC) and liability insurance supplement (LIS). Although these coverages are supposedly optional, the rental car company will do everything within its power to see that you end up buying them. All of these insurances are either unnecessary because you are already covered on other policies or they are incredibly overpriced for the insurance you get.

Here are typical daily and weekly premiums.

	Daily	Weekly
1. Collision Damage Waiver (CDW)	$ 7.50	$ 52.50
2. Personal Accident Insurance (PAI)	3.00	21.00
3. Personal Effects Coverage (PEC)	1.25	8.75
4. Liability Insurance Supplement (LIS)	4.95	34.65
TOTAL	$16.70	$116.90

1. COLLISION DAMAGE WAIVER (CDW)

Year after year, rental car companies require that you become liable for more of the damage caused by a collision or rollover of a rented vehicle. Your deductible on damage to a rental car now ranges from $3,000 to the full value of the car. The rental car company will offer you CDW insurance for about $7.50 a day to cover the deductible.

Here is what they don't tell you. Even without the insurance, you are already covered by the rental car company for fire and theft and under the "Occasional Driver" clause in your automobile policy, you are covered for collision damage. Any deductible you pay will be reimbursed to you by your insurance company based on the limits in your policy.

Strategy #18

CHARGE A RENTAL CAR ON A CREDIT CARD THAT COVERS THE DEDUCTIBLE.

One of the new, valuable credit card services is automatic coverage of the collision deductible when you charge the rental on your credit card. The American Express platinum card covers the first $50,000 and a Diners Club card now covers the first $25,000 of damages. An air travel card issued by the airlines and many MasterCard and VISA cards also cover the deductible up to $3,000 and there is no additional cost to you.

2. PERSONAL ACCIDENT INSURANCE (PAI)

Personal accident insurance is nothing more than an expensive life insurance policy with medical payments. The policy states, "This coverage pays for death directly caused by an automobile accident independent of all other causes." Never take the insurance. You would be paying the equivalent of $1,000 per year for a $175,000 life insurance policy that covers you only a few minutes a day—while you are driving the rental car. The actual value of the insurance is less than $50 per year. You are already covered for medical payments by your hospitalization policy.

3. PERSONAL EFFECTS COVERAGE (PEC)

Personal effects coverage is insurance that covers loss or damage to your personal property in the rental car or hotel room while you are renting the car. Coverage is limited to $525 for you and your immediate family members. Again, an absolute waste of money. The exclusions— what they won't pay for—are almost comical: teeth, contact lenses, furniture, currency, coins, tickets, documents, and perishables or mysterious disappearances. What in the world is left? Your own homeowners policy already gives you the same coverage when you are away from home. Check with your insurance agent.

4. LIABILITY INSURANCE SUPPLEMENT (LIS)

When you rent a car, your automatic liability coverage for injury or death to others is the bare minimum required by the state. For an extra

$4.95 a day, the liability coverage is increased to $1,000,000 or more. Your auto insurance policy already covers you up to its current limits, and by getting the Personal Umbrella Liability Policy described in this chapter, you are covered for $1,000,000 of liability at a fraction of the cost.

You can pay as little as $100 a week to rent a car, and as much as $117 for additional unnecessary insurance coverages. The discount rental car companies in resort areas, such as Florida, are the most misleading in their advertising. By advertising rental rates as low as $99 a week, vacationers end up at the counter only to be threatened into accepting the "optional" insurance.

Rental agents are often paid bonuses for selling the extra insurance, and sales pitches are somewhere between aggressive and obnoxious. Some companies require a deposit of $750 if you don't take the CDW. You may end up taking the insurance just because you're afraid the deposit would put your VISA over the limit.

MOTORCYCLE INSURANCE

Strategy #19
BUY A SEPARATE SIX OR NINE MONTH POLICY TO COVER MOTORCYCLES, MOPEDS, AND SNOWMOBILES.

Motorcycle insurance (including mopeds, snowmobiles, and other miscellaneous vehicles) is similar to auto insurance, even though motorcycles are not classified as automobiles by insurance companies.

Most states requiring auto liability insurance also require motorcycle liability coverage. You should have liability coverage for your motorcycle. A car owner may insure a motorcycle with an endorsement to his auto policy. You are not covered for your motorcycle through your basic auto policy.

Motorcyclists can get coverages for bodily injury and property damage liability, medical payments (usually limited to $500), uninsured motorist coverage, and collision and physical damage coverage. Use the same strategies for your motorcycle as you would with your automobile. You probably will not need coverage for other passengers since they are covered by both the liability portion of your motorcycle policy and by their own hospitalization insurance.

Many insurance companies offer six-month and nine-month policies to motorcyclists and snowmobilers where the equipment is garaged for the winter or summer. Ask your agent; it will save you money.

HOMEOWNERS INSURANCE

Strategy #20
TAKE ONLY THE COVERAGES YOU NEED ON YOUR HOMEOWNERS POLICY.

The risks you take when you own a home are called perils. These perils have been divided into 18 categories. The amount of premium you pay for a homeowners policy is determined by the number of these perils you wish to cover. The more perils covered, the more expensive your policy. Most all homeowners policies cover:

- your home,
- other buildings on the property (i.e. detached garage),
- your personal belongings (other than expensive items like jewelry and furs), and
- living expenses for temporary relocation.

The three major policies are HO-1, HO-2, and HO-5 and the perils covered by each are shown in the following chart.

The advantage of an HO-2 is the coverage for frozen pipes and water damage. This policy is the best value of those living in climates where pipes do freeze. Others living in warmer climates get the best value from HO-1, which costs less.

Mobile home owners pay more for homeowners insurance because mobile homes are more vulnerable to the elements. There is a new homeowners insurance policy, HO-76, which is HO-1 through HO-5 written in simplified language and with a few additions such as credit card coverage.

HOMEOWNERS INSURANCE POLICIES

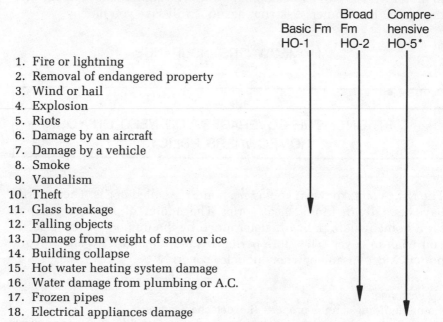

	Basic Fm HO-1	Broad Fm HO-2	Compre- hensive HO-5*
1. Fire or lightning			
2. Removal of endangered property			
3. Wind or hail			
4. Explosion			
5. Riots			
6. Damage by an aircraft			
7. Damage by a vehicle			
8. Smoke			
9. Vandalism			
10. Theft			
11. Glass breakage			
12. Falling objects			
13. Damage from weight of snow or ice			
14. Building collapse			
15. Hot water heating system damage			
16. Water damage from plumbing or A.C.			
17. Frozen pipes			
18. Electrical appliances damage			

*HO-5 covers all possible perils except flood, earthquake, volcano, war, and nuclear accident.

Note: Some policies cover damage to property of guests, others do not. Condominium owners can purchase a special policy HO-6 to cover personal property or damage not covered by the condo master policy.

Strategy #21
DECLINE THE ADDITIONAL COVERAGES ON YOUR HOMEOWNERS POLICY.

You have an option of six additional coverages. These coverages are a poor value and should not be taken.

1. Removal of debris.
2. Damaged property removal.
3. Fire department surcharges—up to $250.
4. Temporary repairs to prevent further damage to property.

5. Trees, shrubs, and plants—covered up to $500 or a maximum of 5% of the dwelling insurance. Since windstorms are excluded this insurance is of little value.
6. Stolen credit cards—up to $500.

Strategy #22
PURCHASE A PERSONAL ARTICLES "FLOATER" TO COVER EXPENSIVE PERSONAL ITEMS.

Your basic policy limits what you can collect for theft or damage of personal articles. Insure expensive jewelry, furs, and other personal property with a personal articles "floater." As your wealth increases and your personal assets increase, make certain your insurance is increased.

Strategy #23
BUY FLOOD OR EARTHQUAKE INSURANCE ONLY IF YOU ARE IN A GOVERNMENT-DESIGNATED FLOOD PLAIN OR EARTHQUAKE ZONE.

Flood and earthquake insurance should be purchased by those in designated potential disaster areas but not by others. To be eligible for flood insurance you must be in an area that practices land use control measures, and in some cases your mortgage company will require the insurance. In some parts of the country earthquake insurance is too expensive to be practical. You can't afford to insure against every possible risk so it pays to weigh the cost against the potential loss.

Strategy #24
VIDEO TAPE YOUR VALUABLES FOR INSURANCE RECORDS.

You can only collect for what you can prove you lost. The best way to provide an acceptable insurance record is to use your video camera to create a video record of furniture, knickknacks, artwork, clothes, stereo and video equipment (including model and serial numbers), musical instruments and everything else of value. While you are taping, verbally record the value of the asset and where and when you bought it. Put the videotape in a safety deposit box along with receipts. Records won't help if they are lost along with the assets. If you don't have a video camera, use your slide or Polaroid camera and a tape recorder.

Strategy #25

BUY REPLACEMENT VALUE COVERAGE, NOT MARKET VALUE COVERAGE, ON YOUR HOME AND CONTENTS.

Replacement value coverage will pay whatever it costs to replace an asset that is lost, destroyed, or stolen. Market value coverage will pay only the current value of the asset after age and wear and tear are deducted. If your five-year-old, $1,000 video player is stolen, the replacement value coverage will pay you $1,000, but market value coverage may net you only $200. Surprisingly, replacement value coverage costs only about $10 more per year.

Make certain your fire insurance is a replacement cost policy and not a market value policy. The value of your home may fluctuate with real estate market conditions, and a market value policy may pay you less than the replacement cost.

Ask for an automatic appreciation clause in your policy that will raise your coverage limits each year without the necessity of checking with your agent.

Strategy #26

CARRY AS FIRE INSURANCE AT LEAST (BUT NOT MORE THAN) 80% OF THE REPLACEMENT COST OF YOUR HOME.

Fire insurance rates are set by considering location, distance from the nearest fire hydrant and fire station, the type of construction, and the age of the home. These are factors over which you have little control.

You can, however, control the amount and kind of insurance you buy which controls your premiums.

Carry enough insurance to cover at least 80%, but not 100% of the replacement value of your home. You are automatically covered for up to 100% of a loss, as long as the policy is written for 80% or more of the value of your home. Never underinsure because if coverage is less than 80% of replacement cost and you have a loss, the policy will pay only a percentage of the loss. Never overinsure because you're paying premium dollars on which you can never collect.

TENANTS INSURANCE

Strategy #27
BUY A SPECIAL TENANTS POLICY, HO-4, IF YOU RENT A HOME OR AN APARTMENT.

The tenants policy (HO-4) is designed for those who rent an apartment or house or own a cooperative apartment. It insures household contents and personal belongings against all of the perils included in the broad form (HO-2), plus additional living expenses. Renters' policies provide a minimum of $4,000 coverage on personal property, and a minimum of $800 for additional living expenses in case the unit becomes uninhabitable. Renters policies also provide liability coverage for injuries, property damage and legal expenses.

OWNERS, LANDLORDS, AND TENANTS LIABILITY INSURANCE (OLT)

Strategy #28
PROTECT YOUR RENTAL PROPERTIES WITH AN OWNERS, LANDLORDS AND TENANTS POLICY (OLT).

Insurance for landlords falls under the general category of public liability insurance. OLT policies cover the liability arising from the ownership and maintenance of a rental property. OLT policies are relatively inexpensive and can be added as a supplement to the fire insurance policy on a rental home or sometimes to your homeowners insurance.

LOAN INSURANCE—CREDIT LIFE AND DISABILITY

Strategy #29

SAY NO TO LOAN INSURANCE—CREDIT LIFE AND DISABILITY.

You can save $1,000 every time you borrow $10,000 for an automobile or any purpose by declining the credit life and disability insurance. Let's say you're buying a $10,000 automobile and financing it at the bank or credit union. The last question the loan officer will ask, right before he approves your application, is "By the way, you do want the credit life and disability insurance, don't you?" You look up, caught off guard, and ask, "What's credit life?" "Well," he says, "Credit life pays off your loan if you die, disability insurance makes the loan payments if you can't work." It all sounds logical until you consider the cost. If you say yes to the insurance, you are overpaying by 800%! Sixty percent of the premiums go as a commission to the financial institution. That should tell you how much the insurance is really worth. Banks, credit unions, and finance companies can actually make more profit from loan insurance than from interest. How do I know? I am an owner of two banks in Florida.

What do most borrowers do? They look up at the loan officer and ask, "Do you really think I ought to take the insurance?" No loan officer has ever answered no, and millions of dollars of unnecessary insurance are sold in the process. The insurance is added to your monthly payments. If the credit life and disability premiums amount to $17 a month, you pay $810 on a 48-month loan, plus over $200 interest, which increases the cost of your automobile over 10%.

Credit life insurance pays only the balance of the loan at the time the insured dies and is, therefore, expensive decreasing term insurance. If your car costs $12,000 and you die owing only one payment of $327, the insurance pays only $327. Your heirs get nothing from the policy; only the financial institution collects.

The abuses of credit life and disability insurance became so rampant in the 70's that a consumer protection law was enacted, preventing a financial institution from making the approval of a loan application contingent on whether the borrower accepts the insurance. A fine and jail sentence are possible for institutions and people who violate the law, but you would never know it from the way the loan officers talk.

If you want a personal loan paid off if something happens to you, don't buy loan insurance, buy inexpensive annually renewable term life insurance. You will save 75% of the premiums.

MORTGAGE LIFE INSURANCE

Strategy #30

REPLACE EXPENSIVE MORTGAGE LIFE INSURANCE WITH INEXPENSIVE TERM INSURANCE.

Mortgage insurance pays off your home mortgage if you die. The logic of mortgage insurance is sound. You want your family to be relieved of mortgage payments if you are not around. The problem is the high cost of the insurance compared to the risk. It is estimated that mortgage insurance companies actually pay out less than 30 cents in claims for every dollar they collect in premiums.

At age 54, $80,000 of mortgage life insurance can cost as much as $1,128 per year. At the same age, you can buy an $80,000 annually renewable term policy to accomplish the same thing for $200 per year, saving $900 a year. The premiums are even less if you add $80,000 to an existing term policy. Mortgage insurance proceeds go directly to the mortgage company but ART proceeds go to your heirs. By correctly investing these proceeds, $80,000 in our example, the mortgage payments can be made until the home is paid for while completely preserving the principal.

MEDICAL INSURANCE

Strategy #31

RAISE THE DEDUCTIBLE ON YOUR MEDICAL INSURANCE TO $1,000 OR EVEN $2,500.

Up to 50% of hospitalization insurance premiums you pay are paid to insure just the first $1,000 or $2,500 of a claim. The insurance you really need is the kind that will pay major medical expenses, those that could cost you thousands or even tens of thousands of dollars and use up the assets you have accumulated. Insurance that covers only your big risks is called major medical and is the only health or hospitalization insurance that makes sense costwise, other than the free plan your employer may provide.

Even a small claim costs an insurance company hundreds of dollars to process—those costs are added to the premiums. If you do have a claim, you have already lost the equivalent of the hospital bill through overpriced premiums. Even if you pay any occasional small hospital bills out of your own pocket, you will save money. You are not paying the cost of administration and paperwork the insurance company must incur.

DISABILITY INSURANCE

Strategy #32

BUY DISABILITY INSURANCE ONLY IF YOU ARE IN POOR HEALTH OR ACCIDENT PRONE.

For people in reasonably good health, putting money in a good investment plan will pay far greater long-term rewards than dumping it into a disability insurance policy.

Disability insurance promises to pay you cash if you become disabled and can't work. The concept is great, but once again, the costs far outweigh the potential benefits. The insurance company has to pay thousands of dollars for administrative and sales expenses, paperwork and medical exams before it even begins paying a claim. These costs are built into the premiums. The restrictions and definitions of disability are so confining that few policyholders ever collect.

Should you decide you want disability insurance anyway, you can cut the high premiums by 50% by increasing the waiting period. The waiting period, similar to a deductible, is the amount of time you must be disabled and unable to work before the insurance takes effect. The usual waiting period is 90 days. By increasing the waiting period to six months or one year, the premiums drop by as much as 50%, while still giving you the most important part—protection against long-term disability.

You don't suddenly lose everything because you become temporarily unable to work. If you are injured on the job, the mandatory workmen's compensation insurance carried by your employer will pay you. Your employer may also have a disability plan as part of your company benefit package. Also, cancel or refuse the disability premium waiver on your life insurance and the credit disability insurance.

SPECIALTY INSURANCE

Strategy #33
DON'T BUY SPECIALTY HEALTH AND LIFE INSURANCE POLICIES.

Avoid health and life insurance policies hyped on television and through the mail. The most popular versions are those that:

- pick up where Medicare leaves off,
- promise low-cost life insurance to those age 55 to 75,
- pay $50 a day, in addition to your hospitalization,
- insure against one disease such as cancer, or
- provide coverage for special groups such as veterans.

The premiums are 400%—too high for the potential payoff and the restrictions guarantee that few will collect. Many of the ads play on the fears rather than the good sense of retired people.

Chapter 4

BETTER LIFE INSURANCE FOR 80% LESS

Insurance—an ingenious modern game of chance in which the player is permitted to enjoy the comfortable conviction that he is beating the man who keeps the table.

Ambrose Bierce
The Devil's Dictionary
1906

Objective: To cut the cost of your life insurance by 80% while increasing financial protection for your family.

Life insurance is a plan whereby you pay money to the company while you are alive and the company pays your chosen beneficiary when you are not. The longer you live, the more the insurance company profits. Life insurance is a must for anyone with family responsibilities and little personal wealth. Because it is misunderstood, overused for underprotection, and sold through marketing gimmicks with little real value, life insurance can also be detrimental to your wealth.

First, here are a few terms that you must understand in order to take control of your life insurance costs.

DEATH BENEFIT. The amount of money that will be paid to the beneficiary if the insured dies; the amount of life insurance. Also called the face value of the policy.

PREMIUM. The amount you pay to the insurance company. Life insurance premiums can be paid in one lump sum (single premium), one check each year (annual premium), or periodically by quarter or by month. Premiums can be for insurance only or partially diverted into investments, prepaid policies, and retirement plans.

POLICY TERM. The period during which the life insurance is in force. The term can range from one year to an entire lifetime.

FEES AND COMMISSIONS. Charges for administrative and selling expenses levied against your premiums or cash value.

SURRENDER CHARGE. The amount of money the insurance company keeps if the policy is cancelled. Surrender charges apply only to policies with investment plans such as whole life and universal life and can run into thousands of dollars.

To determine the amount of life insurance you need, you must first determine if you need life insurance at all.

Strategy #34
IF YOU ARE SINGLE WITH NO DEPENDENTS, DON'T BUY LIFE INSURANCE.

About 30% of all the life insurance in force today is on the lives of single people with no family responsibilities. Who would get the insurance proceeds, the dog or goldfish? Life insurance should be used only to prevent a financial hardship that would be created if the insured dies. If you are single, invest your money for use while you are living.

Strategy #35
NEVER BUY LIFE INSURANCE ON CHILDREN.

The purpose of insurance is to protect against the loss of your financial assets. Although children may be an emotional asset, they certainly are not financial assets unless you have secured them high-paying jobs in television commercials.

Parents buy life insurance on children because they are told by a salesman that it is the loving, responsible thing to do. Insurance on children is a life insurance salesman's dream. The pitch goes something like this: "Because you love your children, you will want life insurance on them, won't you?" If your answer is no, then it sounds as if you don't love your kids. If you love your children, why would it help to collect large sums of money if they died? It wouldn't. Insurance belongs on the income-providing parent(s), not the children.

Another ridiculous salesman's pitch is that if you insure a child while he or she is young, it guarantees the child's insurability later. There is a 99% chance that if a child reaches 18, he or she will be insurable anyway.

Whole life insurance, as a method of providing a $5,000 college education fund for your child, is far too inefficient to be called an investment and should not be considered. A $50,000 life insurance policy on a one-year-old child will cost $250 per year and be worth $5,000 when the child reaches college age. By the time the child reaches 18, your cash value would be $5,000. Two hundred and fifty dollars per year invested correctly in a mutual fund family will create a college fund of $40,000, in the same amount of time.

The same reasoning applies to your spouse. If your spouse is responsible for a significant amount of family income, he or she is a financial asset, and inexpensive term insurance makes sense until the kids are grown. If your spouse does not work, or intends to work only part-time, your spouse is technically a financial liability and insurance is both unnecessary and financially foolish.

Strategy #36
AS YOU GET OLDER, CARRY LESS LIFE INSURANCE.

As you get older, your responsibilities decrease and so does your need for life insurance. Your objective is to become self-insured—to build enough wealth that you have no need for life insurance. The insurance salesman will incorrectly tell you the older you are, the more insurance you need. Why? Because in sales school he was taught that the older you get, the more money you will have that could be spent on premiums.

| Strategy #37 |
| NEVER USE LIFE INSURANCE AS AN INVESTMENT. |

Strip away all of the sales gimmicks and what you have left are only two basic types of life insurance policies: life insurance with a savings plan, and life insurance with no savings plan. Let's first look at those policies that combine insurance and saving.

WHOLE LIFE INSURANCE

Whole life is a plan where your money goes into a "hole," never to be seen again. Whole life was the first major life insurance/investment combination and has literally cheated millions out of billions since its inception.

Only in the last few years has it come to light that "whole life" is not an investment at all. Your cash value is really the property of the insurance company and makes the insurance you are buying over-priced by 600%.

Whole life policies usually have level premiums (equal yearly installments) and claim to build tax-deferred cash value. That claim is a lie. When you die your entire cash value somehow disappears into the coffers of the insurance company. Your beneficiary receives only the face value of the policy or the cash value, whichever is greater, but not both.

Let's say at age 35 a father buys a level premium whole life policy with a death benefit of $100,000. After paying a premium of $1,300 each year for 20 years, he has accumulated $35,400 of cash value. If he dies you would expect his beneficiary to collect $100,000 plus the $35,400 cash value, a total of $135,400. The beneficiary receives only $100,000—not $135,400. The so-called "investment" is no investment at all, but only his heirs will discover the deception because he is gone.

If he decides to borrow the $35,400 of cash value, they've got him again. His death benefit is reduced by the amount he borrows.

The truth about whole life insurance is often enshrouded by appealing promises that turn out to be marketing hot air. Here are a few you will hear and why they are misleading.

THE DISAPPEARING CASH VALUE

At age 35, a father buys a whole life insurance policy under the following terms:

$100,000	Death benefit (face value)
$1,300	Yearly premium
$35,400	Cash value after 20 years

At age 55 he dies.

What he thought his family would receive:		What his family actually received:
$100,000	Death benefit	$100,000
$ 35,400	Cash value	$ 0
$135,400	TOTAL	$100,000

The cash value of $35,400 becomes the property of the insurance company. Whole life is therefore an overpriced term insurance policy.

"YOU CAN BORROW YOUR CASH VALUE."

If you need money, you can borrow your cash value at a low interest rate of 5% to 8%. What a benefit! The insurance company is charging you interest on your own money which you overpaid in premiums.

"YOUR POLICY WILL EVENTUALLY BE PAID UP."

Most everyone loves the idea of a paid-up policy; at a point in time that means no more yearly premiums. In reality, a paid-up policy is created only by overpaying your premiums. The overpayment will eventually be used to pay your future premiums. Therefore, all paid-up policies are just prepaid policies.

"YOU'LL BE EARNING INTEREST."

One of the biggest financial revelations of the century was when someone discovered that whole life policies were paying an average of only 1.3% interest. Worse yet is the fact that you never receive it. Through a slick maneuver, the insurance company has found a way to pay all of the interest, not to the policyholder or beneficiary, but to itself. The interest earned is added to your cash value and the cash value, remember, becomes the property of the insurance company.

"MY INSURANCE POLICY IS A TAX SHELTER."

Another myth is that somehow life insurance enjoys some special tax status. For instance, you are told you can borrow money from your insurance policy tax free. You can borrow money from anywhere tax free—from a bank, through an equity loan on your home, or from your brother-in-law. There are no income taxes on borrowed money.

You are told that insurance proceeds, at the time of death, are income tax exempt. After death, there is no income tax on any part of an estate. Insurance proceeds and the rest of the estate are subject to estate taxes.

"IF YOU BUY LIFE INSURANCE WHEN YOU'RE YOUNG, IT WILL COST LESS."

It is true that yearly premiums are less when you are younger, but only because you will pay greater total premiums over a longer period of time. The same faulty reasoning would apply if an automobile salesman told you, "Finance your car for five years, instead of two. It costs less." Actually, the car, like buying insurance, would cost far more. Only the monthly payments would be lower. The only reason to buy life insurance when you are young is financial protection for your family."

UNIVERSAL LIFE INSURANCE

"Earn 10% to 11%, guaranteed" claim the never-ending parade of universal life ads. Universal life is nothing more than a term insurance policy coupled with an investment plan. The investment can pay fixed interest rates or, in some cases, can be self-directed into mutual funds. The amount of premium above the cost of insurance, fees, and commissions goes into the investment. Universal life insurance makes a poor plan for many reasons.

A 45-year-old man buys a universal life policy combining a $100,000 death benefit with an investment promising a yearly return of 10% for 20 years. He pays $2,000 in premiums per year or $167 a month. He is paid the 10% only on the money that goes into the investment, that is, what is left from the $2,000 premiums after the fees, commissions, and, of course, the cost of the insurance itself are deducted. In a typical universal life policy, the first year fees and commissions alone can amount to $600. He loses 30% of his $2,000 to fees and commissions.

Let's say, tomorrow afternoon you stroll into your bank and put your $2,000 into a certificate of deposit. "No problem," the new accounts officer tells you. "By the way, there is a $600 charge for opening the account." How quickly would you be out the door, into the parking lot, leaving only a trail of dust behind you? Losing the money to life insurance makes no more sense than losing money to the bank. The actual yearly investment return is less than 6% for the first ten years. Each year in a universal life policy, the hidden cost of the insurance increases, further reducing the amount that goes into the investment but you never see it happening because your premium remains the same. The high surrender charge penalty is the insurance company's method of attempting to make it impractical for you to change your mind and drop the policy. Those companies that charge the least in front end fees have the biggest surrender charges. "Well," you might respond, "at least 10% is a fair return when money market rates are 7% to 8%." Is it? More fine print states that the 10% interest rate is guaranteed for the first year only, and then the interest rate you actually can receive drops to as low as 4½%.

SINGLE PREMIUM WHOLE LIFE INSURANCE

Single premium whole life insurance is sold primarily as a tax shelter, not as insurance. The concept is simple enough—you deposit a single payment of between $5,000 and $500,000 into a plan that combines a whole life policy with an investment. You are supposedly able to accumulate earnings over the years, which can then be borrowed with no taxes, to be used as your income during retirement. There are six major drawbacks.

1. You are buying the worst value in life insurance—whole life.
2. You must buy insurance to qualify for the investment, so less than 100% of your money is invested.
3. There are heavy front-end commissions and fees, big surrender charges that reduce the investment benefit, or you receive 8% to 10% per year on an investment that should pay you 12% to 15%, based on the return the insurance company is getting on your money.
4. A bill is pending in Congress already that would tax withdrawals as income. Congress could impose the rules on policies already in force.
5. There is a better tax-sheltered investment, often from the same insurance companies, called an annuity. The annuity earnings are compounded tax free as long as the money is left invested. The best tax-sheltered annuities

are those that offer mutual funds as investment (See Chapter 27, "Self-Directed Annuities").

6. You are told the major benefit is that you may borrow money tax free from your policy. The truth is you may borrow money from anywhere tax free.

TERM INSURANCE—THE RIGHT INSURANCE

Term insurance is pure insurance, no frills, no savings plan. Term is the least expensive life insurance, often 70% to 80% less than the insurance-plus-investment policies. Term pays salesmen far less in commissions and, therefore, is seldom offered if you don't ask. Because insurance policies make poor investments, term insurance is the life insurance choice of all knowledgeable insurance buyers.

There are three types of term insurance.

ANNUALLY RENEWABLE TERM (ART)

You buy a policy for one year at the end of which time you receive a renewal notice for the next year's premium. The younger you are, the lower the rates begin, increasing each year by a few dollars. ART is the least expensive and the best value of the three types of term insurance. The insurance is guaranteed renewable every year as long as you pay your premium. As you get older, your life expectancy decreases, so the premium increases.

DECREASING TERM

With decreasing term, your yearly premiums remain the same but the amount of insurance decreases. Decreasing term is used for both mortgage insurance and credit life insurance and is usually overpriced by 400%.

LEVEL PREMIUM TERM

You choose a policy period, five, ten, or fifteen years, and both your premium and the amount of the insurance remain constant. You are actually overpaying the premiums in the early years so they don't increase in later years—not a good strategy since the younger you are the less assets and positive cash flow you usually have. If you cancel because you find a better deal, you lose all of the overpayments and therefore this kind of term insurance is a poor value for good money managers.

> ### Strategy #38
> ## BUY ENOUGH TERM INSURANCE THAT, IF INVESTED AT 15% PER YEAR, WILL PROVIDE 50% OF CURRENT FAMILY INCOME.

The purpose of life insurance is to keep your family going if you die. Studies have shown that it will cost your spouse and children only 50% as much money if you are gone to maintain about the same lifestyle. Many of your current expenses would be eliminated—expenses like club memberships, family vacations, and entertaining. Life insurance should not be purchased as a get-rich-quick scheme for the surviving family members; you end up worth more dead than alive. The thousands of dollars you save by buying the right amount of the right kind of life insurance should be used during your lifetime to build your wealth, not the insurance company's.

Refer to the "Life Insurance Planning Chart" that follows. Locate your approximate current family income in column A. In column B, you will find the 50% income figure required for your family to fund an investment program at 15% per year to pay your family the amount in column B. Later in this book, you will learn how to invest with a safe annual return of 15% to 25%. If your children are grown, you may reduce the amount of required insurance coverage in C by another 50% as shown in column D. The less responsibility you have, the less insurance needed.

LIFE INSURANCE PLANNING CHART

A	B	C	D
Current Yrly Inc.	Yearly Amt. of Inc. Needed w/o Bread Winner	Amt. of Term Ins. When Invested at 15% to Provide (B)	Amt. of Term Ins. Needed if Children Are Grown
20,000	10,000	65,000	30,000
30,000	15,000	100,000	50,000
50,000	25,000	150,000	75,000
100,000	50,000	350,000	175,000
150,000	75,000	500,000	250,000
200,000	100,000	650,000	375,000

Strategy #39

BUY ANNUALLY RENEWABLE TERM (ART) INSURANCE AND SWITCH COMPANIES EVERY FEW YEARS

Your objective is to buy the least expensive life insurance that provides the greatest financial protection. The ART system will help you accomplish that goal.

Insurance companies, believe it or not, offer the first five years of annual renewable term insurance at less than competitive rates—the way a grocery sells a carton of milk at a loss just to get you in the store. If every company offers the first five years of ART for less than competitive rates, why couldn't you just change companies every five years to take advantage of a new set of lower rates? You can and that's the basis of the ART system.

The "ART Insurance Comparison Chart" compares the rates of three companies that offer the lowest ART rates. You will see some amazing opportunities.

1. The rates for the same person at the same age are dramatically different between companies. The rates vary as much as 30% for the three companies shown. Other companies have rates as much as 100% more than those shown. Compare columns B, D, and F for each age. It pays to shop.
2. If you stay with the same company, your premiums go up significantly each year for ten years (Columns B, D, and F, ages 29 to 38).
3. If you were 29 when you bought your first policy from Federal Kemper, but changed companies after five years and again after seven, you would save hundreds of dollars. You could switch as follows: Columns C, E and G show your new first year premiums.

Company	Ages	1st Year Premium
Federal Kemper	29–34	$115
First Colony	35–37	$136
Jackson National	38+	$158

Information on Companies Used in ART Chart

Federal Kemper	First Colony	Jackson National
Kemper Bldg.	PO Box 1280	5901 Executive Dr.
Long Grove, IL 60049	Lynchburg, VA 24505	Lansing, MI 48910

$100,000 ART INSURANCE COMPARISON CHART

A Age	B Federal Kemper 1st 10 yrs.	C Federal Kemper 1st yr. only	D First Colony 1st 10 yrs.	E First Colony 1st yr. only	F Jackson National 1st 10 yrs.	G Jackson National 1st yr. only
29	115	115	133	133	149	149
30	120		142		155	
31	129		153		161	
32	136	115	163	134	169	149
33	144		172		177	
34	157		190		185	
35	168	116	204	136	193	151
36	186		218		204	
37	200		233		218	
38	215	117	250	136	234	158

Note: Columns C, E and G show your first year premium if you bought the policy at the indicated age.

Had you remained in Federal Kemper for ten years, your tenth year premium would be $215 (Column B). By using the ART switching system as illustrated, your tenth year premium at Jackson National would have been $158 (Column G), a savings of $92 or 37% for that year alone.

Why not just stay with the same company and cancel the old policy and buy a new one every three years? As you might suspect, no company we know of will let you. You may wonder, "If you can save that much money by changing companies every few years, could you save more by changing every year?" Yes, however the money you would save—an extra $10 to $20 per year—might not be worth the extra effort.

Buy the new policy before you cancel existing policies to make certain you are still insurable. The final step is cancelling your existing investment insurance and reinvesting the cash value. The choice is yours. You can use your money to make yourself or the insurance company wealthy, but not both.

Strategy #40
REPLACE YOUR EXISTING WHOLE LIFE AND UNIVERSAL LIFE POLICIES WITH TERM INSURANCE.

There are no valid financial reasons for buying or keeping whole life or universal life policies at any age. You are always better off with term insurance and investing the difference yourself. If your health has deteriorated and you are no longer insurable, you should keep your existing policy. Otherwise, drop the whole life and universal life and replace with term, reinvesting your cash value in mutual funds or other good investments.

Strategy #41
USE THE LIFE-INSURANCE-TO-ANNUITY ROLLOVER RULES TO TAX PROTECT INSURANCE CASH VALUES.

When you drop a whole life or universal life policy, you are subject to taxes on the earnings but not on your principal. If you have a significant amount of earnings or taxable cash value, roll the money into a tax-free annuity with the same company if possible. The tax laws allow the tax-free rollover. Your cash value is now yours and is tax protected. The best annuities are those that offer mutual funds as investments. (See Chapter 27, "Self-Directed Annuities")

Strategy #42
BORROW AND REINVEST YOUR LIFE INSURANCE CASH VALUE.

A second alternative, if your health makes you uninsurable, is to borrow the cash value of your policy at 5% to 8% interest and reinvest at 20% using investment strategies in the investment section of this book. Borrowing your cash value is also a tax free transaction.

Under the new tax laws, interest paid on borrowed insurance money is not deductible if used for personal reasons, but is deductible if the money is used as investment capital. Investing the borrowed cash value makes the interest tax deductible.

Strategy #43

DON'T GIVE LIFE INSURANCE PROCEEDS TO YOUR HEIRS IN A LUMP SUM.

Write your will so that life insurance money is invested according to your instructions, and not given to family members in a lump sum. Only then can you be certain that the money will last until the kids are grown and continue to provide for your spouse. After the kids are grown, you can have the principal split among your family members. In eight out of ten cases studied, lump sum insurance proceeds left to families were totally gone in one to five years through unintentional mismanagement or poor financial advice.

Now you're ready to make your move to straighten out your lifetime life insurance plan. Here is how:

1. Determine the amount of ART insurance you need using Strategy #38.
2. Refer to the Annual Renewable Term Charts to determine the approximate cost and the company with the lowest premiums for a person your age. The charts show the first- and second-year premiums for $100,000, $250,000, and $500,000 of ART for ages 20 to 65 in five year increments.
3. Call the Life Insurance Clearinghouse at 1-800-522-2827. The Life Insurance Clearinghouse is an organization I have personally set up with Buddy Hewell, the Charles J. Given Organization's insurance consultant, to help you buy the least expensive ART life insurance without having to listen to the misleading insurance sales pitches. The Life Insurance Clearinghouse is registered in all states and can get your policy from any of the listed companies at the best rates. There is no charge for this service for readers of this book.

You want to buy insurance as if you expected to die tomorrow and invest as if you expected to live forever. The majority of your financial plan, therefore, should be devoted to living.

ANNUAL RENEWABLE TERM INSURANCE – BEST RATES
$100,000 Policy
Non Smoker

AGE/ Male	ALEXANDER HAMILTON	CONN. NATIONAL	FEDERAL KEMPER	FIRST COLONY*	JACKSON NATIONAL**
20 1st year	$104	$110	$125	$116	N/A
2nd year	113	115	131	126	N/A
25	105	110	125	118	N/A
	115	115	131	100	N/A
30	112	110	125	121	N/A
	125	115	131	108	N/A
35	125	112	125	123	N/A
	143	126	132	112	N/A
40	149	122	134	143	N/A
	175	150	159	146	N/A
45	187	141	160	180	N/A
	239	187	223	183	N/A
50	240	179	227	237	205
	338	246	279	246	260
55	361	230	340	340	273
	476	350	413	367	360
60	540	353	550	568	383
	687	547	708	612	503
65	815	610	968	968	643
	1100	900	1218	994	818
Female					
20 1st year	104	110	106	115	N/A
2nd year	113	115	110	96	N/A
25	104	110	106	116	N/A
	113	115	110	96	N/A
30	105	110	106	119	N/A
	115	115	110	102	N/A
35	112	110	107	121	N/A
	125	117	113	108	N/A
40	125	113	124	126	N/A
	143	129	143	117	N/A
45	149	125	151	149	N/A
	175	157	168	152	N/A
50	187	147	185	189	N/A
	239	197	215	193	N/A
55	240	188	224	278	217
	338	262	273	284	247
60	361	249	392	375	256
	476	381	471	406	335
65	540	389	589	633	363
	687	603	653	676	463

* 20% discount 2nd year if paid with first year premium.
** Minimum premium of $200

ANNUAL RENEWABLE TERM INSURANCE – BEST RATES
$250,000 Policy
Non Smoker

AGE/ Male	ALEXANDER HAMILTON	CONN. NATIONAL	EXECUTIVE LIFE***	JACKSON NATIONAL	PACIFIC FIDELITY***
20 1st year	185	200	N/A	N/A	N/A
2nd year	207	212	N/A	N/A	N/A
25	187	200	N/A	247	N/A
	212	212	N/A	260	N/A
30	205	200	N/A	247	N/A
	237	212	N/A	260	N/A
35	237	205	N/A	255	N/A
	282	240	N/A	275	N/A
40	297	230	N/A	297	N/A
	362	300	N/A	342	N/A
45	392	277	N/A	347	N/A
	522	392	N/A	430	N/A
50	525	372	N/A	430	N/A
	770	540	N/A	567	N/A
55	827	500	500	600	507
	1,115	800	737	817	955
60	1,275	807	837	875	870
	1,642	1,292	1,262	1,175	1,582
65	1,962	1,450	1,427	1,525	1,520
	2,675	2,175	2,397	1,962	2,440
Female					
20 1st year	185	200	N/A	N/A	N/A
2nd year	207	212	N/A	N/A	N/A
25	185	200	N/A	247	N/A
	207	212	N/A	257	N/A
30	187	200	N/A	247	N/A
	212	212	N/A	260	N/A
35	205	200	N/A	247	N/A
	237	217	N/A	260	N/A
40	237	207	N/A	252	N/A
	282	247	N/A	270	N/A
45	297	237	N/A	287	N/A
	362	317	N/A	325	N/A
50	392	292	N/A	337	N/A
	522	417	N/A	412	N/A
55	525	395	N/A	410	N/A
	770	580	N/A	535	N/A
60	827	547	N/A	557	N/A
	1,115	877	N/A	755	865
65	1,275	897	752	800	832
	1,642	1,432	1,142	1,075	1,435

*** Executive Life and Pacific Fidelity have a $500 minimum premium.

ANNUAL RENEWABLE TERM INSURANCE – BEST RATES
$500,000 Policy
Non Smoker

AGE/ Male	ALEXANDER HAMILTON	CONN. NATIONAL	EXECUTIVE LIFE***	JACKSON NATIONAL	PACIFIC FIDELITY***
20 1st year	320	350	N/A	N/A	500
2nd year	365	375	N/A	N/A	840
25	325	350	N/A	445	500
	375	375	N/A	470	840
30	360	350	N/A	445	500
	425	375	N/A	470	840
35	425	360	N/A	460	500
	515	430	N/A	500	840
40	545	410	N/A	545	500
	675	550	N/A	635	840
45	735	505	520	645	500
	995	735	735	810	840
50	1,000	695	655	810	610
	1,490	1,030	1,030	1,085	1,085
55	1,605	950	970	1,150	965
	2,180	1,550	1,450	1,585	1,864
60	2,500	1,565	1,650	1,700	1,690
	3,235	2,535	2,500	2,250	3,115
65	3,876	2,850	2,830	3,000	2,990
	5,300	4,300	4,770	3,875	4,830

Female

AGE/ Female	ALEXANDER HAMILTON	CONN. NATIONAL	EXECUTIVE LIFE***	JACKSON NATIONAL	PACIFIC FIDELITY***
20 1st year	320	350	N/A	N/A	N/A
2nd year	365	375	N/A	N/A	N/A
25	320	350	N/A	445	500
	365	375	N/A	465	840
30	325	350	N/A	445	500
	375	375	N/A	470	840
35	360	350	N/A	445	500
	425	385	N/A	470	840
40	425	365	N/A	455	500
	515	445	N/A	490	840
45	545	425	N/A	525	500
	675	585	N/A	600	840
50	735	535	500	625	500
	995	785	690	775	844
55	1,000	740	620	770	595
	1,490	1,110	960	1,020	920
60	1,605	1,045	880	1,065	900
	2,180	1,705	1,360	1,460	1,680
65	2,500	1,745	1,480	****	1,615
	3,235	2,815	2,260	2,100	2,820

*** Executive Life and Pacific Fidelity have a $500 minimum premium.

REORGANIZING YOUR TOTAL INSURANCE PLAN

A typical family of four can easily pay as much as $5,300 on the myriad of apparently logical insurance options (see Column A, below). By using the life and casualty insurance strategies in Chapters 3 and 4, their insurance costs are cut to $1,850, a savings of $3,450 per year.

Using Column C write in your current insurance premiums. As you use the strategies in these chapters, enter your new reduced premiums in Column D to determine your total savings.

| | | | You | |
| | A | B | C | D |
Type of Insurance	Before	After	Before	After
Life insurance on children	$ 200	$ 0		
Universal Life Insurance	1,500	0		
Term Life Insurance	0	300		
Credit Life Insurance on loans	200	0		
Automobile Insurance	1,100	600		
Specialty Insurance	200	0		
Mortgage Insurance	600	300		
Hospitalization Insurance	600	300		
Homeowners Insurance	300	200		
Rental Car Insurance (vacation)	100	0		
Umbrella Liability Insurance	0	150		
Disability Insurance	500	0		
Other				
Other				
TOTAL	$5,300	$1,850		

Chapter 5

GIVE YOURSELF CREDIT

'Tis against some Men's Principle to pay interest, and seems against others' interest to pay the Principle.

Benjamin Franklin
Poor Richard's Almanac
1753

Objective: Get control of your credit bureau file and establish good credit habits.

The bank must have slipped because it issued me my first credit card just before Christmas in 1965. The timing couldn't have been more appropriate. As in other gift-buying seasons, I was flat broke. I immediately charged $300 for a magnificent Tyco "HO" gauge miniature railroad layout—in one thousand easy-for-a-child-to-assemble pieces. Ever since my mother sold my prized Lionel train set to get money for food I had dreamed of the day when I would have sons of my own old enough to help me disguise my desire to recreate my youth.

The night before Christmas, I was in the attic until 6:30 in the morning putting together the Ping-Pong-table–sized train layout. Time was running out, along with my alertness and patience. The airplane glue, with its high concentration of acetone, put a smile on my face, but made me feel like I was putting all those little plastic pieces together with gloves on. No matter. The boys were elated; Dad was exhausted. It was my Christmas "biggy" and I had pulled it off. Pride lit up the room as chemical smoke poured from the tiny engine, puffing its way through plastic towns, switches, and papier-mâché mountains.

By three o'clock in the afternoon, I was asleep on the couch and the train began a perilous journey. Waking to the sound of a hammer strik-

79

ing metal, I stumbled into the garage to see my son Chuck, still in his blue Christmas robe, carefully dismantling the expensive, heavily financed engine into a hundred pieces. Resisting the temptation to faint, and holding back the tears, I screamed, "Chuck, what are you doing?"

"Dad, this is so neat. I just want to see how it works."

How can you get angry with a curious four year old? The train was gone, like so many Christmas toys, in a few, short hours. But the payments continued through the following Christmas.

There seems to be no end to the young couples I meet who have managed to, quite unintentionally, create the same kind of credit problem, by charging when cash is short and hoping the money will be there when each payment comes due.

There are three uses of credit listed here from worst to best.

Worst—to purchase *perishables*, such as meals, gas, groceries, airline tickets
Better—to purchase *depreciables*, such as automobiles, furniture, clothes
Best—to purchase *appreciables*, such as mutual funds, a home, or other
     investments

Charging perishables is the least desirable and most misused form of credit. Payments linger long after the goods or services are gone. One month after you charge a meal you pay for the potatoes, the next month the steak, and finally the dessert. While buying this month's food, you're paying for last month's feasts.

Depreciable purchases include goods and services that will never again be worth what you paid for them. A better use of credit, yes, but stacking up long-term payments will eventually bury you.

The best use of credit is borrowing money at a low rate and investing at a higher rate of return. Appreciables include a home with a mortgage, margined mutual fund shares, rental real estate, and a leveraged business or IRA. Leverage is the use of borrowed money to make money —often called using OPM (other people's money).

Financial success requires practiced discipline, and there is no better place to practice than with credit management. There are a few simple, but powerful strategies that will allow you to get control of credit.

Here are the winning strategies for perishable purchases:

Strategy #44
PAY OFF CREDIT CARD PERISHABLE PURCHASES EVERY MONTH.

Pay the credit card purchases you make this month with a check next month when you receive the bill. Never wait until you think you have the money—that time may never come. If you charge $100 for gasoline and meals, pay $100.

Strategy #45
DEDUCT A CREDIT CARD CHARGE IN YOUR CHECK REGISTER AS IF YOU MADE THE PURCHASE WITH A CHECK.

Count the money gone—it is. Circle the credit card purchases as you enter them in your check register and deduct the amount from your bank balance. The total of the circled item represents the extra credit card payment you will make at the end of the month. No more end-of-the-month shock. Because you have already deducted your credit card purchases from your balance, you have the money in your checking account to make your payment.

Strategy #46
DEVELOP A POSITIVE CREDIT PROFILE WITH THE "BIG 8."

To develop a positive profile, qualify yourself in as many categories as you can based on the chart on page 82. The more categories under which you qualify, the easier it is to get credit.

You can survive in America if you have poor credit—or worse yet—no credit, but poor credit is a definite handicap to wealth building. It is easier to play the piano with all ten fingers than with bandaged thumbs.

THE "BIG 8"
ELEMENTS OF A POSITIVE CREDIT PROFILE
(In order of importance)

1. A positive up-to-date credit report
2. A home with a mortgage
3. An American Express card and/or Diner's Club card
4. A job you've held for a year or more
5. A current or paid-off bank loan
6. A MasterCard or VISA card
7. A department store credit card
8. A telephone in your name

You must be willing to go public with who and what you are, no matter what the so-called offshore promoters tell you about privacy. Going public is accomplished by making available your financial statement, your tax returns, and your credit bureau data. The first two you furnish, the third will be obtained from the credit bureau by prospective employers and lenders.

Loan and mortgage applications are usually approved or rejected based on a point system. One to six points are assigned to each item in eight different categories. If the number of points you score overall exceeds a certain total, determined by the lender, your loan is approved; if less than the required total, your loan is automatically rejected.

Following is a model of a credit-scoring process taken directly from the procedures book of a finance company that will let you score yourself (page 83). About 18 points is the minimum score required to pass the credit test. The more you score the better your chances.

Owning a home with a mortgage shows stability and scores more points than most items on a credit application. It does not matter if you were required to qualify for the original mortgage, or if you simply assumed a no-qualifying FHA or VA mortgage.

An American Express card has almost as much clout in the financial world as a mortgage. To qualify for the card, you must show an income of over $15,000 a year and pay the balance each month. Diner's Club finishes a close second to American Express. Diner's Club reports on its cardholders to all major credit bureaus; American Express does not.

Factors	Points	Your Score	Factors	Points	Your Score
Marital Status			*Monthly Loan & Credit Cd. Pymts.*		
Married	1	____			
Not Married	0	____	Zero to $200.00	1	____
			Over $200.00	0	____
Age			*Credit History*		
21 to 25	0	____	Loan—most banks	2	____
26 to 64	1	____			
65 and over	0	____	*Residence*		
Monthly Income			Rent Unfurnished	1	____
Up to $600	1	____	Own without Mtge	4	____
$600 to $800	2	____	Own with Mtge	3	____
$800 to $1,000	4	____	Any other	0	____
Over $1,000	6	____	*Previous Residence*		
In Addition			0–5 years	0	____
Phone in Your Name	2	____	6 Years and Up	1	____
Checking or Savings	2	____			

The American Express green card is good; the gold and platinum even better. Always list your American Express or Diner's Club card number first on any credit application. Pay the fee; your credit profile is worth it. If your application is rejected, file a new one every six months until they give you a card, or have a cardholder, such as your parents, issue an extra card on their account until you can qualify on your own.

A current or paid-off bank loan, a MasterCard or VISA, and a department store credit card are indications that others have been willing to extend you credit. If you don't have these credit references, it will pay you to get them whether you need the credit or not.

Your payment habits, good or poor, are shown on your credit report.

Strategy #47

CHECK YOUR CREDIT BUREAU FILE ONCE A YEAR.

The credit bureau is the first place your potential creditors and employers will check. A positive up-to-date credit file is your responsibility, not that of the credit bureau. A positive up-to-date credit bureau file is something you create, not something that happens automatically. You have more control over your file than you may think.

All credit bureaus are governed by the Fair Credit Reporting Act passed by Congress in the mid 70's. In a congressional subcommittee on credit bureau abuses, a story came to light of a man who lost his credit, job, wife (from the pressure), and finally took his own life because of totally incorrect information in his credit file, which he was unable to have removed. With the advent of new laws, the credit power is now in your corner.

My organization conducted a credit bureau accuracy study in 1979. To our surprise, we discovered that 24 out of 25 credit bureau reports contained incomplete or incorrect data. Wait until you see yours! One report showed a man married to his first wife, whom he hadn't seen in eight years, and working for a company that had been out of business for six years.

Every credit bureau, by law, must give you a complete, accurate report of everything, including your credit history and a list of every potential creditor and employer who has been given information from your credit file during the past year. Knowing what others know about you is half the battle.

To obtain a credit report, you are required to identify yourself by completing a mail-in form, or appearing at the credit bureau, and paying a nominal charge of about $10. If you live in a city of over 300,000 people, there may be two or more credit bureaus you will want to check. Look in the yellow pages under "Credit Reporting Agencies."

Credit reports are easy to read once you get the hang of it, and most come with explicit instructions. If you still have trouble, the credit agency is required by law to spend time with you at its office explaining your report.

The credit bureau uses a rating system with the letters "O," "R," or "I," followed by a number from 0 to 9. "O" is a 30-to-90-day open account. "R" represents "revolving accounts" such as credit cards and

CREDIT REPORT CODES

The following codes are used on a standard credit report like the example shown on page 95, "Credit Report."

> *ECOA—These Equal Credit Opportunity Act designators explain who is responsible for the account and the type of participation you have with the account.*

Joint	J
Individual	I
Undesignated	U
Authorized user	A
Terminated	T
Maker	M
Co-maker	C
On Behalf of another person	B
Shared	S

Type of Account

Open Account (30 days or 90 days)	O
Revolving or Option (open-end account)	R
Installment (fixed number of payments)	I

Current Manner of Payment

Too new to rate; approved but not used	0
Pays account as agreed	1
Pays (or paid) in more than 30 days, but not more than 60 days, or not more than one payment past due	2
Pays (or paid) in more than 60 days, but not more than 90 days, or two payments past due	3
Pays (or paid) in more than 90 days, but not more than 120 days, or three payments late	4
Pays (or paid) in more than 120 days	5
Making regular payments under wage earner plan or similar arrangements	7
Repossession	8
Bad debt; placed for collection	9

The type of account and current manner of payment are shown together in the "Credit History" section of a credit report under present status; i.e. R1 means revolving account, pays as agreed.

department store accounts, and "I" is used for "installment credit," such as an automobile or furniture loan. R-1 is the best, R-9 usually means the account was written off by the creditor because of a bankruptcy. Your goal, of course, is to get all of your accounts to R-1 or I-1 status. When you do, the credit world is yours. A few prompt payments will usually upgrade any account. Refer to the sample credit report (page 95) and code explanation (page 85).

Credit reporting agencies do not evaluate your credit file, but make the information available to credit bureau members who may be banks, mortgage companies, department stores, or other issuers of credit.

There are several strategies that will help you control your credit file.

Strategy #48
CORRECT ALL PERSONAL DATA ERRORS ON YOUR CREDIT FILE.

Included in your personal data are your address, Social Security number, employment history, income, and telephone. This part of a credit file is the easiest to correct, but often the most inaccurate. Since 24 out of 25 credit files contain errors, check even the most obvious entries.

Strategy #49
HAVE THE CREDIT BUREAU REVERIFY AND CORRECT ANY INCORRECT CREDIT DATA.

Your credit files may contain information about late payments that weren't late or bad accounts that are not yours. Request that the credit bureau reverify the incorrect data. The credit bureau has 20 days to check and correct the file. Check to be certain the corrected data is entered into your file.

Occasionally, your creditor's records are wrong and the reverified data will remain incorrect. If so, you will begin to get the runaround. Contact the creditor yourself to correct the errors and furnish canceled checks or other necessary information supporting your position. Obtain from the credit bureau a Consumer Dispute form like the one shown on page 96 and list all disagreements with the information in your file.

Strategy #50

HAVE ALL MISSING POSITIVE CREDIT DATA ADDED TO YOUR CREDIT FILE.

You will be surprised when you see your credit file at how much data and how many accounts are missing. Although there is no law or rule that you are required to supply any negative credit data about yourself, you have the right by law and the duty to yourself to have all the positive data and accounts added to your file.

Supply the credit bureau in writing with a list of all charge accounts, credit cards, loans, and mortgages you have kept current. Include the account numbers. Include loans that have been paid off or accounts no longer in use. The credit bureau must, within 20 days, verify the information you have supplied and add it to your file. Recheck your file after 60 days to be certain it includes the new data.

Strategy #51

ADD THE REST OF THE STORY TO YOUR CREDIT FILE.

You have the legal right to add your side of the story to your credit file, that is, why your payments were late, or that credit information in your file is incorrect and is being reverified. Add important information like being unemployed during the period when the payments were late or that you moved and the bills went to the wrong address. One failure of the credit reporting system is that your file often shows how many times you have been 30, 60, or 90 days late in paying, but does not show how long ago. Add to your file the fact that all late payments were prior to a certain date, and why they were late and that payments are now current. Your side of the story can make a difference to your potential creditors and employers.

Strategy #52

HAVE THE CREDIT BUREAU REMOVE ANY DEROGATORY INFORMATION OUTSIDE THE STATUTORY LIMITS.

Negative information can remain in your credit file no longer than seven years, except for bankruptcy, which has a legal credit file life of ten years. You have the right by law to a credit file that does not contain information older than these statutory limits. The credit bureau will remove older data but often only if you request it.

Strategy #53

USE SMALL CLAIMS COURT TO RESOLVE CREDIT DISPUTES.

What if you follow these instructions but can't seem to get a creditor to supply correct information to the credit bureau? Take 'em to court —small claims court, that is. For a small filing fee and without an attorney, you can, in most states, file a suit claiming damages from the incorrect information. You won't have to go to court since it would be far less expensive for the creditor to straighten out the error than to pay an attorney to fight your claim.

Strategy #54

IF YOU ARE REFUSED CREDIT, FIND OUT WHY.

If you get turned down for a loan or mortgage, you have the right by law to know why, and finding out is in your best interest. You must, within ten days of receiving the notice stating denial of credit, contact in writing the company that rejected you after you receive the notice stating denial of credit. The lender must tell you specifically why your application was denied. You can then decide if you should reapply with the same lender supplying new or corrected data or apply some-where else.

Strategy #55

TO GET CREDIT AS A SMALL BUSINESS OWNER, INCORPORATE AND LIST YOURSELF AS AN EMPLOYEE.

If you've ever owned a business, you know that credit is tough to get until you can show substantial income, assets, and longevity. List yourself as an employee of the company instead of the owner and have your accountant verify your income with the lender. An alternative is to incorporate your business. For less than $50 you can incorporate your small business without an attorney by contacting your state corporation commission for the forms and instructions. You then pay yourself a big salary and deduct your expenses as employee business expenses, furnishing copies of W-2 forms instead of tax forms to a prospective lender. Give the lender the phone number of your bookkeeper, accountant, or other involved persons to verify your employment and salary. If you want the credit you must learn to play the game.

Strategy #56

WHEN BORROWING MONEY, NEVER TAKE "NO" FOR AN ANSWER.

Because one store, bank, or mortgage company turns you down doesn't mean everyone will. Make obtaining credit a game and say to yourself, "I will not be denied." I once saw a now successful young lady get turned down by five banks in two days for a $2,000 business loan. The sixth bank said yes. Where would she be today if she had given up after five banks?

Use your good credit to build your wealth. Work on overcoming the stigma of poor credit in the shortest time possible, but most of all, put your credit profile and credit power where it belongs—in your own hands.

STRATEGIES TO REBUILD YOUR CREDIT

Strategy #57

USE A COSIGNER TO HELP (RE)ESTABLISH YOUR CREDIT.

By getting parents or friends to cosign on mortgages, bank loans, or credit cards, creditors will extend credit to you they might otherwise refuse. A positive payment record will eventually qualify you for credit on your own.

Strategy #58

OVERCOME POOR CREDIT WITH A SECURED CREDIT CARD.

If credit troubles are reflected in your life, create enough good credit to offset the poor credit. Establish new credit sources as quickly as you can, and keep ALL payments up to date. Bury the bad among the good.

The easiest way to establish or re-establish your credit is through a secured MasterCard or VISA card. Secured means that you have made a deposit equal to the amount of credit you want, from $300 to $3,000. With some banks or agencies your deposit is put into an interest-earning CD. There is usually an agency fee of about $30 for getting you the credit approval and handling the transaction—well worth it. After you have made regular, timely payments for six months or so, the security requirement is dropped and your deposit returned to you.

After you have made payments, have your account reverified and your credit file updated by the credit bureau.

Contact these three companies for secured cards.

Charles J. Givens Organization
Secured Card
P.O. Box 3111
Orlando, FL 32802
(407) 862-4101
Cards Offered: MasterCard & VISA
Fee: $35

United Credit Network, Inc.
8306 Wilshire Blvd., Suite 19
Beverly Hills, CA 90211
(213)861-5472
Card offered: MasterCard
Fee: $35

Key Federal Savings Bank
PO Box 6057
Newark, DE 19725
(301)939-4840
Cards offered: MasterCard & VISA
Fee: $35

Strategy #59

**TO REHABILITATE CREDIT, BORROW THE BANK'S
MONEY, AND USE IT AS SECURITY FOR A LOAN.**

A banker is a person who will loan you all the money you want as soon as you can prove you don't need it. Banks, however, love to make fully secured loans—to almost anyone. Here is how you get a bank to participate in your credit-building plan. Look the loan officer straight in the face and say, "Mr. Banker, I need your help. I'd like to borrow $1,000. But, before you check my credit, let me tell you you won't like what you see. I would like you to put the $1,000 into a savings account here in your bank and you can put a hold on the money. You will have no risk since you have the money, and by making monthly payments, I can (re)establish my credit."

The cost to you is minimal. Although you are paying interest on the loan, the bank is paying you interest on your savings account. Don't take "no" for an answer. Keep reaffirming that you need the banker's help and will eventually become an excellent customer of the bank. Persistence always overcomes barriers. Once you find a bank that will make the loan, make two payments within the first 30 days. Go to a second bank and repeat the entire process. You can show the loan officer at the second bank the one good credit reference you now have at the first bank. Make two payments at the second bank as well. Now you have two excellent credit references. After 90 days use the money in your savings account to pay off the balance of the loan. Have the credit bureau check your bank loan accounts which now show that your payments were made on time and the loans paid off early.

During one of the shakiest periods of my credit life, I used this credit rehabilitation strategy with great success. I had recently exited from the corporate world and bought a franchise for $5,000 to market motivational programs. Having been a typical medium income, no-cash-on-hand corporate exec, I had to borrow the $5,000 and sell some stock to raise the start-up capital. I sold my home and boat, and ventured off to Gainesville, Florida, where there was no competition. The remaining money went out far faster than sales came in. After two months in Gainesville, a week before Christmas, I was broke. MasterCard and Mobil had demanded their credit cards back. My burgundy Continental Mark III was suddenly repossessed because of late payments. A vacate notice from the apartment manager was stapled to the door—something about overdue rent.

No car, no credit cards, no credit, no rent money, no cash, no Christmas presents—no kidding! The next step was the one-stop source of instant credit in America no matter what your credit history—the pawn shop. With tears in her eyes, my wife Bonnie handed me our only pawnable asset—an $800 set of sterling silver flatware, a Christmas present from her parents the year before. The unconcerned pawnbroker and I played tug-of-war between the measly $80 he originally offered and the $200 I thought I deserved. We finally called it quits at $125, $80 of which went for the kids' Christmas presents, and the other $45 for Christmas dinner.

The first "must" was a rental car—difficult to get without a credit card. I borrowed $40 from a friend and spent the afternoon talking about money with the operator of an independent car rental agency. After two hours I said, "By the way, my wife could use a car while I'm gone the next couple of days." When he asked for a credit card, I told him I didn't have one with me, but was prepared to put down a $40 cash deposit. I could hardly believe my eyes as he pulled out the rental contract with a smile on his face. That little car got me through the next three weeks, until I had the money to take it back.

During the next month, I managed to stall the landlord, feed the family on cereal and fast-food hamburgers, and finally get some regular income from my business. Still no credit, however. I went to a finance company and began: "Look, sir, give me some help. Loan me $300, but don't give me the money. Stick the check in your bottom desk drawer so you have no risk. I'll make payments, and you can give me a good credit report when anyone calls."

"Highly irregular," he said.

"Highly irregular situation," I responded.

After fifteen minutes of all the reasons why not, he finally said, "Why not?" And I was on my way to credit recovery. Later the same day, I went back to his office to sign the papers. Out of habit, I guess, they actually gave me the check. I did not pose a single objection. I used the $300 to open a checking account at a bank down the street and then promptly went over to the loan officer. I began with the "I need your help . . ." story, and told him I was already a customer of the bank, handing him my checking account $300 deposit slip on which the ink was still wet. He loaned me $1,000, and put the money in a savings account. The next day, I wrote checks for two payments of the $300 I had originally put in the bank checking account, and gave them to the teller with payment coupons. I wrote another $50 check to the finance company.

Still I needed a car. A friend drove me to Orlando to a Cadillac leasing agency. Sal, the manager, explained that it was four o'clock and he couldn't run my application through the credit bureau until the next day. I pulled out my aces.

"Sal, I live in Gainesville," I said. "How about if I give you two excellent credit references—one bank and one finance company?" Sal checked and found that I was two payments ahead on each account. Neither bothered to tell him the loans were less than a week old. I drove out of the lot with a beautiful blue metal flake Sedan de Ville. Within another 30 days, I had $4,000 in the bank from my business, the rent paid, a new Cadillac, and much of my credit restored. The next month I went back to Sal and leased another brand new Cadillac for my wife, Bonnie. Nothing is impossible.

YOUR CREDIT BILL OF RIGHTS

According to the Fair Credit Reporting Act and other acts, you have the right to—

1. Obtain from a credit bureau a report of what's in your credit file.
2. Know who has inquired into your credit file—stores, banks, employers, etc.
3. Request reverification by the credit bureau if information is incorrect.
4. Get missing data added to your file.
5. Have detrimental credit information removed from your file after seven years and bankruptcy information after ten years.
6. Put your side of the story in your credit file.
7. Privacy of the information in your file from anyone other than legitimate members of the credit-reporting agency.
8. Have your credit report transferred from one area to another any time you move.
9. Use small claims court to resolve any disputes with the credit bureau about incorrect, inaccurate information in your file.
10. Know exactly why you were refused credit. You must contact the institution refusing credit within ten days.
11. Remain silent about poor credit information that does not currently appear in your file.

CREDIT REPORT

NAME AND ADDRESS OF BUREAU MAKING REPORT CBI ATLANTA REGIONAL CENTER 3660 MAGUIRE BOULEVARD ATLANTA, GA	___ in file ___ single ref. ___trade ___EV&T ___Full ___Pres. Res.
	dat. rec'd. / date mailed / CBR rpt. 09/22/87 / 09/22/87 / inc. verified yes X no

CONFIDENTIAL REPORT	inquired as: Joan Adams	i n file since 07/13/84

report on (surname) **Joan Adams**   ss #: **265-71-4112**   spouses name

Address **100 Blue Lk Dr.**   city: **Atlanta**   state: **GA** zip code: resid. since

	position:	mth.inc.	
Present employer: **Surprise Gift Shop**	MGR	**$1,755**	since **1984**

Date of birth **12/15/55**	number of depndts.	owns	buying X	rents

Former address	city	state	zipcode		from	to

Former employer: **1741, Riversedge, Dr. Atlanta, GA**   position held   mth inc. from   to

Other's employer   dat. verified   postion held   mth inc. from   to

Credit History

firm --	code	date rpted	date opd.	credit limit	term mths	act. bal.	pres.	times	ecoa status	act. number rev'd.
Freedom	4470N119	08/87	09/86	2000	61	2027	R1	10J	I	300436618
Barnett	497BB108	08/87	01/87	13,000	230	12k	I1	07I	I	7099-33280185
GECC-RC	906FF278	08/87	02/87	1.800	79	1626	R1	05I	C	CC735464-W21381
Robinson s	906DC86	07/87	12/86	195		178	R2	05I	I	10627305
Visa	4910N24219	08/87	05/87	1.500	64	1344	R1	01I	A	4060950001048946

Public Records and/or Summary of Other Information

Inquiries--

Con SVC	447AA36	09/22/87	1st at MES	458BB2852	5/14/87
Navy - VISA	4910N24219	05/05/87	GECC	404FF304	03/01/87
Barnett BK	447BB2575	01/14/87	MD Nat. BK	801BB1845	01/13/87
Chrysler	447FA50	01/13/87	Don Mealey	447AU348	01/13/87

CONSUMER DISPUTE FORM

| | Area Code | Telephone No. |

Personal Identification (Please Print or Type)

Name_____
          (Last)   (First)   (Middle Initial)   Suffix (Jr., Sr., etc.)

Present Address _____
                       (Street)   (City)   (State)   (Zip)

Former Address _____
                       (Street)   (City)   (State)   (Zip)

Date of Birth _____ Social Security Number _____
               (Month)   (Day)   (Year)

I RECENTLY RECEIVED A COPY OF THE REPORT CONTAINING MY CREDIT HISTORY, AND I DISAGREE WITH THE FOLLOWING INFORMATION:

CREDIT HISTORY

Name of Business	Account Number	Specific nature of disagreement

Public Record And Other Information Court or Business	Case Number	Nature of disagreement

Other: (I.e. information from other credit bureaus, etc.)	Item	Nature of disagreement

I understand that the information I have disputed will be rechecked when necessary at the source, and I will be notified of the results of this recheck.

_____   _____
          (Signature)   (Date)

Chapter 6

BORROWING MONEY— MORTGAGE AND LOAN STRATEGIES

Live within your income even if you have to borrow money to do it.

Josh Billings
Humorist
(1818–1885)

Objective: Cut the cost of borrowing money by 30% to 50%.

It has been said that you are worth what you owe. At least that's what you're worth to those you owe. Borrowing money has become an American way of life. So let's look at powerful strategies for borrowing money, new types of mortgages that can save you thousands, when it pays to refinance your home, and how to cut your interest 30% by choosing the right term for your automobile and personal loans. None of these strategies requires extra time or effort, only the knowledge, and knowing what to say.

Strategy #60
LIVE FREE BY BUYING INSTEAD OF RENTING.

Before considering a mortgage, you must first decide if owning a home is better than renting. In all of my experience, I have found only two valid reasons for renting: (1) you live with your parents rent-free, or (2) you live in a rent-controlled apartment in a city like New York where you pay $300 a month for a place you would normally rent for $1,000.

Several years ago, I built a computer model to determine what happens financially to a person who buys instead of rents. The parameters included tax rates, interest rates, appreciation, closing costs, and the length of time lived in the home. If you buy and live in a home for at least five years, you live free—your monthly payments, closing costs, insurance and property taxes are returned to you through tax savings and your profit when you sell.

For example let's say you buy a $100,000 home.

Price of house	$100,000
Down Payment	− 10,000
Mortgage Amount	$ 90,000
Mortgage Interest Rate	× 10%
1st Year Interest	$ 9,000
1st Year Property Tax	+ 1,000
	$ 10,000
Income Tax Bracket	× 33%
1st Year Tax Savings	$ 3,300
Yearly Appreciation (6%)	+ $ 6,000
Tax Savings and Appreciation	$ 9,300

The first year interest expense is $9,000 and property taxes are $1000 for a total of $10,000, but your investment return from tax deductions and appreciation is $9,300. Each year the interest decreases until at the end of five years if you sell, you get most or all of your money back. You have lived free. If you rent a $100,000 home for $800 per month, you lose $7,200 per year or $36,000 during the five-year period. Why? There are no tax deductions and no appreciation.

During the next few years, the new tax laws will cause such a shortage of rental housing, you may not be able to afford renting. Rents go up; buying locks in lower payments. If you don't own a home, buy one.

Borrowing mortgage money once was a simple matter of completing the paperwork and waiting to see if you qualified. Today, mortgage decisions include a dozen options. Whether you are buying or refinancing a home, the correct choice of a mortgage is as important as the right choice of the property itself. The last person who should make your decisions is the loan officer, whose motives and profit objectives may be in conflict with yours. Understanding the following mortgage terms and strategies is a prerequisite for taking control.

Fixed-Rate Mortgage (FRM)

If the interest rate remains the same for the term of your mortgage, you have an FRM. Fixed-rate mortgages have been the standard since the 20's. When interest rates began soaring in the early 80's, and mortgage companies became concerned about locking in low fixed interest rates, long-term adjustable rate mortgages were born.

Adjustable Rate Mortgage (ARM)

The interest rate of an adjustable rate mortgage (ARM) changes periodically, based on either a contractual agreement or changes of an economic factor such as Treasury bill rates. ARMs are also called variable rate mortgages. There are two types of ARMs differentiated by the effects of interest rate changes.

A. Adjustable payments—Monthly payments are adjusted up or down to reflect changes in the mortgage interest rate.
B. Adjustable term—The total number of monthly payments is increased or decreased to reflect changes in the mortgage interest rates but the amount of the monthly payments remains constant.

Amortized Mortgage

This is a mortgage with equal monthly payments. The interest portion of the monthly payment decreases and the principal portion of the payment increases with each succeeding month.

Negative Amortization

Negative amortization means that the principal balance is increasing because of monthly payments that are less than the accrued monthly interest. The unpaid interest is converted to principal and added to the mortgage balance.

Cap

The maximum percentage an ARM interest rate may increase over the term of the mortgage. A new law requires the disclosure of the cap but does not regulate the maximum.

Strategy #61

IF THE FIXED RATE INTEREST IS OVER 9¾%, GET THE ARM. IF THE FIXED RATE INTEREST IS UNDER 9¾%, GET THE FRM.

You win with an adjustable rate mortgage when interest rates are low and the mortgage company wins when the rates are high. Mortgage companies are now discovering that mortgage rates are low twice the time they are high, giving the advantage to the mortgagee. The break point is 9¾%.

You can insure that an ARM will give you the advantage if the first year interest rate is at least 2% less than a comparable FRM and has a 5% cap. Most adjustable rate mortgages now have a conversion feature allowing you to change to a fixed rate mortgage without refinancing. Use this feature if you can ever lock in the fixed rate at under 9¾%.

Graduated Payment Mortgage (GPM)

Strategy #62

USE A GRADUATED PAYMENT MORTGAGE TO BUY MORE HOME WITH SMALLER MONTHLY PAYMENTS.

A GPM is a mortgage feature of either a fixed rate or adjustable rate 30-year mortgage, and it offers lower payments in early years with higher payments in later years to allow more buyers to qualify for the loan. Since the payments are often less than the accrued interest, the unpaid interest is added to the principal resulting in negative amortization. Payments go up slightly each year until the mortgage converts to positive amortization and is paid off at the end of the 30-year term.

The smaller payments in the early year of a GPM can help you qualify for or afford a home costing as much as 30% more. As your career flourishes and your income increases over the years, you will be able to afford the increase in payments of a GPM.

Growing Equity Mortgage (GEM)

Strategy #63

USE A GROWING EQUITY MORTGAGE TO PAY OFF YOUR HOME IN HALF THE TIME WITH PAYMENTS YOU CAN AFFORD.

There is a second alternative for saving money on mortgages. Some mortgage lending institutions are now offering a little known special 30-year mortgage called a growing equity mortgage (GEM). The first year's payments are about the same as a 30-year mortgage. Payments then go up each year, but the extra amount of the payment is applied only to the principal so that your mortgage is actually paid off in 15 years, saving thousands in interest payments. The GEM becomes a 15-year mortgage with lower payments in the early years when you need them.

Strategy #64

THE BIGGER YOUR MORTGAGE, THE BETTER YOUR REAL ESTATE INVESTMENT.

Your home is more than a place to live, it is one of the best investments you'll ever make.

There are four positive uses of a mortgage:

1. To increase the return on a real estate investment through the power of leverage
2. To buy a home without paying cash
3. To free up real estate equity for higher return investments
4. To pay off nondeductible consumer loans with tax deductible equity loans

Leverage is the use of other people's money (OPM) and a home mortgage is an easy method of putting OPM to work. Earning $10,000 in a savings account would require an investment of $50,000 for two years at 10%. Thirty percent of your interest would be lost to taxes.

Buy a $100,000 home with $10,000 down payment and if the home appreciates 5% per year you have earned the same $10,000 in two years with no taxes. Your investment return is 50% per year instead of 10%.

Strategy #65
GET A 15-YEAR INSTEAD OF A 30-YEAR MORTGAGE.

You can save tens of thousands in mortgage interest by putting the time value of money on your side. The mortgage company will automatically give you a 30-year term if you don't object. Why? Because 30-year mortgages make mortgage companies rich.

For every $50,000 you borrow at 12% interest for 30 years, your principal and interest will be $515 a month. At the end of five years (60 payments), you will have paid in $30,900, but reduced your principal by only $1000. After 10 years (120 payments), you have paid the mortgage company $62,000—more than the original mortgage amount —but have paid off only about $5,000 of the principal.

Get a 15-year instead of a 30-year mortgage and your monthly payments go up only about 16%. But for every $50,000 you borrow, you will save $80,000 in total interest payments. With the cost of homes today, the shorter mortgage can save you hundreds of thousands during your lifetime. After ten years of making monthly payments on a 15-year mortgage, you have paid 45% of your original principal. After ten years of making monthly payments on a 30-year mortgage, you have paid off only 5% of your principal. You still owe 95% of the original mortgage amount.

No matter how big your payments are today, they will seem much smaller five years from now when your income will have increased and the value of the dollar has been reduced by inflation.

The shorter-term mortgage is an automatic method of using discipline to build your wealth. If, however, you were to take the same amount each month and invest in a no-load mutual fund family or other similar investment, you would earn more.

Strategy #66

CUT YOUR MORTGAGE TERM IN HALF WITH EXTRA PRINCIPAL PAYMENTS.

Refinancing an existing 30-year mortgage for 15 years would result in thousands of dollars in new closing costs. You can pay off your 30-year mortgage in half the time without refinancing by making extra principal payments.

On the first of the month when you write your regular mortgage check, write a second check for the "principal only" portion of the next month's payment. The principal is that tiny number on your amortization schedule. If you didn't get an amortization schedule with your mortgage, your mortgage company, a real estate agent, or a friend with a home computer can print you one.

If you look at the early payments you will be shocked at how much of the payment goes to interest and how little goes to principal. Each month, during the entire mortgage term the principal increases by a few cents and the interest paid decreases by the same amount while your total monthly payment remains the same. There are five columns of importance on a mortgage amortization schedule: payment number, payment amount, principal, interest, and balance. Subtract this month's principal from last month's principal balance and you have the current balance.

Here is a section of a typical amortization schedule showing the breakdown of payment numbers 60 through 63 of a 30-year (360 payment) mortgage.

Principal Payment #	Payment	Principal	Interest	Balance	
60	$500	20.00	480.00	49,000.00	First Month
61	$500	20.30	479.70	48,979.70	
62	$500	20.70	479.30	48,959.00	Second Month
63	$500	21.20	478.80	48,937.80	

Notice how the principal increases slightly each month and the interest decreases by the same amount.

When you write a check for payment 60 of $500, write a second check for $20.30 representing the principal only portion of payment number 61. The following month, write a check for payment number 62 and a second check for $21.20, the principal portion of payment number 63. Mathematically you are moving down your amortization schedule two months at a time. You never pay interest on a payment whose principal is prepaid. The interest on the principal only payment is the amount you have saved.

Paying the exact amount equal to the next month's principal is not a requirement but a convenient way of keeping track of your mortgage balance. Last year I received a letter from a lady who decided to use this strategy on a new 30-year mortgage, sent in an extra check for $200.00 and eliminated 20 payments from her mortgage!

Some mortgage companies limit your minimum extra principal payment to one month's regular payment or allow you to pay off no more then $2,000.00 of your principal in one year without incurring an early payment penalty. Read your mortgage contract to see if you must work with any special rules.

Some financial and real estate writers recommended the bi-monthly mortgage strategy. Instead of making a full payment on the first of the month, you pay half on the first and half on the fifteenth. Since you are making an extra half payment per year, a 30-year mortgage would be paid off in 22 years. This is an example of a strategy that works only on paper since only one in twenty mortgage companies will allow you to split the payment. Using the extra principal payment strategy will pay off a 30-year mortgage in exactly 15 years. The only mortgages on which the mortgage company can refuse extra payments are county bond money mortgages and federal government subsidized mortgages. The government feels that if you have extra money, what are you doing with a subsidized mortgage?

There are three conditions under which you would not make extra principal payments: if your mortgage interest rate is 9% or less; if you plan to live in the home less than three years; or if the house is a rental property.

Never pay off low interest mortgages—those under 9%. Instead, use the extra money in a better investment. If you don't plan to live in the home more than three years, extra principal payments will have little effect. Cutting the interest on rental property is not as important as cash flow. You make the payments on your home, the tenants make the payments on your rental properties.

If you need lower payments in the early years, use the GEM mortgage described earlier.

Often I am asked if it wouldn't be better to keep a longer-term mortgage because the interest is tax deductible. The answer is no. To get $1.00 refunded from a home mortgage interest deduction, you must spend $3.00 in interest (33% bracket). Although the tax deduction is a bonus, interest is still an expense, costing you tens of thousands with or without the deduction.

Strategy #67
NEVER USE MORTGAGE GRACE PERIODS.

Using mortgage grace periods can damage your credit profile. Even though you are not charged a late penalty until after the tenth of the month, paying after the first will be counted as late and could end up on your credit bureau file. Let me share with you my own experience.

After I bought my first 40 rental homes, I found I could create a tremendous float by mailing the mortgage checks so they would arrive at the mortgage company not by the first, but by the tenth of the month. The process also allowed me extra time to collect past due rents to cover the mortgage payments. Using the grace period soon caught up with me. Even though all the mortgage companies gave me until the tenth of the month before a late charge was assessed, payments after the first were counted as late and new mortgages became more difficult to obtain. My payments are now mailed to arrive by the first of the month.

Strategy # 68
REFINANCE YOUR HOME AT A LOWER INTEREST RATE ANY TIME THE NEW INTEREST RATE IS AT LEAST 2% LESS THAN THE OLD INTEREST RATE.

Knowing when to refinance is as important as choosing the right mortgage. Some believe you should never refinance; others will tell you to refinance anytime interest rates drop. Neither is correct.

You cannot save money by refinancing your home every time interest rates drop because of the additional closing costs. The chart below will show you the approximate number of months it takes for low payments to make up for the 3% to 4% closing costs.

Difference in Interest Rate	Number of Months Required
2%	26 Months
3%	22 Months
4%	18 Months

If the difference between interest rates on your old and new mortgage is 2%, 26 months of lower payments will offset the closing costs. It would take 22 months at a 3% difference and 18 months at a 4% difference to offset the closing costs! The lower payments from that point on will save you thousands.

To determine the actual number of months of reduced payments required to offset the new closing costs, divide the closing cost amount by the amount you will save each month with your lower payment.

It would not be wise to refinance a $40,000 mortgage at a 1% difference in interest rates. The amount saved each month would only be $30, and if the new closing costs were $2,000, it would take you 66 months, or 5½ years to catch up. You may sell your home before then. How long you intend to own your home, therefore, is also an important refinancing consideration.

Always ask if the closing costs of a loan or mortgage can be added to the loan amount. Use other people's money whenever possible.

Strategy #69

BORROW YOUR HOME EQUITY FREE BY COMBINING AN EQUITY LOAN WITH A GOOD INVESTMENT PLAN.

Home equity is like money in a shoe box gathering dust in your closet. It may make you feel good, but it is not working for you. There are a dozen good emotional reasons for accumulating a large amount of equity in your home, but not one good financial reason.

My Hungarian relatives lived on the south side of Chicago in an area known as Cottage Grove. Most worked for the Pullman Railroad Car Company until retirement. They lived in three-story row houses that they were somehow able to buy on their small salaries. To save money, they never took expensive vacations, or spent much on themselves. One of life's biggest events after marriage and children was paying off the mortgage and celebrating the event with a mortgage-burning party. In this ethnic neighborhood where half the residents never learned

English, a fire was built in the street in front of the debt-free property. With great fanfare, the proud owners threw their canceled mortgage documents into the flames while the neighbors danced and sang in a joyous circle. Great party, but a losing financial strategy. They may have owned their homes, but that was *all* they owned.

Today millions of Americans are following the same dead end path, living a financially austere life even though they have wealth that could be unlocked from the equity they have built up in their homes. Your home equity, if borrowed and reinvested, can be an excellent source of income. Using a combination of a low interest home equity loan or mortgage and a good safe investment plan that pays over 20% per year, you can borrow your home equity free—with enough income from the reinvested equity to both make your mortgage payments and improve your life-style. For every $50,000 of home equity, you can increase your income $8,000 per year for the rest of your life without depleting the principal. If you have a low interest first mortgage, the "equity loan" is the best alternative for freeing up your home equity. Unlike a regular mortgage, which gives you a fixed amount for a fixed term, the equity loan gives you a line of credit. Money can be borrowed or paid back at any time during the term of the loan, usually by writing a check against your loan account. You only pay interest on the money you borrowed, and you stop paying interest on any portion that you pay back with no prepayment penalty.

Equity loans are available from:

• Savings and loan institutions
• Banks (local and national)
• First and second mortgage companies
• Brokerage firms
• Mortgage brokers (independent mortgage sources)

The equity loan is usually an adjustable rate mortgage.

Shop around; the rates and terms vary from institution to institution. Expect to pay $80 to $140 for a required appraisal and one to five points, which can usually be added to the mortgage amount. Eight points on a 15-year mortgage is the equivalent of 1% interest. Therefore, an 8½% mortgage with four points is the same as a 9% mortgage with no points.

The maximum loan you can obtain is determined by a formula called the loan-to-value ratio (LTV), usually 70% to 90% of the appraised value of your property, less any existing mortgage. If, for example, your home appraises for $110,000, the mortgage company's LTV ratio is

80%, and your first mortgage balance is $45,000, your maximum equity loan would be $43,000.

(LTV × Market Value) − Existing Mortgages = Maximum Loan
(80% × $110,000) − $45,000 = $43,000

The next step is to formulate your investment plan. Your investments must provide a return great enough to make the payments on your loan and give you additional income. The chart below will

BORROW YOUR HOME EQUITY FREE
INVESTMENT PLAN
EQUITY LOAN, 10% INTEREST, 15 YEAR TERM

Investment	Amount Invested	Expected Income %	Cash Income	Deferred Income		
Amt Borrowed/Invested $20,000						
*Yearly Interest = $2,000**						
Mutual Funds[1]	$10,000	20%	$ 2,000	—	Total Income	$ 5,000
Discounted Mtg[2]	$10,000	30%	2,000	$1,000	Interest pymts	− 2,000
			$ 4,000	$1,000	Net Income	$3,000
Amt Borrowed/Invested $50,000						
*Yearly Interest = $5,000**						
Mutual Funds[1]	$25,000	20%	$ 5,000	—	Total Income	$12,500
Discounted Mtg[2]	$25,000	30%	5,000	$2,500	Interest pymts	− 5,000
			$10,000	$2,500	Net Income	$7,500
Amt Borrowed/Invested $100,000						
*Yearly Interest = $10,000**						
Mutual Funds[1]	$50,000	20%	$10,000	—	Total Income	$25,000
Discounted Mtg[2]	$50,000	30%	10,000	$5,000	Interest pymts	− 10,000
			$20,000	$5,000	Net Income	$15,000

* Only the interest portion of the monthly payments is shown since the principal portion of the mortgage payback is your money.
[1] Mutual Funds (Chapter 24)
   No commissions using no-loads funds
   Money Movement Strategy (Chapter 23) used to earn 20% year average
   All earnings can be either withdrawn or reinvested
[2] Discounted Mortgages (Chapter 28)
   Mortgages purchased at 40% discount from face value
   20% is current income from monthly interest received
   10% income is deferred until mortgage matures.

give you suggested investment plans based on the amount of equity you have available. Modify the suggested plans to fit your specific investment needs: maximum growth, maximum income, or maximum tax shelter. Make your plan before you withdraw the money from your equity loan account.

Strategy #70

IF THE RETURN ON A POTENTIAL INVESTMENT IS LESS THAN THE INTEREST RATE ON A LOAN, PAY CASH. IF THE RETURN IS MORE, BORROW TO BUY AND INVEST YOUR CASH.

Automobiles and other rapidly depreciating assets are certainly not investments, but you face the same financing decisions as with mortgages. Should you finance the automobile or other purchase or pay cash? Of course, the question only applies to those who have the cash.

You must first understand an important financial measuring stick called "opportunity cost," or what I call "opportunity lost." If you pay cash, you automatically lose the opportunity to invest that cash. If you could borrow at 12% to buy an automobile, but instead pay cash, your opportunity cost is what you could have earned by investing that same amount of money, minus the 12% interest. If you could have earned 20% in no-load mutual funds (you'll learn how later), your opportunity cost would have been 8% (20% minus 12%). You would be losing an opportunity for earning an additional 8%. In this case, the greater profit would come from borrowing to buy the automobile and investing your dollars in the mutual fund. However, if a 9% bank certificate of deposit is the best investment you know of, you would be better off paying cash for the car. Paying cash instead of financing at 12% is like investing your money at 12% interest. Every financial decision has an opportunity cost and computing your opportunity cost will show you the correct decision.

Strategy #71

FINANCE AUTOMOBILES, FURNITURE, AND OTHER PERSONAL ASSETS NO LONGER THAN 24 TO 36 MONTHS.

In today's world of easy money, you become bombarded with opportunities to pay over time, rather than pay at this time. Choosing a shorter loan term, as with a mortgage, can save you thousands.

When it comes to borrowing, the only two questions Americans have learned to ask are: "How much is my down payment?" and "What are my monthly payments?" The most important element of a loan is your total payments; that's what eats into your lifetime wealth. "The longer the term, the lower the monthly payments" is a true statement, but the law of diminishing returns raises the total cost far beyond the benefit of lower payments. When you lengthen the term of a loan to reduce the payments, the total interest paid increases dramatically.

When you shorten the term, your monthly payments are slightly higher but two positive financial rewards are yours:

1. You pay less total interest; what you buy costs less.
2. A greater percentage of each payment is applied to the principal instead of interest.

Let me show you how the strategy works on an automobile or other personal loan. For example, you buy an automobile on which you

HOW THE TERM AFFECTS YOUR LOAN

	Effect of Choice of Terms			*36 Month Loan Comparison*	
a. Term	**b.** Monthly Payment	**c.** Total Paid	**d.** Total Interest	**e.** Interest Saved	**f.** Increased Payment
24 mos.	$480	$11,520	$1,520	—	—
36 mos.	341	12,300	2,300	—	—
48 mos.	273	13,100	3,100	$ 800	$68/mo.
60 mos.	233	13,960	3,960	1,660	108/mo.

obtain a $10,000 loan at 14%, and you have a choice of terms ranging from 24 months to 60 months.

The chart on page 110 shows the real cost of a loan for terms ranging from 24 to 60 months. Notice that by financing for 60 months instead of 24 months, you will pay $2,440 additional interest or 25% more for your car (Column d $3,960 − $1,520).

Another way to use the chart is to compare a 36-month loan with a 60-month loan. If you get a 36-month loan instead of a 60-month loan you save a total of $1,660 and your payments are only $108 more per month (Columns e & f). In addition, you stop making payments 24 months earlier. The lender always wins with 48- and 60-month loans. You win with 24- or 36-month loans. Use the chart to plan your next financed purchase.

Strategy #72

MAKE EXTRA PRINCIPAL PAYMENTS TO CUT PERSONAL LOAN TERMS AND INTEREST 30% TO 50%.

Not only can you make extra principal payments on a mortgage, you can do the same thing with any high interest loan or to rid yourself quickly of 18% credit card interest.

You can even pay off a 48-month automobile or furniture loan in 24 months by making extra principal payments along with your regular payments. If you just financed $10,000 at 14% interest for 48 months, begin immediately including next month's principal payment along with this month's full payment. Look at the Automobile Loan Amortization Schedule below. Let's say you've made payment number one for $268.27, and you are ready to make payment number two.

AUTOMOBILE LOAN AMORTIZATION SCHEDULE

Month 1 through 5 of a $10,000, 14%, 48 month loan.

Payment #	Amount	Principal	Interest	Balance
1	$268.27	$159.94	$108.33	$9,840.06
2	$268.27	$161.67	$106.60	$9,678.39
3	$268.27	$163.42	$104.85	$9,514.97
4	$268.27	$165.19	$103.08	$9,349.78
5	$268.27	$166.98	$101.29	$9,182.80

The first month of the loan you pay $268.27. The second month you pay:

> check #1—second month's regular payment of $268.27
> check #2—third month's principal of $163.42
> Total = $431.69

The third month you pay:

> check #3—fourth month's regular payment of $268.27
> check #4—fifth month's principal of $166.98
> Total = $435.25

The extra principal payments will pay off the loan in 24 months instead of 48 months. If your lender requires you to pay in increments of full payment amounts, in our example $268.27, make the extra principal payment in that amount every other month.

Strategy #73

TO ELIMINATE HIGH-INTEREST CREDIT CARD DEBT, PAY AN EXTRA $25 TO $100 EACH MONTH, PLUS THE MINIMUM PAYMENT, PLUS THE AMOUNT OF YOUR PURCHASES.

Using credit cards often feels like getting something for nothing, at least until the bill arrives. Credit card interest is often 18% or 1½% per month. and should be a primary target for the "extra principal payment" strategy.

You'll be surprised how quickly you can eliminate your credit card debt with only a few extra dollars each month. Since the monthly interest is computed on your principal balance, making extra principal payments will rapidly decrease your monthly interest and balance.

Let's say, for example, your MasterCard balance is $1,100, your required monthly payment is $60, and you purchased $110 this month. You must send in a check for $220 as follows.

New purchases amount	$110
Required monthly payment	+ $ 60
Additional optional payment	+ $ 50
TOTAL PAYMENT	$220
NEW BALANCE	$880

You'll pay off your balance in half the time! If you have to scrimp and save in some other area—do so. It's imperative that you come up with the extra money this month so you can pay the entire bill in half the time! Otherwise, the credit card debt will never be paid off, exactly what the credit card companies love to have happen.

Strategy #74

REPLACE HIGH INTEREST CREDIT CARDS WITH LOW INTEREST CARDS.

Throw away your 18% MasterCards and VISAs and replace them with low-interest credit cards. The state of Arkansas, for instance, has a usury law that limits the amount of interest that can be charged on any loan, including credit cards. There are banks in Arkansas that have issued MasterCards or VISAs to out-of-state customers at as little as 10½% to 11% interest. Peoples Bank in Bridgeport, Connecticut, has held its rate for out-of-state cardholders to 12½%, and a few others do the same. Following is a list of the least expensive credit cards available. Order your applications today.

Name of Bank	Interest Rate	Type of Card	Yearly Fees	Out of State	Billing
The Charles J. Givens Organization Credit Card Arkansas Federal Savings* PO Box 3111 Orlando, FL 32802 Special Rate for Givens Organization Members Only	10.92	VISA/MC	$37.50	Yes	None
The Charles J. Givens Organization Credit Card Union National Bank* PO Box 3111 Orlando, FL 32802 Open to All	12.50	VISA/MC	$20.00	Yes	None

Name of Bank	Interest Rate	Type of Card	Yearly Fees	Out of State	Billing
People's Bank Box 637 Bridgeport, CT 06601 Application Requests: (800) 423-3273	12.50	VISA/MC	$20.00	Yes	25 days
Home Plan S&L Des Moines, IA Application requests: (515) 270-9459	12.90	VISA/MC	$25.00	Yes	25 days
Empire of America Buffalo, NY Application requests: (716) 845-7000	13.75	VISA Light	$18.00	Yes	None
Republic Bank PO Box 350430 Miami, FL 33135 Application requests: (305) 441-7600	14.00	VISA/MC	$22.00	Yes	25 days
USAA Federal Savings Bank Bank Card Center PO Box 21658 Tulsa, OK 74121 Application requests: (800) 922-9029	14.00	MC	$0	Yes	25 days
Manufacturer's Hanover Bank Box 15147 Wilmington, DE 19850 Application requests: (800) 346-1300					

* Special applications available free from the Charles J. Givens Organization at the address shown.

Chapter 7

SEND YOUR
KIDS TO COLLEGE
FREE!

Experience keeps a dear school, but fools will learn in no other.

Benjamin Franklin
Poor Richard's Almanac
1743

Objective: Combine a college loan with an investment that will cut the real cost of educating your children by 50% to 100%.

The traumas of raising children are no longer limited to diapers, grades, first dates, and first automobiles. The third-biggest expense you'll ever encounter, close behind income taxes and buying a home, is putting your kids through college. The cost of even the most modest four-year college education now exceeds $20,000 with room and board.

My parents began a college fund for me using U.S. Savings Bonds. By the time I was 13, there were several thousand dollars neatly tucked away for an education at M.I.T. Then, in 1953, my parents' business slipped past the point of no return. Their last attempt to save it was to withdraw the college funds and dump the money into the business. Less than a year later, they were bankrupt, and M.I.T. became a faded dream.

Years later, my father did scrape together $300 to enroll me in Millikin University in Decatur, Illinois, but my $27 a week shoe salesman's job didn't provide enough money to keep the education going. Second semester, it was over. I was still paying off the balance of the

115

first semester's tuition and the school would not let me enroll for another term without more money. Ironically, 25 years later, when the college found out that I had become financially successful, they had no shame in asking me for contributions.

My experience is certainly not unusual. Many parents have traditionally found themselves unable or unprepared to finance college educations for their children. Either they intended to save money while the children were growing, or they were sold a life insurance policy that eventually failed to create enough cash value to pay for college. Most educational investment plans are doomed to the same failure. Because of inflation over any 20-year period, parents end up using their lifetime savings or going deeply in debt to finance the education that an 18-year savings plan would not support.

Student loans are difficult to get if you are above the poverty level. Scholarships cannot be depended on and if your child or grandchild is not able to dunk a basketball or scare off a 300-pound defensive lineman, the cost of college will usually put you in financial trouble.

There is a simple plan that will allow you to educate your child, grandchild, or even yourself in any college in America—FREE!

Strategy #75
BUY A HOME THAT WILL PAY OFF A COLLEGE LOAN.

About three months before your child begins college, buy a four-bedroom home, condo, or duplex with as big a mortgage as possible within a few miles of the college campus. Furnish your property in "early Salvation Army" and rent it to four students with leases cosigned by their parents. Then march yourself down to the college financial aid office and ask for a little known type of college financing called the *parent loan*. Finance the entire education using the parent loan plus one of the commercial loans listed at the end of this chapter. Pay the loan off with the profit from the sale of the property when your child graduates. During the four-year term, your property will appreciate dramatically because of the shortage of off-campus housing in almost every college campus area.

Choose a property within a couple of miles of the campus, so that transportation for your resident students is not a problem. The property should be four bedrooms for two reasons: maximum rent while you own the property, and maximum value when you sell. The house should be in good condition, requiring only cosmetic, not major surgery.

Strategy #76

USE THE "PLUS LOAN" TO FINANCE THE FIRST $3,000 PER YEAR OF COLLEGE COSTS.

The parent loan for undergraduate students (PLUS loan) is the easiest to obtain of all the government educational assistance programs, yet the least known. Parent loans are available to parents, grandparents, and even financially independent undergraduate students, and are handled through participating local banks or credit unions. The greatest benefit of the PLUS loan is that you do not have to prove financial need as you would for a guaranteed student loan. The PLUS loan is available to all income brackets, and is usually made directly to parents instead of students. The repayment starts 60 days after the loan is obtained but the money can be borrowed as needed, and you pay only the interest until your child graduates. The interest rate is tied to the 91-day Treasury bill rate.

Most people have never heard of the PLUS loan and most college financial aid offices don't mention it. To learn more about PLUS loans, contact your high school guidance office, the college financial aid office, or the department of education in your state. Ask for the PLUS loan by name.

The PLUS loan will give you a maximum of $3,000 per year up to a total of $15,000. Use one of the commercially available education loans listed at the end of this chapter to finance the balance. The commercial education loans from Mellon Bank and Knight Insurance can be used for up to 100% of college costs and have no restrictions.

Strategy #77

TURN YOUR PROPERTY INTO A MINI STUDENT DORM.

Furnish your property with used, inexpensive furniture from a salvage store. You will want a bed, desk, chest of drawers, lamps, and small bookcase for each bedroom, and basic furniture for the rest of the house. Let students supply their own linens and kitchen utensils. Don't be surprised if you can furnish the entire house for little more than $1,000. All the furnishings are tax deductible.

Strategy #78

RENT YOUR PROPERTY BY THE BEDROOM ON A YEARLY LEASE TO INDIVIDUAL STUDENTS, COSIGNED BY PARENTS.

Renting the property to students is the easiest part of the strategy. Since most students would rather live off campus, there is always a housing shortage. Place ads under the "share" column of the school and local newspapers, as well as posting notices on the school bulletin board. Most college admissions or student housing offices keep a registry of available housing, in which you will want to list your property.

Maximize your income by renting by the bedroom on separate leases. Check with others who own rental property in the area to determine the rent you should charge. You will find you can get $150 to $300 per student, per month, depending on the city, cost of properties in the area, and the shortage of housing. The total rent of $600 to $1,200 per month will be more than adequate to offset the mortgage, taxes, and maintenance costs, and give you extra money for college expenses.

Two caveats about renting to students. First, rent on a full year's lease, not a lease that covers only nine months of the school year, and give each student the option to sublease if he or she will not attend summer school. Secondly, make certain that parents cosign the lease. With a cosigner, you are protected from the problem of collecting for damage or unpaid rent.

Strategy #79

MAKE YOUR SON OR DAUGHTER THE PROPERTY MANAGER.

By making your child the property manager, you can reap tax and business benefits almost immediately. Pay your child a tax deductible salary of about $100 a month, and let him or her handle the regular duties of a property manager including:

* Collecting rents,
* Inspecting the property once a week for cleanliness and damage,
* Renting the property when there is a vacancy,
* Contracting any repair work that needs to be done,
* Reporting to you on the financial and physical condition of your property.

The $1,200 per year you pay your child is tax deductible, since the money is paid for property management. The deduction should save you $360 per year in taxes (28% bracket) or almost $1,500 over the four years. The tax deductible money you pay your student can be used for books, supplies, or food expenses.

Your student may make a couple of tax deductible trips home each year for property management training or business conferences. Of course, the IRS might look at the trip suspiciously, so be certain to document the training or conference. A trip is deductible if it has a legitimate primary business purpose.

You may also travel to inspect any out-of-town property twice per year and take a tax deduction for the cost of the trip. Be certain the primary purpose of the trip is the inspection or maintenance of the property, and the secondary purpose is to visit your child.

Strategy #80

USE THE REAL ESTATE TAX DEDUCTIONS TO GENERATE EXTRA CASH.

The depreciation deductions you claim each year for your mini student dorm give you immediate cash, which can be applied toward college expenses. Using 20% as an estimate of the value of the land, 80% as the estimated value of the house, and assuming you are in the 28% marginal tax bracket, the table below illustrates how much cash you will save in taxes for the four years of college.

Basis of Property	First Year Depreciation	Four Year Depreciation	Four Year Tax Savings
50,000	$1,800	$ 7,200	$2,016
75,000	$2,700	$10,800	$3,024
100,000	$3,600	$14,400	$4,032
150,000	$5,400	$21,600	$6,048

The year you sell the property, be certain to use tax strategies to create enough additional deductions to offset the depreciation recapture you will add to your income. The financial relief of a graduated student will give you the extra money to pay any taxes due on the profits.

Strategy #81
USE THE PROFITS FROM YOUR INVESTMENT TO PAY OFF YOUR LOANS.

When your child graduates, the time has arrived to sell the property. At 8% per year appreciation, the property will be worth $15,000 to $40,000 more at the end of four years, depending on the original price. Because of the demand for housing in college areas, the increase in value of your property will be substantial. The best and simplest way of selling the property for top dollar is to run the following advertisement in the school and city newspapers:

"Send your child to college free—call me for details!"

You'll receive a dozen calls the first day alone. Since you have the proof you can send your child to college free, you will have no problem selling the property to the parents of an incoming freshman. In fact, you'll have several families bidding up the price.

During the past few years, several colleges have sent staff members to my workshops to learn the "free college" strategy, then built condominiums on or near the campus and sold them to parents who then resell them at a profit to other parents four years later. Everyone wants in on the act! Someday, most colleges will adopt the "free college" strategy. Until then, you can use it on your own to pay for one or more expensive college educations.

BEST COLLEGE LOAN SOURCES*

Federal Loans	Interest Rate	Term (years)	Amount	Restrictions
National Direct Student Loan (NDSL)	5%	10	$3,000/yr	Generally, family must have income under $30,000
Guaranteed Student loan (GSL)	8%	10	$2,500/yr	Family must have income under $30,000
Parent Loan for Undergraduate Students (PLUS)	12%	10	$3,000/yr	None
Commercial Loans				
Mellon Bank Edu-Check Program Mellon Bank E. N.A. PO Box 7479 Phila., PA 19101-9990 (800) 322-4417	11¾	8	100% of college costs	None
Knight Insurance Extended Repayment Plan Beacon St. Boston, MA 02108-9901 (617) 267-1500	9¾% 10½%	7½ yr. 10 yr.	100% of college costs	None
Tuition Plan Donovan St. Ext. Concord, NH 03301	15.95%	10	100% of college costs	Available in 38 states.

* Rates in effect as of July 1, 1988, but while rates may change, these sources should remain the best.

In addition to the PLUS loan, there are several other sources of college financial aid. In order to help you plan effectively, the preceding chart will show you the financing options and sources for the best educational loans. You may use the college loans with or without purchasing the real estate. Awareness of your alternatives and proper planning will save you thousands of dollars when educating your children, your grandchildren, or yourself.

Part II

TAX-REDUCING
STRATEGIES

Chapter 8

MAKING YOUR LIFE
LESS TAXING

People who complain about the tax system fall into two categories—men and women.

Barry Steiner
Pay Less Tax Legally
1982

Objective: Cut your income taxes by 50%.

The biggest lifetime expense you'll ever encounter is neither a home nor a college education, but income taxes. What we were never taught is that the amount of income tax you are liable for has little to do with your total income, and everything to do with your knowledge of tax strategies.

The importance of an effective tax plan cannot be overstated. One-third to one-half of all the wealth you will accumulate in your lifetime is dependent on your tax-reducing plan and not your income, investments, or retirement program.

The new tax laws mean a tax increase for two out of three families with an income of over $20,000. All of the flag waving by Congress proclaiming a great tax decrease is purely political, not practical reality. Over 50 once automatic deductions have been eliminated or curtailed and the elimination of income averaging and especially the favorable capital gains tax rates puts a bigger tax burden on investors, retired people, and the upwardly mobile. The best defense is still a good offense—a tax plan that uses the new tax laws to decrease instead of increase your taxes.

Where do we begin? By learning to turn the money you spend into legitimate tax deductions. Up to 60% of your income each year can become tax sheltered by combining personal expenses with tax deduction strategies. Just about every strategy you can logically and legally use to cut your taxes is contained in this and the following chapters.

At 19, I dropped out of Milliken University after one semester, far short of the $300 tuition necessary to remain enrolled. Needing money to help support my mother and brother, I went to work in a foundry dumping "slag"—molten metal waste from the furnaces. If you ever want a job that will motivate you to do something with your life, work in a foundry for a while. That same year I started a rock-and-roll band —Chuck Givens and the Quintones—and I soon was making more money playing music on weekends than I made working in the foundry all week. Then came my first shocking experience with the tax system. My record-keeping skills were almost nonexistent, but I put together what I had and headed for the tax preparer's office. After only five minutes, I left with an assurance I could pick up my completed tax return in a week. When I returned, I got the shock of my life.

"I've got some good news and some bad news," muttered the CPA. "The good news is your tax return is completed. The bad news is you owe the IRS an extra $2,000."

At the tender age of 19, I had never seen $2,000 in one place at one time, and knew that I had absolutely no chance of putting that much money together anytime in the foreseeable future. My mind played visions of police cars and prisons.

In self-defense, I drove to the Federal Building in Decatur, not to turn myself in, but to pick up every publication the IRS would give away free. I was determined to learn something about a tax system that was about to put me under. I didn't realize what I had asked for and carted two full armloads of IRS material to the car. During the next three months, I scoured the pages looking for tax relief. Constantly, it seemed, I came upon possible deductions the CPA had never mentioned. At the end of the three months, right before April 15, I completed another return myself. Based on my calculations, I did not owe the IRS the extra $2,000, and was entitled to a refund of some of the taxes that had been withheld from my paychecks at my full-time job. I was sure I'd made a mistake.

Returning to the CPA's office, I asked, "Where did I go wrong?"

"You're not wrong," he said, "you're absolutely right."

The shock must have registered on my face. "What do you mean?" I said. "You had me scared to death, owing the IRS $2,000 I don't have, and, yet when I do my own return, I get money back."

With a look of disgust, he came halfway out of his chair. "Let me tell you something, son! I am a tax preparer, not your financial adviser. You are paying me to take your numbers and put them on the tax forms. If you don't know how to tell me about what you're doing, I have no reason or responsibility in taking the deductions.''

The light went on; I got it! If I ever wanted to protect myself from overpaying income taxes, I must learn everything possible about the tax system. No one, not even a tax preparer or CPA, was going to do it for me the way it needed to be done. That experience has probably saved me more in income taxes than most people will make in a lifetime.

I have spent the last 25 years learning everything possible about the tax system and how to maximize your spendable income by minimizing your taxes. The tax system is not your enemy, unless you don't understand it. Your objective is to work with the tax system from an ethical business perspective. In business, the objective is to increase profits by reducing expenses. In your personal life, your objective is to increase your spendable income by reducing your taxes.

I am not a tax protester, nor am I out to destroy the American tax system. I love this country and the opportunities it has given me. What I want for America is equality of tax opportunity. Why should only the super-rich know how to make tax laws work in their favor? Equality of tax opportunity will never be achieved through so-called tax reform, but only through education in the form of tax-reducing strategies—the strategies you are about to learn.

Strategy #82
USE ONLY TAX STRATEGIES, NEVER LOOPHOLES OR TAX CHEATING.

In pursuing the dream of lower taxes, it is never necessary to resort to tax cheating, loopholes, or even to question the legality of the tax system. There is a big difference between cheating, loopholes, and strategies.

TAX CHEATING is understating your income or claiming tax deductions for assets you don't own or expenditures you never made. Tax cheating may bring you fame and fortune as in the case of Billie Sol Estes who claimed tax deductions for nonexisting Texas grain bins, but jail and other legal penalties always outweigh the fame and can cost you your fortune.

LOOPHOLES are gray, untested areas of the tax law that allow you to claim "default deductions" that Congress and the IRS might have ruled against had they had the foresight to see the possibilities. Since a specific "no" does not exist, you create a loophole by saying "yes" to a shaky deduction. Loopholes are often sought after by desperate, high-income taxpayers who never took the time to plan. Some loopholes are used purely out of greed, others are taken because of the gambling instinct. There is only one "do" about loopholes, and that is "don't."

TAX STRATEGIES are positive, legal uses of the tax laws to reduce your income taxes. Tax strategies are actions you take that automatically and legally qualify you for additional deductions. These action strategies can include opening an IRA account, starting a small business, buying real estate, and 75 other possibilities. Some tax strategies, like those just mentioned, are straightforward and obvious. Other strategies, like traveling on tax deductible dollars and a tax deductible college education for your children, are just as legal, just as easy to use, but less understood.

One question I am asked over and over again: "Is paying less taxes really legal, patriotic, and moral?" For some reason many people seem to confuse our tax system with the United Fund, whose slogan is "Pay your fair share." By following the tax laws and regulations when you use tax strategies, you automatically pay your fair share, even if your share amounts to zero. Two neighboring families, each with a $30,000 annual income and two children, could both be paying their fair share of income taxes, even if one family paid $5,000 and the other paid nothing at all. It's the way the American tax system was designed.

We have a system that imposes taxes, not on your total income, but on a far smaller number known as your taxable income; your residual income after you subtract your exemptions, adjustments, and deductions. Within the difference between total income and taxable income lie your opportunities for applying legal, powerful tax-reducing strategies.

Not long ago on the Phil Donahue Show, during one of the best national discussions on tax strategies in which I have ever participated, a lady caller said she thought reducing your taxes was cheating. She made $15,000 working, didn't have an IRA, and her husband was even a tax attorney! Her feeling was that she wanted to pay taxes to help the homeless. This may come as a surprise to you, as it did to her, but very few of your federal tax dollars go to the homeless, or many other places you might prefer the money to go. By learning legal strategies for reducing her taxes, she could have given her tax savings directly to the homeless herself.

Another woman in the studio audience felt that paying more taxes was patriotic. The courts say that paying taxes has nothing to do with patriotism whether you pay a lot or none at all. The money goes into the economy whether paid to the government or used by you for a deductible purpose.

The question of legality and morality of tax deductions was settled once and for all over 40 years ago by the United States Circuit Court of Appeals in an opinion written by Judge Learned Hand.

> Anyone may so arrange his affairs that his taxes shall be as low as possible. He is not bound to choose a pattern that will best pay the Treasury. No one owes any public duty to pay more than the law demands.

This decision should govern both your tax plan and your tax attitude. Rearranging your affairs to create deductions where you had none before is the secret to paying less in taxes. All of the tax strategies you will learn will legally and easily reduce your taxes by thousands each year. Your job is to pick those strategies that best suit you and your family. Tax strategies should form one-third of your written financial plan.

How much time is required? Reducing your taxes is basically a do-it-at-home, do-it-yourself, do-it-in-your-spare-time project, requiring no more than a few minutes a week. What you'll soon discover is that one hour spent learning and applying a legal tax strategy will save you $100 to $300 in taxes. That's like having a $100 to $300 per hour tax-free job.

Strategy #83

DETERMINE YOUR TAX BRACKET TO TRACK YOUR TAX SAVINGS.

Our nation has a graduated tax system. That means the more you make, the more they take. Many taxpayers incorrectly believe that by earning more money they can end up with less money because they move into a higher tax bracket. Not so. The higher bracket percentage applies only to the additional income you earn and does not affect the amount of taxes you pay on the amount of money you were already earning. Never fall back on the excuse that you don't want to make more money because you will end up in a higher bracket. Instead, make all the money you can and reduce the taxes you pay by using "Tax Strategies."

The first step is to know your tax brackets. It's like assessing the damage—knowing the percentage of each dollar you earn that is lost forever. For example, if you are in the 28% bracket, you work from 9:00 to 11:30 each day for the government, and the rest of an eight-hour day for yourself.

Your *effective tax bracket* is the percentage of your total income you pay in taxes. If your total income is $40,000 per year and you pay a total of $5,000 in federal, state, and local taxes, your effective tax bracket is 12.5% ($5,000 divided by $40,000 = 12.5%). In tax planning, knowing your effective tax bracket will motivate you to create a good tax plan.

Your *marginal tax bracket* is the percent in taxes you pay on your top dollar of taxable income. It is also the percent of tax you will pay on one additional dollar of income, or conversely, the percentage you will save in taxes for each additional dollar of tax deductions you create.

The chart on page 131, "Tax Rate Schedules Under Tax Reform," will show you your marginal bracket and the amount of tax you will pay based on your taxable income in 1988 and beyond. Your marginal tax bracket is the percentage shown in the right hand column of each schedule.

There are three types of personal income taxes: federal, state, and local. Everyone is subject to federal taxes, but eleven states have no state income tax. Most people are not subject to local income taxes, except in large metropolitan areas such as New York City and Washington, DC.

Most federal income tax deductions are allowed on most state tax returns. The average percentage for those who pay state taxes is 7% applied to taxable income. Add 7% to your federal marginal tax bracket, if you are subject to state income taxes, and you can see why you have so little money left.

TAX RATE SCHEDULES UNDER TAX REFORM

1988 and Beyond

Married Filing Jointly

Taxable Income	Marginal Bracket
0	15%
29,750	28%
71,900	33%
149,250 *	28%

Married Filing Separately

Taxable Income	Marginal Bracket
0	15%
14,875	28%
35,950	33%
74,625 *	28%

Single

Taxable Income	Marginal Bracket
0	15%
17,850	28%
43,150	33%
89,560 *	28%

Head of Household

Taxable Income	Marginal Bracket
0	15%
23,900	28%
61,650	33%
123,790 *	28%

* Plus 5% personal exemption surtax.

Strategy #84

CUT YOUR ADJUSTED GROSS INCOME TO INCREASE
ALLOWABLE DEDUCTIONS AND REDUCE TAXES.

Under the new tax laws the amount of medical and miscellaneous deductions you can claim are partially dependent on your adjusted gross income (AGI). Since medical expenses are deductible only in excess of 7.5% of AGI and miscellaneous expenses such as job-related expenses, are deductible only in excess of 2% of AGI, your goal is to reduce your adjusted gross income.

Use the chart below, "Computing Your Adjusted Gross and Taxable Income," to help you increase certain itemized deductions. Notice that a business loss, IRA contributions and real estate deductions all reduce your adjusted gross income (AGI).

COMPUTING YOUR ADJUSTED GROSS
AND TAXABLE INCOME

Using last year's tax return or an estimate of this year's income and expenses, complete this form to determine your adjusted gross income, taxable income, and marginal tax bracket.

Part 1   Income

A
Included

B
Not Included

A — Included	B — Not Included
$ _____ Wages	$ _____ Tax-free bond interest
_____ Profit from a small business	_____ Tax-free insurance proceeds
_____ Annuity income	_____ Gifts
_____ Pension income	_____ Inheritances
_____ Profit from sale of investments	_____ Social Security (tax-free portion)
_____ Interest or dividend income	_____ Other
_____ Rental income	$ _____ TOTAL (TAX-FREE INCOME)
_____ Royalty payments	
_____ Other	

$ _____ TOTAL TAXABLE INCOME BEFORE DEDUCTIONS

Part 2   Deductions That Reduce Your AGI (adjusted gross income)

$ _____ Loss from small business

_____ Unreimbursed employee travel expenses

_____ Deductible contributions to an IRA or Keogh

_____ Contribution to pension plan of an S corporation

_____ Alimony payments

_____ Premature withdrawal penalty from CD's

_____ Deductions from real estate investments

_____ Other

$ _____ TOTAL AGI DEDUCTIONS

Part 3   AGI & Taxable Income Calculation

Total Taxable Income from Part 1A	+ $ _____
Subtract: AGI Deductions Part 2	− _____
Adjusted Gross Income	$ _____
Subtract:	
Schedule A Deductions (total)*	− _____
Deductions for Dependents ($1,950 each)	− _____
TAXABLE INCOME	$ _____

Part 4   Computing Your Marginal Tax Bracket

Your Federal Bracket (from tax rate schedule)	+ _____ %
Your State Tax Bracket (Estimated)	+ _____ %
YOUR MARGINAL TAX BRACKET	_____ %

You can easily determine your adjusted gross income (AGI) by subtracting Part 2 deductions from Part 1A income. Other Schedule A deductions and deductions for dependents are then subtracted from your adjusted gross income to determine your taxable income.
* Schedule A deductions include interest, medical, charitable contributions, taxes, and miscellaneous deductions often referred to as itemizing.

As you use the tax strategies in this book, keep track of your deductions as you create them. You will notice that as your taxable income gets smaller, your taxes become less and your spendable income increases. The purpose of a good tax plan is having more money to spend.

Chapter 9

TAX RETURN FILING STRATEGIES

Take it off, take it all off!

Gypsy Rose Lee
Entertainer/Author
1936

Objective: Reduce your taxes and chances of an audit at the same time.

The four letter word that keeps most people from becoming better "tax strategists" is *fear*. Most fear in life comes from lack of knowledge, seldom from any real threat. In the case of the IRS, fear is usually founded in fantasy, not fact—fear of an audit, fear of embarrassment, fear of harassment, and worst yet, fear of jail. Unless you are an outright tax cheater, you have nothing to worry about. To succeed financially you must have the confidence to use tax strategies. Confidence and courage come from knowledge of how the tax system really works, and how to use the system in your favor while keeping both the IRS and Congress on your side.

Years ago, when I was designing computer systems for a major corporation, I was a member of an association of computer professionals that included current and former IRS computer systems designers and programmers. Often, late at night, over a beer or two, they would tell me little-known secrets of the IRS computer system. The tax strategies in this chapter are based partially on information obtained at those late night social gatherings and from my experience over the years in working with thousands of taxpayers and tax professionals.

Strategy #85
USE THE LONG FORM—YOU CANNOT PAY MORE IN TAXES, ONLY LESS.

You may be one of the few who thinks you don't need a tax plan because you fill out the short form and can't take deductions. That's the first tax mistake. Those who fill out the short form are paying the absolte maximum tax which can be paid on that level of income.

Always complete the 1040 long form to identify potential tax deductions. If you don't have more than the standard deduction, the long form will point out where your tax plan is lacking. Completing the long form will also familiarize you with the process of turning deductions into dollars. Those who have never completed a long form are those who usually claim they understand little about taxes. Long forms are a necessary part of tax strategy training and are not at all difficult. Use tax publication 17 as your guide. Filing the long form can never cost you more, only the same or less.

Strategy #86
CHOOSE AN AGGRESSIVE TAX PREPARER OR NONE AT ALL.

Whether or not you use a tax preparer is strictly a matter of choice. Almost 60% of taxpayers use a tax preparer and, with the complexity of the new tax laws, more will probably look for help.

A good tax preparer is an aggressive tax preparer, and like four-leaf clovers, they are hard to find. Many tax laws and rules are written to intimidate tax preparers into becoming unnecessarily meek, mild, and conservative, even though these same laws and rules don't apply to you as a taxpayer. If your tax preparer is full of warnings, such as "I wouldn't take that deduction, it might send up a red flag," and short on explanations, the money you are paying for so-called tax advice pales beside the money you are unnecessarily paying in taxes.

The most effective way to choose a tax preparer is to interview several with one key question: "How much in taxes did you pay last year?" If the answer is much more than zero, or a hedge like "None of your business!", you are dealing with a tax loser, not an effective tax preparer. If a tax expert can't help himself pay less tax, how can you expect that he will be able to help you? Another approach is to quiz your friends until you find one who is near the zero tax bracket. Use his or her tax preparer. But even if you use a tax preparer, you must still learn to communicate effectively about taxes.

Strategy #87

INCREASE OR DECREASE YOUR END-OF-YEAR WITHHOLDING TO AVOID PENALTIES OR GET YOUR REFUND FOR CHRISTMAS.

Under the new tax laws, the amount of withholding from your pay-check required to avoid penalties was increased from 80% to 90% of the total taxes due. The IRS decided to waive the new rule for tax year 1987 and maybe 1988, but whether 80% or 90% it is your responsibility to have enough, but not too much, withheld.

If you had too little withheld during the year, you can have any amount of extra money withheld from your end-of-year checks to make up the difference. Every November, pencil in a 1040 form with your approximate income and deductions. If you will be short of the required withholding amount, have your employer withhold extra taxes for your last few pay periods.

If you have had more than 90% withheld, you can reduce your end-of-year withholding to as little as 0 and use the extra money for Christmas.

Strategy #88

PREPARE YOUR OWN RETURN—AT LEAST ONCE.

One question I am often asked at my workshops is "Should I prepare my own return?" The answer is yes—completely once, and partially each year. Without understanding how adjustments, credits and deductions affect your return, you will never feel confident about handling the tax system. You can save yourself both money and time at tax preparation time if you pencil in your income and deductions before you take your papers to a tax preparer. This process will discipline you into becoming a better record keeper as well as operate as a check list to be certain you have everything organized. Your tax preparation will become much easier and the bill much smaller.

There are also hidden traps in the way that your tax preparer may take deductions. Tax preparers may, for instance, choose alternatives for automobile, interest, or investment deductions that save preparation time but give you far less in deductions. You must be in a position to tell your preparer what forms and formulas to use if you want to pay less in taxes.

Strategy #89
TIME YOUR REFUND TO EARN EXTRA INTEREST.

The IRS must send you any refund due within 45 days from the date you file or April 15th, whichever is later. If your refund is late by even one day, you are entitled to interest from the filing date. To get your interest you may have to notify the IRS by sending in a claim. Always calculate the number of days between filing and refund.

Strategy #90
DON'T APPLY THIS YEAR'S REFUND TO NEXT YEAR'S TAXES.

Your 1040 form will give you an option: get your refund in cash or apply your refund to next year's taxes. Never give the IRS the use of your money free! If you end up owing more money because of understated income or interest income you forgot to claim, you will have to pay from your bank account. The IRS will not let you take the additional money owed out of your prepayment. Put your refund in your investment account and let it work for you instead of for the IRS.

Strategy #91
AVOID TAX PENALTIES; DON'T BE CONCERNED ABOUT INTEREST.

Refer to the following "Penalties and Interest on Tax Returns" chart and you will see what it costs to file late, make mistakes, or even cheat.

Mention the word penalty and most taxpayers cringe. The two biggest penalties, negligence and fraud, are also the easiest to avoid. These

PENALTIES AND INTEREST ON TAX RETURNS

Interest (Paid and Received)

Underpayment of tax	3 mo. T-Bill Rate + 3%
Overpayment of tax	3 mo. T-Bill Rate + 2%

Penalties for Tax Law Violations

Civil Violations	Penalty
Unpaid taxes	.5% per month up to 25% + interest
Negligence	5% of underpayment + interest
Failure to file return when due (60 day grace period)	$100 or taxes due
Bad check charge	1% of check
Frivolous or incomplete return	$500
Frivolous lawsuit against the IRS	$5,000
Overvaluation of property	10% to 30% of underpayment
Intent to evade taxes	75% of underpayment + 50% of interest
False withholding information	$500
Failure to file partnership return	$50 ea. partner per month; max. 5 months

Criminal Violations

Willful failure to pay or file	Up to $25,000 + 1 year prison
Willfully falsifying return	Up to $100,000 + 3 years prison
Intent to evade taxes	Up to $100,000 + 5 years prison
False withholding information	Up to $100,000 + 1 year prison

penalties are never assessed arbitrarily or used as a threat, but only to punish taxpayers who intentionally try to cheat or who don't report all income.

The biggest honest taxpayer's penalty is imposed for not having the extra money to pay extra taxes due when filing a return. The penalty is 1 percent per month plus interest of three points over prime. The total interest and penalties paid each month are, therefore, only slightly more than the 18% interest of credit cards you may carry in your wallet. Not pleasant, but not enough to break you either. Interest and penalties are assessed only on the extra taxes due, not on your taxable income.

You must file your tax return or request an extension by April 15th whether or not any taxes are due. The late filing penalty is 5% per month up to 25% maximum. There is no penalty unless you owe money. You have two years to file for a refund and up to three years to amend your return. If you file an amended tax return claiming additional deductions, you will also receive interest on your additional refund from the date you originally filed your return.

All penalties are easily avoided by proper planning and filing an honest return.

Strategy #92
WHEN IN DOUBT, DEDUCT IT.

Most taxpayers think they are doing themselves a favor by being ultra-conservative in taking deductions. Nothing could be further from the truth. If you are tax deduction "shy," not only do you end up spending thousands of dollars in unnecessary taxes, you don't even reduce your chances for audit. Most audits are done at random and have little to do with whether you take all of your allowable deductions or only a few.

If you want to reach your financial goals, you must adopt the winning tax strategy: "WHEN IN DOUBT, DEDUCT IT." Take everything the law allows. Follow the rules, but deduct all gray areas in your favor. Gray areas are not loopholes or an attempt to get around the tax laws, but areas of ambiguity and uncertainty about what Congress or the IRS really meant. You have just as much chance of winning your point as the IRS does. You'll be surprised, as you learn about taxes, at how much of the code is ambiguous. Simple record keeping and tax strategies will always have you prepared to win your point. When you hear a tax preparer say, "I wouldn't take that deduction even though it is legitimate, it might send up a red flag," fire him.

Strategy #93
SIGN YOUR RETURN YOURSELF.

Believe it or not, the IRS audits a greater percentage of returns signed by "experts" than by individual taxpayers. The reason? The IRS found that tax professionals make more mistakes than taxpayers. The statistics are as follows:

- 30% of returns prepared by taxpayers contain errors.
- 40% of returns prepared by CPAs and accountants contain errors.
- 60% of returns prepared by franchised tax preparers contain errors.

If a tax preparer has prepared your return, he must, by law, sign it, but if you simply get tax advice or assistance in preparing your return, you may sign it yourself. Signing your own return cuts your chances of being audited by about 20%, but does not prevent you from taking a professional with you if you are audited.

There is an exception. If you earn over $50,000 per year in total income, your chances of being audited are less if a CPA or tax preparer signs your return. The IRS somehow believes that even though you are smart enough to earn that kind of money, you are not smart enough to prepare your own tax return.

Strategy #94
FILE YOUR RETURN LATER, NOT EARLIER.

The later you file, the less your chances for audit. If you file your tax return each year after April 1st, you have automatically reduced your chances for audit by about 40% over those who file in January, February, and March. The reduced chance for audit is due to a quirk in the IRS's computer program and how it selects returns for possible audit. The IRS will tell you it's not true, but it is. Here's how it works.

The IRS brass meets each year to decide how many returns will be audited for each deduction category. The IRS has only 24,500 auditors and has suffered recent budget cuts like all governmental branches. The number of returns to be selected for each deduction category is programmed into the computer. Returns for possible audit are then selected on a "first come" basis, and when the total number of returns for a category has been chosen, the computer stops selecting. The later you file, the more categories will be full.

Strategy #95
FILE AN AUTOMATIC EXTENSION FORM 4868.

You can reduce your chance for audit even further by filing IRS Form 4868—Automatic Extension of Time to File. The automatic extension gives you an extra four months—until August 15th—to file your tax return for the previous year. Interest is charged on unpaid taxes at less than 1% per month but there is no late filing penalty. Another two-month extension can be requested in writing and is almost always granted moving your required filing date to October 15.

Chapter 10

WINNING THE TAX AUDIT

You pays your money and you takes your chances.

Punch
1846

Objective: Gain the upper hand in a tax audit.

Isn't it strange how the possibility of an audit makes you feel guilty even when you're not?

An audit is nothing more than your opportunity to prove to the IRS that you are a good record keeper. If you're not, your first audit can go a long way in motivating you to become one. Fear of being audited comes from a lack of knowledge, not from any real IRS threat. All of us will be audited once or twice in a lifetime no matter how carefully our returns are filled out. Be prepared rather than scared.

The first time I was audited was 1963. The item in question: a $35 education deduction for a night school course in English Literature. I felt it helped me improve my job skill, which was writing excuse letters to irate customers who had not received their orders. The auditor, a very pleasant lady indeed, said, "English Composition, yes; English Literature, no. No deduction." Since the rest of the return passed, I reluctantly acquiesced and paid the $1.17 in extra taxes. It must have cost the IRS $500 in time and correspondence to collect my money.

Strategy #96
**DON'T REACT TO AN AUDIT AS MORE THAN
IT REALLY IS.**

According to the IRS, an audit is "an impartial review of a tax return to determine its accuracy and completeness." An audit is not an accu-

142

sation that you have done something wrong, only a request for more information. Knowledge of audit objectives and proceedings give you the same level of power and clout that most taxpayers attribute to the IRS. Knowledge can reduce an audit to the impartial review it is supposed to be.

Of course an audit is a hassle. Anything you do that doesn't contribute to your wealth, health, family, relaxation, or goals is a hassle. Grin and bear it. Look at an audit as part of the game, just as painful exercise is part of building a strong body.

Most people try to avoid an audit by being conservative and maintaining a low profile. The thousands of extra dollars a person pays in federal income taxes over the course of a lifetime to avoid one or two audits is simply not worth the price. More importantly, being overconservative doesn't really help reduce your chances for audit.

What are your real chances for being audited in any one year? Out of 96 million individual tax returns, less than 2 million returns are audited—about 2 percent. Even so, it is important to know the rules of the game.

Based on past performance of the IRS, here are your percentage chances for being audited by income and profession.

INDIVIDUALS:

Your Income/Profession	Chance for Audit
Under $50,000	2%
Over $50,000	8%
Professionals	25%
Known criminals	50%

YOUR SMALL BUSINESS:

Business Income	Chance for Audit
Under $10,000	3%
$10,000–$30,000	2%
Over $30,000	7%

If placed on a shelf, the tax code, regulations, and manuals would stretch 40 feet and fill close to fifty thousand pages. It's no wonder the tax system is such a mess; even the IRS is confused. The General Accounting Office of the United States has said that IRS phone representatives give the wrong answer to at least one out of every ten questions asked. *USA Today* hired CPAs to call the IRS with a list of ten questions. The IRS gave the wrong answer 40 percent of the time.

I realize these facts aren't particularly comforting, but at least you can begin to see that IRS professionals are human and make mistakes. Understanding this situation will help you walk into any audit feeling a bit more confident.

Tax returns are chosen for audit using three entirely different parameters. The first parameter is referred to as "Random Selection—the TCMP Audit," which stands for "Taxpayer Compliance Measurement Program," is based on random selection. It doesn't matter how much or how little you make, or what deductions you take, everyone who files a tax return has an equal chance for a TCMP audit.

Each year only about forty thousand out of the 96 million returns are selected for the TCMP audit. The purpose, according to the IRS, is to find out exactly where taxpayers make mistakes, and even where they tend to cheat. The audit is so thorough that if you have children, you may be asked to bring birth certificates to prove they are your dependents. Don't be too concerned. About one-third of TCMP-audited taxpayers walk out the door with a bigger refund check in hand.

The second technique used by the IRS for selecting audit candidates is called "Target Group Selection." IRS experience shows that certain professions have high cash incomes, which shouldn't come as any big surprise. Any profession from which the IRS feels it can collect the greatest amount of extra taxes for the number of man-hours spent has a higher audit profile. These groups include doctors, dentists, lawyers, airline pilots, and accountants—all the people you'd like your son or daughter to marry.

Last but certainly not least, is the "Discriminant Function System" or DFS. DFS is a point system. The deductions on your return are compared to what the IRS considers the "norm" for a person in your profession, in your area, and with your income. The greater the difference between your tax return and the "norm," the higher number of points you are assigned. If your DFS score gets too high, you may be chosen for an audit.

If you are selected by computer, two IRS employees must agree that there is a good chance of collecting additional taxes before you are actually issued an audit notice.

Strategy #97
DELAY AN AUDIT AS LONG AS POSSIBLE.

Keep in mind that the world of the IRS is not a clandestine, behind-the-scenes ring of spies bugging your phone and watching you through infrared binoculars. The IRS is simply a big collection business run by the government, and your success with the system is assured when you take an honest businesslike approach.

If you are picked for an audit, the audit notice will usually be in the form of a computer generated letter. Federal law states that the "time and place for an audit must be convenient to both parties." Your strategy is to delay the audit for as long as possible. You may send a registered letter to the IRS in answer to the audit notice stating, "The time is not convenient." Your response automatically postpones the audit. Eventually, after several postponements, you will receive a letter or call from a "real live person," instead of a computer, asking you to choose the time. By that time you will have all your records in order.

Strategy #98
NEVER GO TO AN AUDIT UNTIL YOU GET THE
REASONS FOR THE AUDIT IN WRITING.

Before you agree to an audit time, get all the following information in writing. The IRS must give you written answers to the following questions, if you ask, before you are required to appear.

Why? Why is the IRS auditing your return? Why does the IRS think it may be able to collect more taxes? Is there an error that can be rectified easily without an office visit? Can you furnish copies of supporting documents by mail?

Which? Which parts of your return are being audited? Ask for a specific answer. The answer the IRS gives to this question limits the audit to these parts of your return. Some of the information you require may come with the audit notice, and some you may have to request yourself, in writing.

What? What papers does the IRS want to see? Take to the audit only the papers requested, not your shoe boxes full of old receipts, contracts, and checks. If the

IRS says bring "everything," request that they be more specific by listing what "everything" includes.

There are some important ground rules you will want to follow during the audit.

Strategy #99

LET THE AUDITOR LOOK AT YOUR DOCUMENTS ONLY ONCE.

The auditor has the right to look at each of your documents only once. Under a recent ruling, if your auditor wants to look at your papers a second time, written permission must be obtained from the U.S. Secretary of the Treasury. It can be done, but the auditor usually won't go to all the trouble if you mention the rule.

Strategy #100

IN AN AUDIT, NEVER PART COMPANY WITH YOUR ORIGINAL DOCUMENTS.

Don't leave original copies of your documents with the IRS. A tax court has ruled that you are still responsible for your records, even if they are lost or misplaced by the IRS. Point the ruling out to the auditor if he or she wants to keep your papers to work on later.

Strategy #101

DON'T LET THE AUDITOR COPY YOUR TAX FILE.

Tax law does not give the IRS blanket permission to build a file from copies of your personal papers. You must produce supporting documents if requested, but not copies for the IRS's file.

Strategy #102

LEARN HOW TO BEHAVE IN AN AUDIT.

It's important to mind your manners when you're being audited. But contrary to what many people believe, you can be aggressive and well-mannered at the same time. Here are the rules to follow:

- Say little; smile a lot. Never volunteer information.
- If you feel strongly about your position, let the auditor know. Often the auditor will let the point go in your favor.
- Provide as much documentation as possible for each point in an audit.
- Don't give up, even if you don't have all the documentation.
- Don't make too many concessions.
- Don't be rushed unless you feel hurrying will work in your favor.
- Don't complain about the tax system; the auditor pays taxes too.
- Don't take your crumpled up receipts in a brown paper bag. That old strategy won't work anymore. Auditors are trained to believe that if you keep your records in a disorganized manner, there must be an error in there somewhere.
- Don't take the Fifth Amendment. Tax protesting is a disaster. The jails and courts are full of people who believed such nonsense would work.
- Don't try to tape-record the conversation. The IRS found from experience that recording tended to fluster auditors. Recording once was a great way to get control of an audit, but now, you will have to go to court to get permission to record. Even if you win, it's not worth the trouble.
- Act with confidence that you're right. You probably are.

Strategy #103

IF YOU DON'T GET WHAT YOU THINK YOU DESERVE, GO BEYOND THE AUDITOR.

If all else fails and you can't get the decision you want, you still have a few cards to play.

STEP 1: ASK FOR THE SUPERVISOR.

Auditors are taught to rule gray areas in the IRS's favor; supervisors are taught to rule gray areas in favor of the taxpayer. Supervisors also have a greater knowledge of the tax law and its application than do auditors. Supervisors are the first level of the public relations effort at the IRS, so they try to please. I cannot tell you how many stories I hear in my workshops of those who have paid extra taxes for denied deductions when the auditor was 100% incorrect, because the individual being audited didn't know what to do next.

STEP 2: CALL THE "PROBLEM RESOLUTION OFFICE."

The P.R.O. was set up to help keep the IRS out of court. The Problem Resolution Office has the power to compromise and resolve taxpayer disputes. You'll find the phone number for the P.R.O. in the phone book under U.S. Government, Internal Revenue Service, Problem Resolution Office.

STEP 3: TAKE 'EM TO COURT.

You may use the small claims tax court to settle any dispute with the IRS once and for all. The taxes in question must be under $10,000. You are not required to take an attorney, and the regular courtroom rules of evidence are relaxed. You present your side of the argument; the IRS presents its side. The impartial judge listens, leaves the courtroom, eats a sandwich, returns and tells you his decision. The decision is final—no appeals.

STEP 4: USE THE APPEALS AND REVIEW SYSTEM.

If the taxes in question are over $10,000, you must use the regular appeals and review system to appeal the auditor's decision. The cost involved will obviously be more, but good planning and understanding of the do's and don't's of taxes will avoid any problem. IRS publications completely outline the appeals and review procedure.

Strategy #104
IF A TAX PREPARER PREPARED YOUR RETURN, TAKE HIM OR HER TO AN AUDIT.

If a tax preparer prepared the return, you should certainly take him or her to the audit. If you feel you are knowledgeable and confident about taxes and your return, you can handle it yourself. But you will want to take a professional if the taxes in question are significant, or if you tend to react emotionally. IRS auditors are not intimidated by tax professionals, but they do speak the same language. If you paid for the service, use it.

Strategy #105
APPLY THE STATUTE OF LIMITATIONS TO AN AUDIT.

Once you file, the IRS has a limited time to challenge your return. The statute of limitations is effective three years from the day your return was due, April 15th or the date the return was filed, if later. If you understate your total income by 25 percent or more, the statute of limitations is six years. If your return is fraudulent, there is no statutory limit to the IRS audit period. If the statutory period has expired, you cannot be audited no matter how badly the IRS might wish to audit you.

The pendulum swings both ways. You also have a limit of three years to amend your return and two years to claim any overpaid taxes, or forgotten deductions.

Strategy #106
AGREE ONLY TO A LIMITED EXTENSION OF AN AUDIT.

If you're being audited and are close to the statutory limit, you will be asked to sign an extension. Instead of signing the form the IRS will give you, which leaves your entire return open to examination past the statutory period, request and sign Form 872, "Limited Extension." This procedure leaves open to examination only the parts of your return in question, which are those specified in the "Limited Extension" form.

Strategy #107
PUT A STOP TO THE HASSLE AUDIT IF YOU'VE BEEN
AUDITED DURING THE PAST THREE YEARS.

If you are audited on any part of your return in one year and the audit produces no change, or only a small change, you should not be audited on the same part of your return for the next three years. The IRS often will not apply this rule unless you bring it up.

Several years ago, during one of my Money Strategies workshops, a young man stood up abruptly stating that he had been audited for the same deductions three years in a row, and was to appear for an audit again on Monday. He decided to test the hassle audit rule based on what he had learned in the workshop. When he pointed out to the auditor that he had been audited three years in a row, the auditor checked the files and said, "You're right; we didn't realize we had audited you last year." The audit was over as quickly as it began.

To sum it up, your best defense in an audit is a good offense. Be civil, knowledgeable, and assertive. Remember, knowledge eliminates both fear AND bigger tax bills! The more you learn about how to report your income and deductions correctly, the less your chances for audit.

Chapter 11

FAMILY TIES

The only difference between death and taxes is that death doesn't get worse every time Congress meets.

Will Rogers
Author/Actor
(1879–1935)

Objective: Reduce taxes by shifting assets between family members. Turn family expenses into tax deductions.

A family is like a business, and great dividends accrue to all family members when the business aspects of a family are recognized. Both business and family rely on income. Business income is derived primarily from the sale of products and services; family income is derived from a lifetime of personal services to your own or someone else's company. Both families and businesses have expenses including housing, transportation, utilities, insurance, storage, payroll (including family allowances and spending money), vacations, negotiations, purchase and sale of assets, communication, praise, discipline, and of course taxes. By applying good business principles to the daily operation of a family, money-making and tax-saving strategies can put thousands of extra dollars into the family coffers.

Strategy #108
SELL YOUR HOME TO YOUR CHILDREN.

Those who reach retirement age usually have a large portion of their assets tied up in their home; they are house rich and often cash poor.

One solution, without moving, is to sell your home to your children once you are over 55 years old.

Both parents and children generate tremendous financial and tax benefits. The parents are able to unlock the equity in their home tax-free without having to move, while the children receive depreciation and other tax deductions as well as the future appreciation of the property. The home, because it is then owned by the children, is a protected part of the parents' estate. If Congress has its way, the maximum amount that will be allowed to pass through an estate, tax-free, will be reduced from the current $600,000 to as low as $200,000. Getting your home, one of your most expensive assets, out of your estate is an important step in your estate plan. Here is how the strategy works:

Parents sell their home to their children at fair market value, determined by appraisal. The children purchase the property with a conventional 80% mortgage. The parents can hold a second mortgage note for all or part of the balance and cosign on the first mortgage if necessary to help the children qualify.

An alternative strategy is for the parents to get a new mortgage or equity loan before selling to the children and then let the children assume the mortgage. The cost of assumption is usually 1% unless the loan is a no-qualifying FHA or VA loan which can be assumed for $45.

For example, if the home is paid for and worth $150,000, parents would receive $120,000 cash from an 80% mortgage.

Parents may elect, using tax form 2119, to take the once per lifetime $125,000 tax exemption to tax protect the accumulated profits from the sale of the home.

Parents rent the home from the children. In order for the children to qualify for the depreciation and other tax deductions, parents must pay them at least 80% of fair market rental value. If the fair market rent is $600, parents must pay at least $480 per month or about $6,000 per year. The rent money parents pay is a portion of the money earned from the reinvested home equity.

Using a combination of investments such as mutual funds and discounted mortgages (see Part III: "Powerful Investment Strategies") and averaging an after-tax net of 15%, parents' income from reinvested home equity would equal $18,000 per year. After paying the $6,000 in rent, parents have increased their tax free income by $12,000 per year or $1,000 per month for the rest of their lives.

Parents may wish to increase their rental payments to the children in order to help equal the payments on the mortgage. The tax deductions they receive will also help offset the mortgage payments. Here is how:

Basis for depreciation	= $120,000 (150,000 purchase price minus 20% land value)
Yearly depreciation deduction	= $ 4,364 (Based on 27½ year depreciation schedule)
Taxes saved at 33% bracket	= $ 1,440 per year

The children now own an appreciating property throwing off generous tax deductions and have built-in property managers, their parents. Parents will want to lease the property back from the children with a lifetime lease, so if parents and children have a spat, parents won't end up in the street. Don't laugh, it has happened.

Strategy #109

BUY A HOME WITH YOUR CHILDREN OR GRANDCHILDREN.

Buying a home with and for your children or grandchildren can be a financially and personally rewarding experience. The children or grandchildren agree to live in and maintain the property as well as make the mortgage payments. Both parents and children get the tax and appreciation benefits of a sound real estate investment with no management headaches.

If you are the co-owner who lives in the property, you enjoy these financial and tax benefits:

• You qualify for a mortgage you might not be able to get on your own.
• Your down payment is reduced or eliminated altogether.
• You can stop renting and start building equity for the future.
• When you sell, you may use the tax deferral rules for rolling over your share of the profits to another home without paying taxes.
• You are allowed a tax deduction for your share of the mortgage interest and property taxes.

If you are the parent or grandparent who co-owns but does not live in the property, you enjoy these financial and tax benefits:

• You can help someone you care about own a home.
• You have a resident property manager.
• There is no vacancy problem.

- You are allowed a tax deduction for your share of the depreciation, interest, tax, and maintenance expenses.

Although the resident owner is not allowed to take depreciation, the nonresident owner can. This strategy can also be used by parties who are not related. Profits on the eventual sale of the property are divided based on the percentage ownership of each party.

ESTATE PROTECTION STRATEGIES

Income taxes are expenses you work to reduce to build your estate and estate taxes are expenses you work to reduce to protect your estate for your surviving family members. The minimum estate tax begins at 55%. The minimum was scheduled to drop to 50%, but the reductions have already been cancelled. The estate tax applies only to money or property given to someone other than your spouse. You may leave to your spouse unlimited amounts of property or cash. What can you do to protect more of your estate? Here are your strategies.

Strategy #110
KEEP YOUR WILL UP-TO-DATE.

Have both your attorney and accountant check your will every three years to see that it conforms to ever-changing rules. Most wills, for instance, were outdated and some provisions rendered invalid by the Economic Recovery Act of 1982. Your potential estate taxes may be increased unnecessarily by the outdated language in your will simply because Congress changes the tax laws!

Strategy #111
CREATE AN IRREVOCABLE TRUST TO PROTECT YOUR ESTATE.

An irrevocable trust allows you to funnel money out of your estate into an investment trust for the future benefit of your heirs, usually your children or grandchildren. You may put into the trust each year up to the gift tax limits explained later with no gift tax now and no estate tax later. Your heirs do not get the money in the trust until your demise or some other stipulated event chosen by you.

There are four important considerations before you create an irrevocable trust.

1. Under the tax reform rules, you cannot receive the income from the trust investments. The money must either accumulate in the trust or be given to the beneficiaries.
2. Irrevocable means you cannot change your mind and get the trust assets back.
3. The Irrevocable Trust usually costs $3,000 or more in attorneys' fees to establish, so it should be used only where proven benefits can be obtained.
4. You don't need the trust if your sole beneficiary is your spouse or your net estate is less than $600,000.

Before even considering such a trust or contacting an attorney, read Norman Dacey's book, *How to Avoid Probate.* Choose an attorney who *specializes* in trusts if you decide to form one.

Strategy #112
USE A DUAL TRUST TO DOUBLE THE TAX-FREE ALLOWANCE OF YOUR ESTATE.

By using a dual trust, you can protect more of your estate. Your estate can be set up in a trust to give your children or grandchildren up to the maximum that can be passed tax free to the next generation—currently $600,000. The balance can be given to the surviving spouse under the unlimited marital deduction rules. Your spouse may then also pass the maximum $600,000 to the next generation without estate taxes. Instead of being able to pass only $600,000 to the next generation tax free, you have increased the tax-free pass through to $1,200,000. The surviving spouse can get the income from the trust with the principal eventually passing to the children.

Strategy #113

GIVE GIFTS TO CHILDREN IN ORDER TO REDUCE ESTATE TAXES.

During your lifetime you can give to each child up to $20,000 per year ($10,000 if single) with no gift taxes. This money or property is then out of your taxable estate. Under the pre-1981 rules, any gift made within three years before death was added back into the estate for tax purposes. This rule has been repealed.

While you are living, you can maintain control of the assets you give the child by putting them into an *inter vivos* or lifetime trust. Control means you can choose where the trust money is invested and whether you or someone else receives the income.

Strategy #114

GIVE CHARITABLE GIFTS IN ORDER TO LOWER ESTATE TAXES.

Consider making charitable gifts while you are living, if you have a project or organization you believe in. Why? You can take the tax deduction while living, which keeps that amount of the gift out of your estate.

Remember, there is more to your tax life than income taxes. Gift tax and estate tax avoidance strategies must always be a part of your overall financial plan.

INVESTMENT DEDUCTION STRATEGIES

Strategy #115
TURN YOUR INVESTMENT PLAN INTO A TAX SHELTER BY DEDUCTING INVESTMENT EXPENSES.

A family investment plan should generate more than current income or a brighter future; it should create hundreds in extra investment expense deductions.

Most taxpayers mistakenly think that expenses associated with their investment plan are no longer deductible. Even the simplest investment plan can generate $500 to $1,000 of yearly deductions.

IRS rules are very clear on the subject:

> Expenses incurred in the production and collection of investment income are deductible as part of Schedule A, Miscellaneous Deductions.

Use the deductible investment expenses checklist (page 158) as a guide to investment expense deductions and investment expense planning. All other investment expenses you incur may be added to the list.

Strategy #116
DEDUCT THE COST OF A VCR OR HOME COMPUTER USED IN INVESTMENT OR TAX PLANNING.

Use your VCR, home computer, or cassette recorder 40% of the time for tax and investment planning and 40% of the cost or market value is deductible.

Keep records of your deductibles and personal usage for 90 days each year to allocate the deductible percentage.

When determining the deduction for your home computer or VCR, use straight-line (alternate MACRS) depreciation over a six-year period unless the asset is *also* used in your small business.

You may first combine the investment and business use percentages in determining your allowable deduction. If used more than 50% of the time for business, you may use the asset expensing method. If used

DEDUCTIBLE INVESTMENT EXPENSES

_____ Accounting fees $ _____
_____ Automobile expenses   _____
_____ Books and audio and videotape courses on investing   _____
_____ Brokerage fees   _____
      (deducted as part of the investment cost when you sell
       investments)
_____ Calculator, adding machine, cassette recorder,   _____
      typewriter
_____ Costs of collecting interest and dividends   _____
_____ Costs of managing investments for a minor   _____
_____ Financial advice on audio and videotapes   _____
      (i.e., The Charles J. Givens Financial Library)
_____ Home computer used for investment planning and   _____
      recordkeeping˙
_____ Investment advice (except for tax-exempt investments)   _____
_____ IRA set-up costs, if billed separately   _____
_____ Legal costs   _____
_____ Meals and entertainment of investment advisors   _____
_____ Proxy fight expenses   _____
_____ Safety deposit box rental   _____
_____ Salary of bookkeeper or others who keep your   _____
      investment records
_____ Subscription to investment publications   _____
_____ Trips to look after investments such as improved real   _____
      estate
_____ Video tape recorder used for investment education and   _____
      advice

NONDEDUCTIBLE INVESTMENT EXPENSES

Costs of travel to stockholder meetings
Costs of trips to investigate prospective rental property
Costs of travel to investment seminars
Home office expenses

less than 50% of the time for business, use the six-year straight-line (alternate MACRS) method.

The percentage from the straight-line depreciation percentage is multiplied times the depreciable basis of the asset. The depreciable basis is the deductible percentage times the cost or market value, whichever is less. Use tax form 4562 and the straight-line table below to calculate your deduction. Enter the investment and tax planning portion of the deduction on Schedule A under miscellaneous deductions. Enter the business deduction portion on Schedule C for a proprietorship or other appropriate business tax form. See Chapter 18, Getting Down to Business, for a more in-depth explanation of depreciation methods.

STRAIGHT LINE

(Alternate MACRS)
Depreciation Table

Year	% Deductible
1	10
2	20
3	20
4	20
5	20
6	10

Strategy #117

TAKE ADVANTAGE OF THE MISCELLANEOUS SCHEDULE A DEDUCTION RULES BY COMBINING OVER 50 POTENTIAL DEDUCTIONS.

DEDUCTIBLE MISCELLANEOUS EXPENSES (SCHEDULE A)

Even though there is a 2% floor on miscellaneous deductions based on your AGI (adjusted gross income), most taxpayers with a little planning can have between $1,000 and $2,000 of allowable deductions because of the wide range of potential deductions included in this category. Here is a partial list to use as your guide.

DEDUCTIBLE MISCELLANEOUS EXPENSES

Unreimbursed Employee Travel Expenses
    Airlines, auto $ _____
    Meals   _____
    Entertainment   _____
Tax advice   _____
Tax preparation   _____
Appraisal fees, casualty losses and contributions   _____
Investment expenses *
    IRA custodial fees   _____
    Safety deposit box   _____
    Investment advice   _____
Employee business expenses (use form 2106) **
    Automobile   _____
    Education   _____
    Legal fees   _____
    Association dues   _____
    Club memberships   _____
    Job hunting and interviews   _____
    Employment agency fees   _____
Office in the home
    Depreciation on rent   _____
    Utilities   _____
    Family salaries for job assistance   _____
Moving expenses   _____

* See Deductible Investment Checklist for complete list
** See Employee Business Deduction Checklist for a complete list

ALLOWABLE MISCELLANEOUS DEDUCTIONS
COMPUTATION CHART

A floor of 2% of adjusted gross income applies to your miscellaneous deductions. All of your expenses above the floor are deductible. Use this chart to estimate your allowable miscellaneous deductions.

Adjusted Gross Income　　　　　　　　　　$ _____

(from last year's return or estimated for this year)

Adjusted Gross Income	Nondeductible Amount of Miscellaneous Expenses
$ 2,000	$ 40
5,000	100
10,000	200
15,000	300
20,000	400
25,000	500
30,000	600
35,000	700
40,000	800
50,000	1,000
60,000	1,200
70,000	1,400
80,000	1,600
90,000	1,800
100,000	2,000
200,000	4,000

Total Miscellaneous Deduction　　　　　$ _____

Nondeductible Amount　　　　　　　　 − $ _____

ALLOWABLE DEDUCTION　　　　　　　　$ _____

Chapter 12

Employee Retirement Plan Strategies

Don't look back. Something may be gaining on you.

Satchel Paige
How to Keep Young
1953

Objective: To create a million dollar retirement plan where you work.

The last million dollar tax shelter may be your IRA or your employer's retirement plan. Retirement plans don't come with instructions for maximizing either tax benefits or profits; and as a result, most participants lose 75% of the potential benefits. You can have total financial freedom when you retire, without sacrificing your current life-style if you learn to use your employer's retirement plan effectively.

A retirement plan can be described in three parts: contributions, investment options, and withdrawal options (see page 163). The questions you must answer to profit from your retirement plans are listed under each category. Check those you cannot answer. They are costing you money.

Retirement plans can be divided into two types: Those you create yourself and those that must be created by your employer. To qualify for either plan you must have "earned income," compensation from a job in the form of a salary, commission or bonus. Income from investments or real estate does not qualify.

UNDERSTANDING YOUR RETIREMENT PLAN OPTIONS

Fill in answers to all questions based on what you know about your retirement plan or learn in this chapter.

Contributions

Do I qualify to contribute to an IRA? How much?   _____

What kind of plan does my employer offer—401(k), 403(b), 457, or SEP?   _____

How much can I deposit each year into all plans?   _____

How much of my contribution is deductible from my taxable income?   _____

Does my employer give me any matching funds? What percent?   _____

Is there a commission or load on my contributions?   _____

Investment Options

What are the choices for investments?   _____

How often can I change investments?   _____

Do I have a choice of sponsors offering different investments?   _____

Should I move my money now to a better investment?   _____

How can I earn 20% instead of less than 10%?   _____

Can I get my employer to put in a better plan?   _____

Withdrawals

At what age can I withdraw my money with no penalty?   _____

What is the penalty if I withdraw before then?   _____

What is the withdrawal method that minimizes the taxes?   _____

Under what conditions, such as disability or financial hardship, can I withdraw my money with no penalty?   _____

Can I borrow from my plan? How much?   _____

Should I withdraw my money in a lump sum, annuity payments, or use the IRA rollover rules?   _____

CONTRIBUTIONS

Strategy #118

CONTRIBUTE THE DEDUCTIBLE MAXIMUM TO AN IRA.

The IRA is the only retirement plan you, as an employee, may create yourself. You deposit your IRA money in investments you select, and you may contribute to an IRA any time before April 15th of the year following the year you earned the qualifying income. Your employer is not involved.

Maximum Contribution:

$2,000	Self
$2,000	Employed Spouse
$ 250	Nonemployed Spouse

Anyone with employment income may contribute the deductible maximum to an IRA regardless of total income, provided neither spouse contributes to an employer-related retirement plan. If you or your spouse contribute to a 401(k), 403(b) or other similar employer-related retirement plan, the following additional rules apply:

A. You may deduct the maximum contribution to your IRA if your adjusted gross income (AGI) is less than $40,000 (couple) or $25,000 (individual), even if you or your spouse contribute to an employer's retirement plan.
B. If you file jointly, you lose the deduction for $200 of your $2,000 contribution for each $1,000 of adjusted gross income over $40,000, and so does your spouse.
C. If you file as an individual, you lose the deduction for $200 of your $2,000 contribution for each $1,000 of adjusted gross income over $25,000.
D. A deductible minimum of $200 may be contributed by any couple or individual whose AGI falls within $1,000 of the deduction phaseout limit.

Even with the ease of creating an IRA and the incredible tax benefits, only 20% of those who qualify have opened the account, and almost no one knows how to use it effectively.

Strategy #119

BORROW THE MONEY FOR YOUR IRA—EVEN IF YOU HAVE IT.

The tax and investment advantages of an IRA are so powerful that if you borrow the money for your account, you'll end up borrowing it free. Let's say this year, you are a little short on cash, and borrow $2,000 from the credit union or bank for your IRA. The interest at 12% for one year would be $240. If you are in the 28% tax bracket, you have already saved 28% of your $2,000 contribution, or $560. The $560 not only pays the $240 interest, but gives you an additional $320 profit. Not a bad day's work. Consider borrowing the money for your IRA even if you have it, so you can keep your money invested elsewhere. The IRS has now ruled that the interest you pay on money borrowed for an IRA is tax deductible even though you are investing in a tax shelter.

Strategy #120

CHOOSE AN IRA WITH A LOW TRUSTEES FEE, $35 OR LESS.

Every IRA must have a trustee, someone certified by the IRS to be responsible for the account. If you put your IRA money in a bank, mutual fund, credit union, or other financial institution, you automatically use the institution's trustee. The required paperwork involved with your IRA is considerable and, therefore, most all institutions or trustees charge an annual fee. The fee can range from five dollars to hundreds of dollars.

Avoid all IRA accounts that charge a percentage. The percentage may seem small when your account is small, but it will amount to hundreds per year as your account grows. Many major brokerage firms and some financial planners charge a percentage.

Strategy #121
CONTRIBUTE THE DEDUCTIBLE MAXIMUM TO YOUR EMPLOYER'S RETIREMENT PLAN.

There are four major types of retirement plans offered by employers and funded through payroll deductions. Locate your plan from the information provided.

1. 401(k)—Deferred Compensation Plan for Corporate Employees
   Employees may contribute up to 25% of their compensation or a maximum of $7,318 per year, tax deferred. The employer may contribute the difference between the employee contribution and $30,000, also tax deferred. The more your employer contributes, the better the plan. The $7,318 limit will be increased for inflation in future years. The best 401(k) plans are those that offer mutual funds as investment options.
2. 403(b)—Deferred Compensation Plan (Tax-sheltered Annuity) for Public School and Nonprofit Organization Employees
   Employees may contribute approximately 20% of compensation up to $9,500 per year, tax deferred. The employer has the option of contributing the difference between the employee contribution and $30,000, also tax deferred, although few, if any, employers use this option. Most public school employees are also covered by a separate pension plan over which the employee has no control. The best 403(b) plans offer mutual funds as investment options.
3. 457—Deferred Compensation Plan for State, County, and City Employees
   Employees may contribute up to $7,500 per year tax deferred. Employers may not contribute. Most municipal employees are also covered by a separate pension plan over which the employer has no control. The best 457 plans offer mutual funds as investment options.
4. 408(k) SEP—Simplified Employee Pension Plan for Employees of Small Companies—Less than 25 Employees
   Employees may contribute up to 15% of compensation or a maximum of $7,000 per year, tax deferred. The employer may contribute the difference between the employee contribution and $30,000, also tax deferred. The more your employer contributes, the better the plan. The best SEP plans are those that offer mutual funds as investment options. SEPs, like IRAs, can be contributed to until April 15th of the year following the tax year.

Strategy #122

USE THE DOUBLE DEDUCTION BENEFITS OF YOUR RETIREMENT PLAN TO BUILD YOUR WEALTH.

In all retirement plans, there are two tax shelters: your contribution is deductible, and the money it earns compounds tax free. This double tax-free compounding effect is what will eventually make you wealthy.

A Deduction for Your Contribution

Within your contribution limits, the money you invest in your plan is deducted from your taxable income for the year. If you are in the 28% federal tax bracket, your tax saving is 28% of your contribution. If your tax bracket is 33%, the tax saving is 33% of your contribution.

IRA		401(k)	
$2,000	IRA contribution	$7,000	401(k) contribution
× 28%	Your tax bracket	× 33%	Your tax bracket (includes 5% surcharge)
$ 560	Tax Savings	$2,310	Tax Savings

Deduction for the Earnings

Your retirement account earnings compound tax free as long as your money remains invested. The concept of "earn now, deal with the taxes later" is known as a tax deferral.

Many supposedly knowledgeable CPAs and accountants have incorrectly advised clients not to contribute to IRAs, since the taxes will be due someday anyway. What nonsense! You pay no taxes on both the amount invested and the income earned from the account. If you were, instead, to invest your money after taxes and then pay taxes on your investment earnings, you would lose twice. As much as 33% is lost to taxes from your initial investment capital and then 33% of what you earn is lost to taxes before your money is reinvested. Let's look at $2,000 of your income invested with or without IRA protection (page 168).

You have $880 more in your account after just one year with IRA tax shelter protection or 44% more based on your original investment. The same is true of all retirement plans.

ONE-YEAR INVESTMENT GROWTH

	With IRA	Without IRA
Amount invested	$2,000	$2,000
Taxes @ 33%	– 0	– 660
Net investment	$2,000	$1,340
Earnings, 1 year, 20%	+ 400	+ 268
Tax on earnings, 33%	0	– 88
Account balance after 1 year	$2,400	$1,520

If you expand the results for five to 30 years, you will see how small investments in retirement accounts make millionaires. Think of it this way. You're going to get older anyway, you might as well be getting older and richer at the same time. Although we have used a $2,000 yearly IRA investment as an example, the wealth-building impact of up to $7,000 invested yearly in your 401(k), 403(b), or other employment-related retirement plan is even greater. Look over "The Power of Tax-Free Compounding" chart below to see how your retirement plan will build your fortune over the next five to 30 years.

THE POWER OF TAX-FREE COMPOUNDING

20% Compounded Annually

$2,000 Invested Yearly in an IRA

Years	With IRA	Without IRA
5	$ 18,000	$ 10,000
10	62,000	29,000
15	173,000	63,000
20	448,000	129,000
25	1,133,000	252,000
30	2,837,000	482,000

$4,000 Invested Yearly in an IRA for You and Your Spouse

Years	With IRA	Without IRA
5	$ 36,000	$ 20,000
10	124,000	58,000
15	346,000	126,000
20	896,000	258,000
25	2,266,000	504,000
30	5,674,000	946,000

$7,000 Invested Yearly/401(k), 403(b) or 457 Employer-related Retirement Plan

Years	With Tax Protection	Without Tax Protection
5	$ 63,000	$ 35,000
10	217,000	101,500
15	602,000	220,500
20	1,568,000	451,500
25	3,965,500	882,000
30	9,929,500	1,687,000

Strategy #123

CONTRIBUTE TO YOUR RETIREMENT PLAN NOW— DON'T WAIT UNTIL LATER.

You can't be too young to start a retirement plan. Read the next statement carefully. It will amaze you.

IF YOU INVEST $2,000 IN A TAX-DEFERRED RETIREMENT ACCOUNT EACH YEAR BETWEEN THE AGES OF 20 AND 26, AND NEVER INVEST ANOTHER CENT, YOU WILL HAVE MORE MONEY WHEN YOU REACH AGE 65 THAN IF YOU WAIT UNTIL YOU ARE 26 AND INVEST $2,000 EVERY YEAR FOR THE NEXT 40 YEARS WITHOUT RETIREMENT ACCOUNT TAX PROTECTION.

INVESTMENT OPTIONS

The new tax rules give you almost unlimited options for where your IRA can be invested. You may, in fact, invest your IRA money in anything except:

1. Collectibles—i.e. art, Persian rugs.
2. Any investment such as mortgaged rental property, where your account would be used as collateral or security for a loan. The IRS treats an IRA used as security for a loan as if you withdrew the money.
3. A business in which you own more than a 5% interest.

Strategy #124
OPEN A SELF-DIRECTED IRA TO EARN 20% PER YEAR.

One of the major benefits of an IRA and often the least used is the ability to choose your investments through a self-directed account. The investment section of this book will show you how to use investments that will earn you 20% instead of the 8% bank IRA rate.

Anyone who qualifies for an IRA may open a self-directed account. A self-directed IRA puts you in control, letting you choose any investment you wish, such as stocks, bonds, mutual funds, discounted mortgages, real estate options, county tax lien certificates, mortgage pools, or even the lot next door to your home. Every IRA must have a trustee. Financial institutions, such as brokerage firms or mutual fund families, have one trustee for all IRAs but you can choose only the investments they sell. If you want to invest your money in real estate, discounted mortgages, or tax liens, you must find an independent trustee. Any bank trust department can legally act as your independent trustee, but many won't. There are now a few financial planners who are IRS registered independent trustees.

Chapter 26, "IRA and Keogh Investment Superstrategies" will show you how to get maximum investment power from your IRA as well as where you can find an independent trustee.

Strategy #125
NEVER INVEST YOUR IRA IN A TAX SHELTER.

An IRA is already tax sheltered. Since you can't take the deduction twice, avoid tax-sheltered investments, which are usually more restrictive. For many years some brokers and financial planners have incorrectly advised clients to put IRA accounts in tax shelters like real estate limited partnerships.

Strategy #126
USE THE TAX-FREE ROLLOVER AND TRANSFER RULES TO TAKE CONTROL OF YOUR RETIREMENT MONEY.

The tax rules allow you to change investments within a company retirement plan or IRA any time you wish. The investment options and number of changes permitted per year are set by your retirement plan sponsor or the financial institution in which your IRA is invested.

IRA Switching Rules

If your IRA is a self-directed account like a mutual fund family or brokerage firm, you may move your money from one investment to another within the same institution as often as you wish. To move from a stock fund to a money market fund, for instance, you would simply contact your account representative and request the switch. There are no tax penalties and the processing charge (if any) should be no more than $5.00.

IRA Transfer and Rollover Rules

If you are dissatisfied with the performance of your IRA and want to transfer the money to a new IRA in a different institution, such as a mutual fund family, you have two options:

A. Trustee to Trustee Transfer

By signing a transfer agreement with the new trustee or institution, the transfer of your IRA can be handled by the institutions. There is no limit to the number of transfers which can be made each year using this method.

B. The IRA Rollover

You may physically withdraw your IRA money and open a new IRA with a different institution with no tax penalty as long as the money is redeposited within 60 days after the date of withdrawal. During the 60 days, you may do anything you wish with your IRA money. You may do a rollover no more than once per 365 days.

Strategy #127

USE THE SWITCHING RULES TO EARN 20% IN YOUR EMPLOYER'S RETIREMENT PLAN.

Ninety percent of all employment-related retirement plans now give you options for investing. Your investment alternatives are actually mutual funds offered through mutual fund families or insurance companies chosen by your employer as sponsors of your retirement plan. Your choices for investments are usually two or more of those shown in the following chart. Notice that the name shown in the retirement plan documents and the salesman's description are often different than the names normally associated with the investment. The investment name, retirement plan name, and salesman's description all mean the same thing. Most company plans allow you to switch investments from one to four times per year. Since your money is tax sheltered, there are no capital gains taxes to pay when you switch.

EMPLOYER RETIREMENT PLAN INVESTMENT OPTIONS

Investment	Retirement Plan Name	Salesman's Description
Stock fund	Equity or variable	High risk
Bond fund	Bond fund	Medium risk
Stock/bond fund	Balanced fund	Medium risk
Money market fund	Variable interest	Low risk
Fixed rate investment	Guaranteed return	Low risk
Company stock	Company stock	N/A

The fixed rate and company stock investments are the only options that are technically not mutual funds. The fixed-rate investment pays a guaranteed or sometimes variable interest rate without the potential for capital appreciation.

Company stock is usually offered to employees at a discount, usually 15%, and often must be held until termination or retirement. The 15% discount is attractive as long as there is an option for selling the stock within a couple of years and moving to another investment. Company stock can also drop in value or become worthless based on the fortunes of your company.

The risk factor terms used by salesmen and the sales materials are often 20 years out of date and do not accurately evaluate the risk potential of the investment.

Although corporations usually offer only one plan, some school systems, like Orange County, Florida, offer over 50 plans and sponsors. If you are employed by an organization that offers more than one plan, you may transfer your money to a new plan sponsor based on the rules of your plan. In many plans, if you change sponsors or withdraw your money during the first five years, you would be charged a back-end load or commission by the sponsor.

Strategy #128

USE THE MONEY MOVEMENT STRATEGY IN YOUR EMPLOYER'S RETIREMENT PLAN TO INCREASE YOUR TAX-DEFERRED EARNINGS TO 20% OR MORE.

The Money Movement Strategy is a formula for switching between the three different types of mutual funds—stock, bond, and money market —to catch only the up cycles of each type of investment and should be used with the mutual funds in a self-directed retirement plan. Chapter 23 will give you complete instructions for using the Money Movement Strategy.

RETIREMENT PLAN WITHDRAWAL OPTIONS

Sooner or later you will stop contributing and start withdrawing and enjoying the money you have accumulated in your retirement plan. That's why you set it up in the first place. If you have followed the strategies as outlined, your retirement accounts will provide you with luxurious living for the balance of your life instead of only an income supplement.

How you make your withdrawals is as important to your wealth as how you planned your contributions and investments.

Strategy #129

USE THE WITHDRAWAL EXCEPTION RULES TO GET MONEY OUT OF YOUR RETIREMENT ACCOUNT BEFORE AGE 59½.

Most employees contribute far too little to retirement plans because they are afraid their money will be tied up until retirement and not available for personal or emergency financial situations. Here are your options for getting money out of your account before retirement.

A. All plans, except an IRA, allow you to withdraw money penalty free to offset a financial hardship or because of death or disability. If you are strapped financially, a committee set up by your employer, using IRS guidelines, can allow you to take money out of your employer's 401(k), 403(b), 457, or SEP. Check with your employer to find out how the rules are applied in your company.

B. Most employer plans now have a loan provision, allowing you to borrow up to $50,000 at any time with no penalties. Even though all 401(k) and 403(b) plans qualify under the tax rules, your employer must offer the borrowing option.

C. You may withdraw money from your IRA any time you wish. If you are under 59½ and withdraw any part of your money, you must pay the 10% penalty on the amount withdrawn. If your account is earning 20% per year, however, the penalty is just six months of interest. All withdrawals of tax-deferred money are added to your taxable income for the year. You can, therefore, successfully use an IRA as a short-term tax shelter, instead of a long-term retirement plan.

D. You may begin withdrawing from your IRA in periodic payments, using the life expectancy payout rules any time you wish with no penalty.

E. If you retire before age 59½ but after you are 55, you're allowed to withdraw your money with no penalty.

F. If a court orders you to pay money to a spouse or child from your retirement account, the withdrawal is not subject to the penalty.

G. If you have extraordinary medical expenses, withdrawals used to pay the medical expenses are not subject to penalties.

H. If you withdraw money from an Employee Stock Option Plan (ESOP) before 1990 that, on the average, has been invested for five years or more when you withdraw, there is no penalty.

I. There is no penalty for the withdrawal of dividends earned in an Employee Stock Option Plan (ESOP).

Strategy #130

**AVOID THE 10% PENALTY BY WITHDRAWING FROM
YOUR RETIREMENT PLAN AFTER AGE 59½.**

There is no 10% penalty applied on a withdrawal after age 59½ no
matter what the reason or method of withdrawal. The amount you
withdraw if part of your or your employer's tax-free contribution is
added to your taxable income for the year. The withdrawal method
you choose, however, will determine the amount of taxes you pay.

Strategy #131

**USE THE LUMP SUM AVERAGING METHOD ONLY IF
YOU NEED THE CASH FROM YOUR RETIREMENT PLAN.**

If money is withdrawn in a lump sum from an employer's retirement
plan, the averaging method option reduces your taxes to a minimum.
The averaging method allows you to treat your lump sum distribution
as if you received an equal portion of the money each year for five or
ten years. Those who were over 50 years old on January 1, 1986, may
elect ten-year averaging at any age. Those under 50 on that date may
use only five-year averaging after age 59½. Lump sum averaging may
now be used only once per lifetime. The old tax law allowed averaging
every time a person changed jobs or retired, no matter what age.

The purpose of lump sum averaging is to prevent your withdrawal
from putting you in a higher tax bracket. Because of the two bracket
system under the new tax laws, the averaging method does not cut
your taxes nearly as much as before tax reform and makes the rollover
option far more attractive.

If your employer's retirement plan withdrawal qualifies for lump
sum averaging, it also qualifies for the tax-free rollover to an IRA.

Strategy #132

USE THE IRA ROLLOVER RULES TO MINIMIZE THE TAXES ON A RETIREMENT PLAN LUMP SUM DISTRIBUTION.

When you change jobs or retire, your objective is to get control of your 401(k), 403(b), 457, or SEP money without paying taxes. The rollover rules allow you to move your entire company retirement plan to any IRA without the $2,000 IRA contribution restriction and without paying taxes. You request a check from your former employer for the amount in your account and you have 60 days from the date you receive the money to deposit it in the IRA.

Strategy #133

OPEN YOUR ROLLOVER IRA IN A NO-LOAD MUTUAL FUND FAMILY.

By using the Money Movement Strategy (Chapter 23) with your rollover account, you will average 20% per year, tax sheltered. If your rollover account is $200,000, you will average $40,000 per year and double your money in under four years.

Strategy #134

AVOID THE EMPLOYER TO EMPLOYER TRANSFER OF YOUR RETIREMENT ACCOUNT.

When you change jobs you have the option of moving your retirement plan from one employer to another with no tax consequences and preserve your right for lump sum averaging. The downside to this option is that your options for investing are limited to those in your new employer's plan. Better to do the IRA rollover! You can usually continue to use a previous employer's plan for one year or more, but your strategy is to get control of the money, which makes this option undesirable.

Strategy #135
NEVER ANNUITIZE YOUR COMPANY RETIREMENT PLAN.

Instead of receiving a lump sum, many plans allow you to use your retirement money to buy a lifetime annuity contract from an insurance company. Based on life expectancy tables published by the insurance company, you receive monthly checks for the rest of your life. Another option allows you to take less initially in your monthly annuity check and guarantees your spouse will receive partial annuity payments if you go first.

The annuity option makes only the insurance companies wealthy and is mathematically your worst withdrawal option even though it sounds appealing. There are three drawbacks to the annuity option.

1. The insurance company annuity tables give you monthly checks that are far smaller than you should receive for an account that size.
2. Your principal in most contracts becomes the property of the insurance company when you die.
3. The monthly check amounts are based on an extremely low investment return on your principal (now owned by the insurance company).

The Mandatory Withdrawal Rules—Minimizing Taxes

All retirement accounts including qualified employer plans and IRAs and Keoghs now have a required uniform starting date for mandatory withdrawals. This withdrawal method is not optional, but a few strategies will enable you to minimize or eliminate the taxes on mandatory withdrawals.

You must start making withdrawals from all your retirement plans by April 1st of the year *following* the year you become 70½ years old. Until 1989 you can defer the mandatory withdrawal from any account except an IRA if you continue working. The minimum yearly withdrawal amount is based on an IRS life expectancy table for you or you and your spouse. The rule of thumb is that your yearly withdrawal will be about 10% of the money in your account.

Strategy #136

CREATE ADDITIONAL TAX DEDUCTIONS TO SHELTER A RETIREMENT ACCOUNT WITHDRAWAL.

By using the tax strategies in the tax section of this book, you can create enough additional tax deductions to make a retirement account withdrawal tax free. Your withdrawal is not directly taxed. The amount of the withdrawal is added to your income for the year and taxed at your highest bracket (i.e. 33%). Every $1,000 of new deductions you create through a small business, family tax strategies, travel deduction strategies, etc., has the effect of tax sheltering $1,000 of your taxable withdrawal.

Strategy #137

TO MINIMIZE A MANDATORY WITHDRAWAL, RECALCULATE YOUR LIFE EXPECTANCY EVERY THREE YEARS.

The longer you live, the better your chances of living longer according to the IRS life expectancy tables. If you are 70½ your life expectancy might be ten years, but if you make it to age 75 it might still be eight years. By recalculating your life expectancy about every three years, you keep the mandatory withdrawal percentage at a bare minimum. You are allowed to elect to recalculate your life expectancy anytime you wish. Tables are available from the IRS. Eventually this calculation will be done automatically by the IRS.

Strategy #138

PRESERVE YOUR RETIREMENT ACCOUNT PRINCIPAL BY USING THE MONEY MOVEMENT STRATEGY.

Prudent investing will allow you to make mandatory withdrawals without touching your accumulated principal. By using an IRA rollover with the Money Movement Strategy (Chapter 23) in a no-load mutual fund family, your account will average 20% per year. If you are withdrawing 10% per year, not only does your principal remain intact, it is actually growing!

Strategies such as these and others you are learning are often overlooked by tax preparers and CPAs, so let this chapter become your retirement plan reference manual.

ENJOY YOUR RETIREMENT MONEY

It is all right to spend the money from your retirement account for pleasure. Withdraw all you want. That's what it is for. Too many successful retired people spend too much time trying to preserve capital instead of spending and enjoying it. You can't take it with you. So far no one has discovered a way to attach a bank vault to a hearse.

Chapter 13

TRAVEL THE WORLD ON
DEDUCTIBLE DOLLARS

*Money is a guarantee that we may have what we want in the
future. Though we need nothing at the moment, it insures
the possibility of satisfying a new desire when it arises.*

Aristotle
Nicomachean Ethics
(384–322 BC)

Objective: Make your vacations and trips tax deductible.

Imagine visiting Honolulu, New York, or even Hong Kong, and having
Uncle Sam pick up one third of your travel expenses. You can enjoy
the privilege by making your vacations and trips tax deductible.

Strategy #139
**USE JOB INTERVIEWS TO MAKE VACATIONS
DEDUCTIBLE.**

If you work for someone else, the easiest way to make your vacations
deductible is with job interviews. The tax code says that if, while you
are traveling, you go on a job interview for the same type of job you
now have, you are entitled to take a tax deduction for up to the entire
amount you spend traveling. Who "entitles" you? Congress. It just
never got around to telling us.

Keeping tax records is easy. Have the personnel department where
you apply make a copy of the job application. When you get home drop

it in your tax file with your airline, hotel, food, and rental car receipts and your trip is deductible. Whether your job is executive, truck driver, nurse, or secretary, the only requirement is that the job you apply for must be the same or similar to the one you have now. If you are between jobs, you may qualify for the deduction by applying for the same type of job as the last one you had.

You may qualify to make all of your travel expenses deductible by following a few, simple IRS rules.

To deduct 100% of expenses, you must spend a minimum of two hours per day or four hours every other day, not including weekends, working on your deductible purpose. Keep the records of the time spent in your daily planner. You may set up multiple interviews, contact a personnel agency, or conduct research at the local library on the companies and the area—all of which counts toward your time requirement.

There is only one outside risk when using the job interview strategy. You might get the job! But that's career advancement, certainly one of your more important goals.

You have created a win-win strategy. You either get the tax deduction or a better job, big promotion, and even palm trees in the wintertime. Your objective is to set up your entire financial life with win-win strategies. No matter what the outcome—you profit. Your spouse may also use the "job interview strategy" to make his or her expenses deductible.

What if you are offered the job and turn it down? Can you still take the tax deduction? That depends. If you were not offered your salary requirements or job terms, you have every right to turn down the position and claim the deduction. If you are offered your terms, it would not be right to take the deduction since the IRS could correctly claim that your job hunting was not a serious endeavor. You are not trying to kid the IRS—it doesn't fool easily—but only to take deductions for which you actually qualify.

Write ahead to line up interviews. Your public library has telephone books for most major cities. Use the form letter on page 182 to set up interviews, and to establish the job search purpose of your trip.

There are unlimited ways to apply the job interview strategy.

A young woman named Lisa, who worked for the governor of the state of Virginia and sang in night clubs around Richmond as a part-time job, had always dreamed of singing on a cruise ship as part of the band. Lisa called Carnival Cruise Lines, and was finally able to talk to a cruise director while he was in port. The cruise director told her she

Magnificent Widgets
101 Lite-My-Way Lane
Phoenix, Arizona

Attn: W. W. Hirem
Personnel Director

Dear Mr. Hirem:

I have been interested in your company for some time and am considering relocating to Phoenix.

    During March, I will be in the area and would appreciate the opportu-
nity to stop by your company to complete an application and possibly
discuss the opportunities available with Magnificent Widgets. If there is
any problem, please let me know. Otherwise, I will phone for an appointment while I am in the area. Thank you.

Sincerely,

---

was welcome to try out with the band, but they were always at sea.
That was just what she had hoped to hear!

    She booked passage on a cruise to Bermuda, during which the band
leader let her entertain the passengers for a few nights as an audition.
Lisa loved it, the band leader thought she was great, but there just
wasn't enough money available to hire another person. Lisa asked the
band leader to put it in writing so she could place the refusal in her
tax file.

    That year, Lisa took a tax deduction for her cruise to Bermuda as a
job interview and the IRS allowed the deduction. The reason is clear;
she did go on a legitimate job interview which she adequately docu-
mented. How fortunate that the job interview was on the cruise, and
the minimum time she could spend on the cruise was one week!

Strategy #140
START A SMALL IMPORTING COMPANY.

You can even make your international travel deductible by starting a
small importing company. Your total investment? Two empty suitcases. Take them with you to Mexico, South America, the Far East, and

even Europe. While you are at your destination, your tax strategy is to go shopping. While visiting the market places and bazaars, you buy the beautiful handicrafts and handmade items that are so inexpensive overseas and so incredibly expensive when you see them in the gift shops and department stores back home. These are your imports and that's what goes in the suitcases. Pick the things you know your friends would love to own.

When you get home, have a party and invite all your friends right down to your distant acquaintances. They are your customers. After you serve the "tax deductible refreshments" bring out all your beautiful imports—with a price tag on them. You will find, like so many who use this strategy that you'll sell out the first night, and make more than enough profit to pay for your next trip. At tax time you may take a deduction on Schedule C for all of your international travel expenses. After all, Tupperware made a billion dollars selling plastic bowls in friendly home parties. Think what you can do with the beautiful items you bring back. Happy bargain hunting!

My first experience at importing came during my first trip to Mexico. I was 26, and two friends and I scraped together enough gas and hotel money to get us from Nashville to Monterrey, Mexico. With the couple of hundred extra expense dollars, I bought leather coats for $8.00 each and beautiful colored ceramic plates that sold in gift shops for $30.00. They cost me just $2.00. Everything I brought back was gone instantly as my friends grabbed for their favorites as if they were at a bargain basement sale.

The government will help you. There is no customs duty on artwork or handicrafts, no matter how much you bring into the country. In any case, you can bring back $400 per person of dutiable items free, and pay only 10% of cost on the next $1,000.

Strategy #141
BECOME AN "OUTSIDE AGENT" FOR A TRAVEL AGENCY.

You can have the benefits of a travel agent or agency without changing careers or starting your own agency. By acting as an "outside agent" for any travel agency, you qualify to receive part of the travel agency's commission—up to 50%. The travel agency normally receives 10% of the cost of the airline tickets, and 15% commission on the ground arrangements such as hotels and tours. Choose a destination you would like to visit, and one that your friends and associates might also enjoy. Print simple brochures or fliers that explain your adventure and distribute them to fellow employees, club members, or even neighbors. The travel agency can furnish you with "shells"—partially printed brochures with color pictures and blank areas for insertion of time, date, and specific information about your trip.

As an outside agent you will have the chance to travel free. You'll usually get one complimentary trip for every 15 people who pay the regular price. The commission income from your trip will show your intent to make a profit and allow you to take a tax deduction for any of your money spent.

After your first successful trip, whether you take three or 50 people, begin planning other trips. You now have the right to travel anywhere to familiarize yourself with possible locations and hotels for group trips. Your travel costs are, of course, deductible.

If your part-time travel enterprise earns you about $6,000 in commissions in any one year, you qualify for free and discounted airline tickets, as well as "familiarization" trips around the world with discounts of as much as 75%. I enjoy travel so much I finally bought a travel agency. While in Amsterdam recently, I pulled out my travel agent's business card at the beautiful Amstel Hotel and was promptly given a 50% discount on my entire stay—from $200 per night to $100 per night. The previous month, I flew on American Airlines round-trip, first-class from Orlando, Florida, to Sacramento, California, for only $300, far less than the regular first-class fare of $1,200. On a recent safari to Africa, the regular cost of the land arrangements was cut in half, from $3,400 per person to $1,700, and the first-class airfare was 75% off, all tax deductible, of course, since I own the travel agency.

During the 70's, I personally took hundreds of people to Hawaii, Mexico, England, Ireland, France, and South America. As an outside agent putting the trips together, I knew I would enjoy myself. My share of the commissions amounted to about $5,000 per week plus free airfare and hotels. Not a bad way to travel.

You can get the same bargains by becoming a successful "outside agent."

Chapter 14

IN YOUR BEST INTEREST

Everything should be made as simple as possible, but not simpler.

Albert Einstein
Physicist
(1879–1955)

Objective: Make consumer interest deductible.

Under the new tax laws, over 50 favorite tax deductions have been changed or eliminated completely. One of the most devastating to taxpayers is the nondeductibility of consumer interest. Consumer interest includes interest paid on credit cards and installment, personal, college, insurance policy, and automobile loans. But the new consumer interest rules do *not* limit the interest deduction for mortgage, investments, and business loans. By converting consumer loans to legitimate mortgage, investment, and business loans, you can preserve your interest deductions.

The consumer interest deduction did not disappear completely with the onset of tax reform but is phased out over a five-year period beginning in 1987. Here are the percentages of consumer interest that are still deductible.

Year	% Deductible
1988	40%
1989	20%
1990	10%
1991	0%

Since $3.00 of tax deductions under tax reform gets you a cash refund of about $1.00, interest deductions dramatically cut the cost of borrowing money. Losing the interest deduction has the same effect as a tax increase.

For a typical family who own their home, interest deductions before tax reform averaged $12,000 or more per year. Here is an example of how you or others are hurt by the new nondeductible interest rules.

FEWER INTEREST DEDUCTIONS MEAN GREATER TAXES

	Interest Rate	Principal	One-Year Interest	Deduction Before Tax Reform	Deduction After Tax Reform
Home mortgage	11%	$ 80,000	$ 8,800	$ 8,800	$8,800
Car loans	13%	12,000	1,560	1,560	0
Credit cards	18%	4,000	720	720	0
Personal loans	12%	5,000	600	600	0
IRA—borrowed	12%	2,000	240	240	0
Margin accounts	10%	4,000	400	400	400
College loans	8%	11,000	880	880	0
TOTALS		$118,000	$13,200	$13,200	$9,200

The amount of deduction lost in the example under the new law is $4,000 ($13,200–$9,200). Under the old law, a $13,200 tax deduction for someone in the 40% tax bracket saved $5,280 in taxes, but under tax reform, with a deduction of $9,200, and a 28% bracket, the tax savings is only $2,576. The family in our example will pay $2,704 more in taxes from the loss of interest deductions alone.

Using the following strategies, you can significantly cut your taxes by making "consumer" interest deductible.

Strategy #142

USE AN EQUITY LOAN OR NEW MORTGAGE TO CREATE DEDUCTIBLE INTEREST.

Mortgages are treated differently than consumer loans when computing deductible interest. Beginning in 1988, the interest is deductible on your first and second home mortgages up to $1,000,000 of total acquisition cost—the price you originally paid for the homes. You may also deduct the interest on up to $100,000 obtained from an equity loan on your homes no matter what the money is used for. For most Americans all interest on refinancing will be deductible. Using the new rules, you can get an equity loan on your first or second home to pay off your nondeductible debt and increase your tax refund in the process.

Example:

Car Loan 1	$10,000
Car Loan 2	6,000
Credit Cards	4,000
Personal Loan	5,000
Total Borrowed	**$25,000**

If the average interest rate on these loans is 12%, one year's interest is $3,000, but the interest is not deductible. Using a qualified home equity loan for $25,000 to pay off the loans, the interest becomes deductible and if you are in the 33% bracket you get $1,000 additional cash back in your next refund check from the $3,000 interest deduction.

Strategy #143
QUALIFY YOUR BOAT OR RV LOAN FOR DEDUCTIBLE INTEREST.

If you own or buy a boat or recreational vehicle which has sleeping and toilet facilities, you may treat the asset as your second home. All of the interest is then deductible up to the acquisition cost limits. As long as the cost of your primary residence plus your boat or RV does not exceed $1,000,000, the interest is fully deductible.

Strategy #144
USE YOUR VACATION HOME AS A SECOND HOME INSTEAD OF A RENTAL PROPERTY.

To qualify your resort or vacation home as a rental property, you cannot use it yourself more than 14 days per year. If you do, you may deduct the mortgage interest expense only up to the amount of rental income. If the property is rented only occasionally, you may get a greater deduction by treating the property as a second home and deducting 100% of the interest.

If your income is too high to benefit from the $25,000 real estate expense deduction, deducting 100% of the mortgage interest on your vacation home is always your best tax alternative.

Strategy #145
BORROW THE MONEY FOR YOUR IRA.

The IRS ruled in 1987 that interest you pay on money borrowed to fund your IRA is deductible even though your IRA is a tax shelter. You take the full deduction for interest you pay, but are not taxed on the current IRA income. Use your money to pay off nondeductible debt and borrow the money for your IRA.
Example:

Bob and Eunice qualify for a $4,000 combined contribution to an IRA. This year they borrow the money from the credit union at 10% for their IRA and use their savings to pay off their VISA bill of $3,000 at 18%. Here is how they benefit.

$4,000	Borrowed for IRA
X .10	Interest—one year
$ 400	Interest paid on borrowed IRA money
X .33	Tax bracket
$ 132	*Refund from deductible interest*

$3,000	VISA bill
X .18	Interest rate on VISA card
$ 540	*Interest saved by paying off VISA bill*

$4,000	IRA money invested in mutual fund
X .20	Return on Investment
$ 800	*Tax sheltered earnings from mutual fund*

$4,000	Amount tax sheltered by IRA
X .33	Tax bracket
$1,320	*Refund from IRA deduction*

$ 132	Refund for deductible IRA interest
540	Interest saved by paying off credit cards
800	Tax sheltered IRA earnings
1,320	Refund from IRA deduction
$2,792	*Total savings and earnings from plan*
−400	Interest paid on IRA loan
$2,392	**Cash saved or earned**

On an investment of $4,000 of borrowed money and using their $3,000 cash to pay off the VISA, Bob and Eunice have earned or saved $2,392 representing an over 50% return the first year on the $4,000 borrowed IRA money.

Borrow the money for your IRA or Keogh account if you don't have it. If you do, borrow the money anyway.

Strategy #146

PAY OFF HIGH NONDEDUCTIBLE INTEREST DEBT WITH LOW NONDEDUCTIBLE INTEREST DEBT.

If you have an insurance policy with an accumulated cash value, borrow on that policy at the 5% guaranteed interest rate and use the low interest money to pay off your high interest personal loans and credit cards. Even though the interest paid on the insurance loan will not be deductible, you may be saving as much as 14% per year interest by substituting low-interest insurance dollars for the high-interest dollars. You can often save more from an interest reduction than from an interest tax deduction.

Strategy #147

PAY CASH FOR CONSUMER GOODS, BORROW TO INVEST.

Since interest on investment loans is deductible, but interest on consumer loans is not, use borrowed money for investments and pay cash for items you would normally charge or finance.

To reorganize your debt for greater deductions, take money out of your mutual funds, CDs, and stocks and use the proceeds to pay off credit cards, car loans, or other nondeductible debt. Sell investments showing current losses first to take advantage of the investment loss deduction.

In a separate transaction, borrow money using an automobile loan, mutual fund margin account, or personal loan to replace your investment capital. The interest on the borrowed money is now deductible as investment interest and you still have about the same amount of money invested. When you borrow to invest, first put the lump sum of borrowed money in a separate bank account and buy your investments from that account. You can then trace the borrowed money directly to your investments to insure the tax deduction.

Strategy #148

SELL APPRECIATED INVESTMENTS TO QUALIFY YOUR INVESTMENT INTEREST EXPENSE AS A DEDUCTION.

Interest on investment loans is fully deductible but only up to the amount of your investment income for the year. Investment income includes interest from CDs or savings accounts, dividends, and capital gains distributions shown on your mutual fund statement.

Each December, check to be certain your investment income will top your investment interest expense. If not, consider selling some appreciated mutual fund shares, stocks or bonds, since the profits count toward your investment income. The appreciated value of an investment you still hold does not count as investment income until you sell.

Strategy #149
CONVERT CONSUMER INTEREST TO BUSINESS INTEREST.

Interest paid on business loans or personal loans to finance assets used full or part time in a business is deductible. The interest deduction is taken on tax Schedule C or other business tax form, so the deduction is not limited by the standard deduction amount on tax Schedule A.

For instance, if you use your personal car financed with a personal loan in your small business and allocate 60% of its use as business, 60% of the interest you pay each year is tax deductible.

Example:

Jenny started a small business at home and used her car 60% of the time for business and 40% for personal purposes. Her car loan is $12,000 at 10% interest. Her total interest cost this year will be about $1,200 of which 60% will be deductible.

$1,200	Total interest paid
X .60	Deductible as business interest
$ 720	Tax deduction
X .33	Tax bracket
$ 238	Taxes saved

Interest you pay on a home computer or VCR loan is also deductible if the asset is used full or part time in your business.

Chapter 15

WORKING FOR TAX DEDUCTIONS

The objective of the employee is to work just hard enough so as not to be fired and the objective of the company is to pay just enough so the employee won't quit.

Unknown

Objective: Use your job to create tax deductions and minimize withholding.

When I was an employee back in the 60's, I was always told that employees get no tax breaks and most employees still believe that. While exorbitant sums are withheld from their paychecks, most act blessed if they get a refund, no matter how small. Employees may "get" no tax breaks, but there are many ways to use a job to "create" sizable tax deductions and significantly reduce withholding taxes.

Strategy #150

USE EMPLOYEE BUSINESS DEDUCTIONS TO TURN YOUR JOB INTO A TAX SHELTER.

CHECKLIST OF EMPLOYEE BUSINESS DEDUCTIONS

Here is a list of what you as an employee may deduct as job-related costs. Check those that do or could apply to you and enter the estimated amounts you spend. Rules for computing some of the deductions are contained in the strategies that follow.

✓			✓		
____ Air Fares	$____		____ Musical Instruments	$____
____ Association Dues	____		____ Parking Fees	____
____ Auto Expenses	____		____ Passport Fees	____
____ Books, Magazines	____		____ Reimbursed Expenses	____
____ Car Insurance	____		____ Repairs	____
____ Christmas Gifts	____		____ Safety Equipment	____
____ Cleaning	____		____ Salary of Assistants	____
____ Club Dues	____		____ Supplies	____
____ Convention Trips	____		____ Tape Recorder	____
____ Correspondence			____ Taxi Fares	____
Courses	____		____ Telephone	____
____ Depreciation	____		____ Tips	____
____ Displays, Samples	____		____ Tolls	____
____ Education	____		____ Tools	____
____ Furniture	____		____ Typewriter/Calculator	____
____ Home Office	____		____ Uniforms	____
____ House-hunting	____		____ Union Dues	____
____ Laundry	____			
____ Legal Expenses	____			
____ Liability Premiums	____		**TOTAL ESTIMATED**	
____ Meals	____		**EMPLOYEE DEDUCTIONS:**	
____ Medical Exams	____			
____ Moving Expenses	____		$____	

Strategy #151
DEDUCT YOUR EMPLOYEE BUSINESS MILEAGE.

When you use your automobile at your employer's request to run errands, drop off the mail, or pick someone up at the airport, and your employer does not reimburse you, you may deduct 22½ cents per mile for the first 15,000 miles and 11 cents per mile for the balance. If you are reimbursed less than 22½ cents per mile, the difference is deductible.

If you work a second job, the mileage between your full-time job and your second job is also deductible.

There are two uses of your automobile that are not deductible under any circumstances—personal use and commuting. "Personal use" includes mileage for vacations, shopping, taking the kids to school, or visiting friends. "Commuting" is driving between your home and your job. Commuting is not deductible, even if you drive to a different company office each day.

There are exceptions for salespeople, inspectors, real estate agents, and construction workers. Use the following rules:

- Your mileage from home to the first location, and from the last location to home is not deductible.
- Mileage between all of your other locations is deductible at 22½ cents per mile.

You claim the actual expenses or the mileage rate on tax form 2106. (See Chapter 18, "Getting Down to Business" for how to calculate your automobile deduction.) You may also claim the employee business portion of your car loan interest on the same form. The personal use portion of the interest is claimed as an itemized deduction on Schedule A. The business portion of the sales tax is added to the cost of the car and depreciated if the actual expense method is used. The sales tax on the personal usage portion of your car is not deductible.

Commuting expenses are not deductible, even if you carry tools or samples in your automobile, unless the items or equipment require a special vehicle, such as a van or truck. Up to three years ago you could deduct mileage if you conducted business on the way to work, or if you sold products or services for a small home business to fellow employees at your full-time job. The IRS has now ruled that commuting mileage is not deductible under any circumstances.

Strategy #152
DEDUCT YOUR JOB-RELATED EDUCATION.

You may take tax deductions for any education, books, tapes, seminars, or adult classes that help you perform your present job more effectively. The deductions include tuition, lab fees, and mileage or other travel expenses.

No deductions are allowed if the education is required to meet the minimum education standards for your job, for example, state licenses for hairdressers, teachers, or CPAs. Although, logically, you would think that required education would be deductible, the deduction applies only to optional job-related education.

You must subtract from your deduction any reimbursements you received from your employer. If you spent, for instance, $500 on job-related education and your employer reimbursed you $100, the balance of $400 is deductible. All job-related expenses work the same way.

Strategy #153
DEDUCT A HOME OFFICE WHEN USED FOR YOUR EMPLOYER.

You may take tax deductions for an office in your home, where you do job-related work, provided:

• the office is your principal office, and
• you have an area set aside that you use "regularly and exclusively" for your employer's benefit.

Even supplies, equipment, or furniture you use in your home office become deductible. If you own your home, you may use the depreciation rules to deduct some of your home office expenses. If you rent, you can deduct a portion of your rent. In both cases you may deduct a portion of your utilities, maintenance, improvements, and telephone.

Under section 143(b) and (c) of tax reform, you can no longer take a deduction for renting your home to your employer. You now take all employee business expense deductions as miscellaneous itemized deduction on Schedule A.

Strategy #154
PAY YOUR SPOUSE OR KIDS TO HELP WITH YOUR JOB.

If your spouse or kids can help you with the work you do at home for your employer, you can create immediate, legitimate tax deductions.

Your spouse could receive an IRA qualifying salary for typing, answering the phone, or preparing reports. Your children might be paid a tax-deductible salary for stuffing envelopes, filing papers, or answering the phone for your employment-related duties.

The procedures and rules for hiring family members are straightforward and completely outlined in Chapter 18, "Getting Down to Business."

Strategy #155
DEDUCT YOUR JOB RELATED TOOLS AND EQUIPMENT.

If your job requires special tools or equipment, and you are required by your employer to furnish these items at your expense, you may deduct the cost. Examples of workers requiring special tools include mechanics, construction workers, nurses or other medical professionals, and repair people.

Strategy #156
DEDUCT YOUR SPECIAL CLOTHES.

If you pay for special clothing or uniforms required for your job and the clothing would not normally be suitable for daily wear, the cost of the clothing is tax deductible. The special gold jackets worn by all Century 21 real estate people, for instance, would qualify as deductible.

Strategy #157
USE FORM 2106 TO CALCULATE YOUR EMPLOYEE BUSINESS EXPENSES.

Whether you travel to make sales, sit behind a desk, or run equipment, Form 2106 is your ticket to computing all of your nonreimbursed, job-related expenses. First list your employee business expenses on Form

2106 and then transfer the total to Schedule A—Miscellaneous Itemized Deductions. To illustrate how to put these deductions together, let's look at a typical example.

Rob Walters is an assistant manager for a small parts company. He seems to be constantly spending his own money on behalf of his company, but never gets totally reimbursed. He stops every evening on the way home to deposit the day's mail at the post office. Deduction: 4 miles a day × 250 days a year = 1,000 miles. Incidental mileage for errands for his boss adds another 400 miles per year. For six months he supplemented his income with a second job at 15 miles a day for 100 days for a total of 1,500 miles.

The company purchased a new computer system during the year and Rob took two night school courses to learn how to operate the system better. Rob's boss said they were necessary courses, but didn't feel the company could afford the tuition. Rob spent $275 of his own money on tuition, books, and supplies, and added on another 300 driving miles for a total of 3,200 employee business miles. Rob spent $84 of his own money on job-related books and magazines, and $60 on a portable calculator, and paid his kids $400 during the year to sort and file.

What are Rob's total deductions?

Automobile (3,200 × .22½)*	$ 720
Education, books, calculator	$ 419
Kids' salaries	$ 400
TOTAL DEDUCTIONS	$1,539

* The mileage rate method is used for the automobile deduction. For an example of the actual expense method deduction, see Chapter 18.

Look at form 2106 (pages 198–99) to see how Rob calculated and claimed his employee business deductions.

Under the new tax rules, the employee business expenses shown on Form 2106 are lumped together with other miscellaneous itemized deductions on Schedule A.

If Rob's employee business expenses are $1,539 (refer to the previous example) and his other miscellaneous itemized deductions are $1,500, his total miscellaneous itemized deductions equal $3,039. Let's say Rob's total income is $40,000, and his adjusted gross income is $20,000. His total deductions of $3,039 are reduced by $400 because 2

Form **2106**	**Employee Business Expenses**	OMB No 1545-0139
Department of the Treasury Internal Revenue Service (X)	▶ See separate instructions. ▶ Attach to Form 1040.	**1987** Attachment Sequence No **54**

| Your name ROBERT WALTERS | Social security number 377 06 2946 | Occupation in which expenses were incurred ASST. MGR. |

Part I   Employee Business Expenses

STEP 1   Enter Your Expenses

		Column A Other than Meals and Entertainment	Column B Meals and Entertainment
1 Vehicle expense from Part II, line 15 or line 22	1	720	
2 Parking fees, tolls, and local transportation, including train, bus, etc.	2	0	
3 Travel expense while away from home, including lodging, airplane, car rental, etc. **Do not** include meals and entertainment	3	0	
4 Business expenses not included in lines 1 through 3. **Do not** include meals and entertainment	4	819	
5 Meals and entertainment expenses. See Instructions	5		0
6 Add lines 1 through 5 and enter the **total expenses** here	6	1539	0

Note: *If you were not reimbursed for any expenses in step 1, skip lines 7 through 13 and enter the amount from line 6 on line 14*

STEP 2   Figure Any Excess Reimbursements To Report in Income

7 Reimbursements for the expenses listed in step 1 that your employer did **not** report to you on Form W-2 or Form 1099	7	0	0
Note: *If, in both columns, line 6 is more than line 7, skip lines 8 and 9 and go to line 10. You do not have excess reimbursements.*			
8 Subtract line 6 from line 7. If zero or less, enter zero	8	0	0
9 Add the amounts on line 8 of both columns and enter the total here. Also add this amount to any amount shown on Form 1040, line 7. This is an **excess reimbursement** reportable as income ▶	9		0

STEP 3   Figure Fully Deductible Reimbursed Expenses

10 Subtract line 7 from line 6. If zero or less, enter zero	10	1539	0
11 Reimbursements or allowances for the expenses in Step 1 that your employer identified to you, included on Form W-2 or Form 1099, and were not subject to withholding tax	11	0	0
Note: *The amount entered on line 11 should also have been reported as income on Form 1040.*			
12 Enter the smaller of line 10 or line 11	12	0	0
13 Add the amounts on line 12 of both columns. Enter here and on Form 1040, line 23. This is your **fully deductible reimbursed expenses** ▶	13		0

STEP 4   Figure Expenses To Deduct as an Itemized Deduction on Schedule A (Form 1040)

14 Subtract line 12 from line 10	14	1539	0
Note: *If both columns of line 14 are zero, do not complete the rest of Part I.*			
15 Enter 20% (.20) of line 14, Column B	15		0
16 Subtract line 15 from line 14	16	1539	0
17 Add the amounts on line 16 of both columns and enter the total here. Also enter the total on Schedule A (Form 1040), line 20 (Qualified Performing Art: ... ...ndicapped employees, see instructions) ▶	17		1539

For Paperwork Reduction Act Notice, see Instructions.   Form **2106** (1987)

170A

Form 2106 (1987)   Page **2**

Part II Vehicle Expenses (Use either your actual expenses (Section C) or the standard mileage rate (Section B).)

Section A.—General Information

		Vehicle 1	Vehicle 2
1	Enter the date vehicle was placed in service	1 1/ 1/ 87	/ /
2	Total mileage vehicle was used during 1987	2 10,500 miles	miles
3	Miles included on line 2 that vehicle was used for business	3 3,200 miles	miles
4	Percent of business use (divide line 3 by line 2)	4 30 %	%
5	Average daily round trip commuting distance	5 12 miles	miles
6	Miles included on line 2 that vehicle was used for commuting	6 3,000 miles	miles
7	Other personal mileage (subtract line 6 plus line 3 from line 2)	7 4,300 miles	miles

8 Do you (or your spouse) have another vehicle available for personal purposes? ☒ Yes ☐ No

9 If your employer provided you with a vehicle, is personal use during off duty hours permitted? ☐ Yes ☐ No ☒ Not applicable

10 Do you have evidence to support your deduction? ☐ Yes ☐ No. If yes, is the evidence written? ☒ Yes ☐ No

Section B.—Standard Mileage Rate (Do not use this section unless you own the vehicle.)

11	Enter the smaller of Part II, line 3 or 15,000 miles	11 3,200 miles
12	Subtract line 11 from Part II, line 3	12 0 miles
13	Multiply line 11 by 22½¢ (.225) (see instructions for a fully depreciated vehicle)	13 720 .-
14	Multiply line 12 by 11¢ (.11)	14 0 .-
15	Add lines 13 and 14. Enter total here and on Part I, line 1	15 720 .-

Section C.—Actual Expenses

		Vehicle 1	Vehicle 2
16	Gasoline, oil, repairs, vehicle insurance, etc	16		
17	Vehicle rentals	17		
18	Value of employer-provided vehicle (applies only if included on Form W-2 at 100% fair rental value, see instructions)	18		
19	Add lines 16 through 18	19		
20	Multiply line 19 by the percentage on Part II, line 4	20		
21	Depreciation from Section D, column (f) (see instructions)	21		
22	Add lines 20 and 21. Enter total here and on Part I, line 1	22		

Section D.—Depreciation of Vehicles (Depreciation can only be claimed for a vehicle you own. If a vehicle is used 50 percent or less in a trade or business, the Section 179 deduction is not allowed and depreciation must be taken using the straight line method over 5 years. For other limitations, see instructions.)

	Cost or other basis (a)	Basis for depreciation (Business use only — see instructions) (b)	Method of figuring depreciation (c)	Depreciation deduction (d)	Section 179 expense (e)	Total column (d) + column (e) (enter in Section C, line 21) (f)
Vehicle 1						
Vehicle 2						

170B

percent of adjusted gross income must be subtracted from the total miscellaneous itemized deductions (2% × $20,000 = $400). The balance is 100% deductible. In our case, Rob is allowed a deduction of $2,639 which saves him about $880 in taxes based on his 33% bracket.

As you can see, employees do get significant deductions, but most never know enough to take them.

Strategy #158

TO REDUCE THE AMOUNT WITHHELD FROM YOUR PAYCHECK, ADD WITHHOLDING ALLOWANCES.

How many times have you said, "If I just didn't have so much withheld from my paycheck, I could . . ." Three out of four employees, including you, can give themselves a tax-free raise of $50 to $300 per month in take-home pay by reducing the amount withheld from their paycheck.

The amount withheld each payday is controlled by an artificial, little-understood unit called the withholding allowance. By federal law, you must complete a W-4 form for your employer when you are first employed and whenever your tax situation changes. You, not your employer, are responsible for determining how much is withheld from your paycheck.

On the W-4 form, called the Employee's Withholding Allowance Certificate, you claim a number of allowances, usually ranging from 0 to 15. Theoretically, if you claim 0 allowances an amount is withheld from your paycheck that by year's end would equal the tax you would owe if you had 0 exemptions or dependents including yourself. Each allowance you claim on the W-4 form will reduce your income tax withholding each year by about the same number of dollars you would save in taxes if you had an additional $2,000 tax deduction. The actual amount of money withheld per "allowance" varies slightly, according to your income.

If you add allowances to your W-4 form, your paycheck gets bigger. If you reduce the number of allowances on your W-4 form, your paycheck gets smaller.

A personal exemption is not the same as an allowance. Claiming allowances is done on the W-4 form, exemptions are claimed on your 1040 tax return. Many people incorrectly believe that you are allowed to claim only one allowance for each dependent in your family. Each dependent is worth one allowance, but you may also claim extra allowances for other tax deductions you already have or can create using tax strategies. Your objective is to get the maximum number of dollars legally possible in every paycheck. By adjusting the number of allowances on your W-4 form based on the following two formulas, you will be able to maximize your take-home pay.

Here are the allowance rules:

- You may legally add any number of allowances to your W-4 form that will enable you to break even with the IRS when you file your tax return. You won't owe the IRS, the IRS won't owe you.
- The number of allowances claimed has little to do with the number of dependents you have and everything to do with the amount of tax deductions you can expect to claim by the end of the year.
- You and/or your working spouse may increase or decrease the number of withholding allowances you claim by completing a new W-4 form in the payroll department or personnel department where you work. Your employer has the form, or you may obtain a copy from the IRS. Your current W-4 form always remains in effect until you make a change.
- If you claim more than nine allowances, your employer is required to send a copy of the form to the IRS. If the IRS can't understand why your taxes will be so low, they may send you a form letter asking you to explain within 30 days why you are claiming so many allowances. If you do not answer the letter, the IRS will ask your employer to reduce your withholding allowances to one until you do explain. You are allowed, however, to claim more than nine allowances if you deserve them.
- If the number of allowances to which you are entitled decreases, you are required to file a new W-4 form within ten days. If the number of withholding allowances to which you are entitled increases, no one is required to notify you.
- If you get a refund each year, you are having too much withheld and need to increase your allowances. If you have to cough up additional cash each year at tax time, you are having too little withheld and should either decrease your allowances or, better still, increase your tax deductions through the use of tax strategies.

Strategy #159

GET NEXT YEAR'S TAX REFUND THIS YEAR.

Ever get a refund? Most American taxpayers do, and somehow feel they have put one over on the IRS. They have not. A refund is nothing more than a return of your own money, which you never owed to the IRS in the first place. You receive no interest and not so much as a thank you letter! You wouldn't loan your money to your bank without interest, why would you loan it interest free to the IRS? The misunderstanding concerning refunds is so universal that 32 million out of a total of 96 million taxpayers receive over 60 billion dollars in refunds each year.

By adding allowances to your W-4 form, you can get next year's refund in this year's paychecks. By completing a new W-4 using the worksheet included on the form, you will be able to determine how many allowances to add to get your refund now. Take the extra money you will be receiving each month and put it into your investment plan.

Strategy #160

ADD ONE ADDITIONAL ALLOWANCE TO YOUR W-4 FORM FOR EACH $2,000 TAX DEDUCTION YOU CREATE.

Through the use of tax strategies, you can create new tax deductions, and will not have to wait until next year to receive the accompanying refund. You can add extra allowances to your employment W-4 form anytime during the year as you create more deductions, and receive your extra refund now.

Here is a typical example of a couple who converted new tax deductions to immediate cash using the W-4 form.

Sally and Bert Adams who have two dependent children calculate that during the current tax year they have or will create a total of $17,000 in new tax deductions to add to their $8,000 mortgage interest and $1,000 property tax deductions. On the W-4 form, these deductions are divided up between worksheet line 1, "Itemized Deductions" and worksheet line 4, "Adjustments to Income."

ITEMIZED DEDUCTIONS—W-4 Worksheet, Line 1

Mortgage Interest	$8,000
Property Taxes	1,000
Net Miscellaneous Deductions	3,000
40% of Personal Interest	2,000
Total Itemized Deductions	**$14,000**

ADJUSTMENTS—W-4 Worksheet, Line 4

IRA	$2,000
Small Business Loss	4,000
Rental Property Loss	6,000
Total Adjustments	**$12,000**

By using the worksheet on the back of his W-4 form, Bert calculates that he qualifies for a total of 14 allowances or eight more allowances than he had last year. With a $35,000 income, the additional allowances will add about $200 per month to his take-home pay, or $2,400 this year in extra tax-free cash. Look at the following W-4 form, and you will see how the allowances are calculated.

When you have created tax deductions that equal the income from your job, you may declare yourself legally exempt from income tax withholding by checking one of the exempt boxes on the front of any W-4 form, line 6a and 6b. Under the tax reform, you cannot claim yourself totally exempt if you have any nonwage income such as investment interest.

Use your tax plan and W-4 as your ticket to instant wealth.

19**88** Form W-4

Department of the Treasury
Internal Revenue Service

Purpose. You must complete Form W-4 so that your employer can withhold the correct amount of Federal income tax from your pay.

Exemption From Withholding. To be exempt, you must have owed no Federal income tax last year **and** must not expect to owe any this year. You may not claim exempt status if you can be claimed as a dependent of another person, have any nonwage income, and expect your total income to be more than $500. If exempt, only complete the certificate at the bottom of this page.

Basic Instructions. Employees who are not exempt should complete the Personal Allowances Worksheet. Additional worksheets are provided on page 2 for employees to adjust their withholding allowances based on itemized deductions, adjustments to income, or two-earner/two-job situations. For accuracy, complete all worksheets

that apply to your situation. The worksheets on this form are designed to help you figure the number of withholding allowances you are entitled to claim. However, you may claim fewer allowances than this.

Head of household. Generally, you may claim Head of household filing status on your tax return only if you are unmarried and pay more than 50% of the costs of keeping up a home for yourself and your dependent(s) or other qualifying individuals.

Nonwage Income. If you have a large amount of nonwage income, from sources such as interest or dividends, you should consider making estimated tax payments using Form 1040-ES. Otherwise, you may find that you owe additional tax at the end of the year.

Two-Earner/Two-Jobs. If you have a working spouse or more than one job, figure the total

number of allowances you are entitled to claim on all jobs using worksheets from only one Form W-4. This total should be divided among all jobs. Your withholding will usually be most accurate when all allowances are claimed on the W-4 filed for the highest paying job and zero allowances are claimed for the others.

Advance Earned Income Credit. If you are eligible for this credit, you can receive it added to your paycheck throughout the year. For details, obtain Form W-5 from your employer.

Check Your Withholding. After your W-4 takes effect, you can use **Publication 919,** Is My Withholding Correct for 1988?, to see how the dollar amount you are having withheld compares to your estimated total annual tax. Call 1-800-424-3676 (in Hawaii and Alaska, check your local telephone directory) to obtain this publication.

Personal Allowances Worksheet

A	Enter "1" for **yourself** if no one else can claim you as a dependent . . . . **A**	1
B	Enter "1" if: 1. You are single and have only one job; or	**B** ____
	2. You are married, have only one job, and your spouse does not work; or	
	3. Your wages from a second job or your spouse's wages (or the total of both) are $2,500 or less.	
C	Enter "1" for your **spouse.** But, you may choose to enter "0" if you are married and have either a working spouse or more than one job (this may help you avoid having too little tax withheld) . . . . **C**	1
D	Enter number of **dependents** (other than your spouse or yourself) whom you will claim on your tax return . . . . **D**	2
E	Enter "1" if you will file as a **head of household** on your tax return (see conditions under "Head of Household," above) . **E**	____
F	Enter "1" if you have at least $1,500 of **child or dependent care expenses** for which you plan to claim a credit . . **F**	____
G	Add lines A through F and enter total here . . . . ▶ **G**	4

For accuracy, do all worksheets that apply.
- If you plan to **itemize or claim adjustments to income** and want to reduce your withholding, turn to the Deductions and Adjustments Worksheet on page 2.
- If you are **single** and have **more than one job** and your combined earnings from all jobs exceed $25,000 OR if you are **married** and have a **working spouse or more than one job,** and the combined earnings from all jobs exceed $40,000, then turn to the Two-Earner/Two-Job Worksheet on page 2 if you want to avoid having too little tax withheld.
- If **neither** of the above situations applies to you, **stop here** and enter the number from line G on line 4 of Form W-4 below.

- - - - - - - - - - - - - - - **Cut here and give the certificate to your employer. Keep the top portion for your records.** - - - - - - - - - - - - - - -

Form **W-4**	**Employee's Withholding Allowance Certificate**	OMB No 1545-0010
Department of the Treasury Internal Revenue Service	▶ **For Privacy Act and Paperwork Reduction Act Notice, see reverse.**	19**88**

1 Type or print your first name and middle initial	Last name	2 Your social security number
BERT J.	ADAMS	339-084-2164

Home address (number and street or rural route)		
991 TEMPECO	**3** Marital Status	☐ Single ☒ Married
City or town, state, and ZIP code		☐ Married, but withhold at higher Single rate.
ALTAMONTE SPRINGS, FL 32714		**Note:** If married, but legally separated, or spouse is a nonresident alien, check the Single box.

4 Total number of allowances you are claiming (from line G above or from the Worksheets on back if they apply) . .	**4**	14	
5 Additional amount, if any, you want deducted from each pay	**5**	$ 0	

6 I claim exemption from withholding because (check boxes below that apply):
- **a** ☐ Last year I did not owe any Federal income tax and had a right to a full refund of **ALL** income tax withheld, **AND**
- **b** ☐ This year I do not expect to owe any Federal income tax and expect to have a right to a full refund of **ALL** income tax withheld.
- **c** If both **a** and **b** apply and you satisfy the additional conditions outlined above under "Exemption From Withholding," enter the year effective and "EXEMPT" here. Do not complete lines 4 and 5 above . . . ▶ | Year 19 |

7 Are you a full-time student? (**Note:** Full-time students are **not** automatically exempt.) . . . . ☐ Yes ☒ No

Under penalties of perjury, I certify that I am entitled to the number of withholding allowances claimed on this certificate or, if claiming exemption from withholding, that I am entitled to claim the exempt status

Employee's signature ▶	Date ▶ 1-15	198 8

8 Employer's name and address (**Employer: Complete 8, 9, and 10 only if sending to IRS**)	9 Office code	10 Employer identification number

175A

Form W-4 (1988)   **Page 2**

Deductions and Adjustments Worksheet

Note: *Use this worksheet only if you plan to itemize deductions or claim adjustments to income on your 1988 tax return.*

1	Enter an estimate of your 1988 itemized deductions. These include: qualifying home mortgage interest, 40% of personal interest, charitable contributions, state and local taxes (but not sales taxes), medical expenses in excess of 7.5% of your income, and miscellaneous deductions (most miscellaneous deductions are now deductible only in excess of 2% of your income)	1	$ 14,000
2	Enter: { $5,000 if married filing jointly or qualifying widow(er) $4,400 if head of household $3,000 if single $2,500 if married filing separately }	2	$ 5,000
3	**Subtract** line 2 from line 1. If line 2 is greater than line 1, enter zero	3	$ 9,000
4	Enter an estimate of your 1988 adjustments to income. These include alimony paid and deductible IRA contributions	4	$ 12,000
5	**Add** lines 3 and 4 and enter the total	5	$ 21,000
6	Enter an estimate of your 1988 nonwage income (such as dividends or interest income)	6	$ 0
7	**Subtract** line 6 from line 5. Enter the result, but not less than zero	7	$ 21,000
8	**Divide** the amount on line 7 by $2,000 and enter the result here. Drop any fraction	8	10
9	Enter the number from Personal Allowances Worksheet, line G, on page 1	9	4
10	**Add** lines 8 and 9 and enter the total here. If you plan to use the Two-Earner/Two-Job Worksheet, also enter the total on line 1, below. Otherwise, **stop here** and enter this total on Form W-4, line 4 on page 1 10		14

Two-Earner/Two-Job Worksheet

Note: *Use this worksheet only if the instructions at line G on page 1 direct you here.*

1	Enter the number from line G on page 1 (or from line 10 above if you used the Deductions and Adjustments Worksheet)	1	
2	Find the number in **Table 1** below that applies to the **LOWEST** paying job and enter it here . .	2	
3	If line 1 is **GREATER THAN OR EQUAL TO** line 2, subtract line 2 from line 1. Enter the result here (if zero, enter "0") and on Form W-4, line 4, on page 1. **DO NOT** use the rest of this worksheet.	3	

Note: *If line 1 is LESS THAN line 2, enter "0" on Form W-4, line 4, on page 1. Complete lines 4–9 to calculate the additional dollar withholding necessary to avoid a year-end tax bill.*

4	Enter the number from line 2 of this worksheet	4	
5	Enter the number from line 1 of this worksheet	5	
6	**Subtract** line 5 from line 4	6	
7	Find the amount in **Table 2** below that applies to the **HIGHEST** paying job and enter it here	7	$
8	**Multiply** line 7 by line 6 and enter the result here. This is the additional annual withholding amount needed.	8	$
9	**Divide** line 8 by the number of pay periods each year. (For example, divide by 26 if you are paid every other week.) Enter the result here and on Form W-4, line 5, page 1. This is the additional amount to be withheld from each paycheck	9	$

Table 1: Two-Earner/Two-Job Worksheet

Married Filing Jointly		All Others	
If wages from **LOWEST** paying job are—	Enter on line 2 above	If wages from **LOWEST** paying job are—	Enter on line 2 above
0 - $4,000	0	0 - $4,000	0
4,001 - 8,000	1	4,001 - 8,000	1
8,001 - 18,000	2	8,001 - 13,000	2
18,001 - 21,000	3	13,001 - 15,000	3
21,001 - 23,000	4	15,001 - 19,000	4
23,001 - 25,000	5	19,001 and over	5
25,001 - 27,000	6		
27,001 - 32,000	7		
32,001 - 38,000	8		
38,001 - 42,000	9		
42,001 and over	10		

Table 2: Two-Earner/Two-Job Worksheet

Married Filing Jointly		All Others	
If wages from **HIGHEST** paying job are—	Enter on line 7 above	If wages from **HIGHEST** paying job are—	Enter on line 7 above
0 - $40,000	$300	0 - $23,000	$300
40,001 - 80,000	550	23,001 - 48,000	550
80,001 and over	650	48,001 and over	650

Privacy Act and Paperwork Reduction Act Notice.—We ask for this information to carry out the Internal Revenue laws of the United States. We may give the information to the Department of Justice for civil or criminal litigation and to cities, states, and the District of Columbia for use in administering their tax laws. You are required to give this information to your employer.

175B

Chapter 16

TURN YOUR HOME INTO A TAX HAVEN

He worked like hell in the country so he could live in the city, where he worked like hell so he could live in the country.

Don Marquis
Journalist
(1878–1937)

Objective: Generate thousands in extra tax deductions from your principal residence.

You don't have to look far to find tax deductions; thousands of dollars of deductions can be found right under your roof. In this chapter, you'll learn several tax-saving strategies available to you simply because you are a homeowner. If you are not a homeowner, your first priority is to become one and these strategies should help motivate you.

Strategy #161
TURN YOUR HOME IMPROVEMENTS INTO TAX DEDUCTIONS.

Your home improvements become a tax shelter when you sell your home. If you own a home, you already realize how easy it is to pour thousands of dollars into your property to make your home environment just the way you want it to be. Improvements are any expenses that add to the value of your home and are differentiated in the tax law

206

from repairs. Improvements make your home more valuable; repairs only help maintain the current value. Following are examples of home improvements and home repairs to assist you in understanding the difference.

Home Improvement (Deductible)	Home Repair (Nondeductible)
paneling a room	replacing a scratched or broken panel
new shrubbery	replacing dead shrubbery
installing a fence	painting a fence
carpeting a room	replacing or cleaning your carpet
paving a driveway	repairing cracks in your driveway
adding a room	painting a room

"Upgrading" can also turn nondeductible "repairs" into deductible "improvements." If you upgrade something that needs repairing, such as a hot water heater, roofing, or carpet, the difference between the repair cost and the upgrade cost is considered an improvement and is deductible. Examples of upgrades include the following:

- Replacing a 30-gallon hot water heater with a 60-gallon, energy-efficient hot water heater.
- Replacing asphalt shingle roofing with expensive spanish tile or cedar shake roofing.
- Replacing $4 per yard standard carpeting with $16 per yard plush Antron IV carpeting.

Remember, the difference is deductible.

If you upgrade a part of your home that does not need repairing, the entire cost may be considered an improvement. Improvement expenses include all labor that is not your own or your spouse's. Making a home improvement provides you with a great opportunity to use the family tax strategy—"Hire Your Children and Grandchildren." You may not be able to deduct the work you personally do on your home, but you can hire your children and grandchildren to help with the work and deduct amounts paid to them.

Take the deduction for improvements on Form 2119 when you sell your home. Keep receipts for all home improvements.

Strategy #162

DEDUCT LAST MINUTE PRESALE FIX-UP EXPENSES.

Before you sell a home, there are usually repairs and fix-up expenses ranging from a few hundred to several thousand dollars—all necessary to get your home in salable condition. Any normal nondeductible repairs you make within a 90-day period before you sell your home are tax deductible on tax form 2119, line eight.

Strategy #163

USE THE TAX DEFERRAL OPTION TO AVOID TAXES WHEN YOU SELL YOUR HOME.

Congress has passed special rules for homeowners that make it possible to enjoy huge cash profits from the sale of a personal residence without becoming liable for immediate taxes. In order to qualify for the homeowners tax deferral, you must buy or build another personal residence of equal or greater value within 24 months of the sale of your first home. The 24-month purchase period of the new home can begin before or after the sale of your current home, so you actually enjoy a 48-month qualifying period.

Using the "homeowners tax deferral" rules means you pay no taxes now, but you must report your profit by using tax form 2119. The cost basis of the new home you purchased is reduced by the amount of the profit from the sale of your first home. Should you sell a home sometime in the future and not buy another home that qualifies for the homeowners tax deferral, you would be liable for taxes on all of the accumulated profits. Your strategy, therefore, is to always own a home and buy a more expensive home each time you sell. All of the equity you accumulate from home to home is tax sheltered as long as you use this strategy.

If the purchase price of the new home you buy is less than the sale price of your old home, you must claim the difference as profit. The difference is taxable in the year your new home is purchased. Let's say you sell your home, which cost $70,000, for $90,000 and decide to buy a condo for $85,000. Your profit on the sale is $20,000: How much can you defer using the homeowner deferral rules? Since the purchase price of the new residence is $5,000 less than the sale price of your previous home, you must claim the $5,000 as taxable profit this year. Therefore, $15,000 ($20,000 profit − $5,000 taxable) is the amount you can defer from taxes.

If, because of separation or divorce, you sell your home and split the profits with your ex-spouse, you are only required to buy a home costing half as much as the one you sold.

If you don't buy another home within 24 months, you will be liable for taxes on the profits of the home you sold plus any deferred profits from the sale of previous homes you have owned.

Strategy #164

DON'T INVEST THE PROFITS FROM THE SALE OF YOUR OLD HOME INTO YOUR NEW HOME.

To qualify for the homeowners tax deferral, you are not required to reinvest any of your profit from the sale of your old home into the new home, only to buy a home of equal or greater value.

Therefore, when you sell your home, use the profits in a powerful investment program that will earn more than the interest you would pay on a home mortgage. Buy your new home using as big a mortgage as possible.

Let's look at the home sale of Martin and Marie Jones of Kansas City, to see how the tax deferral process actually works.

The Joneses sell their home for $110,000. They originally purchased the home eight years ago for $65,000. The pre-sale fix-up expenses were $1,000, and they paid Jacob Realty $7,000 in commissions for selling the home. Their new home costs $120,000, so, using the homeowner's tax deferral rules, there is no taxable gain on the sale of their old home. They are able to defer or postpone the taxes on their profit of $38,000 ($110,000 sale price − $7,000 commission − $65,000 cost = $38,000 cash profit).

The Joneses report the transactions involving the sale of the old residence and purchase of their new residence on tax form 2119 in order to qualify for the homeowner's tax deferral. See the sample form on page 210.

On their new $120,000 home the Joneses can either make a down

Form **2119**	**Sale or Exchange of Principal Residence**	OMB No 1545-0072
	► See instructions on back.	**1987**
Department of the Treasury Internal Revenue Service (X)	► Attach to Form 1040 for year of sale (see instruction B).	Attachment Sequence No **22**

Name(s) as shown on Form 1040 · MARTIN AND MARIE JONES   Your social security number   776 24 3394

Do not include expenses that you deduct as moving expenses.

1 a Date former residence sold ► 3-24-87

  b Enter the face amount of any mortgage, note (for example, second trust), or other financial instrument on which you will receive periodic payments of principal or interest from this sale ►   0

		Yes	No
2 a	If you bought or built a new residence, enter date you occupied it; otherwise enter "None" ► None		
b	Are any rooms in either residence rented out or used for business for which a deduction is allowed? (If "Yes," see instructions.)		X
3 a	Were you 55 or over on date of sale?		X
b	Was your spouse 55 or over on date of sale? If you answered "No" to 3a and 3b, do not complete 3c through 3f and Part II.		X
c	Did the person who answered "Yes" to 3a or 3b own and use the property sold as his or her principal residence for a total of at least 3 years (except for short absences) of the 5-year period before the sale?	–	
d	If you answered "Yes" to 3c, do you elect to take the once in a lifetime exclusion of the gain on the sale?	–	
e	At time of sale, was the residence owned by: ☐ you, ☐ your spouse, ☒ both of you?		
f	Social security number of spouse, at time of sale, if different from number on Form 1040 ► (Enter "None" if you were not married at time of sale.)		

Part I   **Computation of Gain**

4	Selling price of residence (Do not include personal property items.)	**4**	110,000 –
5	Expense of sale (Include sales commissions, advertising, legal, etc.)	**5**	7,000 –
6	Subtract line 5 from line 4. This is the amount realized	**6**	103,000 –
7	Basis of residence sold	**7**	65,000 –
8	Gain on sale (subtract line 7 from line 6). If zero or less, enter zero and do not complete the rest of form. Enter the gain from this line on Schedule D, line 3 or 10,* unless you bought another principal residence or checked "Yes" to 3d. Then continue with this form	**8**	38,000 –

  If you haven't replaced your residence, do you plan to do so within the replacement period? ☐ Yes ☐ No
  (If "Yes" see instruction B.)

Part II   **Age 55 or Over One-Time Exclusion**

Complete this part only if you checked "yes" to 3(d) to elect the once in a lifetime exclusion; otherwise, skip to Part III.

9	Enter the smaller of line 8 or $125,000 ($62,500, if married filing separate return)	**9**	
10	Gain (subtract line 9 from line 8). If zero, do not complete rest of form. Enter the gain from this line on Schedule D, line 10,* unless you bought another principal residence. Then continue with this form	**10**	

Part III   **Gain To Be Postponed and Adjusted Basis of New Residence**

Complete this part if you bought another principal residence.

11	Fixing-up expenses (see instructions for time limits)	**11**	1,000 –
12	Adjusted sales price (subtract line 11 from line 6)	**12**	102,000 –
13	Cost of new residence	**13**	120,000 –
14	Gain taxable this year (subtract line 13 plus line 9 (if applicable) from line 12). If result is zero or less, enter zero. Do not enter more than line 8 or line 10 (if applicable). Enter the gain from this line on Schedule D, line 3 or 10*	**14**	0 –
15	Gain to be postponed (Subtract line 14 from line 8. However, if Part II applies, subtract line 14 from line 10.)	**15**	38,000 –
16	Adjusted basis of new residence (subtract line 15 from line 13)	**16**	82,000 –

***Caution:** If you completed Form 6252 for the residence in 1a, do not enter your taxable gain from Form 2119 on Schedule D

For Paperwork Reduction Act Notice, see back of form.   Form **2119** (1987)

179A

payment using the $38,000 profit from the first home or make a minimum down payment of $12,000. In either case the fixed interest rate is 10%. What should they do?

The correct strategy in real estate is to maximize your cash available for more liquid investments. Real estate ties up your money long term. The Joneses should take the $26,000 difference in the down payments and invest the money in mutual funds or discounted mortgages that will return 20% or more. The difference in mortgage payments can be made using part of the investment income. At a 20% investment return, the $26,000 will generate $5,200 while the $26,000 extra mortgage amount will cost only $2,600 per year in tax deductible interest.

Strategy #165

TAKE THE ONCE-PER-LIFETIME $125,000 TAX EXCLUSION TO SAVE AS MUCH AS $40,000 IN TAXES.

You can create your own tax-free retirement program using your home and a special tax exemption created by Congress.

Once you, or your spouse, reach age 55 and sell your home, you may elect to exclude from taxes up to $125,000 of the accumulated profits. The full exclusion, if you are in the 33% bracket, will save you over $40,000 cash in taxes. Your strategy is to apply the homeowners tax deferral rules from home to home until you or your spouse are over age 55. When you sell after 55, use form 2119 to permanently tax exempt up to $125,000 of the accumulated profits. To qualify, you must have lived in the home for any three out of the five previous years before selling. You may use the exclusion as an individual or as a couple only once per lifetime.

If you and the person you are planning to marry are over age 55 and both own homes, you would be smart to both take the exclusion by selling your homes and making your profits tax exempt before you marry. Use tax form 2119, part two to claim your exemption.

An unusual court case involved a divorced couple who jointly owned a property on which the accumulated profit totaled $250,000. After their divorce, their home was sold and they each claimed the full $125,000 exclusion. The IRS said no. In an appeal, the tax court ruled in favor of the couple and allowed the full $250,000 exclusion based on the court's interpretation of the tax laws.

Since the exemption can be used only once per lifetime, continue to use the homeowner's deferral rules from home to home until you have accumulated close to the $125,000 exemption limit even if you are over age 55.

Strategy #166
CREATE A DEDUCTIBLE OFFICE AT HOME.

There is a myth perpetrated by unknowledgeable tax preparers that establishing a business office in your home will either flag you for an audit or cause you to be taxed on the home office deductions when you sell your home. Both premises are absolutely false. In his first term of office, President Reagan stressed the importance of the free enterprise system and encouraged regulations that would make it easier to begin a small business with little or no red tape. At the same time he pressured the IRS to reverse its position on home businesses and allow tax deductions without hassle for the expenses involved. Since 1982, the IRS has reversed many of its positions relative to a tax deductible office in the home, but most people, including many tax professionals are not aware of the positive changes that have taken place. Here are the current rules for deducting an office in your home.

RULE 1: Items you may deduct for an office in your home include utilities, repairs, maintenance, improvements, decorating, insurance, and depreciation if you own the property, or a portion of the rent, utilities, and improvements if you are a tenant.

RULE 2: To take the deduction for office in the home you must meet any one of the following conditions:

- Your home office is the primary office for your business and you do not have another office in the same city or area. You may not claim a deduction for an office in the home if you are a realtor, or a professional with another office, or if you have office space in a retail shop, warehouse, or plant. Teachers may not claim a deduction for an office in the home even if they grade papers or talk to students at home.
- You regularly see clients or patients in your home.
- You take care of children in your home or conduct home parties or sales meetings for your multi-level marketing business.
- You have an office in your home which is the primary and only office you use on behalf of your employer.

RULE 3: You may also take tax deductions if you rent out a room or rooms in your home to college students or tenants.

RULE 4: You must use the area you call your office "regularly and exclusively" for business, although the area does not have to be a separate room. You may also deduct an area you use exclusively for a workshop or storage.

The IRS has denied the deduction to those who use their office area for other purposes, such as watching television or storage of personal items. The IRS will normally not ask to visit your home for inspection, but you will want to follow the correct procedures.

RULE 5: You may compute the deductible percentage of your expenses in one of two ways. Choose the method that gives you the greatest tax deduction.

Method #1—Divide the number of rooms you use for tax deductible purposes by the total number of rooms in your home or apartment, not counting bathrooms. One out of five rooms used for deductible purpose would give you a 20% deduction.

Method #2—Divide the square footage of the area you use for tax deductible purposes by the total number of square feet in your home or apartment. A 2,000 square foot home with a 400 square foot area set aside for a deductible purpose would give you the same 20%.

RULE 6: Since you have already deducted interest on your home mortgage and property taxes as personal tax deductions, you must reduce your total home office deductions by the amount of personal deductions you have already taken for the deductible areas. See IRS publication 334 for the formula.

RULE 7: Your tax deduction is limited to the total amount of income your business earned during the year.

RULE 8: You are not penalized for home office deductions when you sell your home, provided you do not have an office or business area in your home the year you sell. Get rid of your home office the year before you intend to sell your home. Up to 1982, if you took the depreciation deduction, you would not be able to defer the entire profit from the sale of your home if you bought another home. You may, under current tax law, defer the entire profit.

GETTING THE MOST FROM THE HOME YOU OWN

1. Always own a home; don't rent.
2. Turn your home improvements into tax deductions when you sell.

3. Deduct all fix-up expenses you incur within 90 days of the date you sell your home.
4. When you sell, always buy another home of equal or greater value to defer taxes on the profits.
5. After age 55, use the $125,000 exclusion rule to make your accumulated profits tax exempt.
6. Don't invest the profits from the sale of your old home into the new home. Make the minimum down payment and put your cash in better investments.
7. Use a part of your home as the main office for your small business.
8. Use form 2119 to claim all deferrals, improvements, and exclusions when you sell a home.

Chapter 17

MAKE YOUR BOAT, PLANE, OR RV TAX DEDUCTIBLE

True, you can't take it with you, but then, that's not the place where it comes in handy.

Unknown

Objective: Find big tax deductions for your recreational assets.

The great outdoors! Who can resist it? Exploring rivers, lakes, and cruising ocean waters for the big catch, while waiting for the camera crew of *American Sportsman* to arrive; donning the wings of eagles and flying three-dimensionally free in a personal and private plane; getting close to nature at the seashore, or high in the mountains in your own plush home on wheels. These are the dreams that inspire us to work harder. Vacations and leisure time activities cost money. But from my own experience, I can assure you that you can easily reduce the cost of owning and operating recreational assets up to 30% by making your boat, plane, or motor home legally tax deductible.

There are two uses of recreational vehicles that qualify them for tax deductions. The first is direct use in a small business; the second is third-party leasing.

Strategy #167
USE YOUR BOAT, PLANE OR MOTOR HOME IN YOUR SMALL BUSINESS TO CREATE TAX DEDUCTIONS.

What is now a hobby—flying, fishing, or sailing—can be turned into a tax deductible small business enterprise simply by showing the intent to make a profit. The tax code stipulates that assets used in a business that contribute directly to the production of income are tax deductible, even if you own them personally. Entertainment expenses, such as food, clean-up, and fuel, are deductible as business expenses. Depreciation, however, is not deductible unless you find a business use other than entertainment. Here is a good example.

My friend Tom lives and breathes fishing. He would rather fish than eat, except for eating fish. Year after year, weekend after weekend, he trailers his 23-foot Sea Craft behind his Ford van from his home in Richmond, Virginia, to the fertile fishing grounds of the Chesapeake Bay over a hundred miles away. Continually pouring money into gas, maintenance, fishing tackle, and motel expenses left Tom feeling as if he was working for his boat, instead of the other way around.

One day, while bobbing about in two-foot swells, Tom and I began to discuss what he could legally do to be able to take tax deductions for some of his expenses. Tom was already selling his catch of sea bass and bluefish to local restaurants, often at a handsome profit, which meant that he was in a tax deductible business. He had never thought of taking the deductions.

Tom also wrote to manufacturers of fishing rods, reels, and lures, to see if he could become a distributor, and received several enthusiastic replies, especially from the smaller companies. He was excited and well on his way. He bought several samples at wholesale (50% off) and began to show them to fellow fishermen. He used his boat to house, display, and demonstrate his new line of fishing equipment. Not only has Tom picked up some unexpected income from his venture, his expensive hobby has now become a personally and financially reward-

Item	Cost	Cash Spent	Annual Tax Deduction	% Business Use
Boat	$26,000	$ 4,000	$ 6,500	50%
Boat fuel	1,800	1,800	900	50%
Van fuel	900	900	450	50%
Sample costs	750	750	750	100%
Cost of van	12,000	2,000	3,000	50%
Motels, food	2,800	2,800	1,400	50%
TOTALS		$11,250	$13,000	

ing, tax deductible small business. Look how Tom benefited the first year alone from his small fishing-related business (table page 216).

Because Tom is in the 40% tax bracket (33% federal and 7% state), he received an additional refund of $5,200 (40% of his $13,000 deduction), significantly reducing the cost of his former hobby.

Here's another creative example of how to make your recreational assets deductible. Bart, a member of my organization, always loved flying, but didn't feel he could afford to own a plane. He estimated that he could buy a used, four-seater Cessna for about $22,000. Even though the cost of fuel and maintenance was slightly out of his budget at the time, Bart reasoned that if he could make a good part of his expenses tax deductible, he could afford the plane immediately.

Bart combined his interest in flying with another interest, photography, and started a small business he calls "Aerial Photos by Bart." He printed brochures and business cards and contacted realtors, the Chamber of Commerce, and the city planning commission about his new venture. He also ran ads in the classified section of the newspaper offering to give guided air tours for new families moving into the area. (For this he was required to get an additional license.) His weekend, part-time business is thriving, and he was able to convert two hobbies into a fun and profitable business. Most of all, he was able to afford his dream of owning his own plane.

There are countless ways to use recreational assets in a small business and take advantage of the tax deductions and profit potential. Here are a few ideas:

- Using your plane for flying lessons
- Sailing lessons on your sailboat
- Chartered fishing trips on your fishing boat
- Water-skiing lessons using your boat and tax deductible skis
- Using your motor home as the principal office for your small business or to display your products or services
- Using your motor home as a traveling billboard with your ad painted on the side

You may also deduct the business use percentage of the interest you pay on the loan to purchase recreational assets, since business but not personal interest is deductible.

Strategy #168
USE THIRD PARTY LEASING TO MAKE RECREATIONAL ASSETS DEDUCTIBLE.

A second method of making your recreational assets deductible and depreciable is "third party leasing," which means offering your boat, motor home, or airplane for rent at "fair market rental value," using someone other than yourself as the leasing agent.

Why not just rent it yourself? The IRS has ruled that if you attempt to rent your recreational assets yourself, your deductions are limited to twice the amount of time the asset is actually rented. If you rented the asset four weeks per year, even though it was available for rent all year, your deduction for depreciation and other expenses would be limited to eight weeks, instead of 52.

When you are renting through a third party—another company normally in the business of leasing—your recreational asset is considered to be used for business purposes the entire time the asset is available for rent, whether rented or not. If you use the asset for two weeks per year and it is available for rent the balance of 50 weeks, you would be allowed 11½ months or $^{23}/_{24}$ of the total available tax deductions, including asset expensing and depreciation.

Leasing agents can be found for boats at most marinas; for planes at flight services or the FBO at any airport; and, for motor homes, in the Yellow Pages under "motor homes—renting and leasing."

If you operate your leasing activity as an investor, your current deductions will be limited by the passive-investment rules. You can claim deductions each year only up to the amount of your passive income.

If you are active in the leasing activity, approving all leases, formulating a business plan, contracting for maintenance, doing regular inspections and keeping the business records yourself, you will qualify to take all the deductions, including depreciation, against current income.

Even with the passive loss rules you may use the current tax deduction to shelter up to 100% of the leasing income.

Take the deductions and show your income on tax schedule "C."

Of course, if your boat or motor home means so much to you that you don't want anyone else to use it, you'll just have to pay the bills yourself!

Strategy #169

DEDUCT THE INTEREST ON YOUR BOAT OR MOTOR HOME AS A SECOND HOME.

The new tax rules allow you to deduct the mortgage interest on both a first and second personal home up to $1,000,000 of acquisition cost. Normally, we think of a home as bricks and wood on a stationary concrete foundation. However, the writers of tax reform chose to define a home as almost anything with living quarters. Why then wouldn't the definition include a sailboat, yacht, or motor home with living quarters? It does, at least, until someone decides to change the law. Living quarters include a galley or kitchen, bathroom facilities and sleeping quarters. If a boat or motor home you own or buy fits this definition, deduct the loan interest on tax Schedule A.

Chapter 18

GETTING DOWN TO BUSINESS

*By working hard eight hours a day, you may eventually get
to be boss and work hard twelve hours a day.*

Robert Frost
Poet
(1874–1963)

Objective: Start a small business for fun, profit, and huge tax deductions.

America was firmly established in the 1700s as the country of independent small business people, the country for turning dreams into reality and wealth. For 200 years the American business principle has survived and prospered, and today small business falls under Congress's favored tax status. During the past ten years while 2 million smokestack industry jobs were lost or eliminated, small business accounted for all of the 10 million new jobs that are absorbing men and women into the work force. Whether you start small and stay small or eventually become a corporate giant, the tax benefits alone are worth starting a small business.

While I was in the Soviet Union in 1985, I had a lengthy conversation with one of the Soviet tourist guides. "What do you do," I asked "if you want to start your own business in the Soviet Union?"

"Defect to the West," she answered matter-of-factly.

How fortunate, I thought, that we live in a country where small business opportunities are so easy to come by.

My father started his first business when he was ten, sitting in the limbs of oak trees in La Grange, Illinois, waiting for rattlesnakes to come along so he could trap them with a forked stick around the base

220

of the head. He would then stuff them into a burlap bag and cart the snakes off to a local laboratory where they were sold for 17 cents apiece. He was always positive, aggressive, and incredibly calm under pressure—three winning characteristics for all successful entrepreneurs.

My own entrepreneurial experience has taught me that success in business is 80% marketing and only 20% dependent on your product or service.

My first crack at the wonderful world of self-employment was a carry-out food service founded by me and my neighbor, J. Allen Furguson. I was 11. Al had a gas hot plate and refrigerator in his basement. So during the summer months we fixed lunch for all the neighborhood housewives who hated to cook three meals a day. Day after day we cooked a batch of hotdogs and hamburgers and delivered them semi-hot throughout the neighborhood for a quarter apiece. After gutsy negotiations with the grocer on the corner, we could buy three pounds of hamburger for a dollar, instead of the normal 38 cents a pound, and a loaf of bread for 14 cents. Soon I was hooked. I liked the independence and freedom of choice that business brings. Unfortunately, I didn't stick with it. Why should I have worked for pennies when I could live in luxury off my 50 cents a week allowance? Besides, there was baseball.

There are many great returns for starting your own business. Here are some of them:

- Sense of accomplishment,
- Desire for wealth or greater income,
- A sense of freedom and independence,
- An opportunity to be creative,
- A chance to meet people,
- A chance to turn work into fun,
- A chance to be your own boss,
- And, most important for our discussion, transforming personal expenses into legitimate tax deductions.

Strategy #170
TURN ANY SMALL BUSINESS INTO A TREMENDOUS TAX SHELTER.

A business can be part-time or full time, require a large capital investment or no investment, can have no employees or many employees, and can be run out of a home, apartment, retail store, or office.

The small business strategy should be considered by everyone who works for someone else or who is retired. The possibilities are endless and so are the financial opportunities and benefits—if you understand the rules. A small business, even run part-time from home, can create $6,000 to $10,000 of tax shelter every year, no matter how profitable your business is or isn't.

In a small business, the personal things you own and do become fully or partially tax decuctible. To emphasize the importance of a small business as part of your tax strategy, here is a list of what can become deductible through your small business that is not normally deductible:

- Your automobile or van
- Your automobile expenses—gas, insurance, parking, and tolls
- Your interest on loans for assets used in your business
- Your home
- Your children or spouse
- Your boat, motor home, or airplane
- Your home computer
- Your domestic and foreign travel
- Your health club or country club membership
- Your entertainment
- Your video tape recorder
- Your income from your job or investments
- Your books and subscriptions
- Your educational audio and video tape courses
- Your calculator, typewriter, cassette recorder
- Your repairs to your automobile or other equipment
- Your utilities and telephone
- Your gifts to customers, potential customers, and associates
- Your investment in a small business retirement plan

These deductions are just a sampling of the tax power of operating a small business. There are many more deduction possibilities. If you are not getting tax deductions for these expenses, plan to start a small business immediately even part-time. If you already have a small business or if you are a professional, there are strategies and tax techniques we will cover that your tax advisers never told you about.

Any business idea creates the opportunity to succeed financially. Small businesses started with little capital and winning ideas have resulted in the creation of thousands of new millionaires and multi-million dollar corporations; McDonalds, Apple Computer, and Texas Instruments are well-known examples. As the old Coca-Cola bottles stated so clearly, "No deposit, no return." If you don't experiment with new ideas you have no chance of success at all.

For those who are beginners, we will first concentrate on starting a part-time business. You'll discover how to make your life legally tax deductible through the small business tax umbrella. If you own your own business already, use the strategies in this chapter as your business tax strategy checklist.

When you have a small business, almost every related business activity becomes legally tax deductible, even if you derive pleasure or fun in the process. If the business initially generates little income, it may still generate hundreds or thousands of dollars of tax deductions which can be used to shelter income from your job, investments, or retirement plan.

Strategy #171

BEGIN A SMALL BUSINESS AS A "SOLE PROPRIETORSHIP" INSTEAD OF AS A CORPORATION.

The easiest form of business to create is a "sole proprietorship," that is, you or your spouse doing business. You use your Social Security number as the business I.D. for tax purposes and you don't even report to the IRS that you are a business until you file "Schedule C" the following year. Most at home, part-time businesses should start as sole proprietorships. The cost of incorporating and the paperwork involved are not worth the expense at this point. As your business grows, and becomes highly profitable, you can then consider incorporation. An inexpensive small business liability policy will protect you from personal liability.

Strategy #172
USE BUSINESS "PAPER" LOSSES TO TAX SHELTER JOB AND INVESTMENT INCOME.

With a sole proprietorship, you *are* your business; all tax deductions in excess of business income reduce your personal taxes. Look on the front of a 1040 individual tax return and you'll notice that business profit or loss is included with your other income from your job or investments. A business becomes a personal tax shelter when your business shows a "paper" loss. Your personal taxable income is reduced by the amount of the loss and your personal income taxes are reduced accordingly. The same is true of an "S" Corporation, a corporation treated for tax purposes as an individual. Even though your business operates as a corporation, all income or losses flow through your personal tax return. If your first year business income is $2,000 but your deductible expenses are $10,000, the $8,000 difference reduces your taxable income from your job, investments, or retirement account.

Strategy #173
OPERATE YOUR ACTIVITY AS A BUSINESS, NOT AS A HOBBY.

A business, according to the IRS, is any activity conducted on a regular basis with the intent to make a profit, but you are not required to make a profit in order to claim the tax deductions. In order to be a business you must have a product or service which you offer regularly to the public. For tax purposes, you are a business if you sell a product or service whether you actually call yourself a business or not.

Intent to make a profit is what differentiates a "business" from a "hobby." A hobby is an activity that may produce income, but is operated for pleasure without the intent of making a profit.

As a business, you may deduct all of your ordinary and necessary operating expenses, no matter how great or small your income. If you have more income during the year than expenses, the difference is your taxable profit. If you have more expenses than income, the difference is your tax loss. With a hobby, you may deduct your expenses, but only up to the amount of your income. Therefore, with a hobby there can be no "loss" for tax purposes.

You show your intent to operate as a business by:

• Talking regularly to potential or actual customers and keeping a list.
• Opening a separate bank account.
• Keeping good records of income and expenses.

Use the "Business Start-Up Checklist" to get your small business off and running in the shortest possible time.

BUSINESS START-UP CHECKLIST

__ Obtain publication 334, "Tax Guide for Small Business" from the IRS and read it thoroughly.

__ Choose a business idea based on your interests, abilities, and the amount of time you want to spend.

__ Choose a business form—sole proprietorship, partnership, or corporation. Sole proprietorship is the simplest.

__ Set up your business record-keeping system. Simple record-keeping books are available at any office supply store. Get IRS publication 583.

__ Choose a business name. If your name is included in the business name, most states do not require you to file under the fictitious name statute.

__ Set up an interest-bearing business checking account using one of the asset management account sources listed in the investment section of this book.

__ Print business cards and flyers.

__ Offer your product or services for sale to friends and others.

__ Learn everything you can about business from books, magazines, tape courses, seminars, and trade publications.

__ Get business educational materials from the Small Business Association and the Charles J. Givens Organization.

Have fun. It's only work if you don't like what you are doing.

Strategy #174

SHOW A PROFIT THREE OUT OF FIVE YEARS TO QUALIFY FOR CONTINUING TAX DEDUCTIONS.

An activity is automatically considered a business if it produces a profit in any three out of five years. Many taxpayers, as well as tax professionals, incorrectly believe that the three out of five rule means that if your business is still showing an operating loss after two years, you automatically lose all future tax deductions. Not true. The first two years are considered the "ruling period" in determining whether your activity is a business or a hobby and are used by the IRS as a guideline only.

At the end of two years, if you are still showing a loss, you can use one of these many strategies.

1. Work hard to show a profit during the next three years and use the three profitable years as the beginning of the next ruling period.
2. File an IRS form called "Automatic Extension of Ruling Period" which gives you an automatic extra year in which to show a profit.
3. Start another business, after all, this is America. Your ruling period starts over.
4. Continue to run your business at a loss but be prepared to show the IRS that you have the intent to make a profit and have a reasonable chance of eventually doing so by putting together a written business plan.
5. Choose a business activity such as timber or breeding which has a five-year instead of three-year initial ruling period.
6. Continue your activity, but as a hobby, taking deductions only up to your level of income.
7. Close the business. You will still keep your tax deductions.

There are so many myths and misunderstandings about how to start and run a business, the confusion prevents many people from ever getting started.

Here are the real business facts:

- You don't need to operate your business full time or incorporate to take tax deductions.
- There are no requirements regarding how much money you must invest or that you must invest any money at all.

- If you are a "sole proprietorship," you do not need a tax I.D. number; your Social Security number will suffice, as long as you have three employees or less.
- You are allowed to take deductions on assets you buy and use in your small business even if you buy the assets on credit.
- If you use assets part-time in a business you may deduct part of the cost.
- Investments such as real estate do not fall under the three- out of five-year profit rule, but real estate should be treated as an investment, not a small business.
- Managing your own investments or collectibles is not considered a business, but does qualify you for investment tax deductions.
- Having a small business does not flag your return for audit.
- You may claim more tax deductions than income.
- Your automobile or other assets do not have to be in a business name to become deductible.
- Record keeping and tax forms for a small business are easy.
- You don't need special licenses or permits before you can take tax deductions.

Strategy #175

CHOOSE A SMALL BUSINESS IDEA THAT IS EXCITING, FUN, AND IN ALIGNMENT WITH YOUR INTERESTS AND ABILITIES.

There are no limits to the number of ideas for creating a small business, even those that require little or no capital. If you need ideas for your small business venture, use the "Small Business Ideas" chart (page 228) to get your mind moving.

The important thing is to pick something you love to do or make and turn it into a small business.

MAXIMIZING BUSINESS DEDUCTIONS

The following strategies will help you create the maximum deductions for your small business.

SMALL BUSINESS IDEAS

Services:

Automobile tune up
Automobile washing, waxing
Carpet cleaning
Care for ill or elderly
Catering
Clown for children's parties
Consulting (in anything)
Dance instruction
Day-care for children
Doing anything for anyone
Flower arranging
Foreign language teaching
Interior decorating
Lawn maintenance
Maintenance for real estate
  investigators
Manager for musical groups
Office janitorial service
Painting/wall papering
Party organizer for adults or
  children
Pet boarding
Photography—portraits,
  weddings
Real estate sales
Real estate property management
Roommate locating

Tool, saw, and scissor
  sharpening
Teaching—golf, tennis, music
Tutoring
Typing
Videotaping—parties, weddings

Products:

Cake baking and decorating
Candle making
Catering
Christmas tree ornament making
Dressmaking
Jewelry making
Making and delivering office
  lunches
Quilt making
Used books or records—buying
  and selling
Woodworking from your
  woodworking shop

Multilevel marketing:

A. L. Williams
Amway
Herbalife
Prepaid legal services
Shacklee products

Strategy #176
BEGIN MARKETING IMMEDIATELY TO MAKE BUSINESS START-UP COSTS DEDUCTIBLE THIS YEAR.

Business start-up costs that you incur prior to marketing a product or service must be deducted or amortized over a five-year period at 20% per year. Expenses you incur after your business begins are fully deductible in the year you spend the money. Begin marketing your product or service immediately to establish the starting date of your business. All expenses will then be deductible in the current year.

Strategy #177
HIRE YOUR SPOUSE AND CREATE A DEDUCTIBLE IRA.

You can create up to a $2,000 tax deduction each year by hiring your nonworking spouse to work in your small business, and using your spouse's salary to open a fully deductible IRA.

George is a salesman for a small sportswear company which has no retirement plan. He contributes to a company retirement plan each year, but would like to be able to contribute $2,000 to an IRA for his wife, Sally. George hires Sally to do his paperwork and filing, and help him with correspondence, and pays her by check $300 per month. George pays no additional taxes, nor does Sally, since they file jointly. What is income to Sally is a deduction for George. Sally puts the first $2,000 she earns into an IRA, saving the family over $600 in taxes.

Under tax reform, your spouse may contribute $2,000 to an IRA if he or she earns less than $10,000 even if you do not qualify. There are other benefits as well. When you employ your spouse, certain everyday expenses become tax deductible: life insurance, health insurance, tuition for job-related education, and job-related travel and entertainment.

You can also hire parents or other adult family members. Ted's father, Ben, resides in a nursing home. Ben's only disability involves physical limitations of his legs. In addition to the money from Ben's Social Security check, Ted was paying the nursing home $500 per month ($6,000 per year), none of which was tax deductible. Ted started

a small mail order business in his home and hired his father to stuff
and address five hundred envelopes per week. Ted pays Ben $500 each
month for the work, and Ben pays his own $500 monthly nursing
expense. Ted now has a $6,000 yearly tax deduction and Ben derives
a sense of real worth by actively participating in his son's business
venture. Ben is within the Social Security earnings limit and pays no
taxes on the income.

Strategy #178

QUALIFY YOUR SPOUSE FOR
SOCIAL SECURITY BENEFITS.

A new tax law requires the payment of F.I.C.A. Social Security taxes
when one spouse hires another. You can turn the new rule into greater
retirement income.

Herb worked all his life at General Electric, while his wife, Ethel,
managed the home and raised the kids. Although Ethel worked hard
for the family, she doesn't qualify for Social Security benefits. Herb
started a small part-time sports equipment business and hired Ethel to
manage the business and correspond with the customers. Herb pays
Ethel a salary of $10,000 a year, from which she contributes to the
family expenses. By paying Social Security taxes for ten quarters, Ethel
qualifies to receive Social Security income when she reaches age 65.

You can choose to avoid the payment of extra Social Security taxes
by making your spouse a co-owner instead of an employee of the business.

Strategy #179

HIRE YOUR CHILDREN AND GRANDCHILDREN AND
MAKE ALLOWANCES AND GIFTS DEDUCTIBLE.

As a teenager, I arose at four A.M. every morning to deliver the *Chicago
Tribune* to west-end subscribers in my hometown of Decatur, Illinois.
When everyone paid, my net profit was $7.40 a week for a daily four-
mile bike ride. Eventually, my father offered me an evening job with

his home improvement business. I was moving up the corporate lad-
der. Instead of riding four miles in the morning, I began riding four
miles every afternoon to the C. J. Givens Company, where my after–
office hours responsibilities included sweeping floors and taking
phone messges. Boy, did that make me feel important! I felt more like
a business executive than a part-time janitor. My father also felt great,
taking a tax deduction for each of the five dollars he paid me once a
week.

If you have or start a small business, even part-time, you can hire
your children or grandchildren and turn nondeductible allowances,
gifts, and expensive handouts into tax deductible salaries. Depending
on their ages, the kids can perform any number of tasks including:

- Cleaning the business office
- Washing the business automobile
- Answering the phone when you are away
- Stuffing and addressing envelopes
- Keeping track of inventory
- Delivering products
- Running business errands
- Entering data on the computer

You can pay deductible salaries to children to perform jobs either
for your small business or to help you in your regular employment.
Children are not required to file a tax return if they earn less than
$3,000. Give your family employee a 1099 form at the end of the year.
Use IRS circular E as your guide.

Pay two children or grandchildren salaries of $20 per week each for
three or four hours of work instead of giving them nondeductible allowances, gifts, and handouts, and you have created a $2,000 per year
legal tax deduction. The money the kids earn can be used for school
lunches, clothes, entertainment, investments, or even an IRA.

As an example, hire your two children to work in your small business and pay them each $20 per week: $10 is used for entertainment
and allowances, $10 each goes into an investment account in their
name. Your tax deduction is the amount you pay the children. Two
children × $20 per week each × 52 weeks = $2,080; 30% bracket ×
$2,080 deduction = $624 cash tax saving.

The kids are involved, having fun, learning responsibility, and you
are pocketing over $600 a year from the tax savings.

Bob Vorse, another member of my organization, hired his 11-year-old son who had a knack for computer programming. He started a small business and hired his son, Jeff, at $10 per hour to write simple business programs. Jeff works three hours a week. Can Bob legally take a tax deduction for the $30 per week he pays his son? Yes, as long as Jeff actually does the work. Bob would have to pay a programmer from outside the family as much as $25 to $50 an hour for programming services, so he is within the rules. It doesn't matter that Jeff is only 11.

By using this strategy, Bob created a $1,500 per year tax deduction. (50 weeks × $30 per week). His home computer is now tax deductible because he is using it in his small business, and he is enjoying the benefit of working on an important project together with his son. Since the $1,500 is Jeff's only income, Jeff pays no income tax.

Often I'm asked if the IRS frowns on the hiring of family members. Not at all. The procedures and rules for hiring family members are well established in tax law, and make hiring family members less troublesome than hiring other employees.

Here are the rules that quailfy you for family member tax deductions:

1. The family members must do the work for which they are paid. It would not be honest to pay a family member for work not performed simply to claim a tax deduction.
2. You may pay a family member a deductible salary of up to the amount you would have to pay a nonfamily member to do the same job. The pay cannot be excessive on work performed. Squelch any tendency to overpay a family member in order to claim a greater tax deduction. Someone from outside the family must be paid a minimum wage, so no matter how menial the job, minimum wage is not unreasonable.
3. Salaries paid to children under 18 are not subject to Social Security tax.
4. No Federal Income Tax Withholding is required if the family member is paid under $4,450 per year.
5. You are not required to pay Federal Unemployment Insurance on family members.
6. Salaries are treated as tax deductible wages by you as the employer, and as taxable income by your family member employees. You lose the tax advantages if you pay wages to a family member who is in a higher tax bracket than you.
7. The pay must be periodic. Pay family members by check at least once a month, as you would any employee. If you were to pay a year's worth of wages in the last month of the year, it would look suspicious to the IRS. If you pay by cash have someone else keep a written record of the payments.

Strategy #180

BEAT THE KIDDIE TAX WITH A CHILDREN'S IRA.

Under tax reform, the first $500 per year of investment income for children is not taxed, the next $500 is taxed at 11% and any balance above $1,000 is taxed at the parent's high tax rate. These new rules make it difficult to build a college fund or to transfer investments and assets to your children and grandchildren.

Salaries you pay your children can help circumvent this so-called "Kiddie Tax," if you put the money in an IRA. Even though a child does not pay taxes on a salary unless the salary is over $3,000, any earnings of over $1,000 per year from the investment of the salary will be taxed at the parent's rate.

You can beat the new rule by opening an IRA for your child. There is no age limit on an IRA, but the money must come from employment. Since IRAs are tax deferrals and have no current taxable income, the child may earn over $1,000 from IRA investments with no taxes. The money compounds completely tax free until it is withdrawn.

There is a 10% penalty on any withdrawal from an IRA before age 59½, but that equals only six months earnings if the IRA is invested at 20% per year. You can build a $50,000 college education fund by depositing only $2,000 for each of nine years in the child's IRA and using any of the 20% per year investment strategies you will learn later in this book. There is a double tax deduction. Parents get the salary deduction and the child gets the IRA deduction.

Over the years I've seen families become incredibly creative with this strategy. A few years ago, a young couple approached me after a workshop, wanting to start their own small business and hire their son. Unfortunately, he was only seven months old, barely old enough to walk and talk, let alone work. Many months later I saw the couple again and they were beaming, "Well, we've done it; we now employ our son in our small business."

My curiosity was piqued. "What can a toddler that age possibly do for a living?" I asked.

"After your lecture, we went to a baby furniture store and got the owner to agree to let us sell his baby furniture for a commission at home parties. That's our small business. We pay our son $40 a week to model the cribs and bassinets. The $2,000 per year salary is tax deductible and we are putting the money away in an IRA just like you suggested for his tax deductible college education."

This couple achieved two objectives: funding their child's education, and creating a $2,000 per year tax deduction in the process. Because they are in the 28% tax bracket, they save $560 each year in taxes. The child pays no taxes because the money is a salary and invested through the child's IRA.

Strategy #181
PAY YOUR CHILD A SALARY OF UP TO $3,000 AND STILL CLAIM A DEPENDENCY EXEMPTION.

Each exemption for a dependent you claim on your tax return is worth a $1,950 tax deduction beginning in 1989, saving you up to $650 on taxes. The new standard deduction rules, which replaced the old zero-bracket amount, let a child earn up to $3,000 of salary income without you losing the child as a dependent.

If you claim your child as a dependent he cannot claim himself. You as the person in the higher tax bracket should claim the dependency exemption for your child.

Strategy #182
USE YOUR AUTOMOBILE IN YOUR SMALL BUSINESS TO MAKE IT DEDUCTIBLE.

Because your automobile represents one of your largest personal expenses, it is also one of your biggest potential tax deductions. One of 12 methods of making an automobile deductible is to use it in your small business.

If you use your automobile 100% of the time for business, 100% of the mileage or expense is deductible. The 100% rule would apply to a two-car family who allocates one car for personal use and the second, usually more expensive car, for business. If you use one automobile for both personal and business purposes, you must allocate by percentage the amount of deductible business use and nondeductible personal use, for example, 55% business use, 45% personal use. By putting a permanent advertisement on the side of your vehicle, you increase the percentage of deductible business use, up to 80% or more.

Strategy #183

CHOOSE THE AUTOMOBILE DEDUCTION METHOD THAT GIVES YOU THE GREATEST DEDUCTION.

There are two methods of deductions for using an automobile in your business.

METHOD #1—You may deduct the cost of the automobile through:
      Asset expensing
      Depreciation

Plus you may deduct operating expenses, including:

Gas	Cleaning
Insurance	Interest
Licenses	Parking
Maintenance	Taxes
Tires	Tolls

METHOD #2—You may use the standard mileage rate in lieu of depreciation and operating expenses.

The IRS standard mileage rate deduction.

First 15,000 business miles	.22½ per mile
Over 15,000 business miles	.11 per mile

In addition to the standard mileage rate you may deduct interest, property tax, parking and tolls.

Once you have chosen the deduction method you wish to use, you may not change for the life of the car.

Complete your tax deduction using both methods. Use tax form 2106 as your worksheet but take the deductions on Schedule C and the depreciation for the actual expense method on form 4562. Use whichever method gives you the greatest deduction, usually the actual expense method. Tax preparers often choose the mileage rate method because it is easier to compute. Always compute the deduction both ways yourself.

Method #1 deductions can actually exceed the amount of money you have spent in payments on your car or other assets. (See Strategies #186 & 187 for how to take the asset-expensing and depreciation deductions.)

Strategy #184

BUY AN AUTOMOBILE INSTEAD OF LEASING FOR GREATER DEDUCTIONS.

You are usually better off buying than leasing a business automobile if you make it tax deductible. Leasing allows you to write off only the business percentage of the lease payment. Owning allows you to use the asset-expensing and depreciation deductions which will usually be greater than the lease deductions. Automobiles can now be depreciated over five years using MACRS (Modified Accelerated Cost Recovery System).

Depreciation actually extends into the sixth year because of the half year convention explained later. As a shortcut in determining the maximum amount of your automobile deduction, use the following table and tax form 4562. Apply the amounts in the table against the declining business depreciation basis of the automobile.

AUTOMOBILE DEPRECIATION
SIMPLIFIED CALCULATION TABLE (MACRS METHOD)

Year	Lower of:
1	20% or $2,560
2	32% or $4,100
3	19.2% or $2,450
4	11.52% or $1,475
5	11.52% or $1,475
6	5.76% or $1,475

The dollar figure in the "Lower of" column represents the maximum annual automobile depreciation and is meant to keep owners of luxury cars from overdoing their deductions. If only a percentage of your car is used for business, for example 60%, your first year limit would be 60% of $2,560 or $1,536. You must use your automobile more than 50% of the time for business in order to use the MACRS method. Otherwise, the straight line method (alternate MACRS) must be used. In addition, the operating costs and business portion of the interest on your car loan are also deductible.

Because of the elimination of tax credits under tax reform, leasing companies, usually set up as investor tax shelters, are being forced to raise their rates. By substituting longer lease periods, for example, five years instead of three, your payments look smaller but it will cost you additional thousands to get out of the lease if you want to get rid of the car. You are stuck with the car for the lease term whether you want it or not.

Strategy #185
USE YOUR PERSONAL ASSETS IN YOUR BUSINESS TO MAKE THEM DEDUCTIBLE.

Using your personal equipment, such as home computers, videotape recorders, cassette recorders, calculators, tools, or furniture in your business will make these assets deductible. If you already own the assets when you begin using them in your business, your tax deduction is computed by depreciating the entire cost or market value (whichever is less) over a five-year period using the MACRS method based on the percentage of time you use your assets for business.

If you buy an asset and begin using it immediately in your business, even part-time, you may use the asset-expensing rules discussed later to deduct up to a maximum of $10,000 in the current tax year and depreciate any balance of the cost over the five-year recovery period, including the current year as the first year of the recovery period. To use the asset-expensing rules, you must use the equipment at least 50% of the time in your business; the rest can be personal.

It is important to understand the difference between personal and business use. Here are some examples.

Your computer is used for business when used for record keeping, business projections or computing your business tax deductions. Your videotape recorder is used for business when you buy or rent videotapes that relate to any phase of your business. Your video camera is deductible if you use it at conventions, lectures, for practicing sales presentations or in any other way that relates to your business. Computer and video supplies are fully deductible when used for business purposes. The furniture in your business office, whether at home or at a separate location, is deductible. Your typewriter, filing cabinet, calculator, or cassette recorder are also deductible if used in your small business.

Any tools or equipment are deductible when used even part-time for a business purpose, such as:

• Musical instruments used in a band.
• A lathe and drill press in a home woodworking shop.
• A sewing machine used in making quilts or other items to sell.
• Steam cleaning machine used in a part-time carpet-cleaning business.
• Cameras and darkroom equipment used in a photography business.

Your tax deduction is computed based on the percentage of time you use the equipment for business. For instance:

Business Item	Cost	Business Use	Maximum Deduction
Videotape recorder	$ 800	× 60%	= $ 480
Video camera	700	× 60%	= 420
Home computer	2,500	× 80%	= 2,000
Office furniture	1,500	× 100%	= 1,500
Tools & equipment	600	× 100%	= 600
Typewriter	250	× 100%	= 250
TOTAL	$6,350		= $5,250

If your federal plus state bracket is 40%, using the previous list as an example, your total cash savings would be $2,100 or 40% of the maximum deduction of $5,250. You spent $6,350 on the assets and the government returned to you $2,100. You saved 40% of the cost because of the tax deductions. You have therefore recovered in cash 40% of the total cost of some of your major purchases.

Strategy #186

USE THE ASSET-EXPENSING RULES FOR IMMEDIATE DEDUCTIONS ON ASSETS YOU BUY.

Section 179 of the Internal Revenue Code says you may treat the first $10,000 of assets you buy each year and use in your business as a currently deductible expense instead of a capital expenditure which would be subject to long-term depreciation. This process is called asset expensing. The choice is yours, but unless you don't need the deductions you will want to use the following asset-expensing rules instead of depreciating.

1. The total amount to be expensed cannot exceed $10,000 in one year.
2. The assets must be placed in service, not just purchased that year.
3. If you place in service more than $200,000 of assets you lose the expensing benefits. That means the asset-expensing rules were designed to benefit small business only.
4. The total amount you can expense using Section 179 is limited to the taxable income of the business not counting the Section 179 deductible. If your business is showing a loss, you may still take the deduction as depreciation. You may carry any unused expensing deductions forward to the next year.
5. If you file separately, you and your spouse are still limited to the maximum of $10,000.
6. The asset-expensing deduction for an automobile cannot exceed $2,560. The balance must be depreciated.
7. If you use the asset for both personal and business use, you are eligible to expense the business portion, provided the business percentage is greater than 50%.
8. You may use asset expensing only in the year you place the property in service.
9. Each asset is treated separately and you must specify on tax form 4562, "Depreciation and Amortization," which items you intend to expense.
10. You cannot amend your previous tax returns after the due date to change depreciation to expensing.
11. You can use asset expensing on any depreciable, nonreal estate property used in your business with a life of three years or more.
12. You cannot use asset expensing on property held as or used in investments.
13. Asset expensing is in lieu of depreciation for the portion of an asset that you choose to expense.

14. If the usage of an asset you expense drops below the 50% business usage anytime during the property's normal recovery period, you would have to add the deduction you took to your income for the year. Use form 4797— "Gains and Losses from Business Assets." You can then claim the lost expensing deductions as depreciation up to the depreciation limits.
15. If you are in a partnership or "S" Corp. each partner or stockholder can claim up to the $10,000 limit from the same business.
16. For additional information on asset expensing refer to IRS publications 334 and 534.

Your strategy is to find a legitimate business use for assets you buy. As long as 50% of the use is for business, you may use the asset-expensing rules for up to $10,000 in deductions each year.

Strategy #187

TAKE DEPRECIATION DEDUCTIONS FOR ASSETS YOU ALREADY OWN AND USE IN A BUSINESS.

Depreciation means deducting the cost of the business portion of an asset over the "life" or recovery period set by the IRS. It is a slower method of taking deductions than asset expensing but gives you the same amount of overall deduction.

To figure your depreciation for an asset used in a business you must know:

1. THE BASIS—the basis is a measure of the value of an investment for tax purposes. Your original basis is usually the amount you paid for the property. As you depreciate an asset, your depreciation deductions reduce the basis. When you inherit or receive property as a gift, your basis is generally the market value when you received the asset. Improvements increase the basis. If you convert personal property to business use, your basis is the fair market value of the property on the date you make the change.

2. DATE PLACED IN SERVICE—the date you begin using the property in your business determines the amount of depreciation deduction you get the first year. Three- , five- , or seven-year recovery period assets are treated as if placed in service on July first no matter when placed in service. You get one half year's depreciation deduction the first year.

This formula is called the half-year convention. Real estate assets are subject to a mid-month convention.

3. THE RECOVERY PERIOD—the recovery period is the number of years over which you must take your depreciation deductions. The shorter the recovery period, the more deductions you may take each year. In a small business you are usually concerned with the recovery period for cars, computers, office equipment, and videotape recorders. All have a five-year recovery period. The recovery period for furniture and fixtures is seven years. The MACRS Depreciation Recovery Period table will show you the recovery period for depreciating other assets as well as those mentioned.

MACRS
DEPRECIATION RECOVERY PERIOD TABLE

3	year	Tractor trailer trucks
		Race horses over 2 years old
		Any horse over 12 years old
5	year	Cars, light trucks
		Computers
		Office equipment
		Videotape recorders
7	year	Furniture and fixtures
		Farm buildings
27.5	year	Residential rental property
31.5	year	Commercial and business real estate

4. DEPRECIATION METHOD—the depreciation method is the formula you choose or in some cases must use to determine the amount of deduction each year. For property placed in service from 1980 to 1987, the Accelerated Cost Recovery System (ACRS) was the standard. After tax reform, the standard is the Modified Accelerated Cost Recovery System (MACRS).

Here is how MACRS works. For property in the three- , five- , and seven-year recovery period classes, you use the double declining balance formula. To determine your deduction you divide the number two by the recovery period and multiply the quotient by the basis or cost of the property.

For example, you want to depreciate your home computer which cost $4,000 and is used 100% of the time for your small business. Computers have a recovery period of five years. What is your first year's depreciation deduction?

$$\frac{2.00}{5 \text{ years}} = 40\% \qquad \text{Percent deductible first year.}$$
$$.40 \times \$4,000 = \$1,600 \quad \text{Amount of deduction first year.}$$

The second year you subtract $1,600 from $4,000 and take a deduction for 40% of the new basis.

$$.40 \times \$2,400 = \$960 \quad \text{Amount of deduction second year.}$$

Strategy #188
CONVERT TO STRAIGHT-LINE DEPRECIATION WHEN MORE DEDUCTIONS WILL BE GENERATED BY THIS METHOD.

The amount of depreciation taken using the MACRS method drops each year. When the straight-line depreciation rate exceeds the double declining balance rate, you may choose to switch to the straight line method for the remaining years. The following chart will show you the double declining balance percentage to use for three-, five- and 7-year property and the year in which it is best to switch to the straight-line method. Straight-line depreciation is the easiest to understand since straight-line means that the same amount of depreciation is taken each year for the life of the asset. Straight-line is computed by dividing the basis by the number of years in the recovery period.

DEPRECIATION CHART

Recovery Period	Declining Balance %	Year to Switch to SL
3-year	66.67%	3rd
5-year	40.00%	4th
7-year	28.57%	5th

Strategy #189
USE TAX FORM 4562 TO COMPUTE AND CLAIM ALL
ASSET-EXPENSING AND DEPRECIATION DEDUCTIONS.

Your key to both asset-expensing and depreciation deductions is Tax Form 4562 (page 244). The total amount of your form 4562 deduction is entered on line 12, "Depreciation" on Schedule C for sole proprietors and in the similar space on partnership and corporate returns.

EXAMPLE:

Jim and Sue start a small business in which they use their home computer 60% of the time. The cost of the computer was $3,000 and it was purchased this year. They also buy a second car which they allocate 100% of the time for business—cost $13,000. They realize the maximum deduction the first year is $2,560 for an automobile. Other equipment already owned such as furniture and small machinery used in the business has a value of $4,000 when placed in service and qualifies as seven-year class depreciable property. How much is their total form 4562 deduction?

ANSWER:

The $3,000 computer can be asset-expensed at a business use of 60% giving a total deduction of $1,800. This amount goes in Part 1, Section A of form 4562. The $2,560 asset-expensing deduction for the automobile goes in the same place. The $4,000 equipment qualifies for a 28.57% depreciation deduction the first year amounting to $1,143. This amount goes in Part 1, line 6c under seven-year property on form 4652. See the sample form 4562 that follows for how all these pieces fit together. The total depreciation deduction is $5,503 their first year in business, saving them over $1,800 in taxes!

Strategy #190
USE PERSONAL ASSETS IN YOUR BUSINESS TO CLAIM
THE SALES TAX DEDUCTION.

Beginning in 1987, the deduction of state and local sales taxes on personal purchases is no longer allowed. The sales tax is deductible,

Form **4562**	**Depreciation and Amortization**	OMB No 1545-0172
Department of the Treasury Internal Revenue Service (X)	▶ **See separate instructions.** ▶ **Attach this form to your return.**	**1987** Attachment Sequence No. **67**
Name(s) as shown on return JIM AND SUE FELDMAN		Identifying number 331-84-2946
Business or activity to which this form relates		

Part I **Depreciation** (Do not use this part for automobiles, certain other vehicles, computers, and property used for entertainment, recreation, or amusement. Instead, use Part III.)

Section A.—Election To Expense Depreciable Assets Placed in Service During This Tax Year (Section 179)

	(a) Description of property	(b) Date placed in service	(c) Cost	(d) Expense deduction
1	Computer	5-14-88	3,000	1,800
	Automobile	3-01-88	13,000	2,560
2	Listed property—Enter total from Part III, Section A, column (h).			
3	Total (add lines 1 and 2, but do not enter more than $10,000)			4,360
4	Enter the amount, if any, by which the cost of all section 179 property placed in service during this tax year is more than $200,000			0
5	Subtract line 4 from line 3. If result is less than zero, enter zero. (See instructions for other limitations)			4,360

Section B.—Depreciation

	(a) Class of property	(b) Date placed in service	(c) Basis for depreciation (Business use only — see instructions)	(d) Recovery period	(e) Method of figuring depreciation	(f) Deduction
6	Accelerated Cost Recovery System (ACRS) (see instructions): *For assets placed in service* **ONLY** *during tax year beginning in 1987*					
a	3-year property					
b	5-year property					
c	7-year property		4,000	7	DDB	1,143
d	10-year property					
e	15-year property					
f	20-year property					
g	Residential rental property					
h	Nonresidential real property					
7	Listed property—Enter total from Part III, Section A, column (g).					
8	ACRS deduction for assets placed in service prior to 1987 (see instructions)					

Section C.—Other Depreciation

9	Property subject to section 168(f)(1) election (see instructions)	
10	Other depreciation (see instructions)	

Section D.—Summary

11	Total (add deductions on lines 5 through 10). Enter here and on the Depreciation line of your return (Partnerships and S corporations—Do NOT include any amounts entered on line 5.)	5,503
12	For assets above placed in service during the current year, enter the portion of the basis attributable to additional section 263A costs (See instructions for who must use.)	

Part II **Amortization**

	(a) Description of property	(b) Date acquired	(c) Cost or other basis	(d) Code section	(e) Amortization period or percentage	(f) Amortization for this year
1	Amortization for property placed in service **only** during tax year beginning in 1987					
2	Amortization for property placed in service prior to 1987					
3	Total. Enter here and on Other Deductions or Other Expenses line of your return					

See **Paperwork Reduction Act Notice** on page 1 of the separate instructions.   Form **4562** (1987)

212A

however, if you use the purchased items in your business or investments. Sales tax paid on business supplies is deductible that year as an expense. Sales tax paid to buy a capital asset such as a car used in a business is added to the basis and depreciated.

For example, if you buy a $10,000 car in a state with a 6% sales tax and use it personally, the $600 tax is not deductible. If it is your second car that is used 80% for business, you add 80% of the $600 sales tax, $480, to the basis for depreciation. Since an automobile is depreciated over five years with 40% of the deduction taken the first year, the same 40% applies to the deductible sales tax.

Strategy #191
USE THE SIMPLIFIED 90-DAY RECORD METHOD TO ALLOCATE BUSINESS AND PERSONAL USE OF ASSETS.

The new record-keeping requirements are not complicated. For home computers and video recorders/cameras, the simplest, most effective system is to keep a pocket size spiral notebook by the equipment. You need only three columns.

1. Date
2. Amount of time used
3. B for business/P for personal

The IRS now allows you to keep the log for three months, and if the percentage of business usage remains consistent, you may use the same percentage for the balance of the year, without further record keeping. Before tax reform, Congress created a mandatory "Adequate Contemporaneous" record-keeping rule that required you to keep detailed records of personal and business use for the entire year. Since no one in Congress could spell it let alone wanted to use it, the record-keeping rules were changed.

Strategy #192

CREATE A DEDUCTIBLE OFFICE IN YOUR HOME.

If you start a small business at home, use part of your home for a deductible office and storage area.

The rules and strategies are explained in Chapter 16 "Turn Your Home Into a Tax Haven."

Strategy #193

MAKE YOUR SOCIAL CLUB, COUNTRY CLUB, AND HEALTH CLUB MEMBERSHIPS DEDUCTIBLE THROUGH BUSINESS USE.

If you use your club 50% of the time or more for business purposes, you may deduct the business percentage of the yearly dues. Initiation fees are not deductible, but entertainment expenses at the club are (subject to the 80% deductibility rule). Entertaining current or prospective clients is considered business use.

The required record keeping is simple. Keep a club section in your appointment book that lists the dates you use your club and if the use was personal, business, or a combination. Also keep track of entertainment expenses, such as drinks, green fees, tennis court fees, and meals. If you are prospecting for clients or customers, list the names of the people you talk to, whether they become customers or not. The dues deduction is taken under "dues and subscriptions" on Schedule C or other business tax form. Entertaining deductions are taken under "entertainment."

Strategy #194

TAKE A DEDUCTION FOR YOUR BUSINESS RELATED BOOKS, MAGAZINES, NEWSLETTERS, AND TAPE COURSES

Purchasing books, magazines, newsletters, or audio and videotape courses that relate to business make these items tax deductible. Much of what you already read may be tax deductible if you start a small business. Here are some examples of worthwhile business-related publications which you can deduct.

Magazines:

Forbes

Venture

Money

Entrepreneur

Time

Nation's Business

Newsweek

Fortune

Newsletters:

The Charles J. Givens Financial Digest

Kiplinger Washington Letter

Kiplinger Tax Letter

Decker Reports (Public Speaking)

Executive Wealth Advisory

Tax Hotline

Books:

There are dozens of books currently available at your bookstore in the business and social sciences sections that relate to starting a business, business management, business ideas, marketing, advertising, accounting, record keeping, and success attitudes, including:

Megatrends

What They Don't Teach You at Harvard Business School

In Search of Excellence

John Naisbitt

Mark H. McCormack

Thomas J. Peters and Robert H. Waterman

Think and Grow Rich   Napoleon Hill
Magic of Thinking Big   David J. Schwartz

Audio and Videotape Courses, Seminars, and Workshops:

High impact, adult education in the future will not be done in traditional classrooms spanning several years, weeks, or evenings, but will use new types of media and meeting facilities. Keeping up and getting ahead is already being done at home with audio and videocassettes or in multimillion dollar hotel meeting and conference rooms, through seminars and workshops. When this education relates to your business (or even present job) the cost is deductible.

Strategy #195
TAKE DEDUCTIONS FOR REPAIRS TO BUSINESS ASSETS.

Repairs to assets are deductible when the assets are used even part-time in your business. When you use your assets only for personal reasons your repairs and maintenance are not deductible.

Strategy #196
TAKE DEDUCTIONS FOR YOUR BUSINESS TRAVEL EXPENSES.

Planning your trips or vacations around a legitimate business purpose makes your travel expenses tax deductible. What better way to travel than with tax savings covering part of the cost. When it comes to business travel deductions, a few simple IRS rules will keep you from being audited or losing the deductions. Although you may have as much personal fun as you wish on your trips, the primary purpose of the deductible trip must be business related.

The expense of your spouse or other family members on the trip are deductible if they are co-owners or employees of the business and have a business purpose for being there. Your spouse or other family members are not deductible if they are simply traveling with you. Your spouse's expenses are deductible if your spouse is involved in business-related entertaining, but not if the only function is secretarial, such as typing or making appointments, something a local person could do at far less expense.

You may deduct as business travel expenses hotels, rental cars, airline fares, automobile expenses, meals, entertainment, laundry, and any other related expenses. The main categories or purposes of deductible business travel are:

- Attending a convention or conference,
- Attending a trade show or association meeting,
- Attending a business-related educational program,
- Setting up distributors for your product or services,
- Buying trips for products to resell,
- A stockholders or partners meeting, even in a small, closely held business,
- Traveling to a business meeting on a cruise ship,
- Meetings with current or potential investors, and
- Visits and discussions with owners of similar business as a learning experience.

HERE ARE THE IRS RULES FOR COMBINED BUSINESS AND VACATION TRIPS:

1. Trips within the United States

A. If the primary purpose of the trip is business, you may deduct 100% of the costs of your transportation (i.e., airlines, automobile) even if you spend time playing. If the main purpose was personal, there is no deduction for transportation.

B. The amount of time you spend on business is the most important factor in determining deductibility. Also important is the fact that you had to be in that spot to conduct business or to attend a convention.

C. Even if you extend your trip for a few purely vacation days, your transportation costs are fully deductible.

2. Trips Outside the United States

A. You may deduct 100% of your travel expenses even though you vacationed provided you can show that: 1. the primary purpose was business; 2. you had no control over the assignment of the trip. That means that your company sent you and you are not either a managing executive or own more than 10% of the company.

B. Special rules for small business owners and managing executives: You may deduct 100% of the transportation costs if:
   1. The trip outside the United States was one week or less, not counting the day you leave but counting the day you return.
   2. The trip lasted more than one week you spent three days on business for every one day of purely vacation time.
   3. You spent more than 25% of the time as pure vacation days you may deduct the business percentage of the trip. Any day on which you conducted any legitimate business is counted as a business day.
   4. You conduct business on Friday and Monday, but not on the weekends, you can count the weekend as two business days. If business is conducted on Friday and Tuesday, the weekend counts as personal days.

3. Conventions and Seminars

A. Travel to investment seminars is no longer deductible, but travel to business seminars is.
B. Keep a complete itinerary of the convention or seminar as part of your records.
C. Be prepared to show what you learned or experienced was directly connected to your business.
D. You must do more than just view video tapes of lectures at your convenience to qualify for the deductions.

4. Foreign Conventions and Cruise Expenses

A. To take the deduction you must be able to show the convention was directly related to your business and that there was a reason for the meeting to be held outside of the United States.
B. Conventions in Canada and Mexico are not considered to be foreign conventions.
C. You may even use the "inside the U.S." rules for conventions held in Puerto Rico, U.S. Virgin Islands, Barbados, Guam and Jamaica.
D. Attend a deductible convention on a U.S.-registered cruise ship. You may deduct up to $2,000 per year for attending cruise ship conventions if all ports of call are in the United States or its possessions, and if the ship is U.S.-registered. Good examples of trips to book under these deduction rules are:
   1. Hawaiian Island cruises
   2. U.S. Mainland-to-Alaska cruises
   3. Mississippi River boat cruises
E. If you travel for business using a cruise ship as your mode of transportation to your destination, you may deduct up to twice the highest federal

government per diem paid to government employees travelling within the United States. The highest federal per diem is $126 per day, so you may deduct up to $252 per day per person. For example, if you travel to the Virgin Islands on a cruise ship to attend a business convention or seminar in the Islands, your transportation cost deduction is up to $252 per day.

If family members or others travel with you, but have no business purpose, you may still deduct full auto mileage, auto rental, and hotel expenses which you would have incurred if you had traveled alone. You may deduct only your food and airfare, not that of other nonbusiness related family members. You may not deduct unrelated recreational and entertainment expenses such as sightseeing, ski-lift, or theater tickets.

You do not have to spend the entire day conducting business to qualify the day as a business day. If part of the the trip is business related with several days devoted to personal purposes only, you should apportion the expenses between deductible business expenses and nondeductible personal expenses. Required expenses such as airfare would still be fully deductible if the primary purpose of the trip is business related.

Keep good records and notes on your receipts if the expense is related to the business portion or personal portion of your trip.

Strategy #197
MAKE INTEREST DEDUCTIBLE AS A BUSINESS EXPENSE.

Tax deductions for interest are possible when you treat interest paid as a business and not a personal expense. Business interest is deductible, consumer or personal interest is not.

When you borrow money to purchase an automobile, video recorder, computer, or other asset for use even part-time in your business, the business interest portion can be deducted. Your small business once again creates deductions out of previously nondeductible expenses.

Strategy #198
CONSIDER AN "S" CORPORATION ELECTION.

Although most new, do-it-at-home businesses should be set up as sole proprietorships, what should you do if you now have a small closely held corporation? Keep it. The process of setting up the business and record-keeping system is already complete.

Tax reform changes the rules enough to consider changing a small "C" corporation to "S" corporation. An "S" corporation from a legal standpoint is not much different than a "C" corporation, but from a tax standpoint the "S" corporation operates like a partnership or proprietorship. Business income and losses in an "S" corporation are taxed only once at the owner's personal tax rate. An "S" corporation cannot have more than 35 shareholders, is limited to one class of stock, and cannot have any nonresident foreign shareholders or subsidiaries. There are two tax benefits of an "S" corporation that make the need for reconsideration clear:

1. Individual and "S" corporation maximum tax rates after 1987 are 28% (except for high income individuals—max 33%) while the "C" corporation maximum tax rate is 34%.
2. The Alternative Minimum Tax (AMT) rate for "C" corporations is much stiffer beginning in 1987 with an increase from 15% to 20%. In addition, "C" corporations must add back to income more tax preferences before computing the AMT, which can significantly raise taxes. On the other hand, an "S" corporation completely circumvents the corporate Alternative Minimum Tax.

Strategy #199
CUT YOUR SELF-EMPLOYMENT TAX BY INCREASING YOUR BUSINESS DEDUCTIONS.

In 1988, small business owners paid self-employment tax (SET) at 13.02% on the first $45,000 of net earnings or a maximum of $5,859. The self-employment tax is a Social Security tax for individuals who work for themselves. The good news is SET qualifies you for Social

Security payments later on; the bad news is you can probably use the money now more than later.

Those subject to self-employment tax include small business owners, independent contractors, and professionals. Members of the clergy can get an exemption. The key word in reducing your SET is "net" income. Only your bottom line self-employment profit (i.e., line 31 of Schedule "C") is subject to SET. Your strategy is to maximize your small business tax deductions. Each $1,000 of deductions that reduces your net profit further below the $45,000 level will save you $130.20 of self-employment tax. If your business net income is already in the hundreds of thousands—too much to reduce your taxable net below the $45,000 threshold—you won't miss the $5,859 anyway.

Strategy #200
USE YOUR SMALL BUSINESS TO CREATE AN INVESTMENT/RETIREMENT TAX SHELTER.

One of the greatest advantages of a profitable small business is the opportunity to create a retirement tax shelter. The rules are so liberal for small business owners that as much as $30,000 to $90,000 per year can be contributed to "defined contribution" and "defined benefit" Keogh plans and excluded from current taxable income.

If your small business or profession is showing a profit, you want to contribute the maximum possible into your plan. The following chart will show you, based on your business form, which plans you are qualified to have.

QUALIFIED RETIREMENT PLANS FOR SMALL BUSINESS OWNERS

	IRA	SEP	Keogh Defined Contrib.	Keogh Defined Benefits	401(k) Salary Deferral
Sole proprietorship	Yes	Yes	Yes	Yes	No
Partnership	Yes	Yes	Yes	Yes	No
"S" corporation	No	Yes	Yes	Yes	Yes
"C" corporation	No	Yes	Yes	Yes	Yes

The more you pour into your plan, the lower your taxable income for the year. With a Keogh, you must have the account opened by the end of the year, but have until April 15th to contribute the money.

Strategy #201
USE ONLY A SELF-DIRECTED SMALL BUSINESS RETIREMENT PLAN.

Another great advantage of owning your own business is total control of where your money is invested. All no-load mutual fund families offer retirement plans for small business owners and self-employed professionals. The use of the Money Movement strategy in your self-directed retirement plan will earn you over 20% per year, no commissions, and no current taxes. See Chapter 23.

Strategy #202
USE THE SEP TO MAXIMIZE YOUR SELF-EMPLOYMENT RETIREMENT CONTRIBUTIONS WITHOUT MATCHING EMPLOYEE CONTRIBUTIONS.

As your business grows, you face the problem with most self-employment retirement plans of having to pay in the same percentage for employees as you pay for yourself. Under the current rules, if you want to avoid matching contributions for employees, the Simplified Employee Pension Plan (SEP) is your best bet.

TAX DEDUCTION STRATEGIES CHECKLIST FOR SMALL BUSINESS OWNERS

Starting a small business is fun, and certainly tax deductible. Here is a summary of the strategies for maximizing your tax deductions.

1. Hire your kids to work in the business to make allowances tax deductible.
2. Hire your spouse to work in the business to create a $2,000 tax deductible IRA account.

3. Use your automobile in your business to create deductions through asset expensing, depreciation, gas, repairs, insurance, parking, and interest.
4. Use your home computer, videotape recorder, cassette recorder, furniture, typewriter or other assets, even part-time, in your business and make them tax deductible.
5. Set up your business office in your home so that part of your mortgage, rent, utilities and other domestic expenses become deductible.
6. Use your social or athletic club at least 50% of the time for business purposes, such as meetings, entertaining, finding new customers, and that part of the dues becomes deductible.
7. Books, subscriptions, newsletters, or tape courses which relate to business in general or to your particular business are deductible.
8. Repairs to any asset you use in your business are deductible.
9. A trip planned around a business purpose, such as staff meetings, visiting customers or suppliers, setting up a sales organization, becomes deductible.
10. If you borrow the money for a business/pleasure trip, the interest is deductible.
11. Using your boat, plane, or motor home directly in a business creates deductions.
12. Interest deducted as a business expense rather than a personal expense will give you interest deductions you might otherwise lose.
13. Consider an "S" Corporation election if you now have a small closely held "C" corporation.

Part III

POWERFUL
INVESTMENT
STRATEGIES

Chapter 19

THE SECRETS OF
POWERFUL INVESTING

*The man who is a bear on the future of the United States
will always go broke.*

J. P. Morgan
Financier
1895

Objective: Accomplish the three major investment objectives:

1. **20% Safe Investment Return**
2. **No Commissions**
3. **No Taxes**

Investing is putting your money instead of your muscle to work; yet, if
there is any area of managing and making money that most people foul
up, not just once, but over an entire lifetime, it is investing.

One of my personal fortunes was lost by listening to the dubious
advice of a financial salesman. At 26, after losing a million dollars in
my recording studio fire, I decided to build my next fortune through
investing. Genesco, the apparel conglomerate for which I designed
computer software systems, offered a magnificent stock incentive plan
to its management employees. My first 200 shares were bought for me
by the company with another 200 shares on the payment-a-month plan.
After buying in at $21 per share, the stock began to split periodically
and grow rapidly in value. Being close to management computer systems, I began to see loopholes that would legally allow me to get my
hands on hundreds of shares of Genesco stock financed totally by the
company. With two thousand shares of stock, for which I had paid
nothing but a few monthly payments, I was accumulating tens of thou-

sands of dollars in stock equity during the company's most expansive era, and the stock skyrocketed to $70 per share.

I was hooked on the stock market. I thought I couldn't lose. What a learning experience I was in for! Borrowing money on everything I owned, including my home and cars, I bought shares in all the new stock issues of the mid-60's. Margin accounts and undercollateralized loans enabled me to run $60,000 of borrowed capital into a stock fortune of $800,000 in just three years. I even considered a leisurely, full-time career as an investor. Then the roof fell in. Every morning, the newspaper would show my newly found fortune dwindling at an ever increasing rate. Every afternoon, I was in contact with the holders of my notes and margin accounts who wanted instant replacement for their disappearing collateral. My margin calls seemed to have margin calls! Companies in which I had invested heavily, like Performance Systems (Minnie Pearl Fried Chicken) and Continental Strategics, went bankrupt leaving me only memories and worthless stock certificates. I was forced to trade my new custom-designed Cadillac for a three-year-old Volkswagen Beetle, rather than have the car repossessed for lack of payments. My home was finally sold with barely enough equity to pay back most of the borrowed money. The entire fortune was gone. I had tasted both the bitter and the sweet of investing and vowed that I would never again risk my money until I knew how to win without the risk of losing.

The investment principles I discovered over the next few years were enough to build a lifetime investment fortune without investment mistakes and these principles can do the same for you. Powerful investing is one of the easiest of all strategies to master, but the misinformation, lack of information, potential for loss and outright fraud that exist in the arena of investing are enough to destroy any good financial plan. Traditional investing has become a mixture of storing money and legalized gambling. Players are the usual losers, financial institutions the winners.

Powerful investing is not like saving money. In America, savers die broke hoping for a pitiful 6% to 10% return that is instantly eaten up by taxes and inflation. Smart investors, on the other hand, have learned to earn 20% per year safely with no taxes and no commissions. How? By using the ten best and safest investments in America, those you won't find at banks, brokerage firms, financial planners, or insurance agents. If the financial salesman's office is your only source of information, not only are you dealing with second-class investments, you will more than likely lose.

The ten best investments and the average yearly returns you can expect are listed below. In this section, you will learn all the strategies for successfully using each of these great investments.

Your objective as an investor is to put your money to work safely and effectively, making yourself rich instead of making financial institutions rich. Through your choice of these investments you can enjoy income, tax shelter and maximum growth or any combination you choose.

THE TEN BEST INVESTMENTS

Investment	Strategy	Average Yearly Return
1. Asset management checking account	Legal float debit card	8%–14%
2. No load mutual funds	Money Movement	25%
3. Mutual fund margin account	Leverage	25%
4. IRA/Keogh account	Self-directed accounts	25%
5. Your own home	Leverage and personal use	20%
6. Employer's retirement	Money Movement payroll deducted	20%
7. Self-directed annuities	Money Movement	25%
8. Discounted mortgages	Guaranteed interest tax deferral	30%
9. Liened property sales	High government guaranteed interest and leverage	20%
10. Residential real estate	Leverage and tax shelter	30%

THE IMPORTANCE OF INVESTING

If you don't expect to win a lottery, and you don't have the option of inheriting vast sums of money, you have only five ways to increase your wealth:

1. Putting yourself to work—Employment,
2. Putting other people to work—Business,
3. Putting your ideas to work—Inventing, marketing, or consulting,

4. Putting your money to work—Investing,
5. Putting other people's money to work—Leverage.

Working for someone else is the first money-making experience for most of us, beyond birthday gifts, and the tooth fairy. There are two limiting considerations when you put your financial future in the hands of the "company."

- Your success is directly tied to the success and attitude of your employer, over which you have no control.
- Your income and life-style are limited by your experience, age, education, the opportunity for advancement, and your ability to sell yourself on the job.

If there are any two words that no longer belong together, they are "job" and "security." Putting together a powerful investment program will put an end to the lifelong dependency on others (employers or the government), even if you don't want the responsibility of starting your own company. In the 80's, a powerful investment plan is as essential to your life-style as a home or automobile. It can be your ticket to freedom, both during your working years and after retirement.

There are two approaches to investing—putting your money to work, and putting other people's money to work.

You put your money to work when you invest in:

- Stocks,
- Bonds,
- Mutual funds,
- Certificates of deposit,
- IRAs,
- Treasury bills,
- Company retirement programs,
- Or any other direct investment using your own money.

You put other people's money to work when you:

- Buy a home with a mortgage,
- Use a brokerage firm or mutual fund margin account,
- Take an option on a piece of real estate,
- Borrow money for your business,
- Invest in leveraged limited partnerships,
- Borrow the equity on your home to reinvest,
- Expect any financial rewards from the use of borrowed capital.

Putting your own money to work is direct and easy to understand, but limits your benefits to the profits that can be generated by your own capital. Putting other people's money to work can be more profitable, but can also be more risky and difficult to understand. The main benefit of OPM (other people's money) is that you can create profits and/or tax deductions far beyond what your own capital can generate. Using OPM is a step you will certainly want to consider once you have mastered the basics of investing your own money.

There are three major objectives of a sound investment plan that can be converted to strategies.

Strategy #203
EARN 20% PER YEAR SAFELY BY USING ONLY THE TEN BEST INVESTMENTS.

Normal investment profits can be more than doubled with knowledge and without additional time or risk by using a combination of the ten best and safest investments. Chapter by chapter in this section we will cover them all. The last chapter will show you how to choose those that are right for your investment plan and objectives.

Strategy #204
PAY NO OR LOW COMMISSIONS BY WORKING DIRECTLY WITH GOVERNMENT AND FINANCIAL INSTITUTIONS.

You cannot split your money with everyone else and expect to end up with much for yourself. Small investors eliminate commissions by dealing directly with financial institutions and eliminating middlemen, such as brokers and financial planners. Paying unnecessary commissions is like throwing $20 bills into your fireplace to heat your home. The job will get done but at far too great a cost.

Strategy #205

USE TAX SHELTERS AND TAX STRATEGIES TO PROTECT YOUR INVESTMENT INCOME.

Most investors think the only strategies for investing without paying taxes are retirement programs or low interest tax exempt bonds. Any investment income can be tax sheltered. You have the choices of using automatically tax-sheltered investments, such as annuities and real estate, or creating tax deductions to match your investment income using any of the tax strategies in Part II of this book. Both methods can make your investments tax deferred or even tax free.

Whether you are a novice or a seasoned investor, you'll find all the secrets to building a powerful investment plan right here. There are no prerequisites. Your job is to organize or reorganize your investment dollars around a combination of these powerful, safe investments. Your decisions on which investments to choose will depend on your investment experience or lack of it, your financial goals, and the amount of capital you have. All ten investments are intended to re-move risk and are appropriate no matter what your age.

Personal knowledge will eliminate risk and fear in your investment plan. Risk occurs most frequently when you act solely on the advice of others, without sufficient knowledge, making decisions without taking control.

THE GREATEST RISKS ARE TAKEN, NOT THROUGH THE INVESTMENTS CHOSEN, BUT THROUGH THE LACK OF PERSONAL KNOWLEDGE OF HOW TO USE INVESTMENT STRATEGIES CORRECTLY.

Chapter 20

THE TEN BIGGEST
INVESTMENT MISTAKES

The trouble with the profit system is that it has always been highly unprofitable to most people.

E. B. White
One Man's Meat
1944

Objective: Learn to recognize investment schemes, scams, and bad advice.

By understanding the ten worst investments and how they earn that distinction, you will find it easier to develop your winning approach to investment wealth. Left out of the ten worst investment list are those that border on fraud or are actually fraudulent. The investments chosen for our list are considered legitimate, but have downside risks or costs that far outweigh any apparent benefits.

Strategy #206
KEEP YOUR MONEY OUT OF VACANT LAND.

Nondeveloped land, sometimes called vacant or raw land, will continue to be a depressed investment for the next five years. The lowered value is caused by the shift in agricultural production from small farms to major farming operations. In addition, land, unless leased, produces no income but does create negative cash flow through property taxes and loan interest. A lot in an appreciating area, or one on which you eventually intend to build, is an exception and can be a good investment.

Strategy #207
DON'T THROW AWAY MONEY IN TIME-SHARING.

Time-sharing is a real estate investment, usually one condominium unit, co-owned by as many as 25 investors. Each investor may personally use his unit during designated weeks, which are chosen as part of the transaction. Two unit weeks are usually sold for between $8,000 and $25,000. Owners, instead of being confined to the use of their own unit usually have the right to trade for the use of other units in other complexes.

Time-sharing has a bad reputation because of developer defaults and bankruptcies. To combat the well deserved negative press, developers have coined a new term, "interval ownership," to replace "time-sharing," but a rose by any other name is—well, you know. The latest marketing twist is the "membership" concept. The purchaser owns nothing except the right to use a unit for a week or two each year. Because the purchaser owns nothing, the price is often half of the cost of time-sharing. Is this concept sellable? Right. Is it a good value? Wrong!

There are *four* major drawbacks of time-sharing:

THE COST

A developer who sells two weeks to 25 investors for $10,000 each has generated $250,000 for one unit. The cost plus reasonable profit for building the unit may have been only $80,000, so the purchasers have overpaid by 300%. The payments at 12% interest would be $1,200 per year, plus maintenance fees. Renting luxury accommodations at most resorts costs far less, with no maintenance fees or headaches of ownership.

THE MAINTENANCE FEES

The developer charges yearly maintenance fees per owner of $300 to $500, built in, of course, to the monthly payments. One of the developer's goals is always to sell out the project and retire comfortably on the income from maintenance fees never used for maintenance.

THE PROMISES

There are already on record hundreds of defaults because the developer wasn't able to sell enough "unit weeks." The developer goes bankrupt, the project remains uncompleted, leaving the unit purchasers holding the bag. Purchasers usually lose their down payment, plus any monthly payments already made. If the purchaser paid cash, the entire amount may be lost.

THE INVESTMENT PITCH

The salesman usually infers that the purchaser is making a good investment and that the unit weeks eventually can be sold at a big profit. Today there are thousands of unit weeks on the market that can't be sold at any price.

Strategy #208
NEVER USE LIFE INSURANCE AS AN INVESTMENT.

Buy life insurance as if you were going to die tomorrow, and invest as if you were going to live forever. Life insurance and investing, both necessary parts of a good financial plan, have little in common. Life insurance companies got into the investment business for one major reason: *There are bigger profits in selling investments than in selling insurance.*

Unlike your bank, which can tie your money up for only a few days to a few years, insurance companies have discovered methods to tie up your money for almost your entire lifetime at a low rate of return. Put $2,000 into a universal life policy and withdraw your money after one year and the surrender charge can be as much as $1,000! (See Chapter 4.)

Your strategy is to buy term insurance and build your investment wealth by choosing the correct investments and strategies yourself.

Strategy #209

STAY AWAY FROM INDIVIDUAL STOCKS AND BONDS.

Buying 100 to 1000 shares of a stock, or pumping $1,000 to $2,500 into one or two bond issues, is eight times riskier than investing in stocks and bonds through mutual funds. Buying individual stocks and bonds also means paying commissions. You pay no commissions by using one of the over 300 no-load mutual funds you will learn about later.

Strategy #210

NEVER INVEST IN BONDS WHEN INTEREST RATES ARE RISING.

Bonds are good investments only when they are appreciating due to declining interest rates. When the Prime Rate is rising, any long-term bond will lose 10% of its principal value for every 1% increase in the Prime Rate. From March, 1987, to October, 1987, while the Prime Rate rose from 7½% to 9¼%, bond investments dropped 10% to 20% in value. Stay away from financial advisers who tell you bonds are always a good safe investment for those who want income.

Bond investments include:

Individual Bonds—corporate, tax exempt, zero coupon, GNMAs.

Bond Mutual Funds—high yield, fixed income, government securities.

Strategy #211

DON'T INVEST IN INFLATION HEDGES SUCH AS PRECIOUS METALS.

Precious metals (gold and silver) are investments only for the most aggressive investors. Traditionally, gold and silver have been called a hedge against inflation. Inflation hedges are always investment losers.

One hundred years ago in 1887, one ounce of gold would buy one average men's custom-tailored suit. Today at about $400 per ounce, one ounce of gold will buy—you guessed it—one average men's custom-tailored suit. With all the fluctuations in price, the real value of gold hasn't changed in a hundred years. Your loss in an inflation hedge comes when you sell your investment and pay 28% capital gains tax on your profits.

Scared investors often invest in precious metals as a hedge against economic collapse or hyperinflation, basing their reasoning on the Great Depression. The Great Depression was not even close to an economic collapse; 75% of all workers remained employed and real estate appreciated an average of 3% per year even in 1933 and 1934. Of course, no depression is a pleasant time, but it was not the end-all doom period it was painted to be. There is no impending economic collapse, no matter how many books and newsletters predict one. Therefore, all defensive investing will cause investment losses.

Strategy #212
DON'T FALL FOR INVESTMENT PHONE PITCHES.

Now you can buy your investments over the phone, but don't! Dozens of phone "boiler rooms" have been created to sell off-the-wall investments. High pressure sales pitches are conducted by highly commissioned phone room managers using minimum wage telephone solicitors. The bait is the belief you are being let in on some new investment secret or opportunity not generally known to the public. Included in the wide range of these investment pitches are:

precious metals	tracts of land in desolate areas
commodities	bids on government land leases
cellular phone lotteries	industrial grade diamonds

These schemes make big promises and deliver little, other than opportunity to lose your money. Incredibly enough, tens of thousands of investors fall for these investment gimmicks every year.

Strategy #213
NEVER USE A COMMISSIONED FINANCIAL SALESMAN AS A FINANCIAL ADVISER.

Paying big commissions will turn almost any winning investment plan into a marginal one at best, often into a loser. Today's smart investor learns to work directly with financial institutions like no-load mutual fund families, eliminating the need for the middleman. A commissioned investment salesman should never be used as a financial adviser for two reasons:

Bias—The salesman will always recommend as your investment solution the investments he or she sells, whether or not these are the investments you should be using.

Lack of Investment Knowledge—Brokers and other licensed salesmen are required to know only two things: the securities laws and how to sell investments successfully. Too many strategies recommended by investment salesmen are either too risky or 20 years out of date.

The Wall Street Journal published an article, based on a copy of a brokerage firm memo that stated the only requirement to keep your job as a broker with the firm is to produce $100,000 in commissions for the company. A better approach would be for each firm to require its salesmen to produce a 20% after commission return for investors and to collect commissions only on investments that actually return what the salesmen promise. Most brokers and financial planners have appalling records when it comes to making investors any real investment wealth.

Some "certified" financial planners have taken only a home-study course, and most have very little money of their own to manage. If you want to learn how to make money, you will learn the most from someone who has plenty of it.

Strategy #214
DON'T OVERLEVERAGE IN VOLATILE INVESTMENTS LIKE COMMODITIES.

Commodities are the riskiest of all legal investments. Greed is the commodities' drawing card. Investors can put up as little as 5% of the purchase price of the investment in order to control the entire investment. An investor can buy a $10,000 commodities contract for only $500. The leverage seems interesting until you look at the validity of the investment. The average price fluctuation in the commodities market is 1% every day. If the investor puts up only 5% and is leveraged by a factor of 20 to 1, the value of his investment will fluctuate an average of 20% per day—great news if the price goes up, disaster if the price of the commodity drops. Even if the price drop is small, the investor's capital may be wiped out. This condition in Las Vegas is known as the "Gambler's Ruin." Ninety-five percent of commodity players eventually lose money. There is no safe strategy for profiting in commodities. When the value of the investment drops below the 5% margin requirement, the investor is required to put up more money or lose the investment and receive a bill for the difference. These margin calls have wiped out the entire assets of many investors.

Strategy #215
AVOID OPTIONS AS A LEVERAGED OR HEDGED INVESTMENT.

An *option* is a right to buy or sell a specified number of shares of stock at a specified price on or before a specific day. A *put* is the right to sell. A *call* is the right to buy.

The investor pays a price for the option, which is forfeited if he or she does not exercise the option. The price an investor pays for the option is usually 2% to 10% of the price of the stock. Seventy-two percent of options are never exercised. The only realistic use of an option for a conservative investor would be to protect the profit on a stock already owned that could not or should not be sold at the present time.

Examples:

A. An employee is going to leave a company in six months and wants to cash in his stock, but cannot sell until he leaves. He is concerned that the price will drop during that period. He buys a "put" on his company stock, which gives him the right to sell at a guaranteed price. The cost of the option is like buying insurance.
B. An investor has a huge profit on a stock, is concerned the market is about to drop, but wants to sell the following year to defer the capital gains tax for 12 months. He buys a put to protect his profits from a market drop. If the market drops he exercises his right to sell at the higher price, otherwise his risk is limited to losing the money he paid for the option.

There are now many mutual funds that use options as their primary investment or as a hedge against fluctuating prices. The mutual funds that use options as a hedge have poor overall performance records.

Strategy #216
LEARN TO RECOGNIZE BAD INVESTMENT ADVICE.

How do you really know when your broker or financial planner is just a commissioned wolf in sheep's clothing? You can tell by the statements he or she makes and the strategies you are told to employ. You should recognize the following statements as bad investment advice:

THE BIGGEST LIES IN THE INVESTMENT BUSINESS

"Stocks and bonds are a good long-term investment."
There is no such thing as a good long-term investment. The best investments change as the economy and interest rates change.

"We'll diversify into different investments—some stocks, some bonds for safety."
Stocks and bonds are good investments at different times but not at the same time.

"Government securities are always a good safe investment for those who want income."
Government securities are bonds. Bonds drop about 10% in principal value for every 1% increase in the Prime Rate. Never invest in government securities when the Prime Rate is going up.

"Tax-exempt bonds are a good investment anytime you want a tax-free income."
Tax-exempt bonds usually pay only 7% to 8% tax-free interest. It would be better to invest in a mutual fund earning 25%, pay the taxes of about 8% maximum, and end up with a 17% profit after taxes.

"It always requires bigger risks to make bigger profits."
Only amateur financial advisers believe this. Bigger profits in the range of 20% to 30% can easily be attained using knowledge and not risk. The ten investment strategies in this section will earn you over 20% safely.

"This investment is a hedge against inflation."
If you just keep pace with inflation, your before-tax profit is zero. After you pay capital gains taxes on the phantom gains, you end up with a guaranteed 28% loss.

"By using dollar cost averaging, we can avoid the fluctuations in the market and end up with potentially bigger profits."
Dollar cost averaging is the practice of making equal investments at equal intervals in the same stock, bond, or mutual fund. This strategy violates two rules of successful investing:
   1. There is no such thing as a good long-term investment.
   2. Every economy has one best type of investment.

"I've got a hot tip on a good stock."
Hot tips ruin most unaware investors. Stock brokers are always the least informed in a brokerage firm hierarchy and their "hot tips" usually lose investors' money.

"Single-premium life insurance is one of the best tax shelters."
Single-premium life insurance is a second-class tax shelter because you must buy whole life insurance before you can make the investment. The best tax shelter, usually available from the same company, is a self-directed annuity, which allows you to invest in tax-sheltered mutual funds without the requirement of buying insurance. (See "Self-Directed Annuities," Chapter 27.) Salesmen often neglect to tell you about the annuities because they pay only a fraction of the commission earned through the sales of single-premium life insurance plans.

"Zero coupon bonds are a great investment for your children."
Zero coupon bonds are sold as investments for tax shelters and children because salesmen know you'll buy them. If not in a tax shelter, you or the kids would pay taxes on interest you do not receive. The

best way to invest for children under 14 is mutual funds, averaging over 20% until the child earns over $1,000 a year and then through self-directed annuities as a tax shelter. Even with a 10% one-time withdrawal penalty the child's account will average over 20% per year instead of 10% per year earned with zero coupon bonds. (See "Self-Directed Annuities," Chapter 27.)

"Life insurance proceeds are tax exempt."
Since deceased people don't pay income taxes, there is no income tax to pay but even insurance proceeds are subject to estate taxes (See "Better Life Insurance for 80% Less," Chapter 4.)

"You should pay commissions because you get better financial advice."
A good financial adviser or money manager will earn you 20% per year after commissions but those of this caliber manage portfolios of $1,000,000 or more and spend most of their time on the ski slopes of Aspen. If you have less than a million, you won't qualify to work with the best portfolio managers. One reason this book was written is to give you the same caliber of help, even if you don't have the big dollars.

"We should make some conservative investments and then take a few risks."
No risks are necessary for a knowledgeable investor. Using the winning investment strategies in this book, even a novice investor can expect to earn 20% to 30% per year while avoiding the pitfalls and risks.

"A bank trust department should become the trustee for your estate."
Bank trust departments have the worst track records of any estate managers, often losing 50% of an estate in five to ten years. Use as your trustee an attorney, friend, or relative who will follow exactly the strategies you are learning now for building and preserving your estate.

"It is not possible to average 20% per year safely."
Nonsense. Tens of thousands of investors who have followed my strategies for two years or more have averaged 20% to 30% safely. These strategies work, work for everyone, and work all the time.

Half the battle of successful investing is ridding yourself of common false or outdated investment beliefs, most of which we have reviewed in this chapter. From now on we will concentrate on the winning investment strategies.

Chapter 21

THE 10% SOLUTION

I've been rich and I've been poor. Believe me, rich is better.

Sophie Tucker
Entertainer
(1884–1966)

Objective: Get your million dollar investment plan started on a shoe-string.

Ninety percent of the families in America are still living paycheck-to-paycheck, always finding too much month left over at the end of the money. Paycheck-to-paycheck is a symptom, not of a lack of income, but of a lack of skills needed to build wealth. You begin to feel as if there is no level of income you cannot outspend.

It is true, that without the discipline to take control of your financial future there is no level of income you cannot outspend. Budgeting is certainly not the answer. The two most difficult personal promises to keep are certainly budgeting and dieting. Neither produces any instant reward or positive feedback so necessary for continued motivation. Budgeting is a plan requiring self-sacrifice now for some vague reward sometime in the not-so-foreseeable future. Budgeting never worked for me and it probably doesn't work any better for you. But there is a strategy I've discovered that allows you, without sacrifice, to build an investment fortune for your future. I call it the "10% Solution."

Strategy #217

**USE THE 10% SOLUTION TO GO FROM
PAYCHECK TO PROSPERITY.**

Beginning with your next paycheck, take 10% right off the top and send it to a mutual fund family (see Chapter 24). Do the same with

275

every paycheck for the rest of your life. Write yourself the first check each month before you pay the rent, mortgage, car payment, or buy the groceries. We were all taught to handle obligations backwards; to pay everyone else first and then enjoy and invest what was left over. The problem? There is never anything left over.

Always pay yourself first. The less money you think you have, the more important the strategy. Make the 10% Solution a personal challenge. Do it now. Don't wait for it to happen.

The one mutual fund family that will allow you to invest with no minimums is Twentieth Century Investors, Kansas City, MO. Send 10% out of each paycheck to Twentieth Century and use the Money Movement Strategy (Chapter 23) to choose the right kind of mutual fund for the current economy. You will double your money every three to four years. Do like everyone else and put the same 10% of your check in a bank or credit union account and you will double your money only once every ten years! Twentieth Century will now debit your bank account automatically every month for the amount you want to invest—automatic wealth building.

"What do you mean, take 10% out of my paycheck?," you may be thinking. "I'm already spending 120%!" If you are, you won't even miss the other 10%. No one ever makes excuses for success. Excuses are only necessary when we forget or fail to do something. Excuses won't build wealth, action will. All successful people have discovered the same success principle: "Do it Now."

Strategy #218
STORE 20% OF ONE YEAR'S INCOME AS ATTITUDE MONEY.

Have you ever noticed how directly your attitude is related to your bank account balance? You have if you are still on the paycheck-to-paycheck treadmill. A positive attitude and financial self-confidence are two of the most important wealth-building tools. The easiest method of maintaining the winning attitude that comes from cash in the bank is never to be without it.

Using the 10% Solution, make deposits in your mutual fund account until the balance is equal to 20% of one year's take-home pay. In writing, promise yourself you will never touch the money—not for overdue bills, emergencies, or any other logical reason. Why? As soon as the money goes, so does your attitude. You will find it far easier, attitude-wise, to have overdue bills with money available to pay them if you wanted to, than to have your bills totally paid and be back in the paycheck-to-paycheck rut.

You will always encounter tough months where the money goes out faster than it comes in. Your 20% is your attitude money, your dependable shelter during financial storms—never, never touch it no matter how tough it gets. Your more stable attitude will propel you past your short-term financial dilemmas.

Once you have reached the 20% quota, you won't have to deposit another dime in the account. If your goal is to double your income every four years or so, your 20% account invested correctly also will double in the same amount of time. Open a separate account for your future 10% deposits.

Strategy #219
USE THE "RULE OF 76" TO DETERMINE THE DOUBLING POWER OF YOUR MONEY.

How long does it take to double your money in an investment?—a long time in a 7% bank account, not so long if you're earning over 20% per year in a mutual fund family. But how long? The "Rule of 76" is the easiest way to determine the answer. Divide the number 76 by the expected return on your investment and the result is the number of years required to double your money if all of the earnings are reinvested and compounding. The short-term doubling power of money invested at 15% to 25% should give you the motivation to get your 10% Solution strategy started immediately.

Using investment strategies like mutual funds, money movement, discounted mortgages, and tax lien certificates covered in this part you will soon be doubling your money every three to four years, even starting with only 10% out of every paycheck.

Let's look at it another way. For every $1,000 you invest this year at 15% to 25%, the following chart will show you how much you will have accumulated during periods ranging from five to 20 years. What you see in the chart can be accomplished with just $83.33 per month, ($1,000 per year), the amount that someone with a net income of

$833.00 per month would deposit in the 10% Solution. Who said you have to have big money to make big money?

THE RULE OF 76
INVESTMENT TIME REQUIRED
TO DOUBLE YOUR MONEY

$ Invested @	Number of years
25%	3.0
20%	3.8
15%	5.0
10%	7.6
9%	8.4
8%	9.5
7%	10.8
6%	12.75

INVESTMENT OF $1,000/AMOUNT AFTER:

Investment Return	5 yrs	10 yrs	15 yrs	20 yrs
15%	$2,010	$4,050	$ 8,150	$16,380
20%	2,480	6,190	15,400	38,340
25%	3,051	9,313	28,422	86,736

In my twenties, I wondered what it was I didn't seem to understand about getting wealthy. Why did some people seem to have the Midas Touch, while I was still running to the bank with each paycheck to cover the checks I had written the previous week? I had been taught that hard work would build wealth; but I couldn't work any harder. I had been holding down at least two jobs since I was 18 and there were no more hours in the day.

Then, one day, I found an answer in "Ripley's Believe It or Not" which said:

> If you sell a five-pound bar of iron right out of the blast furnace, it will be worth $6.00. If you turn the iron into fishing weights, they will be

worth $25.00. Transform your iron into fishing hooks, and they will sell for $250. Hammer the iron into hunting knife blades and you'll get $2,500. If, however, you transform your iron bar into watch springs, they will be worth $250,000—one quarter of a million dollars.

I suddenly realized that working smarter instead of harder is what creates wealth. It doesn't matter what you are worth now, what matters is what you do with what you've got. Time and knowledge will do the work for you. Strategies like the 10% Solution help you turn your five-pound bar of iron into watch springs.

Begin your 10% Solution with your next paycheck!

Chapter 22

THE ASSET MANAGEMENT ACCOUNT (AMA)

Most bankers dwell in marble halls, which they get to dwell in because they encourage deposits and discourage withdrawals.

Ogden Nash
Poet
(1902–1971)

Objective: Couple the convenience of checking with the power of an investment.

There are 15 government-insured, no-minimum-checking accounts in which you can often earn twice the interest your bank will pay. These Asset Management Accounts (AMAs), cannot be found at banks, savings and loans, or credit unions. They are national checking accounts and represent money management systems of the future that are available today.

Asset Management Accounts are available through brokerage firms, mutual funds, or other large financial institutions. Some AMAs require as little as a $1,000 minimum deposit, while others like those offered at Merrill Lynch, E. F. Hutton, and Shearson want $10,000 to $25,000 just to open the account. The Consolidated Asset Management (CAM) account has no minimum deposit requirement. Edward D. Jones' "Full Service" account requires only a $1,000 deposit and as little as a $500 minimum balance. Additional deposits can be made at any time. Asset management accounts have no minimum check requirement or limit to the number of checks you can write. Money market funds and bank money market accounts offer only limited checking.

Strategy #220

USE AN ASSET MANAGEMENT ACCOUNT TO DOUBLE THE INTEREST YOU RECEIVE FROM A BANK CHECKING ACCOUNT.

There are two profits in an asset management account. The first is the variable interest paid on your account balance. Interest rates in asset management accounts have averaged between 6.5% and 18% since 1980 and often pay 2% to 5% more than CDs. The second profit is an additional ½% to 1% created by the daily compounding.

Strategy #221

CHOOSE AN ASSET MANAGEMENT ACCOUNT THAT GIVES YOU MAXIMUM LEGAL FLOAT.

AMAs are national checking accounts and often your checks must travel thousands of miles before they are processed. When you write a check from your AMA, you'll discover that it takes 10 to 14 days before the amount is deducted from your account balance. During the entire time, you're earning interest on money you've already spent! This delay is called legal float—the investor's dream. Some of the accounts like Merrill Lynch's AMA account now process checks locally, reducing the legal float to that of a local bank check, two days. Others, like Edward D. Jones and the CAM account, still give you maximum float time.

Legal float is so lucrative that it has enabled traveler's check companies like American Express to generate millions in profits—all with other people's money. Have you ever wondered what really happens when you buy traveler's checks? You give the bank or traveler's check company "real" money and they give you "play" money (traveler's checks) in return. A traveler's check represents a 100% interest-free loan to the company until you use those checks. On any day of the year, these companies have accumulated and reinvested millions of interest-free dollars using the principle of legal float.

Corporations dealing in large sums of money have also cashed in on legal float. When I was designing computer systems for Genesco in the mid-60's, their sales were approaching a billion a year. The company wrote checks for over $50 million dollars a month. What if they could just get a few days extra float on all that money? The computer department came up with the solution. We had checking accounts in 32 banks across the country from Washington State to Florida. When the accounts payable checks were written, the computer first looked at the address of the vendor to whom the check was to be written, then wrote the check on the bank farthest away. If the vendor was in New York, the check might be written on a bank in Walla Walla, Washington. The first year the company earned millions of extra dollars through the effective use of legal float.

Although legal float may never earn you millions, it is a painless way of earning extra interest.

Strategy #222
WRITE ALL YOUR BILL-PAYING CHECKS FROM YOUR ASSET MANAGEMENT ACCOUNT.

To take advantage of legal float, simply write all your checks from your AMA. An AMA should not be used as a place to store money unless the current interest rate is over 10½%. Deposit each month just enough to cover the checks you intend to write. Over the past five years, you would have earned in an Asset Management Account 2½ times what you earned in a bank checking account. Here is a comparison:

	Bank	Asset Management Account				
Year	Checking account interest	Compounded interest		Legal float		Total interest
1982	5.25%	15%	+	3%	=	18%
1983	5.25%	12%	+	3%	=	15%
1984	5.25%	10%	+	3%	=	13%
1985	5.50%	8%	+	2%	=	10%
1986	5.50%	7%	+	2%	=	9%
1987	5.50%	7%	+	2%	=	9%
TOTAL	26.75%	59%	+	15%	=	74%

Strategy #223

CHOOSE A SIPC-INSURED ASSET MANAGEMENT ACCOUNT.

Most of the asset management accounts have SIPC insurance (Security Investors Protection Corporation). SIPC insurance is to brokerage firms, mutual funds, asset management accounts, and other financial institutions, what FDIC insurance is to banks. Accounts are insured up to $2,000,000 with additional insurance available to $5,000,000.

Strategy #224

CHOOSE AN ASSET MANAGEMENT ACCOUNT THAT OFFERS A DEBIT CARD.

The debit card is a plastic check which has the universal acceptance of a credit card but no end-of-the-month bill. A debit card looks like a VISA card, runs through the merchant's machine like a VISA Card, but doesn't charge anything. The merchant can't tell the difference. When the merchant slip gets to your asset management account, the amount you paid is deducted directly from your account balance—a monthly bill and no check to write.

Nine of the asset management accounts issue VISA debit cards, while others, including Shearson, Paine Webber, and Smith Barney, issue American Express credit cards which cannot be used as a debit card. The debit card is too good a financial management tool to be without and should be a consideration in determining which AMA is for you.

STRATEGY #225

CHOOSE AN AMA WITH A LOW YEARLY FEE.

Yearly fees of $0 to $65 are charged on all AMA accounts, except the Charles Schwab and IDS accounts, which have no fee. Charles Schwab, however, requires you to trade in other securities to keep your AMA open. A yearly fee of over $50 is unreasonable since there are alternatives. Because your asset management account is really an investment account, the yearly fees are tax deductible as a miscellaneous investment expense.

To choose your asset management account, use the comparison chart at the end of this chapter. One important decision is determining if you have the required initial deposit amount and can maintain the required balance.

After you have made your initial deposit, a much smaller minimum balance is usually required to keep the account open and earning interest. Check the chart to determine the minimum balance requirements of the various accounts. All the accounts are good. Simply pick the one that fits you best, with the convenience and services you need.

Call the toll-free telephone number listed or the local office in your area for the accounts in which you are interested. Refer to the account by name and ask them to send you a prospectus. Contained in the prospectus is everything you need to know about the account. To open your account, simply fill out the account application card and mail with a check for at least the minimum deposit. You will receive a checkbook similar to your bank checkbook along with your initial deposit receipt.

Strategy #226
USE AN ASSET MANAGEMENT ACCOUNT FOR YOUR SMALL BUSINESS CHECKING ACCOUNT.

Many of the AMAs also offer checking privileges to small businesses. From the "Asset Management Account Comparison Chart" you'll notice that those who offer business accounts include the CAM account, Edward J. Jones, IDS, Fidelity, Citibank, and most of the brokerage firm accounts. You can enjoy the legal float and debit card privileges for your small business by opening a separate business account at the AMA of your choice.

Asset management accounts prove that there are always better money management alternatives if you know where to look.

ASSET MANAGEMENT ACCOUNT COMPARISON CHART

Sponsor's Name	Account Name	Information Number	Minimum Initial Deposit	Minimum Balance Required	Checks Returned	Yearly Fee	Debit/Credit Card	Margin Accounts Available	Business Accounts Available
Consolidated Asset Mgt.	CAM	800 423-2345	Any	None	No	0	None	No	Yes
Edward D. Jones	Full Service	314 851-2000	1,000	500	Yes	20	VISA	No	Yes
Kemper	Money Plus	800 621-1048	5,000	None	Yes	50	VISA	No	No
IDS Financial	IDS Cash Mgt.	800 328-8300	2,000	300	No	0	None	No	Yes
Schwab	Schwab One	800 648-5300	5,000	500	No	0	VISA	No	No
Fidelity	Ultra Service	800 343-8721	5,000	5,000	Yes	36	MC/VISA	Yes	Yes
Citibank	Focus	800 752-0800	10,000	10,000	Yes	60	VISA	Yes	Yes
Dean Witter	Active Asset	800 222-3326	10,000	None	No	80	VISA	Yes	Yes
E.F. Hutton	Asset Reserve	800 334-4636	10,000	5,000	Yes	36	None	Yes	Yes
Pru-Bache	Command Acct.	800 222-4321	10,000	None	No	50	VISA	Yes	Yes
Thom.-McK.	Asset Director	800 221-3626	10,000	None	No	30	VISA	Yes	Yes
Shearson AMEX	Fin. Mgt.	800 221-3636	15,000	8,000	No	50	None	Yes	Yes
Paine Webber	Resource Mgt.	800 432-9607	15,000	None	No	50	MC	Yes	Yes
Merrill Lynch	Cash Mgt.	800 262-4636	20,000	None	No	65	VISA	Yes	Yes
Smith Barney	Vantage	800 221-3434	20,000	None	Yes	40	None	Yes	Yes
A. G. Edwards	Total Asset	800 325-8380	25,000	10,000	No	25	VISA	Yes	No

Note: Branches located in most major cities have local area phone numbers. Please check with individual sponsors for updates and changes.

Chapter 23

THE MONEY MOVEMENT STRATEGY

You don't buy a stock because it has real value. You buy it because you feel there is always a greater fool down the street who will pay more than you paid.

Donald J. Stockings
Securities and Exchange Commisison
1925

Objective: Time your investments in stocks, bonds, and money market instruments to safely average 20% + per year.

The Money Movement Strategy allows you to reach the three important investment objectives:

1. To earn 20% per year safely.
2. To pay no commissions.
3. To pay minimum taxes on your earnings.

Every investor dreams of being in the right place at the right time—to get in on the beginning of a bull market and out before a bear market or to own bonds when they are appreciating and to sell them before they drop. The Money Movement Strategy times your investment moves to accomplish these goals.

There are a few simple strategies for successful stock, bond, and money market investing that will turn you into a wealthy investor in a short time. Violate any of these rules and you will eventually lose money.

Strategy #227
NEVER STORE MONEY.

A futile effort made by most conservative investors is the search for a good long-term investment. There are good investments and there are long-term investments, but when it comes to stocks and bonds there are no good long-term investments. The best investment this year will become the worst investment in two or three years as inflation and interest rates change. To become a successful investor, you must be willing to move your money, but only once every year or two.

Strategy #228
INVEST IN STOCKS, BONDS, AND MONEY MARKET INSTRUMENTS ONLY THROUGH MUTUAL FUNDS.

A mutual fund is a group of a hundred or more stocks, bonds or money market investments, all managed by the same company. When you invest in mutual funds, you own a small share of the fund's entire investment portfolio. Mutual funds give you the benefits of a diversified portfolio of stocks, bonds, or money market instruments without the risks, costs, or required expertise. Benefits of mutual fund investing make such a strong case that there is virtually no reason to invest in individual stocks, bonds, or money market instruments.

Here are the reasons for using mutual funds.

1. Professional Management—Mutual fund managers are among the most knowledgeable financial people in the country. A full-time pro, not you, is responsible for choosing the stocks, bonds, or other investments held by the fund.
2. Safety—A mutual fund is a group or portfolio of over one hundred stocks, bonds, or money market instruments all managed by the same company. You, as an investor, own shares in the entire portfolio. Because of the incredible diversification, a mutual fund investment is mathematically eight times safer than investing in any one stock or bond. The safety factor of mutual funds was clearly demonstrated in the stock market drop of October 19, 1987. While many well respected stocks dropped as much as 40%, the average stock mutual fund dropped only 16%.

3. Easy-to-Evaluate—The track record of every mutual fund is a matter of public record. You simply check your newspaper for the previous day's closing price (NAV) just as you would for a stock. There is currently no effective way to evaluate stock brokers, financial planners, or investment counselors.
4. Control—Only those who are willing to exercise a measure of control over their investments can safely and consistently earn big profits. Those who turn control over to a broker, financial planner, or other investment salesman generally do poorly. Mutual funds are an excellent vehicle for exercising control.
5. Income—You can choose to receive periodic income from any type of mutual fund: stock, bond, or money market.
6. Liquidity—You can withdraw part or all of your money anytime you wish and within 24 hours.
7. Investment Options—Your investment options are almost limitless through mutual funds. You can invest in stocks, bonds, money market instruments, overseas companies, and even precious metals.

Strategy #229
USE ONLY THE NO-LOAD MUTUAL FUNDS.

A true no-load mutual fund charges no commissions when you invest, and no commissions when you withdraw your money. Out of the over 2,000 mutual funds, 300 are no-load.

Where does the mutual fund make its money? All mutual funds, whether they charge commissions or not, charge about 1% per year for management fees and expenses. For this low fee the mutual fund:

• Chooses the investments.
• Watches the markets for you eight hours a day.
• Keeps all necessary records of your account.
• Sends you periodic statements, usually monthly, about your account.

No-load funds give you a great deal of investment help for very little money. The net asset value per share (NAV), quoted in the newspaper or on your statement, already reflects the deduction of the management fee.

A load is a sales commission and not a management fee. The load is paid to a broker, brokerage firm, financial planner, insurance agent, or anyone else who "sells" you the investment. By working directly with a no-load mutual fund and eliminating the middleman, you save up to 9% in commissions. Remember, you can't be splitting your money with everyone else and end up with much for yourself.

The important question is: Does paying a commission in any way earn you extra profits? The answer is no. Studies for over 20 years have shown that no-load and load funds perform equally when the sales charge is disregarded. Often there are more no-load than load funds in the list of top 20 best performing funds. When you do include sales commissions in calculating mutual fund performance, load funds earn less.

There are three classifications of load mutual funds:

High-Load Mutual Funds

Those that charge 4–9% commissions paid from the money you invest or withdraw. The front-end load means you pay commissions when you invest, reducing your principal. A back-end load means you pay commissions when you withdraw your money, reducing your earnings. Many back-end load funds become no-load funds after your money has been invested for five years or more. Is there ever a time when your best choice of mutual funds might be a load fund? Yes, but only a back-end load fund. Let's say you want ongoing advice from a certain successful financial adviser but want to avoid paying commissions for the advice. When you invest in a back-end load fund, the adviser gets paid a commission by the mutual fund instead of you. As long as you stay with the fund for at least five years, you pay no commissions even when you withdraw your money. If you withdraw your money during the first five years, you are charged a yearly decreasing commission which enables the fund to recoup some of the money it paid to the adviser.

When using the Money Movement Strategy in your employer-sponsored retirement plan, you may have no choice but to use the load funds offered in the plan. The tax benefits will offset by many times the penalty of the load.

You will also use back-end load mutual funds if you invest in self-directed annuities. (See Chapter 27, "Self Directed Annuities.")

Low-Load Mutual Funds

Those that charge 3% or less when you invest or withdraw your money. There are low-load funds that do make good choices for aggressive investors, like Fidelity's sector funds. Conservative investors should avoid low-load funds altogether. Most low-load funds do not pay commissions to salesmen but keep the money for advertising and extra profits.

12b-1 Funds

Mutual funds that charge an extra 1% per year to offset marketing costs but are otherwise no-load.

Even though the Securities and Exchange Commission has permitted the 12b-1 charge for several years, very few mutual funds actually apply it. Those who sell load mutual funds will lead you to believe that it is better to pay 6–9% up front rather than the 1% 12b-1 fee each year. Mathematically that is not true. When you pay an 8% commission up front, only 92% of your money is actually invested. If you used a 12b-1 fund, 100% of your money is invested and the 1% fee is deducted from the earnings. Avoid the 12b-1 funds in favor of the no-load funds.

The Mutual Fund Family Facts Sheets (Appendix I) indicate whether a fund charges a load of any type. Those that are high-load are omitted.

Strategy #230
CHOOSE THE RIGHT TYPE OF MUTUAL FUND FOR EACH ECONOMY.

If the secret to safely investing in stocks and bonds is mutual funds, then the secret to making money in mutual funds is knowing that there are three entirely different types of funds—stock, bond, and money market. The Money Movement Strategy matches the right investment to the right economic climate creating an average investment return of over 20% per year.

Strategy #231
INVEST IN ONLY ONE TYPE OF MUTUAL FUND AT A TIME.

One and only one type of mutual fund is right for each economy. One major mistake made by most investors, often on the advice of an investment salesman, is overdiversification: dividing investment capital among stocks, bonds, government securities, and money market funds. Overdiversification can cost as much in lost profits as underdiversification. An overly diversified investment plan operates like a seesaw; when one side goes up, the other goes down.

Strategy #232

USE THE PRIME INTEREST RATE TO IDENTIFY THE SAFEST AND BEST MUTUAL FUND INVESTMENT FOR EACH ECONOMY.

What factor identifies the current economy and therefore the correct investments? Interest rates. More specifically the Prime Interest Rate. Eighty percent of the long-term increase or decrease in the value of stocks, bonds, and money market instruments is caused by changes in interest rates and is predictable. Short-term, nonpredictable increases or decreases are caused by speculation.

The Prime Rate is the easiest of the interest rates to follow. Any change makes front page headlines. The Prime Rate moves slowly and does not change direction often as stock prices do. Looking at the "Prime Rate Direction Charges Chart" and the "Prime Rate Changes" graph on page 299, you will notice that, if we consider direction changes of at least ½%, the Prime Rate has changed direction only 11 times in ten years. Twice during the last ten years the Prime Rate has continued in the same direction for more than two consecutive years, and changed directions on average of once every 11 months.

You must watch two components of the Prime Rate to choose the right investment:

1. Prime Rate Level—High or Low.
2. Prime Rate Direction—Up or Down

Refer to the "Money Movement Strategy" chart (page 292) and you'll see a curve that represents typical changes of prime interest rates over a three- to five-year period. This is one prime rate cycle. On the chart we've smoothed out the curve to demonstrate how the money movement strategy works. The actual changes are shown on the graph of Prime Rate Changes (page 299). The three shaded areas on the "Money Movement Strategy" chart each represent one of the three investment climates. Notice that there are three places during the cycle where the shading changes. At each of these points you must move your money from one investment to another to maintain maximum safety and continued profits.

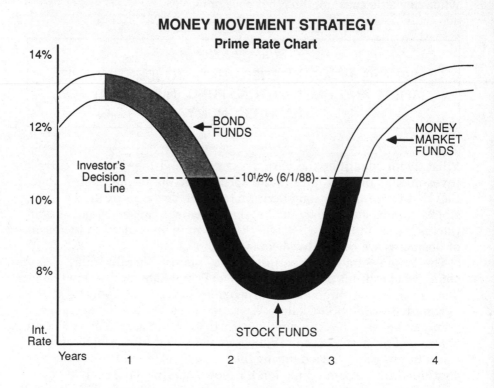

MONEY MOVEMENT STRATEGY
Prime Rate Chart

Strategy #233

INVEST IN STOCK MUTUAL FUNDS ANYTIME THE PRIME RATE IS BELOW THE INVESTOR'S DECISION LINE.

There is always one of the three types of mutual funds—stock, bond, or money market—that will give you an average investment return of 20% per year or more. The Prime Interest Rate indicates which one.

The points on the Money Movement Strategy chart where the shading changes are the points where you must move your money. Two of the three points are on the horizontal dotted line across the middle of the chart called the Investor's Decision Line (currently shown at

10½%). The Investor's Decision Line does change but only once every few years. The area below the Investor's Decision Line defines a *bull* market, a time when most stocks and stock mutual funds are on the rise. It is the point at which the big institutional investors get into the stock market, when the Prime Rate is dropping, and out of the stock market when the Prime Rate is rising. Currently over 80% of stocks are owned by just three groups of institutional investors: mutual funds, pension funds, and big corporations. When the big guys buy, stocks go up; when the big guys sell, stocks go down.

When is the correct time to invest in a stock mutual fund? Any time the Prime Rate is below the Investor's Decision Line. During those years, no matter how widely the Dow Jones stock average fluctuates, the stock market and stock mutual funds will grow an average of 20% or more for the period. During this period there will be unpredictable corrections. The Money Movement Strategy allows you to react to these corrections logically rather than emotionally.

The greatest stock market correction in history came as a shock to the world on October 19, 1987 when the Dow dropped 508 points. During a bull market, however, major corrections are a normal part of the cycle, not a cause for panic. Although big publicity has been attached to the correction of October 19th it is only one of six major corrections since 1982. Here are the others which attracted far less attention.

DOW CORRECTIONS SINCE 1982

Year	Duration	Dow Begin	Dow End	% Drop
1982	Nov. 3–Nov. 23	1065	991	7%
1984	Jan. 6–July 24	1287	1087	16%
1986	July 2–Aug. 1	1909	1764	8%
1987	Apr. 6–May 20	2406	2216	8%
1987	Aug. 25–Oct. 15	2722	2413	11%
1987	Oct. 19–Oct. 19	2246	1738	23%

The important thing to remember is that during this same period the stock market overall achieved record growth. Within months after each correction, there was a major gain in the Dow average. For example, by March 1988 the Dow had recovered 60% of what it lost on Oct. 19, 1987.

January 1985 was the last time the Prime Rate dropped below the current Investor's Decision Line of 10½%. If you were a member of my organization at that time, you were told in your monthly newsletter: "The Prime Rate is below 10½%, move your money to stock mutual funds." Those that did made an average of 40% in 1985, 30% in 1986, and an average of 3% in 1987 even with the biggest stock market drop in history. The total three-year return was 73% or 24% per year. That's how the Money Movement Strategy will protect you and make you a wealthy investor.

Strategy #234

MOVE YOUR MONEY TO A MONEY MARKET FUND WHEN THE PRIME RATE MOVES ABOVE THE INVESTOR'S DECISION LINE.

How do you know when a bull market is really over? When the Prime Rate is rising and reaches the Investor's Decision Line. At that time move your money out of stock mutual funds and into money market mutual funds. When the Prime Rate is above the horizontal Investor's Decision Line, money market funds will not only give you the best return but will also be the safest investment. Can you ever make money in a money market fund? Of course. In 1981, with the Prime Rate averaging 18%, money market funds were paying as much as 20% interest! Of course when the Prime Rate is at 11% and you are in a money market fund you are averaging only about 11% on your money, but you are protected from the coming bear market in stocks and the radical drops in bond prices.

There is always one type of mutual fund in which you will earn an average of 20% or more over time; in 1981 it was the money market funds, in 1982 and 1984 it was bond mutual funds. In 1983 and the average of 1985, 1986, 1987 and 1988, the right investment was stock mutual funds. The Money Movement Strategy will always have you at the right place at the right time and overcome the problems of short-term market drops.

Strategy #235
MOVE YOUR MONEY TO A BOND FUND WHEN THE PRIME RATE IS HIGH AND COMING DOWN.

As long as the Prime Rate is over the Investor's Decision Line and moving up, stay in money market funds. When the Prime Rate changes direction and starts downward, move your money to the third and last investment in the Prime Rate cycle, a bond mutual fund.

Bond mutual funds are always the best investment when the Prime Rate is high and coming down. During that period you will earn two profits from bonds—interest and appreciation. The appreciation can be your big profit, averaging more than 20% per year.

There are two principles that guide this aspect of the Money Movement Strategy:

When the Prime Rate Drops 1%, Bonds appreciate 10%.

Prime down "one," bonds and bond mutual funds up "ten." Ten to one is the best leverage you'll ever get in a safe investment plan. A good example was 1982, when the Prime Rate dropped 5%, from 16½% to 11½%, and the average bond mutual fund appreciated 40%. Tax-free bond funds actually out-performed the regular bond funds that year.

Why are bonds and government securities a poor investment so much of the time? Because the opposite of the foregoing principle is also true.

When the Prime Rate Rises 1%, Bonds Depreciate 10%.

Prime up "one," bonds and bond mutual funds down "ten." Never invest in bonds, tax-exempt bonds, GNMAs, or government securities when the Prime Rate is going up. Your principal may be decreasing faster than you are earning interest. Most financial salesmen will incorrectly tell you to hold onto 7% or 8% bonds even when principal is falling because "you haven't lost anything unless you sell and, after all, you are still getting the interest payments." You have lost. You've lost the opportunity to reinvest your money in bonds paying 12% to 13% when the Prime Rate goes up. Your bond or bond fund value can drop as much as 50%, due to increasing interest rates, locking you into unwanted low interest bonds.

The Money Movement Strategy will produce the greatest profits when the Prime Rate is dropping, often 30% or more per year in stocks or bonds. When the Prime Rate is rising Money Movement becomes more of a defensive strategy and profits are in the 10% to 15% range. During these periods consider discounted mortgages as your source of 20% returns (Chapter 28).

The Money Movement Strategy is not intended as a get-rich-quick scheme. It is a lifelong strategy for reducing risk and maximizing investment profits. The Money Movement Strategy will allow you to average 20% per year, year after year—without having to watch your money day by day. It is the right mutual fund strategy for both conservative and aggressive investors.

There are four investments in which you can successfully use the Money Movement Strategy in mutual funds. Three are tax shelters—all are covered in this book.

1. No-load mutual fund families   Chapter 24
2. Your IRA or Keogh account   Chapters 12 and 26
3. Self-directed annuities   Chapter 27
4. Your employer's 401(k) or 403(b) retirement plan   Chapter 12

The following chart lists the "Prime Rate History" from October 1977 to March 1988. It also lists the correct investments during this period according to Money Movement Strategy. If you had made these investments, you would have profited by an average of 20% per year.

PRIME RATE HISTORY

Year	Date		Prime Rate	Correct Investment	Year	Date		Prime Rate	Correct Investment
1977	Oct.	7	7½	MM		Aug.	31	9¼	MM
		24	7¾	MM		Sept.	15	9½	MM
1978	Jan.	10	8	MM			28	9¾	MM
	May	5	8¼	MM		Oct.	13	10	MM
		26	8½	MM			27	10½	MM
	June	16	8¾	MM		Nov.	1	10½	MM
		30	9	MM			6	10¾	MM

PRIME RATE HISTORY (*cont.*)

Year	Date		Prime Rate	Correct Investment	Year	Date		Prime Rate	Correct Investment
	Nov.	17	11	MM		Sept.	8	12	MM
		24	11½	MM			12	12½	MM
	Dec.	26	11¾	MM			19	12½	MM
1979	June	19	11½	MM			26	13	MM
	July	27	11¾	MM		Oct.	1	13½	MM
	Aug.	16	12	MM			17	14	MM
		28	12¼	MM			29	14½	MM
	Sept.	7	12¾	MM		Nov.	6	15½	MM
		14	13	MM			17	16¼	MM
		21	12¼	MM			21	17	MM
		28	13½	MM			26	17¾	MM
	Oct.	9	14½	MM	1980	Dec.	2	18½	MM
		23	15	MM			5	19	MM
	Nov.	1	15¼	MM			10	20	MM
		9	15½	MM	1981	Jan.	2	20½	MM
		16	15¾	MM			9	20	MM
		30	15½	MM		Feb.	3	19½	BF
	Dec.	7	15¼	MM			23	19	BF
1980	Feb.	19	15¼	MM		March	10	18	BF
		22	16½	MM			17	17½	BF
		29	16¾	MM		April	2	17	BF
	March	4	17¼	MM			24	17½	BF
		7	17¾	MM		May	19		MM
		14	18½	MM			30	17½	MM
		19	19	MM			11	19½	MM
		28	19½	MM			19	20	MM
	April	2	20	MM			22	20½	MM
		18	19½	MM		June	3	20	MM
	May	1	19	BF		July	8	20½	MM
		2	18½	BF		Sept.	15	20	MM
		7	17½	BF			22	19	MM
		16	16½	BF		Oct.	5	19	BF
		23	14½	BF			13	18	BF
		30	14	BF		Nov.	3	17½	BF
	June	6	13	BF			9	17	BF
		13	12½	BF			17	17	BF
		20	12	BF			20	16½	BF
	July	7	11½	BF			24	16	BF
	Aug.	22	11¼	BF		Dec.	1	15¾	BF
		27	11½	BF	1982	Feb.	2	16½	BF

PRIME RATE HISTORY (*cont.*)

Year	Date		Prime Rate	Correct Investment	Year	Date		Prime Rate	Correct Investment
		18	17	BF		Oct.	17	12½	MM
		23	16½	BF			29	12	BF
	July	20	16	BF		Nov.	9	11¾	BF
		29	15½	BF			28	11¼	BF
	Aug.	2	15	BF		Dec.	20	10¾	BF
		16	14½	BF	1985	Jan.	15	10½	BF
		18	14	BF		May	20	10	SF
		23	13½	BF		June	18	9½	SF
	Sept.	30	13½	BF	1986	March	7	9	SF
	Oct.	7	13	BF		April	21	8½	SF
		14	12	BF		July	14	8	SF
	Nov.	22	11½	BF		Aug.	1	7½	SF
1983	Jan.	11	11	SF	1987	March	31	7¾	SF
	Feb.	28	10½	SF		May	1	8	SF
	Aug.	8	11	SF		May	15	8¼	SF
1984	March	19	11½	MM		Sept.	4	8¾	SF
	April	5	12	MM		Oct.	6	9¼	SF
	May	8	12½	MM		Oct.	22	9	SF
	June	25	13	MM		Nov.	5	8¾	SF
	Sept.	27	12¾	MM	1988	Feb.	2	8½	SF
						May	16	9	SF

MM = Money Market Funds
SF = Stock Funds
BF = Bond Funds

PRIME RATE CHANGES
Oct. 1977 – Mar. 1988

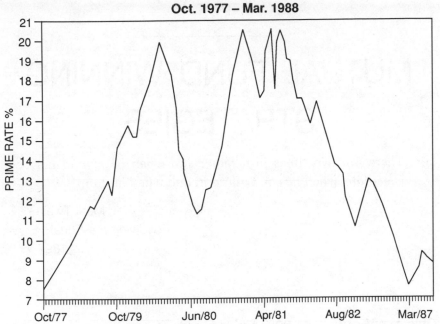

PRIME RATE DIRECTION CHANGES CHART 1978 TO 1988

Date	From	To	Direction	# of Mos.
Jan. 1978 to Apr. 1980	8.00%	20.00%	up	28
Apr. 1980 to Aug. 1980	11.00%	11.00%	down	4
Aug. 1980 to Jan. 1981	11.00%	21.50%	up	5
Jan. 1981 to Apr. 1981	21.50%	17.00%	down	3
Apr. 1981 to Jun. 1981	17.00%	20.00%	up	2
Jun. 1981 to Feb. 1982	20.00%	15.75%	down	8
Feb. 1982 to Feb. 1982	15.75%	17.00%	up	1
Feb. 1982 to Aug. 1983	17.00%	10.50%	down	18
Aug. 1983 to Sep. 1984	10.50%	13.00%	up	13
Sep. 1984 to Mar. 1987	13.00%	7.50%	down	30
Mar. 1987 to Nov. 1987	7.50%	9.25%	up	8
Nov. 1987 to May 1988	9.25%	8.50%	down	4
May 1988 to —	8.50%	9.00%	up	—

Chapter 24

MUTUAL FUND WINNING STRATEGIES

There are two times in a man's life when he should not speculate: when he can't afford it, and when he can.

Mark Twain
Following the Equator
1897

Objective: Earn a safe 20% per year with no commissions in a liquid investment.

Strategy #236
USE THE MONEY MOVEMENT STRATEGY IN NO-LOAD MUTUAL FUND FAMILIES.

One of the easiest investments in which to apply the Money Movement Strategy is a no-load mutual fund family. A mutual fund is an investment company registered with the S.E.C. (Securities and Exchange Commission) and managed by a professional fund manager. The mutual fund buys a portfolio of stocks, bonds, or money market instruments and you, as an investor, own a share of the entire portfolio. Mutual funds are open-ended, that is, they can sell unlimited numbers of shares to new investors. The mutual fund promises to redeem shares upon notice at the current net asset value (NAV). A mutual fund family is a group of mutual funds all under the same management.

MUTUAL FUND DEFINITIONS

To profit from mutual fund investments, there are certain terms and definitions you must understand. These are the mutual fund terms that allow you to maneuver your investment.

Account

Your investment arrangement and record with the mutual fund. Your account is initially the amount of your investment minus any front-end commissions. Your account increases in value when the fund's assets increase or when you invest more money. Your account decreases in value when the fund's assets decrease, you withdraw money, or the fund's management expense is deducted. You receive a periodic statement of your account.

Adviser

An organization or person employed and paid by the mutual fund to give professional investment advice to the fund.

Asked Price

The price at which you can buy shares in a mutual fund, also known as the offering price. This price is the current net asset value per share (NAV) plus any sales charge.

Bid Price

The price at which the mutual fund will buy back your shares. The bid, also called the redemption price, is the current net asset value per share (NAV). Back-end loads or commissions, if any, are subtracted from the total amount you receive when you sell.

Capital Gains or Losses

Your profit or loss from the sale of your mutual fund shares. Capital gains and losses are created when investments are sold by either you or the mutual fund. When the mutual fund sells investments, the profits or losses are taxable transactions and your taxable share appears on your account statement. When you sell your shares in a fund or move to another fund, you have created taxable gains or losses unless your mutual fund is tax sheltered.

Cash Position

The amount of the fund's assets that are not invested in stocks or bonds but are put in the bank or in short-term investments. If a stock fund manager thinks stocks may go down, he will sell stocks and maintain a bigger "cash position" with the intent of buying stocks at a reduced price later. If the stock goes up and the fund maintains a big cash position, it will be out-performed by those funds that stayed more "fully invested."

Certificate

The printed record showing ownership of mutual fund shares, similar to a stock certificate. Because of a unique computerized record of your account maintained by the fund, certificates are seldom issued unless the shares are going to be pledged for a loan or margin account.

Distributions

The payments to shareholders of capital gains or dividends in the form of cash or additional mutual fund shares.

CAPITAL GAINS DISTRIBUTIONS. Payments made to mutual fund shareholders representing profits earned by the fund when stocks or bonds are sold. These profits are paid at the shareholder's option, in cash or as additional shares in the fund. In the past, capital gains were distributed once per year, but because mutual funds must now distribute 90% of capital gains to avoid taxation; some will go to a quarterly distribution system. You pay taxes on capital gains distributions even if the money is reinvested. All mutual fund capital gains distributions are treated as long-term for tax purposes.

Although the total net asset value of the fund remains the same before and after a distribution, the per share NAV drops as more shares are issued to each shareholder representing the capital gains per share. For example:

BEFORE DISTRIBUTION

1,000,000 shares at $11 per share = $11,000,000 net assets of fund

Capital gains distribution $1,000,000

AFTER DISTRIBUTION

1,100,000 shares at $10 per share = $11,000,000 net assets of fund

The total assets remain the same but the number of shares and the NAV per share change proportionately.

DIVIDEND DISTRIBUTIONS. The distribution of dividends and interest from investments to the mutual fund shareholders. The distribution methods are the same as with capital gains distributions.

EX-DIVIDEND DATE. The date on which declared distributions are deducted from the fund's assets. On that day the share price drops but since each shareholder receives more shares, the amount in the shareholder's account remains the same.

Exchange Privilege

The right of a mutual fund shareholder to transfer his money from one fund to another within the same family. The two types of exchanging are:

- Telephone Switching—Your money can be moved by a telephone call.
- Mail Exchanging—You write to the fund to move your money.

An exchange is actually the sale of shares in one fund and the purchase of shares in another. The transaction is taxable unless your investment is protected by a tax shelter like an IRA or self-directed annuity.

Management Company

The entity which manages the fund. Often a fund family itself will have different officials than those that actually manage the fund. The "adviser" described earlier gives investment advice; the management company handles the business.

Net Assets

A mutual fund's total assets minus current liabilities.

Net Asset Value Per Share (NAV)

The mutual fund's total assets minus current liabilities, divided by the number of shares outstanding.

Payroll Deduction Plan

A plan where mutual fund contributions are deducted from your paycheck and sent by your employer directly to the fund.

Performance

The percentage change in a fund's net asset value per share (NAV) over a period of time. Performance is a method of comparing different mutual funds.

Portfolio

All the securities owned by a mutual fund.

Portfolio Turnover

The percentage of a mutual fund's investments that were changed during the year (sold and the money reinvested). The total can be from 0 to over 100%. Most aggressive funds have higher portfolio turnovers.

Prospectus

The official brochure issued by a mutual fund that describes how the fund works, how it manages its money, the objectives of the fund, how you invest and withdraw your money, and how much the fund charges in fees and commissions. Much of the information is required by the Securities and Exchange Commission. The important information from the prospectus for the recommended no-load families is in the Mutual Fund Family Fact Sheets in Appendix I.

Reinvestment Privilege

The right of a mutual fund shareholder to have interest dividends and capital gains automatically used to purchase additional shares of the fund.

In addition to these terms, you must know the three categories and many subcategories of mutual funds. Knowing the difference and when to use each is the basic secret of mutual fund investment success.

MUTUAL FUND CATEGORIES

All mutual funds fall into three basic categories.

- Stock mutual funds
- Bond mutual funds
- Money market mutual funds

Each category has many subcategories that are identified by a two-digit code used throughout this chapter in all references and charts (see page 324 for key).

STOCK MUTUAL FUNDS

A stock represents ownership of a portion of a company's assets. Individual stocks are bought and sold through stock brokers who are connected by computer to the major exchanges, such as the New York or American Stock Exchanges. Stocks not listed on the exchanges are traded broker-to-broker through the National Association of Securities Dealers (NASD). The brokers receive commissions for handling investors' stock trades. The per share price of a company's stock increases or decreases, based on supply and demand. If there are more buyers than sellers, the price goes up. If there are more sellers than buyers, the price drops.

A mutual fund that invests primarily in stocks is a stock mutual fund. Stock mutual funds are classified into many subcategories and are named by their investment objectives and the type of stocks in which they invest. Since few stock funds use the term "stock" in the fund name, you, as the investor, must understand the terms that identify a stock fund and its investment philosophy.

Growth Fund (SG)

A stock mutual fund that invests primarily in common stocks with good growth potential.

Aggressive Growth Fund (SA)

A stock mutual fund that uses aggressive and sometimes volatile techniques in an attempt to increase profits. These aggressive techniques include leverage, short selling, and buying warrants and options.

Growth and Income Funds (SI)

A stock fund that attempts to give investors capital growth and income at the same time. The fund invests in stocks that are lower in price so that the dividend yield is higher. Dividend yield is the amount of dividends paid per share divided by the price of one share. The lower the price, the higher the yield.

BEST PERFORMING GROWTH STOCK FUNDS 1986*

(In Recommended Families)

Family	Fund	% Growth
USAA	Cornerstone	41
Boston Co.	Capital Appreciation	23
T. Rowe Price	Growth Stock	22
GIT	Select Growth	22
Babson	Value	21
Twentieth Century	Select	20
Lexington	Research	20
Founders	Growth	20
Babson	Growth	19
Rushmore	Stock	18

* 1986 figures used as more representative than 1987

BEST PERFORMING AGGRESSIVE GROWTH STOCK FUNDS 1986*

(In Recommended Families)

Family	Fund	% Growth
Strong	Opportunity	60
Constellation	Growth	29
Twentieth Century	Gift Trust	28
Twentieth Century	Vista	25
Fidelity	Magellan	24
Value Line	Lev. Growth	23
Lexington	Growth	21
Hartwell	Leverage	19
Founders	Special	19
Twentieth Century	Growth	19

* 1986 figures used as more representative than 1987

These conservative (SI) funds slightly outperformed the growth and aggressive growth funds from 1981 to 1986. The average dividends paid by the three main types of stock funds in 1986 stacked up like this:

- Aggressive growth funds (SA) 1.0%
- Growth funds(SG) 2.0%
- Growth and income funds (SI) 3.3%

Because of the small difference in actual yield between types of funds, the better performance of growth and income funds was based on other factors. To get higher yields, (SI) fund managers looked for under-priced, undervalued stocks in good, solid, well-established companies. The lower the price, the higher the percentage dividend yield. This approach creates a great potential for growth once the stock price begins to recover and is the reason growth and income funds have performed so well.

BEST PERFORMING GROWTH AND INCOME FUNDS 1986*

(In Recommended Families)

Family	Fund	% Growth
Scudder	Growth & Income	35
Vanguard	Windsor II	22
Vanguard	Windsor I	20
Vanguard	Index Trust	18
Fidelity	Equity Fund	17
Founder's	Mutual	17
AARP	Growth & Income	17
Fidelity	Fidelity Fund	16
Dreyfus	Dreyfus Fund	16
Safeco	Equity	13

* 1986 figures used as more representative than 1987

Although (SI) funds are often considered the best choice for conservative investors, they are a good choice for all but aggressive investors.

Equity Income Funds (SE)

Combination stock and bond funds that have a primary goal of income and a secondary goal of growth. There are about 40 no-load and low-load equity income funds whose assets on the average are invested as follows:

- 40%   High dividend-paying stocks
- 50%   Bonds
- 10%   Cash

The equity income funds perform well when the prime rate is dropping because both stocks and bonds are appreciating plus the yield from interest and dividends (i.e., 6.2% in 1986). They are poor performers when the prime rate is going up because any stock gains are automatically wiped out by bond losses.

Also included in the equity income funds category are the qualified dividend funds set up for corporate investments only. Tax reform allows corporations to earn tax-free 70% of dividends received from investments in other corporations (85% under pre-tax reform rules). Several mutual funds have been created for this specific purpose.

SPECIALTY STOCK MUTUAL FUNDS

Specialty stock mutual funds buy stocks using a special selection process, leverage, or other type of investment formula not used by the regular stock funds, and are generally for only more knowledgeable and speculative investors. The following is a description of major categories of specialty stock funds.

Option Fund (SO)

A mutual fund that buys stock options instead of stocks. An option is the right to buy or sell a specific number of shares of a stock at a fixed price by a specific date. Some option funds buy stocks and then attempt to hedge against a price drop by purchasing "puts" or options to sell on the same stock. Option funds have not been particularly successful during the past ten years.

BEST PERFORMING EQUITY INCOME FUNDS 1986*

(In Recommended Families)

Family	Fund	% Growth
Strong	Income	30
T. Rowe Price	Equity Income	27
Dreyfus	Convertible Sec.	23
Vanguard	Qualified Dividend **	21
Fidelity	Qualified Dividend **	21
Fidelity	Puritan	21
Safeco	Income	21
Bull & Bear	Equity Income	19
Vanguard	Wellington	18
Vanguard	Wellesley	18
Stein Rowe	Total Return	17
Value Line	Convertible	17
Flex Fund	Corp Income **	17
Value Line	Income	16

* 1986 figures used more representative of stock funds than 1987.
** Qualified dividend funds set up for corporations only to take advantage of the 70% dividend tax exclusion

Index Fund (SX)

A mutual fund that theoretically owns all of the stocks in the Standard and Poor's 500 or other index. The growth, therefore, is the same as that of the index. During the past five years, the S&P 500 average has outperformed the average growth and aggressive growth mutual funds. Investors who guess at which mutual funds will be good performers will generally earn less than an index fund. Investors who use knowledge and good mutual fund advice will always outperform the S&P 500 and the index funds. Vanguard's Index Trust is an example of an index fund.

BEST PERFORMING BALANCED FUNDS 1986*

(In Recommended Families)

Family	Fund	% Growth
Stein Roe	Total Return Fund	17
Vanguard	Star Fund	14
Strong	Investment Fund	18
Fidelity	Balanced Fund	18
Vanguard	Wellington Fund	18

* 1986 figures used as more representative of stock funds than 1987.

Balanced Fund (SB)

These mutual funds invest in a combination of stocks, bonds, and preferred stocks and violate the rule: "Every economy has one best investment." Knowledgeable investors avoid the overdiversified balanced fund that are big losers when interest rates are rising.

Closed-End Fund

Closed-end funds, sometimes called "trusts," issue a fixed number of shares and are publicly traded on the stock exchanges. Unlike the open-ended funds, which are the more familiar mutual funds, closed-end funds do not issue or redeem shares from investors. The current share price of a closed-end fund is not the NAV (net asset value per share), but a price based on supply and demand. Poor overall performance is the best reason to avoid the closed-end funds.

Social Conscience Fund

There are two no-load funds that invest in stock of companies organized for social good, or that seek to avoid companies involved in war materials, liquor, tobacco, gambling, or South Africa. The two stock funds are PAX World Fund and Dreyfus Third Century. These funds have had an average to poor track record and should be used only by those whose social consciences match the objectives of the funds.

Industry Fund

Funds that purchase stocks related to only one industry are called industry funds. Some industry funds, like the health funds, have been great performers because of the overall growth or profits of that single industry. Others, like the high tech funds, have been at times the big losers.

Industry funds are for aggressive investors, and should be used only during periods when the Prime Rate is dropping. Some industry funds have never done well, like the "Gaming Fund" (gambling stocks) organized in 1978 and liquidated in 1982.

Industries represented by industry funds include: high tech, computer software, drugs, computers, bio tech, health, chemicals, energy, financial, housing, leisure, defense, restaurants, life insurance, automotive, paper, broadcast media, banking, air transport, and industrial materials.

Sector Fund (SS)

When you put several industry funds under one mutual fund family and allow switching between these as well as money market funds, you have sector funds. Sector fund investing allows the choosing of more specific stocks with the safety of diversification. The Fidelity family has 35 sector funds called "Select" funds and Vanguard has five Sector funds it calls "Special" funds. Sector funds are good choices for aggressive investors.

EMERGING GROWTH FUNDS

FAMILY	FUND
Babson	Enterprise
Stein Roe	Capital Opportunities
T. Rowe Price	Horizons
Stein Roe	Discovery
Scudder	Development
Fidelity	O.T.C.

Emerging Company Growth Fund

Stock funds that buy shares in new companies with good future potential. These funds are volatile and far riskier than regular stock funds because of the unpredictability of small company performance, and should be avoided by conservative investors. These funds were good performers the first six months of 1988 as the stock market recovered.

Precious Metal Fund (SP)

These funds buy the stocks of mining companies involved in the extraction of gold, silver, platinum, and other precious metals. They are volatile funds and should be used only by more aggressive investors. Overall, the performance of the gold funds has been greater than the growth or aggressive growth stock funds even with some bad years. The increase or decrease in value of precious metal funds follows the market price of the metals and not the prime rate, and makes these funds unpredictable. Invest in precious metal funds only with good, dependable advice.

Multi-Fund (SB)

A multi-fund is a mutual fund that invests in shares of other mutual funds. An example is Vanguard's Star Fund, which invests in other Vanguard stock, bond, and money market funds. These funds have a poor track record because of overdiversification. Multi-funds are sometimes classified as "balanced funds" discussed earlier.

BOND MUTUAL FUNDS

A bond investment represents a loan made by an investor to a corporation or government agency for a term ranging from one to thirty years. Bonds normally pay guaranteed interest rates like certificates of deposit, but unlike CDs, bond values go up and down daily due to changes in marketplace interest rates. A bond may sell at a premium (more than its face value) or at a discount (less than its face value). At the end of the term, the issuer guarantees to pay the investor the face value of the bond.

A mutual fund that invests primarily in bonds is a bond mutual fund. These can be classified into several subcategories.

High Yield Fund (BL)

A bond fund investing in corporate bonds with supposedly higher than usual interest rates and often lower than usual ratings.

Fixed Income Funds (BL)

A bond fund that invests most of its assets in long-term bonds.

GNMA Fund (BG)

A bond fund that invests in mortgage bonds issued by the Government National Mortgage Association.

Government Securities Fund (BG)

A bond fund that invests in GNMA's and bonds issued by other government agencies.

MONEY MARKET MUTUAL FUNDS

Money market funds are mutual funds that invest in short-term, super-safe, interest-bearing instruments. The maturity date of these securities is between one day and one year. The interest rates paid daily to money market fund investors is a composite of all the rates on instruments held by the fund and has, in the last eight years, ranged from a low of 6% to a high of 18% annually. Money market funds make good investments when interest rates are over 10½% and poor investments when interest rates are less.

Money market funds are not the same as money market accounts. Money market account is a fancy name for bank savings plans that pay variable instead of fixed interest. The banks use the name in an effort to confuse investors and to lure money away from the money market funds.

Money market funds were originally created in 1972 with the birth of the Reserve Fund. The objective was to offer small investors the opportunity to get better-than-bank rates on money market instruments, formerly available only to investors with $100,000 or more. In 1974 the Fidelity Daily Income Trust pioneered the concept of check-writing in a money market fund. Many money market funds now allow you to write up to three checks per month, with a $250 to $500 minimum.

The per share value of a money market fund is always $1; so your principal value does not increase or decrease. The interest earned by your shares is added to your account as additional $1 shares, unless you withdraw the money. Newspapers quote money market funds in terms annualized by daily interest paid.

Money market funds have been created both by mutual fund families and stock brokerage firms. The following descriptions center on those no-load money market funds which are part of mutual fund families.

Regular Money Market Funds (MM)

Invest in:

U.S. GOVERNMENT SECURITIES. Short-term debt instruments issued by the U.S. Treasury and other government agencies.

BANK JUMBO CERTIFICATES OF DEPOSIT. Loans of $1,000,000 or more made to banks.

BANKERS' ACCEPTANCES. Short-term bank guarantees designed to finance imports and exports. The importer does not want to pay a foreign company until goods are received. An exporter does not want to ship the goods until he is guaranteed he will receive his money when the goods are delivered. Bankers' acceptances are the guarantees and are risk free.

COMMERCIAL PAPER. Unsecured but virtually risk-free short-term notes issued by large creditworthy corporations and finance companies. Maturity dates are up to nine months.

REPURCHASE AGREEMENTS. A security sold by a brokerage firm to finance its transactions with a written guarantee to repurchase the security on a specific date, at the same price, plus interest. Repurchase agreements have a maturity of less than one week.

Tax-Exempt Money Market Funds (MX)

These special money market funds invest in tax-exempt municipal securities that mature within one year. The average maturity of these tax-exempt securities is 75 days compared with 45 days for a regular money market fund. Tax-exempt money market funds, because of very low interest rates, are not good investments even for those in higher tax brackets.

Insured Money Market Funds (MI)

Money market funds like Vanguard's money market trust and Vanguard's insured portfolio are insured, but you pay the insurance with reduced interest. Money market funds are already safe enough that the insurance is a waste of money.

Asset Management Accounts

The natural outgrowth of money market funds are the asset management accounts which have unlimited checking and offer other financial services such as "debit cards." (See Chapter 22)

Now that you have an overall picture of the diversity of mutual funds available, let's look at the strategies that will put these funds to work for you.

Strategy #237

INVEST ONLY IN FUNDS THAT HAVE MORE THAN $25 MILLION AND LESS THAN $3 BILLION IN ASSETS.

The size of a mutual fund should be considered in your investment strategy. If a fund has under $25 million in assets there is a good chance it cannot afford to hire or keep the best of the fund managers. You do not want your capital used to provide the training ground for a new fund manager.

Getting too big also has a downside. If a stock mutual fund has over $3 billion in assets, it loses flexibility. Much of the success of a stock fund in beating the stock indices is created by portfolio turnover— moving money in and out of cash positions in anticipation of market drops or gains. A fund manager can't move money fast enough if the fund is too large.

A good example is the Fidelity Magellan Fund, which in 1987 grew to 11 billion dollars. Magellan was the best performing fund for the previous ten years and by imposing a low-load of 3% raised enough advertising capital to make itself famous. The more Magellan advertised the more capital flowed in. In an interview with *The Wall Street Journal*, Fund Manager Peter Lynch speculated that the fund would be unlikely to maintain its performance record of the past. I began warning members of my organization in the winter of 1987 that Magellan could get itself in performance trouble if the stock market took a sudden turn. On October 19, 1987, it happened. The Dow dropped 508 points. While the average mutual fund dropped only 16%, Magellan was a big loser with a drop of 32%.

Big mutual funds have an option. They can close the existing fund to new investors and start a new one with new management but an identical investment philosophy. The Vanguard family closed its super successful Windsor fund to new investors when it got too big and created the Windsor II fund. Windsor II actually outperformed Windsor I in 1986.

In the Mutual Fund Family Fact Sheets (Appendix I) you'll find each fund's total assets.

Funds and families with too little assets are shown in the "Not Recommended" chart on page 320 as "too small."

Strategy #238
INVEST IN GOOD PERFORMING NO-LOAD FUNDS WITH TELEPHONE SWITCHING.

Choosing the right fund and fund family is easy once you know what you are looking for. All the information you need is in the Fund Family Fact Sheets in Appendix I. Following is a step-by-step process for choosing your mutual fund.

1. Choose for convenience a fund that is part of a family with at least one:
   A. Stock fund
   B. Bond fund
   C. Money market fund
2. Choose a no-load or low-load fund.
3. Choose a mutual fund that has a minimum required initial deposit within your investing limits.
4. Choose the right type of mutual fund for the current economy by using the Money Movement Strategy (Chapter 23).
5. Choose a fund that has assets of more than $25 million and less than $3 billion.
6. Choose a mutual fund based on its track record for the type of economy in which you intend to use it, not its five-year or ten-year total performance record.
7. If you want income, choose a fund that offers a periodic withdrawal plan. The minimum investment for periodic withdrawals is shown in the Fund

Family Fact Sheets, Appendix I. All types of funds have periodic with-drawal plans.

8. If your account is an IRA or Keogh, check the Fund Family Fact Sheets, Appendix I, for minimum required investment and yearly fee.

9. Choose a fund that qualifies for a Schwab Margin Account if you plan to use the margin account strategy (See Chapter 25).

There are 28 fund families that meet these criteria. They are listed in the "No-load Mutual Funds Recommended for Use With the Money Movement Strategy" chart on page 321. There are almost 75 mutual fund families that do not qualify under these criteria for one or more reasons and you will find these in the "Mutual Funds Not Recom-mended for Use With the Money Movement Strategy" list on page 320.

Strategy #239
USE THE FUND FAMILY FACT SHEETS TO CHOOSE THE BEST FUND AND FUND FAMILY FOR YOU.

From the Fund Family Fact Sheets, Appendix I, choose two or three mutual fund families that meet the above criteria and your own special needs and objectives. There is no one right choice, so don't waste time trying to find it.

If you're beginning with 10% of your paycheck, or opening a small account for children or grandchildren, the logical choice is the Twen-tieth Century family of funds which has no minimum investment. Twentieth Century is also a good choice for teaching your children to invest correctly.

If you are an aggressive investor, looking for maximum flexibility with aggressive growth or sector funds, your choice may be the Fidelity funds. Stein Roe and Scudder funds also tend to lean more toward the aggressive side.

Fidelity funds are not necessarily a first choice for beginners. If you were to call Fidelity and ask for a prospectus on every fund they offer, you would be reading for months. Fidelity has over a hundred different funds.

For conservative investors, Vanguard or Dreyfus funds might be ideal choices. How do you know if you're a conservative investor? Your money is probably in all the wrong places. Remain conservative, but remember there are two kinds of conservative investors: conserva-tive winners and conservative losers.

Call the mutual fund family's number and request a prospectus for each fund by name. If you don't receive it on a timely basis, call again. All of the recommended fund families have toll-free numbers (shown in the "recommended funds" list on page 321). If you live in the state in which a fund is located, use the in-state number.

The prospectus will tell you everything about the fund, including the investments owned. It is not necessary to read through all the required technical gibberish, but read carefully the instructions pertaining to investing, moving, and withdrawing your money. To save you countless hours of researching the mutual fund families, you will find all of this information in the Mutual Fund Family Fact Sheets (Appendix I). To open an account, complete and send the application with your check to the address listed in the prospectus. Specify by name the fund in which you want your money initially invested.

Although past performance is no guarantee of future performance, a mutual fund's track record should be an important factor in your choice. Use the performance histories in the Mutual Fund Family Fact Sheets, Appendix I along with the Prime Rate Direction Changes Chart on page 299 to compare fund performance. For instance, if you want to know what would have happened to the value of your shares in any fund during 1985 and 1986, first determine where your money should have been invested according to the Prime Rate History Chart on p. 296. Both were years of declining interest rates and a time for stocks, so you would check only stock fund performance. The Prime Rate fell from a high of 11% to a low of 9% during 1985 and to 7½% by August 1986. As you might expect from your understanding of the Money Movement Strategy, one of the greatest surges in stock market history began and lasted until October 1987. When the smoke cleared, recommended stock funds appreciated 40% in 1985, 30% in 1986, and about 3% in 1987, even after the stock market drop of October 19th.

Money market funds averaged less than 7%. Government securities funds, heavily pushed by brokers, averaged only 9% in 1985 and less in 1986, and lost 10% to 15% of principal in the first half of 1987 because of rising interest rates. International stock funds were big winners, averaging a total of 100% in 1985 and 1986 due to the declining value of the dollar. Bond mutual funds performed reasonably well during 1985 and 1986 with the Prime Rate dropping, but lost much of their gains in 1987 and 1988 when the Prime Rate began to rise.

Tracking Your Mutual Fund Investments

The current value in dollars of one share of a mutual fund is known as its *net asset value* per share (NAV). You have daily access to the net asset value of any fund through the financial pages of major newspapers. The NAV is listed under "Mutual Funds" near the stock market quotes. The mutual funds are listed by family. For example, all of Value Line's funds are listed together alphabetically under "V", all of the Fidelity funds are listed alphabetically under "F".

Look to the right of the fund name and you'll find two price columns. Load funds will have a price in both columns. The higher figure is the price at which you could purchase one share, the lower figure represents the price at which you could sell one share. The difference between the two prices represents the commission charged by loaded funds. If the commission is 8%, there will be an 8% difference between the two prices. No-load funds have no commissions and only one column will show a price. The other column will contain a dash (-) or "N.L." (no-load). (See page 325.)

If you purchased your shares at $10.00 each (100 shares for each $1,000 you invested), and the share price increased over the next six months to $12.00 per share, you have made a 20% profit on your money. When dividends are earned for one or more stocks in your stock fund, or interest is earned and reinvested in a bond fund, you will be credited with more shares unless you request a cash distribution. Make note of how many shares you receive when you first invest and check each month on your statement to see if you have been issued more shares. Even if it appears you have made only 10% on your money from the price change alone, you may discover that you now have 15% more shares and have actually earned 25% total return. The current net asset value per share (NAV) is not information enough to determine your profit or loss. Profits from capital gains distributions, dividends, and interest are usually given to investors as additional shares. On the distribution dates, the number of shares owned by each investor will increase, but if you look at NAV per share alone, your profit from distributions will not be reflected. To find the true value of your investment, multiply the number of shares shown on your last statement by the current NAV and compare to the amount of money you originally invested. On many statements, the total current value of your account is shown.

Each month, you will receive a complete statement showing your status in the fund at the end of the previous month. The statement is easy to use, easy to follow, and is one major benefit of investing through a mutual fund family.

A no-load mutual fund family investment is a must investment for everyone. Get yours started or reorganized today.

MUTUAL FUND FAMILIES *NOT* RECOMMENDED FOR USE WITH THE MONEY MOVEMENT STRATEGY

Mutual Fund Family	Reason
Bankers System Financial Services	Too small
Bartlett and Company	No stock or MM fund
Benham Management	No stock fund
Claremont Company	No money market fund
Decision Funds	Not open to all investors
Depositors Investment Trust	No money market
Dividend Funds	Too small
Federated Research	Closed-end trust
Fiduciary Management	No money market fund
Flex Fund	Poor overall performance
General Funds	Not open to all investors
Gentel Equity Mortgage	No money market fund
Gradison & Company	No bond funds
Heine Securities	No money market fund
Ivy	No money market fund
Janus Capital	No bond fund
Legg Mason	No bond fund
Lehman Management	No bond fund
Lepercq, de Neufize & Co.	Too small/No MM Fund
Loomis Gayles & Co.	S. fund closed to new investors
Horace Man Funds	Not open to all investors
M.A.S. Funds	Not open to all investors
Meritor Investor Co.	Family too new/too small
New Beginnings Fund	No money market fund
Nicholas Co., Inc.	No money market fund
North Star	No money market fund
Prudential-Bache	No stock fund
Quest Advisory Corp.	No money market fund
Reich & Tang	No bond fund
Reserve Management Co.	No bond fund
State Farm Investment Mgmt.	Not open to all investors
Sleadman Security Corp.	Too small/No MM fund
Unified Management Corp.	Too small
United Missouri Bank	Too small
United State Trust Co.	Too small
Weiss Peck & Greer	No money market fund

NO-LOAD MUTUAL FUNDS RECOMMENDED FOR USE WITH THE MONEY MOVEMENT STRATEGY

Name	# of Funds	Phone Toll-free	In state	Address	City	State	Zip
1. AARP	7	(800) 253-AARP		175 Federal St.	Boston	MA	02110
2. AMA ADVISORS	6	(800) 523-0864	(215) 825-0400	Sentry Parkway West	Bluebell	PE	19422
3. AXE HOUGHTON MGMNT.	4	(800) 431-1030	(914) 631-8131	400 Benedict Ave.	Terrytown	NY	10591
4. BABSON	9	(800) 821-5591	(816) 471-5200	2400 Pershing Rd.	Kansas City	MO	64108
5. BOSTON COMPANY	10	(800) 225-5267		One Boston Place	Boston	MA	02106
6. BULL AND BEAR	8	(800) 847-4200	(212) 363-1100	11 Hanover Square	New York	NY	10005
7. CALVERT	5	(800) 368-2748	(301) 951-4820	1700 Pennsylvania Ave.	Washington	DC	20006
8. COLUMBIA	6	(800) 547-1037	(503) 222-3600	PO Box 1350, 1301 S.W. 5th Ave.	Portland	OR	97207
9. DREYFUS	24	(800) 645-6561	(718) 895-1206	666 Old Country Rd.	Garden City	NY	11530
10. FIDELITY	88	(800) 544-6666	(617) 523-1919	82 Devonshire St.	Boston	MA	02109
11. FINANCIAL PROGRAMS	19	(800) 525-8085	(800) 525-9769	PO Box 2040	Denver	CO	80201
12. FOUNDERS	6	(800) 525-2420	(303) 394-4404	3033 East First Ave, Suite 810	Denver	CO	80206
13. GOV. INVESTORS TRUST	10	(800) 336-3063	(800) 572-2050	1655 No. Fort Myer Drive	Arlington	VA	22209
14. LEXINGTON	8	(800) 526-0057	(201) 845-7300	PO Box 1515	Saddle Brook	NJ	07662
15. MONEY MANAGEMENT ASS.	9	(800) 343-3355	(301) 657-1500	4922 Fairmont Ave.	Bethesda	MD	20814
16. NEUBERGER AND BERMAN	9	(800) 367-0776	(212) 850-8300	342 Madison Ave.	New York	NY	10173
17. NEWTON	3	(800) 247-7039	(800) 242-7229	2 Plaza East, Suite 150	Milwaukee	WI	53202
18. T. ROWE PRICE	23	(800) 638-5660	(301) 547-2308	11 E. Pratt St.	Baltimore	MD	21202
19. SAFECO	8	(800) 426-6730	(800) 562-6810	SAFECO Plaza	Seattle	WA	98105
20. SCUDDER	25	(800) 225-2470	(617) 482-3990	175 Federal St.	Boston	MA	02110
21. SELECTED FUNDS	4	(800) 621-7321	(800) 572-4437	230 W. Monroe, Suite 2800	Chicago	IL	60606
22. STEIN ROE	15	(800) 621-0615	(312) 368-7800	PO Box 1162	Chicago	IL	60690
23. STRONG	8	(800) 368-3863	(414) 765-0620	815 E. Mason St.	Milwaukee	WI	53202
24. TWENTIETH CENTURY	10	(800) 345-2021	(816) 531-5575	PO Box 200	Kansas City	MO	64141
25. UNITED SERVICE	10	(800) 824-4653	(512) 696-1234	PO Box 29467	San Antonio	TX	78229
26. USAA	10	(800) 531-8000	(512) 498-8000	USAA Building	San Antonio	TX	78288
27. VALUE LINE	10	(800) 223-0818	(212) 687-3965	711 Third Ave	New York	NY	10017
28. VANGUARD	39	(800) 622-7447	(215) 645-6000	PO Box 2600	Valley Forge	PA	19482

THE BULL MARKET TOP TEN NO-LOAD
AND LOW-LOAD FUNDS 8/82–8/87*

Fund	Type	NL/ LL**	5 yr. Growth %	Yrly Avg.
1. Vanguard World	International	NL	445	89
2. Fidelity Magellan	Agg. growth	LL	435	87
3. Loomis Sayles Capital	Agg. growth	NL	375	75
4. Scudder International	International	NL	360	72
5. Fidelity Select Health	Sector	LL	355	71
6. T. Rowe Price International	International	NL	340	68
7. Newberger Manhattan	Growth	NL	340	68
8. Twentieth Century Select	Growth	NL	335	67
9. Vanguard Windsor Federated	Growth & income	NL	330	66
10. Stock Trust	Growth & income	NL	320	64

* Stocks registered above average performance from 1982 to 1987 up to the sharp decline of October 19, 1987. Although using the Money Movement Strategy you would not have stayed strictly in stock funds, it is interesting to see how the best stock funds in the recommended mutual fund families performed during the period.

** During the five-year period, of the Top 20 best performing mutual funds, 13 were no-load (NL) and 7 were load funds (LL).

MUTUAL FUND PERFORMANCE 10 YEARS

Type of Fund	78	79	80	81	82	83	84	85	86	87
All										
Stock funds	12	30	34	−1	24	21	−2	27	15	2
Bond funds	1	3	3	5	29	10	11	20	14	2
Money market	7	11	13	17	13	9	10	8	6	6
Stock										
Aggressive growth	17	41	48	−5	25	20	−10	28	11	1
Growth	12	30	32	−1	23	22	1	27	13	2
Growth—income	7	20	27	1	23	23	6	26	15	1
Precious metals	9	152	57	−26	43	−1	−28	−7	37	31
International	23	17	38	−6	−1	33	−5	52	59	15
Bond										
Fixed income	1	3	3	5	29	10	11	20	14	2
Tax free	−3	−1	−12	−8	39	11	8	19	18	−1
Income	5	14	18	5	25	17	9	24	16	−3
Money Market										
General	7	11	13	17	13	9	10	8	6	6
Tax free	—	—	—	7	7	5	6	5	4	4

MUTUAL FUND RETURNS

(5 Year and 10 Year)

Type of Fund	Returns 5 Yr	10 Yr	10 Year Average
All			
Stock funds	92	191	19
Bond funds	55	96	10
Money market funds	37	98	10
Stock			
Aggressive growth	84	210	21
Growth	93	189	19
Growth—income	95	173	17
Precious metals	74	309	31
International	177	248	25
Bond			
Fixed income	55	96	10
Tax free	55	70	7
Income	80	147	15
Money Market			
General	37	98	10
Tax free	23	—	—

MUTUAL FUND TRACKING CHART

(Use this page to track mutual funds over the next few years.)

Type of Fund	'88	'89	'90	'91	'92	'93	'94	'95	'96	'97
All										
Stock funds	—	—	—	—	—	—	—	—	—	—
Bond funds	—	—	—	—	—	—	—	—	—	—
Money market	—	—	—	—	—	—	—	—	—	—
Stock										
Aggressive growth	—	—	—	—	—	—	—	—	—	—
Growth	—	—	—	—	—	—	—	—	—	—
Growth—income	—	—	—	—	—	—	—	—	—	—
Precious metals	—	—	—	—	—	—	—	—	—	—
International	—	—	—	—	—	—	—	—	—	—
Bond										
Fixed income	—	—	—	—	—	—	—	—	—	—
Tax free	—	—	—	—	—	—	—	—	—	—
Income	—	—	—	—	—	—	—	—	—	—
Money market										
General	—	—	—	—	—	—	—	—	—	—
Tax free	—	—	—	—	—	—	—	—	—	—

MUTUAL FUND CATEGORY CODES

Stock Funds | Code

	Code
Stock—growth	SG
Stock—aggressive growth	SA
Stock—sector	SS
Stock—precious metals	SP
Stock—growth and income	SI
Stock—equity income	SE
Stock—balanced	SB
Stock—option	SO
Stock—index	SX

Bond Funds

Bond—long-term corporate	BL
Bond—short/medium-terms corporate	BS
Bond—long-term tax exempt	BX
Bond—short/medium terms tax exempt	BY
Bond—government/GNMA	BG

Money Market Funds

Money market—regular	MM
Money market—tax exempt	MX
Money market—government	MG
Money market—insured	MI

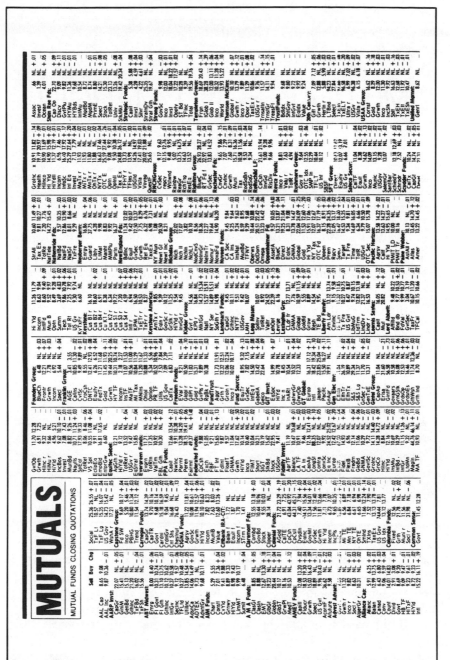

Chapter 25

MUTUAL FUND MARGIN ACCOUNTS

How I Made My Fortune?

It was really quite simple. I bought an apple for five cents, spent the evening polishing it, and sold it the next day for 10 cents. With this I bought two apples, spent the evening polishing them, and sold them for 20 cents. And so it went until I had amassed $1.60. It was then that my wife's father died and left us a million dollars.

Anonymous Capitalist

Objective: Use O.P.M. to increase the earning power of mutual funds.

Strategy #240
USE A MUTUAL FUND MARGIN ACCOUNT TO INCREASE YOUR INVESTMENT CAPITAL.

One of the most powerful uses of credit is to borrow money at a low interest rate and invest at a higher rate. The difference between the cost of the money and your investment return is your profit. Most businesses, investment fortunes, and even countries have been developed on borrowed money, and yet investing with borrowed money, or leverage, is still a foreign concept to most Americans. If your objective is to build wealth in the shortest possible time, with the least effort and greatest return, then investing borrowed money is a must.

A margin account is a line of credit with a broker or mutual fund that allows you to borrow money for investing or other purposes using your existing investments—stocks, bonds, or mutual fund shares—as collateral. The Securities and Exchange Commission recently lifted its long-standing ban on the use of mutual fund shares as collateral for margin accounts, and a new world of building bigger profits using borrowed money opened up to smart investors. A mutual fund margin account allows you to increase your mutual fund investment capital with your signature only. The important question is: How safe is a mutual fund margin account?

If shares of stocks, bonds or mutual funds decrease in value past the legal minimum margin requirement—the amount of collateral you must maintain on your loan—you will receive a "margin call" requiring you to put up more collateral. A mutual fund margin account is actually a safer method of using borrowed money to buy securities than a broker's margin account. The stock market drop of "Black Monday," October 19, 1987, is the best example. While the Dow plummeted 22% (508 points in one day) and many well respected stocks dropped 40% or more, the average, well managed, mutual fund dropped only 16% and still finished the year with a 3% gain.

In addition, a mutual fund must drop in price 50% before you get a margin call. The average stock mutual fund, during the worst stock market drop in history, dropped only 16%. The only exceptions were the giant mutual funds like Fidelity's Magellan with 11 billion dollars and no chance to move money fast enough. Magellan dropped 32%, but was already off of our recommended list more than a year before, when its assets exceeded 3 billion.

The interest rate you pay on the margin account is the broker's loan rate, which is only 1 or 2 percent above the Prime Rate. If the margin account interest rate is 10% and you are earning an average of 25% per year in your mutual fund family, your net profit is 15% after paying the interest on the borrowed money. Your interest is also tax deductible. Under tax reform, interest on money you borrow to invest is deductible up to the amount of your total investment income. You do not have to repay the principal or interest as long as the market value of your pledged shares is within the margin limits. Interest is generally charged to your account and compounded monthly.

Strategy #241

USE A MUTUAL FUND MARGIN ACCOUNT TO FREE UP CAPITAL FOR OTHER INVESTMENTS.

If you own mutual fund shares and wish to borrow money (margin your shares) to buy more shares, you can borrow 50% of the market value of your existing shares depending on S.E.C. margin requirements in effect at the time. For example, if you have 500 shares of a mutual fund whose NAV is $10 per share, the market value of your shares is $5000. You may borrow up to $2500 to buy more shares of any fund.

If you own shares of a mutual fund and want to use the shares as collateral for a personal loan for purposes other than buying investments, you may borrow up to the same 50% of the market value of your existing shares.

You cannot open a mutual fund margin account with every mutual fund, but you can through one of two discount brokerage firms that will allow you to margin shares of over 200 different mutual funds.

CHARLES SCHWAB (1-800-648-5300). Charles Schwab is a discount broker, a division of BankAmerica, and was the leader in creating mutual fund margin accounts. You may use the Schwab margin account to buy or margin any of the over 250 no-load mutual funds and fund families which Schwab represents. (See Charles Schwab Mutual Fund Margin Accounts at the end of the chapter.)

If you buy your original shares directly from a mutual fund, and wish a Schwab margin account, ask the fund for the Certificate of Ownership which you then give to Schwab for collateral. The Charles Schwab organization now has offices in most states and major cities.

FIDELITY BROKERAGE (1-800-544-6767). If you buy or own any of Fidelity's over 50 stock, bond, and money market funds, you may margin any of your shares through Fidelity. You may also margin shares of other mutual funds or fund families through Fidelity's nationwide discount brokerage service.

Here is how your profit picture develops with or without a mutual fund margin account.

Example 1:

You own or buy $10,000 worth of shares in a stock mutual fund. The margin allowance in effect is 50%. In January, using the Charles Schwab or Fidelity margin accounts, you buy an additional $5,000 worth of mutual fund shares. During the year, the fund shares increase 28%. What is your profit with and without the margin account if the broker's margin account interest is 10%?

With the Margin Account		Without Margin Account	
Original Shares	$10,000	Original Shares	$10,000
Financed Shares	5,000	Financed Shares	0
TOTAL INVESTMENT	$15,000	TOTAL INVESTMENT	$10,000
28% Increase	$ 4,200	28% Increase	$ 2,800
Minus 10% Interest	− 500	Interest	0
NET PROFIT	$ 3,700	NET PROFIT	$ 2,800
Profit Percentage	37%	Profit Percentage	28%

The profit in both cases is calculated on your original $10,000 cash investment. Using the mutual fund margin account, you have increased your net profit to 37% in a mutual fund that returned only 28%. You earned an additional $900 or 9% on your $10,000 investment.

Example 2:

Let's say you own the same $10,000 in shares during the same time period, but instead borrowed 50% of the value to buy a piece of real estate. You borrowed $5,000 and used the money for the down payment and closing on residential real estate property you purchased for $80,000. Tax savings from depreciation are calculated using the 27.5 year depreciation schedule for a person in the 28% bracket. Appreciation is calculated at 5% for the year. The appreciation of the mutual fund shares is 20%.

Mutual Fund Profits

Total Investment	$10,000
	× .20
20% Profit	$ 2,000

Real Estate Profits—$80,000 Property

Your Own Investment	0
Borrowed Money Invested	$5,000
Total Investment	$5,000
Tax Savings—Depreciation	$ 644
Appreciation (5%)	$4,000
Real Estate Profit	$4,644

Combined Profits and Costs

Profit—Mutual Fund	$2,000
Profit—Real Estate	$4,644
Minus Margin Interest (10%)	$− 500
Net Profit	$6,144
Profit Percentage	61%

By using borrowed money from your mutual fund margin account to buy a piece of real estate, you have achieved a 61% return on your original $10,000 capital in one year.

Mutual fund margin accounts should be considered by every investor wishing to maximize profits in the minimum amount of time. Used correctly they are one of the safest wealth-building accelerators.

CHARLES SCHWAB MUTUAL FUND MARGIN ACCOUNTS

AMA Advisors
Classic Growth
Income
Axe-Houghton Mgmt.
Stock Fund
Fund B Inc.
Income Fund Inc.
Money Market
Babson Funds
(not available)
Boston Co. Advisors
(not available)
Bull & Bear Group
Special Equity
Capital Growth
Equity Income
Golcorda Inv.
High Yield
Tax-Free Inc.
US Gov. Guar. Sec.
Dollar Res.
Calvert Group
Equity
Social Inv. MM
Columbia Funds
Special
Growth
Municipal Bond

Fixed Inc. Sec.
US Gov. Guar. Sec.
Daily Inc.
Dreyfus Corp.
Strategic Agg.
New Leaders
Growth Opp.
Third Century
Fund
Convertible Sec.
Mass TE Bond
NY Tax Exempt
CAL TE Bond
Insured TE Bond
Tax Exempt Bond
A Bond Plus
GNMA
Pk. Ave. NY TE Int.
Int. Tax Exempt
Pk. Ave. TE MM
CAL TE Money
Tax Exempt MM
Pacific Horizon MM
MM inst. Gov. Sec.
Pacific Horizon Gov.
Dollar Int'l.
Liquid Assets
Pacific Horizon

Financial Programs
Dyanamics
Industrial Fund
Industrial Inc.
Strategic Gold
Strategic Tech.
Strat. Health
Strat. Energy
Strat. Financial
Strat. Leisure
World of Tech.
Strat. Utilities
Strat. European
Strat. Pacific
Bond Sh. US Gov.
Bond Select Inc.
Tax Free Inc.
Bond Sh. High YLD.
Daily Inc. Shares
Tax Free Money
Founders
Frontier
Special
Growth
Blue Chip
Equity Income
Fidelity
OTC

Capital App.
Growth Co.
Magellan
Value
Contra Fund
Trend
Tr. Port Growth
Growth & Income
Fidelity Fund
Health Care Del.
Equity Inc.
Real Estate
Puritan
Balanced
Qualified Div.
Convertible Sec.
Tr. Equity Port. Inc.
Sel. Prec. Metals
Sel. Amer. Gold
Sel. Energy Serv.
Sel. Chemicals
Sel. Tech.
Sel. Software
Sel. Computers
Sel. Electronics
Sel. Telecomm.
Sel. BioTech.
Sel. Defense

CHARLES SCHWAB MUTUAL FUND MARGIN ACCOUNTS (*cont.*)

Sel. Automation
Sel. Health
Sel. Air Trans.
Sel. Trans.
Sel. Automotive
Sel. Cap. Goods
Sel. Ind. Mat.
Sel. Paper Forest
Sel. Housing
Sel. Food & Agr.
Sel. Bdcast & Media
Sel. Energy
Sel. Life & Ins.
Sel. Prop. Cas.
Sel. Broker
Sel. Financial
Sel. Reg. Banks
Sel. S&L
Sel. Leisure
Sel. Rest.
Sel. Retail
Sel. Elect. Util.
Sel. Utilities
Global Bond
NY TF Yld. Municip.
CAL Free HY
Ltd. Term Municip.
Penn Free HY Municip.

High Inc.
High Yield Municip.
Agg. Tax Free
Texas Tax Free
Mass Free Municip.
Minn. Tax Free
Mich Tax Free
Ohio Tax Free
Munic. Bond
NY Tax Free Ins.
CAL Ins. TF
Insured Tax Free
Short Term
GNMA
Short Term TF
Flexible Bond
Mort. Sec.
Thrift Trust
Mass TF Money
NY TF Money
CAL TF Money

Lexington Mgmnt. Corp.
Growth
Research
Gold Fund
GNMA Inc.
Gov. Inv. Trust
(not available)

Money Mgmt. Assoc.
(not available)
Newton
Growth
Income
Newberger
Guardian Mutual
T. Rowe Price
New Horizons
New Amer.
New Era
Growth Stock
Growth Inc.
Equity Inc.
GNMA
Tax Free Inc.
High Yield
Int'l Bond
New Income
Tax Free Short Int.
Select Funds
Special Shares
Amer. Shares
Srong Corneliuson Cap.
Opportunity
Total Return
Investment
Income

Safeco Mgmt Co.
Growth
Equity
Income
CAL TF Inc.
Muni Bond
Stein, Roe & Farnham
Special
Farn. Cap. Opp.
Farn. Stock
Total Return
Scudder
Development
Cap. Growth
Int'l
Global
Growth & Inc.
NY TF
Managed Municip.
Tax Free 1993
Target General 1990
Target Gen. 1987
Target US Gov 1990
Target US Gov 1987
Twentieth Century
(not available)
USAA Inv. Mgmt.
(not available)

332

United Services Advisors
Lo Cap.
Growth
Good & Bad Time
Income
Gold Shares
Prospector
New Prospect
Tax Free
GNMA

Value Line Inc.
Lev. Growth
Spec. Sit.
Fund
Income
Convertible
US Gov. Sec.
TE MM

Vanguard
Naess & Thomas
Explorer
Explorer II
WL Morgan
Word US
Index Trust
Windsor
Windsor II

Trustees Commingled
Star
Word Int.
Qualified Div. I
Qualified Div. II
Qualified Div. III
Fixed Inv. HI yld.
Bond Market
Fixed Inc. GNMA
Fixed Inc. US Treas.
Fixed Inc. Short Term
Spec. Gold
Spec. Tech.
Spec. Health

Spec. Service
Spec. Energy
Muni Hi. Yld.
Penn. Ins. FF
NY Ins. TF
CAL Ins. TF
Municip. lg-Term
Municip. lg-Term
Municip. Inter. Term
Municip. Short Term
Wellesley Inc.
Wellington
Convertible Sec.
Fixed Inc. Inv. Grade

333

Chapter 26

IRA AND KEOGH
INVESTMENT
SUPERSTRATEGIES

*A banker is a fellow who lends you his umbrella when the
sun is shining and wants it back the minute it rains.*

Mark Twain
Writer
1897

**Objective: Earn over 20% per year in nontraditional IRA and Keogh
investments.**

In this chapter I will show some nontraditional investments for your
retirement money that will build your tax-free wealth two to four times
faster than a bank's IRA/Keogh accounts.

```
                        Strategy #242
            LOCATE AN INDEPENDENT TRUSTEE FOR
                      YOUR IRA/KEOGH.
```

The maximum flexibility in an IRA/Keogh is achieved with an independent trustee, a custodian that will allow you to invest your account
in anything legal. The only IRA/Keogh investments specifically excluded by law are:

- Precious metals other than U.S. gold and silver coins.
- Any investment that requires the use of your IRA/Keogh money as collateral for a loan—i.e., rental properties.
- A business in which you have more than a 5% interest.
- Collectibles—i.e., art, stamps.

Almost anything else is fair game.
An independent trustee can be found at:

BANK TRUST DEPARTMENTS—Any bank trust department can act as trustee for your account and allow you to put your money in any of the investments suggested later in this chapter. You may have to check several banks before you find one that will work for you. The bank will charge you a fee per transaction of about $50 plus any legal fees. Any bank trust department, by law, can legally act as your trustee; some will, some won't.

MAJOR FINANCIAL PLANNING FIRMS—Many big financial planning firms are now getting one of their associates registered as an independent trustee. Fees are about the same as bank trust departments.

Here are two suggestions:

First Trust Corporation
444 Sherman St.
Denver, CO 80203
1-800-525-2124
1-800-233-0407 (CO)

Retirement Accounts, Inc.
P.O. Box 3017
Winter Park, FL 32790
1-800-325-4352
1-800-432-1268 (FL)
    Available only through financial planners.

Some of the investment options suggested below, like mutual funds and land lease partnerships come with a built-in trustee; to use others, you must open your account with an independent trustee.

Strategy #243
INVEST YOUR IRA/KEOGH IN MUTUAL FUND FAMILIES.

Using a combination of a mutual fund family and the Money Movement Strategy in Chapter 23, you can average 20% or more per year by moving your money among stock, bond and money market funds.

When you open an IRA or Keogh in a mutual fund family, you automatically get a self-directed account. All mutual fund families have IRA/Keogh options and the low yearly trustees fees range from $5 to about $30. The use of the Money Movement Strategy, discussed in Chapters 23 and 24, will guide you in choosing the mutual fund family that's right for you and your IRA/Keogh.

Strategy #244
INVEST YOUR IRA/KEOGH IN LAND LEASE LIMITED PARTNERSHIPS.

Investing in a land lease limited partnership can produce high income and capital appreciation for your IRA/Keogh. Here's how it works. A limited partnership buys a piece of prime commercial real estate using investors' IRA or Keogh money. The investors own the real estate and then lease the land to a developer to build an office building, shopping center, apartment building, or bank. The owners of the building make lease payments to the land lease partnership representing usually 8% to 10% of the investment each year. The income to the partnership is not taxed because of the IRA/Keogh status of the invested capital. When the partnership sells the property, the investors get a share of the profits.

There are no taxes on the profitable sale of the investment as long as the profits are redeposited in the tax-sheltered account. The total return can be as high as 15% to 20% per year, all tax sheltered. The profits and original investment can be used to buy a new piece of land and the process begun again.

For more information on land lease partnerships for your IRA/Keogh, you can contact:

Delta Capital Corp.
520 Crown Oak Centre Drive
Longwood, FL 32750
(407) 331-8004

Strategy #245
INVEST YOUR IRA/KEOGH IN VACANT LAND OR LOTS.

If you have your eye on a piece of investment land or maybe a lot in your neighborhood, you can use your self-directed IRA/Keogh money to purchase the property. You may hold the property as long as you wish and when you sell, even at a huge profit, your profit is tax sheltered by your IRA or Keogh. You must, however, pay cash or obtain a loan which does not use your IRA/Keogh money as collateral. If your IRA/Keogh is used as collateral for a loan or mortgage, the transaction is counted as a withdrawal, triggering both income taxes and, if you're under 59½, the 10% early withdrawal penalty.

Strategy #246
INVEST YOUR IRA/KEOGH IN REAL ESTATE OPTIONS ON LAND.

You can invest your IRA or Keogh in a highly leveraged short-term real estate option on land and enjoy huge profits without current taxes. A real estate option is a contract which gives you the exclusive right to purchase a piece of property at a specified price anytime within a specified term ranging from one month to several years. For the privilege, you make an option deposit of 1% to 10% based on your ability to negotiate. If you buy the property, your option money is applied to the purchase price. If you choose not to buy, the seller keeps the property and your option money. The major benefit of the option strategy is the almost outrageous profits you can generate with relatively small risk. Only your option deposit is at risk; you are not obligated to buy the property.

In 1982, my friend Don opened his $2,000 IRA at a local bank using the bank trust department as an independent trustee. He then put a 60-day option on a $1,000,000, prime 50-acre piece of land near Disney World in Orlando, Florida, where he lives. The option deposit money used was the $2,000 from his IRA. The trustee for his IRA handled the investment. In other words, Don tied up the 50-acre property for $2,000 for a period of 60 days. If he bought the property, the $2,000 would apply to the purchase and his guaranteed purchase price was $1,000,000. If Don backed out for any reason, all he would lose would be his $2,000 option deposit.

Don never intended to purchase the land. Instead, during the 60-day option period, he assembled a group of investors. Per Don's instructions, investors put together a $400,000 down payment to purchase the property, not for the $1,000,000 option price, but for $1,200,000, the appraised value of the land. At closing, $200,000 of the investors' money was paid to the seller as a down payment with an $800,000 note for the balance. The balance of $200,000 of the down payment was Don's profit on the transaction.

Within 60 days, Don had taken an option on a $1,000,000 piece of property for a $2,000 cash outlay and sold the option to the investors for a $200,000 cash profit. Best of all, because the $2,000 option money came out of Don's IRA, the $200,000 profit was deposited in his IRA tax free until he withdraws the money. The moral of this story: ALTHOUGH YOUR IRA CONTRIBUTION EACH YEAR IS LIMITED TO $2,000, THERE IS NO LIMIT TO THE TAX SHELTERED PROFITS YOU CAN EARN.

Strategy #247
INVEST YOUR IRA/KEOGH IN REAL ESTATE OPTIONS ON RESIDENTIAL RENTAL PROPERTIES.

Another way to use real estate options to your advantage is through a two- to three-year option on a single family home, duplex, or condo. For beginners, a longer-term real estate option on a residential property is much easier and less risky than a short-term option on a piece of land.

Using the Sunday paper or a realtor, locate an owner who is having trouble selling his property and would be willing to give you a two-year, but preferably a three-year, option to purchase his property at today's price and lease you the property at fair market rent. The owners, even if unable to sell now, would then have the income to make their mortgage payments. You will be surprised how many options you can put together in a short period of time, because an option solves an owner's short-term problem—cash flow. Your cash flow will be neutral or positive because the owner must lease you the property at fair market rent, the same rent you can get when you sublease to a tenant.

There are two documents required: the option contract giving you the right to purchase the property, and the lease contract giving you the right to use the property during the option period. Insert a sublease clause in the lease agreement specifying that you may rent the property to a third person. Tell the owner you will agree to be responsible for all minor maintenance and will act as manager of the property in consideration for your right to sublease. Of course, if you intend to live in the property, there is no need for the sublease clause.

Have the trustee of your self-directed IRA/Keogh account handle the investment of your funds. You should be able to option a $70,000 to $120,000 property for no more than a $1,000 to $2,000 option deposit. You can usually get the owner to accept the option money as the first and last month's rent, further reducing your cash outlay.

During the option period, you have two choices: buy the property yourself or sell the property at a profit to someone else. If your option deposit is $1,000 and three years later you sell your option to someone else at a $10,000 profit, you have made a 1000% return on your money. Take your $10,000 nontaxed profit and place a three-year option on ten more properties at $1,000 each. If the profit was the same $10,000 after the next three years, you will have nontaxed profits totalling $110,000 after six years, or a return of 11,000% on your orginal $1,000 investment and all tax sheltered.

A retirement account is not required when using option strategies, but does provide tax shelter for your big cash profits.

Chapter 27

SELF-DIRECTED ANNUITIES

Go around asking a lot of damn-fool questions. Only through curiosity can we discover opportunities.

Clarence Birdseye
Inventor
(1886–1956)

Objective: Combine the 20% earning power of the Money Movement Strategy with America's best tax shelter.

One of the best, safest, and easiest to use tax shelters remaining after tax reform, and an ideal investment for the Money Movement Strategy, is a self-directed annuity, which is actually a tax-sheltered mutual fund family.

Think of an annuity as an umbrella over your investment, protecting your profits from taxes. As long as you leave your money invested in any annuity, your money compounds tax free. When you withdraw part or all of your money, you add the profits but not the principal to your taxable income for that year.

The annuity tax shelters we are about to cover are nonqualified annuities, meaning that they are not employment related. (See Chapter 12 for employment-related annuities.)

Strategy #248
USE A SELF-DIRECTED ANNUITY TO EARN 20% PER YEAR WITH NO COMMISSIONS OR TAXES.

A self-directed annuity is a tax-sheltered mutual fund family in which you have a choice of investments. There are 1,100 annuities that have only one investment choice, a fixed interest account, but there are only a few self-directed annuities. All of the self-directed annuities offer you the same three investment choices—stock, bond, and money market mutual funds. Because of the tax-shelter feature, you can move your money from one fund to another, with no tax liability. You may also, in most annuities, withdraw up to 10% of your money each year for whatever purpose you wish without penalties or commissions, although you would be liable for any income taxes.

The annuity was originally a retirement program offered by the insurance companies with its origins in the pre-IRA days when most people retired broke. The insurance companies claimed that no income taxes should be paid on the interest earned until the money was withdrawn. There was no basis in tax law for that position, but because of the awesome political power of the insurance companies, Congress allowed the tax-deferred status by not specifically denying it. Congress finally decided to tackle the issue in the Economic Recovery Act of the early 80's, which not only legitimized the annuity concept, but in the process, made self-directed annuities one of the best, safest, and most powerful tax shelters in America.

Few brokers or financial planners will recommend self-directed annuities because of the low commissions (or none at all) paid on the initial investment. Instead, financial salesmen recommend single premium life insurance, a lesser investment that pays high commissions.

The first rule of annuity investments is to use them last, only after you have contributed the legal maximum into your IRA, Keogh, or other tax-deferred, employment-related retirement programs. The money you invest in an IRA or Keogh, remember, is tax deferred. In an annuity, only the investment earnings are tax deferred; you have already paid taxes on the money you invest. (Teachers' and state employees' job-related tax-sheltered annuities are an exception.)

All of the self-directed annuities listed at the end of this chapter give you three or more choices for investing your money. When you open your account, tell the company which of their investments you have chosen; never let them tell you. Once you open your account, you manage your money using the Money Movement Strategy with an expectation of averaging 20% currently tax free.

You may contribute to some annuities until you are 90. Unlike most retirement plans which require you to stop contributing when you are 70½, you can contribute to some annuities for an additional 20 years.

Under tax reform, you must begin withdrawing about 10% of your money each year after you reach age 70½. When you withdraw, you will be given two options: take the money out in lump sums or allow the account to annuitize, which means the company will guarantee to pay you a monthly income for a specified number of years or even for the rest of your life. Under tax reform, there is a penalty of 10% on all amounts withdrawn from an annuity before age 59½. The penalty is overcome in three to five years from the tax-free compounding, so the penalty should not be a deterrent to using an annuity even as a short-term investment.

Strategy #249
NEVER ANNUITIZE YOUR ANNUITY ACCOUNT.

Annuitizing means you agree to accept periodic payments over the balance of your lifetime. Sounds appealing until you realize the payment schedule is weighted in favor of the company. Always withdraw your money as required so no part of it becomes the property of the insurance company. You may withdraw in a lump sum anytime or use the minimum per year withdrawal requirements when you reach age 70½ as defined by law.

Strategy #250
USE THE TAX-FREE ROLLOVER RULES TO MOVE YOUR ANNUITY TO ANOTHER COMPANY.

What if you become dissatisfied with one company's annuity program and wish to move to another? You may move your money to another company using the tax-free rollover rules without any tax penalty. You would, however, be subject to any withdrawal penalty imposed by the insurance company for early withdrawal. You may move your money from investment to investment within a self-directed annuity without becoming liable for any taxes and, in most instances, without commissions.

Strategy #251
MAKE YOUR ANNUITY ACCOUNT WITHDRAWALS TAX FREE BY CREATING "EQUIVALENT" TAX DEDUCTIONS.

One annuity benefit was lost in the Economic Recovery Act: treating the first money you withdrew from your annuity as nontaxable principal instead of taxable interest. The rules now require that when you make a withdrawal, the first money withdrawn is treated as taxable profits instead of nontaxable principal. Your strategy is clear. Any year you withdraw money from your annuity, create an equal amount of tax deductions using any tax strategies you choose. One will offset the other and, in essence, your withdrawal will be tax free.

How to Invest in a Self-Directed Annuity

Investing in an annuity is as simple as opening a bank account. Call several companies that offer self-directed annuities, using the telephone numbers listed in the Self-Directed Annuities Planning Chart at the end of this chapter. Ask for a prospectus. Check the Planning Chart or the prospectus to determine your different options for investments. Be certain you have all the options necessary for using the money movement strategy: stock funds, bond funds, and a money market fund (or fixed-rate investment). Determine what procedure—letter or phone call—is required to move your money from one fund to another, and how often you are allowed to change investments. Complete the application for the annuity you choose, and mail it along with your check. Use the list of questions on page 345 to evaluate any annuity.

Strategy #252
INVEST IN AN ANNUITY ONLY WITH FUNDS YOU PLAN TO LEAVE INVESTED FOR FIVE YEARS OR LONGER.

Annuities are commission free if you leave your money invested long enough. To discourage you from moving your money in and out, most annuities have a decreasing load or commission. If you withdraw your money the first year, the maximum commission of 5–9% would be deducted. The commissions usually decrease by 1 percent each year until the withdrawal charge reaches zero. Make certain there is no commission or front-end load when you invest.

Strategy #253
USE YOUR SELF-DIRECTED ANNUITY AS AN ESTATE PLANNING TOOL.

The major goal in planning your estate is to pass to your heirs as much of your wealth as possible by not letting the government and the attorneys get their hands on it. Currently, you can distribute, undisturbed by the tax collector, any amount of an estate to a surviving spouse or up to $600,000 in assets to other beneficiaries. Annuities are great estate-planning tools because they avoid probate. Annuities, like insurance contracts, allow you to nominate a beneficiary who would receive your annuity money without probate or attorney's fees. It is, however, counted as part of the estate for estate tax purposes.

Strategy #254
USE A SELF-DIRECTED ANNUITY TO BEAT THE KIDDIE TAX FOR CHILDREN UNDER 14.

If you are a parent or grandparent, one of your biggest concerns about tax reform should be the low-taxed investment earnings limit for children under 14. When income from investments totals over $1,000, the child automatically pays taxes on the excess at the parents' tax rate, even though the child files a separate return. That means investment income for children can be taxed at over 30% instead of the child's rate of 0 to 15%. A child would pay in taxes more than double what an adult with the same income would pay.

The new rules make it difficult to create a college investment fund or to move some of your wealth to the lower tax bracket of children and grandchildren. If a child is under 14 and earns more than $1,000 from an investment account in one year, the excess is taxed at the parents' tax rate.

A self-directed annuity is one solution to this problem. By law, there are no current taxes due on the earnings from an annuity so the earnings from even a child's college fund investment compound tax free until the money is withdrawn.

Tax protect all of a child's income over $1,000 by using a self-directed annuity. When the child reaches college age and starts withdrawing the money, there is a 10% penalty. The tax-free compounding makes up for the penalty in about three years. If the child's annuity is self-directed using the Money Movement Strategy (Chapter 23), 10% is only six months of the average 20% one year return.

Strategy #255

ROLLOVER YOUR CASH VALUE LIFE INSURANCE, TAX-FREE, INTO A SELF-DIRECTED ANNUITY.

Questions to Ask When Choosing Self-Directed Annuities:

Q: What is the minimum investment?

A: The minimum investment required must be within your investment capital range. Some annuities require a larger lump sum, others will accept monthly installments. Check the Self-Directed Annuity Planning Chart at the end of this chapter.

Q: Can I add money any time I wish? What minimum?

A: It is advantageous to be able to add money to an existing account, like you do in a bank savings account. Again, check the chart.

Q: Is the annuity insured or registered in the state of New York?

A: Insurance protects you against bankruptcy or fraud of the issuing company. If the annuity is registered in the state of New York, the New York Insurance Commission has done the work of being certain the annuity is insured and you are protected no matter where you live. Otherwise check the A.M. Best Rating.

Q: How often can I move my money within the annuity and what is the procedure?

A: Some annuities have telephone switching; in others you must put your request in writing. Some annuities may limit the number of times you can move your money each year, others will not. Although you will not be moving your money often, flexibility is always on your side. Check the chart.

Q: What is the load or commission charged?

A: Your objective is to find an annuity with no commission when you invest, no commission when you move money within the annuity, and a yearly decreasing commission if you withdraw. Look for a maximum 6% withdrawal commission decreasing 1% each year to zero. In addition, annuities level charges against the account including a fixed charge and a percentage amount similar to the mutual fund management fee. The total charges should be no more than 1.5% per year. Check the chart.

Q: What different investments are available with the annuity?

A: To use the Money Movement Strategy, you need a minimum of a stock fund, a bond fund, and a money market or fixed rate fund. Check the chart.

Q: Can I withdraw 10% a year during the early years with no commissions?

A: Most annuities allow the penalty-free withdrawal of 10% a year. The money you withdraw is added to your income for the year. In that way, part of your earnings can be withdrawn for income or other purposes while the rest remains tax sheltered.

If you have been investing your money in low-interest, highly taxed bank certificates of deposit or you are considering single-premium life insurance, a self-directed annuity is a far better alternative.

Self-directed annuities are a must investment when your desire is to create safe, tax-sheltered investments for yourself, your children, or your grandchildren.

SELF-DIRECTED ANNUITIES PLANNING CHART

Definitions and Description of Terms Used

GENERAL INFORMATION

Company—The name of the company which issues the annuity.

Annuity Name—The name of the annuity plan offered by the company.

Issue Ages to—The last year in which you can deposit money into the annuity.

Minimum Initial Deposit—The minimum investment required to open the account.

SP = Single Premium, one-time investment required to open account. Install = The amount required to open the account, if you intend to add monthly installments to your investment.

Additional Deposits—The minimum amount you can add to your account. "None" means no additional investment can be made.

Retirement Plans Available—The retirement plans that can be used with the annuity, including IRA, Keogh, 403(b), 401(k), 457.

Statements—How often you receive a statement of your account.

States not approved—Those states in which the company is not licensed to sell.

FEES

Mortality Fees/Expenses—Represents the percentage per year charged against your account balance for expenses.

Load—The percentage charged against your account as a load or commission. The average is .5%.

Administrative Fees—A flat charge assessed against your account for administrative expenses. The average is $30 per year.

Transfer Charge—The amount you are charged, if any, to move your money from one investment to another.

SAFETY

Year Founded—The year the company began doing business.

Assets—The amount of assets in billions managed by the company.

A.M. Best Rating—The safety rating assigned by the A.M. Best Company. All companies in the charts are acceptable.

FLEXIBILITY

Investment Options—The different mutual funds or accounts in which you can invest your money.

Transfer—When, how often, and how much of your money you can move from investment to investment.

Written or Phone—The method(s) you can use to move your money from one investment to another. "Written" requires a letter or special form; "phone" requires only a phone call and gives maximum convenience.

PERFORMANCE

The percent growth for the year shown of each type of investment offered. Where more than one investment is included in a category, the average is shown.

SELF-DIRECTED ANNUITIES PLANNING CHART

Company	Mass Mutual	Guardian	Anchor Nat'l	Keystone	Security Benefit
Annuity Name	Flex Annuity V	Value Guard II	Am. Pathway II	Key Flex	Vari-Flex
General Info					
Issue—Ages To	75	75	85	80	75
Min. Initial Deposit	$25,000	$3,000	$1,500	$5,000	$2,500 SP/$500 Install
Additional Deposits	None	$100 Min.	$25 Min.	0	$25
Retiremt Plans Avail.	All	All	All Except 457	All	All
Statements	Quarterly	Annual	Quarterly	Quarterly	Monthly
States Not Approved	NY	ID, ME, VT, W.V.	NY	NY	NY
Fees					
Mortality Expenses	1.24%	1.5%	1.3%	1.2%	1.2%
Investment Fees	0.50%	0.6%	0.6%	0.7%	0.5%
Admin. Fees	$30	$35	$30	$30	$30
Transfer Charges	0	0	0	0	1st free, $10 after
Safety					
Year Founded	1851	1860	1965	1957	1892
Assets	$18 Billion	$4 Billion	$2 Billion	$3 Billion	$3 Billion
A.M. Best Rating	A + Superior	A + Superior	A Excellent	A + Superior	A + Superior

Flexibility					
Investment Options	Equity (SG)	Centurian (SG)	Growth (SG)	Growth Stock (SG)	Growth (SG)
	Managed Bond (BL)	Stock (SG)	Growth/Income (SI)	Aggr. Growth (SA)	Growth/Income (SI)
	Blend (SI)	Bond (BL)	High Yld Bond (BL)	Managed Assets (SG)	High Grade Bond (BL)
	Money Mkt (MM)	Money Mkt (MM)	Gov't AAA (BG)	High Yld Bond (BL)	High Yld (BL)
	Fixed Interest (FI)	Strategic (AG)	Money Mkt (MM)	Mort. Securities (BG)	Money Mkt (MM)
		Asset Mgt Trust (MM)	Fixed Interest (FI)	Money Mkt (MM)	Fixed Interest (FI)
				Fixed Interest (FI)	
Transfer	V = 1 per 90 days; F = 25% per year	V = 1 per 30 days	V = 6 times per year; F = 25% per year; $500 min.	5 per year	V = 1 per 30 days; F = once per year
Written or Phone	Written	Either	Written	Either	Written

Performance	85	86	87	85	86	87	85	86	87	85	86	87	85	86	87
Stock	29%	18%	1%	32%	17%	-1%	19%	29%	7%	15%	9%	-8%	21%	5%	5%
Bond	18%	13%	1%	22%	15%	-1%	24%	18%	4%	23%	7%	5%	15%	3%	7%
Stock/Bond	25%	17%	2%	32%	17%	-4%	36%	20%	-1%	27%	18%	2%	23%	18%	12%
Money Mkt	7%	5%	5%	N/A	6%	5%	6%	5%	5%	6%	5%	8%	6%	5%	5%
Fixed	—	—	8%	—	—	—	—	—	9%	—	—	8%	—	—	8%

Liquidity					
Back-End Load	5-4-3-2-1	5-5-4-3-2-1	5% Rolling/7 years	5-4-3-2-1	8-7-6-5-4-3-2-1
Charged Against	Total	Deposits	Total	Deposits	Deposits
Yrly No-Fee Withdr.	10% of Acct	10% of Deposits	10% of Deposits	All Appreciation	10% of Deposits
Phone Number	(413) 788-8411	(800) 221-3253	(602) 955-0300	(617) 338-3703	(913) 295-3000

SELF-DIRECTED ANNUITIES PLANNING CHART

Company	Pruco Life	Kemper Invest	Great West	Great American	Aetna	Nationwide
Annuity Name	Discov. Plus	Advantage II	Maxim	Uni-Flex	Acct B/C	Best of Amer II
General Info						
Issue—Ages To	76	100	80	60	90	78
Min. Initial Deposit	$10,000	$2,500	$50	$10,000	$10,000 SP/$1,000 install	$1,500
Additional Deposits	None	$500	$50	$5,000	$1,000 or $85 mo. install	$10
Retirem't Plans Avail.	All	All	All	All	All	All
Statements	Annual	Quarterly	Quarterly	Quarterly	Quarterly	Quarterly
States Not Approved	NY	NY	NY, RI	—	—	—
Fees						
Mortality Expenses	.9%	1.3%	1.4%	1.0%	1.5%	1.36%
Investment Fees	.4%	0.6%	0.4%	0	0	0
Admin. Fees	$35	$25	$35	$20	SP = 0/F = $20	$30
Transfer Charges	0	0	0	0	$10	0
Safety						
Year Founded	1873	1947	1891	1937	1863	1929
Assets	$104 Billion	$4 Billion	$14 Billion	$1 Billion	$70 Billion	$18 Billion
A.M. Best Rating	A + Superior	A Excellent	A + Superior	A + Superior	A + Superior	A + Superior

Flexibility

Investment Options	Common Stock (SG) Bond (BL) High Yld (BL) Aggr. Mgt. Flex (AG) Cons. Mgt. Flex (SI) Real Estate (RE) Money Mkt (MM) Fixed Interest (FI)			Equity Income (SI) Total Return (SB) Money Mkt (MM) Fixed Interest (FI)			Growth (SG) Total Return (SB) Bond (BL) Gov't Guarantee (BG) Money Mkt (MM)			Stock (SG) Bond (BL) Money Mkt (MM) Fixed Interest (FI)			Variable (SG) Income Shares (BL) Encore (SG) Fixed Interest (FI)			Stock (SG) Gov't Bond (BG) Money Mkt (MM) Fixed Income (FI)		
Transfer	V = 4 per year; F = 25% per year			Min. $500			1 per 30 days; Min. $500			V = 1 per 90 days; F = 20% per 6 mos.			Anytime			V = Anytime All; F = 25% year					
Written or Phone	Either			Either			Either			Written			Either			Either					
Performance	85	86	87	85	86	87	85	86	87	85	86	87	85	86	87	85	86	87			
Stock	32%	16%	2%	24%	8%	.5%	25%	12%	4%	25%	9%	3%	30%	17%	4%	32%	19%	12%			
Bond	19%	14%	5%	20%	16%	5%	20%	15%	1%	16%	12%	1%	21%	13%	3%	15%	14%	4%			
Stock/Bond	26%	15%	-2%	27%	14%	-.5%	12%	9%	3%	—	—	—	—	—	4%	—	—	—			
Money Mkt	8%	7%	7%	7%	5%	5%	6%	5%	5%	7%	6%	6%	7%	6%	5%	7%	5%	4%			
Fixed	—	—	9%	—	—	8%	—	—	—	—	—	9%	—	—	8%	—	—	8%			
Liquidity																					
Back-End Load	9-8-7-6-5-4			6-5-4-3-2-1			5-5-5-5-5			8-7-6-5-4-3-0			5-4-3-2-2			5% (8) Rolling Deposits					
Charged Against	Total			Total			Deposits			Total			Total			Deposits					
Yrly No-Fee Withdr.	10% of Deposits			10% of Account			100% Appreciation			10% of Account			None			5% of Deposits					
Phone Number	(602) 264-7892			(312) 781-1121			(303) 889-3000			(214) 953-7111			(203) 273-4326			(614) 249-5134					

LIQUIDITY

Back-end load—The year-by-year decreasing commission charged if you withdraw your money.

Example: 5-4-3-2-1 and means that 5% is charged if you withdraw your money the first year and decreases by one percentage point each year until it reaches zero in the sixth year and after.

Charged against—The amount of your account against which the back-end load is charged. "Deposits" means that the load is charged against your deposits but not the appreciation. "Total" means the load is charged against your total withdrawal or account balance.

Chapter 28

DISCOUNTED MORTGAGES

A broker is a man who runs your fortune into a shoestring.

Alexander Woollcott
Wit's End
(1887–1943)

Objective: Earn 30% per year guaranteed and secured.

Strategy #256
**INVEST IN DISCOUNTED MORTGAGES FOR A
GUARANTEED 30% RETURN.**

What if there was an investment that paid a guaranteed interest rate of 30% each year, in which your principal was 100% secured? There is such an investment, but you'll never find it at brokerage firms, banks, or financial planners. The investment is discounted mortgages—usually second mortgages—that you locate, negotiate, and purchase yourself.

Occasionally, an investment opportunity arises, created by unusual economic conditions. During 1979 to 1984, the years of super high interest rates, homeowners who wanted to sell found there were not many willing buyers. High interest rates meant that the buyer's payments would be too high if a new mortgage was obtained. "Creative financing" replaced location, as the most important words in real estate. In order to entice a purchaser and help that buyer avoid the costs of refinancing, the seller would allow the buyer to assume the existing low interest first mortgage, and then take back a second mortgage for a large part of the down payment. Second mortgages were most often used when the first mortgage was a fully assumable nonqualifying FHA

353

or VA mortgage. There were thousands of properties in every area sold in this manner.

Sellers normally do not like mortgages; they want cash, and as a result, tire quickly of owning a mortgage that is paid in periodic payments. The seller's desire to get cash out of a mortgage creates an unequalled investment opportunity.

Strategy #257

WHEN MAKING AN OFFER FOR A MORTGAGE, BEGIN BY OFFERING NO MORE THAN 60% OF FACE VALUE.

Because there is no ready-made market for mortgages, sellers are forced to sell mortgages at a discount of 30% to 50% from the face value, and the price is determined by agreement between the seller and buyer of the mortgage. When making a cash offer for a mortgage, begin by offering 60% of the face value. You may either stick to your 60% offer or negotiate up to 75%, but usually not more. You'll be surprised by how many good mortgages you can buy for 60 cents on the dollar.

HOW YOU MAKE YOUR MONEY

If a seller sold his home two years ago and took back a $10,000 interest-only 12% second mortgage for seven years, and you purchase the mortgage for 60% of face value, you pay $6,000 for the mortgage. When the mortgage term is up in five years, you receive the entire face value, $10,000, which is $4,000 more than the $6,000 you invested. Until maturity, the interest of 12% is paid to you. The 12% interest, remember, is based on the $10,000 face value of the mortgage and amounts to $1,200 each year. Since you have only $6,000 invested, but still receive the full $1,200 interest annually, your return is 20%. Your total annualized return from the interest plus the discount is 30%.

Here is an example of how your return is earned and computed when you buy a discounted mortgage:

Face value	$10,000
Purchase price	$ 6,000
Balance of term	five years
Original interest rate	12%

Return on Discounted Mortgage as a Percentage

Your interest rate	20.00%
Earnings from discount (annualized)	10.75%
Annual return	30.75%

Return on Discounted Mortgage in Dollars

Interest ($1,200 year × 5 years)	$ 6,000
Discount	4,000
Total profit	$10,000

In this example, you would have earned $10,000 during five years on a $6,000 investment or about 30% per year—guaranteed.

Once you get the hang of it, you'll wonder why every investor isn't looking for and buying discounted mortgages.

You won't buy discounted mortgages at financial institutions, nor will you normally find them advertised in the newspaper. Where do you look?

Strategy #258
USE THE COURTHOUSE AS A DISCOUNTED MORTGAGE SOURCE.

The easiest method of locating unlimited numbers of mortgages, which you can buy at a discount, is at the county courthouse.

Spend a couple of hours in the real estate records room, where you'll find all real estate transactions in date order on microfilm. Sit down at a microfilm reader and, beginning with 1986 and working backwards locate second mortgages on residential properties. You'll find dozens of them, ranging from $2,000 to $50,000. All the information you need is normally on the screen.

The mortgagor—Person to whom the money is owed.
The mortgagee—Person responsible for the payments.
The address of the property—so you can evaluate it.
The amount of the mortgage.
The terms of the mortgage—payments, interest, due date.

In many states, second mortgages are referred to as deeds of trust or second deeds of trust. You will find the people who work in the county courthouses are usually very helpful, and they will show you how to work the equipment and find the records you are looking for.

Make a list of 10 or 20 that look promising and are within your investment capital range. Remember, your goal is to buy a mortgage at 30% to 40% less than face value. That is what is meant by "discounted."

When you get home, let your fingers do the walking. Look up the telephone numbers of the mortgagors. If you can't find one, call the mortgagee and ask for the phone number of the person to whom they make their second mortgage payment.

Call the mortgagor and use these words to open the conversation:
"Hi, Mrs. Smith?"
"Yes."
"My name is [your name] and I understand you are holding a mortgage for $[amount] on the property located at [address]. Is that correct?"
"Yes, why do you want to know?"
"Well, Mrs. Smith, I'm an investor and I would like to buy your mortgage for cash. Does that interest you?"

Four out of five will say "yes." You then set up an appointment and negotiate the discount amount by beginning your offer at about 60 cents on the dollar. For a mortgage with a $10,000 balance, you would offer $6,000 cash. The longer the mortgage has to run, the more receptive the mortgageholder will be.

Why would a person sell a mortgage to you at a discount? Because most Americans are such poor money managers, they need cash now far more than they need payments over time, even if the payments will produce more income. You'll find that one out of three mortgageholders will sell to you at a 30% to 40% discount.

Strategy #259
RUN NEWSPAPER ADS IN SEARCH OF MORTGAGES YOU CAN BUY AT A DISCOUNT.

You can spend a few tax deductible dollars running ads to search for people who want cash for their mortgages. The ads can be placed in the classified section or as a larger display ad with such captions as:

"Cash for your mortgage."

"I buy mortgages."

"Investor wants to buy first and second mortgages."

"Want to sell your second mortgage?"

Most who have tried the newspaper route find it a long, slow, but eventually successful process, generating one to five calls per week and one or two mortgages a month.

Strategy #260
MAKE FRIENDS WITH REAL ESTATE PROFESSIONALS WHO WILL CALL YOU WHEN THEY LEARN OF A MORTGAGE FOR SALE.

You can cultivate a mortgage garden of real estate agents and brokers. Since there is no ready-made market for discounted mortgages, the first person a mortgage holder would think to call is someone in the real estate business. By making friends with several real estate professionals and letting them know of your interest in purchasing discounted mortgages, you'll discover a never-ending supply.

Many years ago, when I was first getting into investment real estate, I enrolled in an adult night school course called "Real Estate Financing." The people I met in that one class, mostly real estate professionals, were worth thousands of dollars to me. From friendly conversations that ensued on class breaks, I bought several properties at a bargain, found a property manager, a handyman for inexpensive repairs, got several new clients for my printing and publishing companies, and bought several discounted mortgages.

Strategy #261

WHEN BUYING DISCOUNTED MORTGAGES, EXPECT THE BEST, ARM YOURSELF FOR THE WORST, AND TALK TO YOUR ATTORNEY FIRST.

Your outside risk when buying discounted mortgages is that the mortgagee won't make the payments and you may have to foreclose on the property to protect your investment—not a problem if you plan effectively.

Before you buy a discounted mortgage, have a chat with a competent real estate attorney who is familiar with the real estate laws and practices in your area. Develop a contingency plan for how he will handle collection if the mortgagee is late with the payments. If the mortgage is in default over one day, your attorney should serve immediate notice that you intend to foreclose. You will seldom have a real problem if you act immediately. As a holder of a mortgage, never get into the welfare business by allowing other people's problems to influence you into letting them be late with their payments. No matter how you feel emotionally, the only 100% sure method of protecting yourself and collecting every dime is to act, act immediately, and act in the strongest way possible. If you want to help people financially, do it through a contribution to your favorite charity, never by mixing business and charity; you'll always lose. Once you learn to act immediately and consistently, the mortgagee will find a way to make the payments on time because he knows you mean business.

If, in a rare case, the property does go to foreclosure because payments either weren't made on the first mortgage or on your second mortgage, you and your attorney will want to choose one of three options:

1. Bring the payments current on the first mortgage to prevent the first mortgage holder from foreclosing while you are handling the situation. When you buy a mortgage, always send a certified letter to the first mortgage holder stating that you are the holder of a second mortgage and want to be notified anytime a payment is late. Although not required by law, the first mortgage holder will generally comply with your request.
2. Convince the mortgagee he should immediately deed the property to you using a Quit Claim Deed to avoid the embarrassment and ordeal of a fore-

closure, and to preserve his credit standing. This alternative is often the best.

3. If the property goes to auction, bid an amount equal to the existing first mortgage plus the amount of your second mortgage. If someone outbids you, they will have to pay every cent owed to you. If you win the bid with the highest offer, you would have to put 10% of the bid into escrow and have about 30 days to produce the balance. Check the rules for your area. Your bank will help you with some short-term financing while you refinance or sell the property to get your money back. In this case, the worst that can happen is that you have purchased a property worth at a minimum 20% more than you bid at foreclosure.

Strategy #262
BUY DISCOUNTED MORTGAGES WITH NO MORE THAN AN 80% LOAN-TO-VALUE RATIO.

Every commercial mortgage company has an upper limit on how much money it will loan on a first or second mortgage. The formula for calculating the maximum loan amount is known as the loan-to-value (L.T.V.) ratio. You will want to adopt your own L.T.V. I recommend you use 80% as your loan-to-value ratio, as I do.

The L.T.V. is the maximum percentage of the market value of a property you would be willing to finance. The maximum amount you would pay for a mortgage should be no more than 80% of the market value of the property, less any other mortgage amounts. If a property is appraised at $100,000, the sum of all mortgages including yours would have to total less than $80,000 or you would not want to purchase the mortgage. If the first mortgage is $60,000 and the mortgage you are purchasing is $10,000, the total of the mortgage amounts would be $70,000. This would be perfectly acceptable because $70,000 is less than the $80,000, 80% maximum. If the mortgage on the property is $75,000 and the mortgage you wanted to buy has a face value of $15,000, the loan-to-value ratio of 80% or $80,000 would be exceeded and you would not purchase the mortgage.

Strategy #263

CHECK THE CREDIT HISTORY OF THE MORTGAGEE BEFORE BUYING A DISCOUNTED MORTGAGE.

Carefully check the credit rating and credit history of the mortgagee, the person who will be responsible for making the payments. Good credit habits are likely to continue; poor credit habits on the part of the mortgagee may come back to haunt you. Since the mortgagee has been making payments to the mortgage seller for some time, obtain proof of the timeliness of the payments. Mortgages that have a payment history are called "seasoned" mortgages.

If you have over $15,000 of total investment capital, discounted mortgages should be a serious consideration. You will find mortgages available between $2,000 and $50,000. Begin immediately by going through the motions of locating possible mortgage purchases even if you don't intend to buy one just now. You'll get a feel for the process without being required to make a commitment. Even if you grow to love discounted second mortgages as an income and wealth producer, invest no more than 30% to 50% of your capital in mortgages, since your investment is tied up from two to ten years.

The final step in purchasing a mortgage is to have your attorney handle the mortgage transfer and record the mortgage at the courthouse, giving you a priority claim against most other subsequent loans or mortgages.

Discounted mortgages are one of the best investment choices for reinvesting equity you have borrowed from your home (See Chapter 6).

The high guaranteed and secured investment return of discounted mortgages certainly qualifies them for our list of the "ten best investments."

Chapter 29

TAX LIEN CERTIFICATES

The art of getting rich is found not in saving, but in being at the right spot at the right time.

Ralph Waldo Emerson
The Conduct of Life
1860

Objective: Earn 15% to 50% government-guaranteed interest.

Strategy #264
INVEST IN TAX LIEN CERTIFICATES FOR SAFETY AND MAXIMUM INTEREST.

The highest government-guaranteed interest paid on any investment is a tax lien certificate. There are 500 government agencies, usually county taxing authorities, that issue tax lien certificates with government-guaranteed interest of 15% to 50%. A tax lien can be any amount from $20 to $50,000.

A tax lien certificate is an encumbrance on real estate placed by a government taxing authority and sold to an investor. Here's how the investment opportunity is created. Let's say a neighbor of yours moved away, rented out the house, but hasn't paid the property taxes. After one notice or less the county puts a lien on the property for the amount of the unpaid taxes. The lien, recorded at the courthouse, means the property cannot be mortgaged, sold, or otherwise disposed of by the owner until the back taxes are paid.

The lien gives the county some control over the property but not any money. More and more counties are selling tax lien certificates to compensate for unpaid taxes at courthouse auctions. You, as an interested investor, go to the court house on auction days to bid on the certifi-cates. The bid, or investment, is the amount of the unpaid taxes.

The state sets the maximum interest rate. In Florida, where I live, the interest rate is 18% per year; in other states like Michigan, it is as high as 50% per year. Since the lien will not be taken off the property until the taxes plus interest are paid, your investment is virtually government-guaranteed.

Many tax liens are sold at the maximum guaranteed rate; others go for a lesser rate. Why? Because the hope of the bidders is that the owner won't pay the back taxes, and the investor will end up with a valuable property instead of the interest. The winning bid in most states is the lowest interest rate; in other states the interest rate remains constant but the amount of the investment is bid up.

What happens if you own a tax lien certificate and the owner never pays the taxes? That is the investor's dream. In some states, after three delinquent tax years, the property will either be sold at public auction to the highest bidder, or in many states the holder of the tax lien certificate simply applies for and receives a deed to the property. In the case of an auction, you show up at the auction and bid the amount of your investment (the unpaid taxes) plus all interest due you. If you are outbid, the high bidder must, by law, pay you the amount of your investment plus all unpaid taxes. If you are the high bidder, you get the title to the property. All previous mortgages and liens are wiped out except federal tax liens, if any. The appraised value of the property could be as much as two to one hundred times your investment.

Strategy #265
BUY A PIECE OF REAL ESTATE AT A HUGE DISCOUNT AT A TAX LIEN AUCTION.

At a tax lien auction, the property itself and not a tax certificate is sold. Maybe you'd like to buy a lot in your neighborhood or a bargain prop-erty you can fix up and live in or rent out. The courthouse steps should be your bargain basement shopping area. In most states, properties with delinquent real-estate taxes are eventually sold at auction at the courthouse. When you win a bid, you will usually have to put 10% down and you'll have 0 to 30 days to come up with the balance. If you don't have the money, it is relatively easy to get a bank, mortgage company or an investor to underwrite your liened property purchases. Have the bank mortgage company or investor commit to giving you the money within the 30-day period before you bid.

Strategy #266
EXAMINE THE PROPERTY BEFORE YOU BID AT A TAX LIEN AUCTION.

Always know what you're bidding on at any auction. Before you go to a tax lien or liened property sale, examine the property, neighborhood, and courthouse records. Buy liens or properties only in appreciating areas. The best price on the wrong property brings more headaches than profits.

Check the courthouse records for any mortgages, IRS liens, or other encumbrances. The only lien that is senior to a tax lien is an IRS lien. The recorded mortgages on a property will give you an indication of whom you will be bidding against. Normally any mortgage holder will appear at the auction to bid an amount to cover their mortgage plus any senior liens or mortgages. That way, they will either be paid off by a higher bidder or get title to the property to secure their investment. If the mortgage holder does not show up, and the winning bid is less than the amount of the mortgages, the mortgage holders lose all or part of their investment. The taxing authority will publish a complete description of the properties that will be sold at the next auction. Some areas will put you on a mailing list, others will only put notices in legal papers.

Strategy #267
BID NO MORE THAN 70% OF THE MARKET VALUE AT A LIENED PROPERTY AUCTION.

Often you can buy a piece of land or even an improved property at a tax lien auction for as little as $.10 on the dollar.

In no case would you want to bid more than 70% of the value of the property so you could resell quickly at a profit if that were your objective. Your choices when you win a bid are to hold the property as an investment, sell it for a quick profit, or in the case of a home, to live in the property. The choice is yours.

Recently I saw a $500,000 property in North Carolina go at a tax sale for $9,500. A property in New York was bought at an auction for $950 in unpaid taxes and sold six years later for 1.3 million! Although these incredible profits are the rare examples, you can see the upside potential without the downside risk.

Tax lien certificates give you the excitement of gambling with no chance of losing. To help you get started, Appendix II lists the addresses and phone numbers of government agencies that sell tax lien certificates or tax liened properties. Call or write to them for the auction dates. Specific information for 30 states is also included.

By calling your local taxing authority, you can obtain the local rules and procedures governing the sale of tax lien certificates or tax liened properties in your area.

Some states do not sell tax lien certificates, which may necessitate your doing some traveling to nearby states in order to bid. If so, your travel expenses are deductible as a miscellaneous investment expense.

TAX LIENED PROPERTIES

Checklist for Investors

1. Check your local county or taxing authority for where and when the auctions are held.
2. If you are interested in tax certificates instead of bidding on the properties, find the closest state where certificates are offered.
3. Find out if you can get on a mailing list, or if not, where and when the properties are advertised.
4. Determine which properties you are interested in. Verify that the property is actually where it is supposed to be and is in the condition described. Most taxing authorities make plot maps available at a small charge.
5. Check with the taxing authority to determine the total amount of taxes, interest, penalties, and costs due, not just those listed in the minimum bid.
6. Check the Department of Records to be certain there are no federal liens, such as an IRS lien against the property.
7. Find out if you must preregister and put up a deposit on properties on which you intend to bid.
8. Find out the procedure and costs involved in getting title to a property you win in an auction.
9. Ascertain the minimum possible bid.

10. Decide in advance your maximum bid so you don't get carried away with enthusiasm.
11. Find out how your deed or certificate should be recorded.
12. In the case of a tax lien certificate, determine the notices and procedures required, if the owner never pays the taxes.

Example of the rules for investing in tax lien certificates. Each state and county has slightly different rules.

SEMINOLE COUNTY, FLORIDA, TAX CERTIFICATE SALE RULES

1. The 1988 Tax Certificate sale will begin in Room W120 and will continue on a day to day basis, until all certificates are sold. There will be a one hour recess for lunch from 12:00 until 1:00 P.M. ·
2. Bidding is for the rate of interest only and may commence at a maximum rate of 18% and bid inversely to a low of zero percent. Face amount of certificate is: tax plus cost, as advertised. The advertised figure is the amount due for each certificate purchased.
3. Bidders are asked to wait until the Auctioneer has finished calling an item before bidding.
4. The first bid recognized by the Auctioneer is the official bid.
5. A reasonable deposit of 10% of the bid amount (to be determined by the Tax Collector) is required at the close of your bid.
6. Purchase of a tax certificate in no way permits the certificate holder to enter the property or intimidate the landowner. The landowner has a period of two years from the date the tax became delinquent to redeem the tax certificate. The redemption is done through the Office of the Tax Collector only.
7. In the event an error is discovered in the tax certificate, it may be cancelled or corrected by Authority of the Department of Revenue. In this case 8% simple interest will be paid, except as revised by law.
8. When a tax certificate is redeemed and the interest earned on the tax certificate is less than five percent of the face amount, then a mandatory charge of five percent shall be levied upon the tax certificate. The person redeeming the tax certificate shall pay the interest rate bid or the mandatory charge, whichever is greater. This shall apply to all tax certificates except those with an interest rate bid of zero percent. Considering the exceptions mentioned, the interest rate bid shall prevail for the life of the tax certificate. Redemption is made through the Tax Collector's Office only.
9. The life of a tax certificate is seven (7) years.
10. Tax certificates must represent taxes which are two years delinquent before a tax deed application may be made. Taxes become delinquent on April 1st each year, as per Florida Statutes.

11. The name given at the sale is the name that will appear on the tax certificate. All redemption notices will be mailed to the address given at the sale. Subsequent changes of address must be filed with the Office of the Tax Collector only.

12. Tax certificates will be sent by certified mail after the sale is balanced and certified. Interest will be earned from the date of the tax certificate sale.

13. All tax certificates which are transferred, must be recorded in the Office of the Tax Collector. There will be $2.00 fee for transfers.

14. For further information and assignment of a bidder number, contact the Office of the Tax Collector at (407) 321-1130 ext. 638 or 641.

Chapter 30

POWERFUL INVESTING—
HOW TO STRUCTURE
YOUR INVESTMENT PLAN

He is poor whose expenses exceed his income.

Jean de La Bruyere
(1645–1696)

Objective: Choose the investments that will accomplish your goals in the shortest time.

Strategy #268

**CHOOSE FROM THE TEN BEST INVESTMENTS FOR
MAXIMUM GROWTH, MAXIMUM TAX SHELTER, OR
MAXIMUM INCOME.**

Other than safety, there are only four different objectives of a powerful investment plan. Maximum growth, maximum tax shelter, and maximum income are the three financial objectives; convenience is the fourth.

In all good investment plans safety should be the key factor and is created through your choice of investments and your knowledge of investment strategies. Maximum growth is the result of reinvesting the profits you are earning while paying no commissions or taxes or through the use of borrowed money. In the early years of your investment plan maximum growth is usually the main objective; in later

367

years you will want to concentrate on maximizing your income. Tax shelter is always a part of any good investment plan. In structuring your investment plan, you must first determine which of the four objectives are most important to you: growth, income, tax shelter, or convenience. Safety is built into all the investment strategies we have discussed. If your objective is income, liquidity or the ability to take money out of your investment is also important.

The "Ten Best Investments Rating Chart" (page 369) rates each of our investments using the numbers 0 to 3. Zero means "none at all," such as "no tax shelter"; 3 means maximum, such as "maximum growth." All the investments listed are very safe when used as directed. Growth means an increase in the value of your original investment. Income means that income is available should you choose to take it, or in some cases like the mutual fund, the income could be reinvested. In summary, here are the reasons why these investments are the "ten best":

An **ASSET MANAGEMENT ACCOUNT** should be used as your primary checking account offering convenience, ease of record keeping and "legal float."

A **NO-LOAD MUTUAL FUND FAMILY** account can be used as a highly liquid, high return investment. If growth is your objective, pump 10% of all of your net job income into a mutual fund family and reinvest the earnings. If income is your objective, you may set up your mutual fund account to send you a predetermined amount of income each month, regardless of the monthly earnings of the account. The first $5,000 of investment capital should be invested in mutual funds.

The **MUTUAL FUND MARGIN ACCOUNT** is a leveraged growth tool and can be used to the maximum by all aggressive investors, and to a lesser degree by conservative investors.

SELF-DIRECTED ANNUITIES combine high return with tax shelter, but the money should be kept invested for five years or more to eliminate commissions. All conservative and retired investors with $10,000 or more of capital should use annuities as part of their plan. After age 59½, there is no 10% withdrawal penalty. Aggressive investors with $50,000 or less will opt instead for the high returns and income from the mutual fund margin accounts and discounted mortgages, and, if adjusted gross income is less than $100,000, build tax shelter using personally held investment real estate. With over $50,000 of investment capital, annuities become a must for all investors.

If you qualify for an **IRA/KEOGH, 401(k)** Salary Deferral Plan or a **403(b)** Public Employees Tax Sheltered Annuity, put every dime you

TEN BEST INVESTMENTS RATING CHART

	Growth	Income	Tax Shelter	Conven.	Safety[6]	Liquidity
Asset Management Account	0	1	0	3	3	3
No-Load Mutual Fund Family	3	3	1	2	3	3
Mutual Fund Margin Account[1]	3	3	1	2	2	2
Self-Directed Annuity	3	0	3	2	3	1
Self-Directed IRA/ KEOGH	3	0	3	3	3	1
401(k) Deferred Compensation	3	0	3	3	3	1
403(b) Tax- Sheltered Annuity	3	0	3	3	3	1
Discounted Mortgage[2]	3	3	2	1	3	0
Your Own Home[3]	3	0	3	2	3	1
Rental Real Estate Residential[4]	3	0	3	1	2	1
Tax Lien Certificate Liened Properties[5]	3	3	0	1	3	0

Notes:
1. Tax shelter in a mutual fund is the nontaxable appreciation of stocks or bonds held but not sold by the fund. Tax shelter in a mutual fund margin account is the deductible interest on the loan.
2. Growth in a discounted mortgage represents the difference in purchase at a discount and the amount of payoff when the mortgage matures. Tax shelter in a discounted mortgage is the discounted amount on which the taxes are deferred until maturity. The income is taxable in the year received.
3. The tax shelter on your own home includes deductible taxes and interest as well as the tax-deferred appreciation.
4. Rental real estate should be purchased for growth and tax shelter, not income. The income objective is neutral cash flow. The tax shelter on residential rental real estate includes depreciation and deductible expenses.
5. The growth in a tax lien certificate is represented by the opportunity to purchase property based on the taxes due if the owner does not redeem the property. The income from a liened property is the guaranteed interest paid when the property is redeemed by the original owner. There is no income on a liened property purchase.
6. The high degree of safety indicated is based on the use of the strategies covered in this book.

can afford into the plan, even if you have to borrow money to live on. Job-related retirement programs, when used correctly, will automatically make you rich over time.

DISCOUNTED MORTGAGES should be used by everyone with more than $10,000 investment capital who desires maximum income, 20% to 30%, at a guaranteed interest rate.

Your own **HOME** is the one real estate investment you should always own because of both tax shelter and growth. You are renting mortgage money instead of renting a property.

INVESTMENT REAL ESTATE is a tax shelter alternative for those who have an adjusted gross income of under $100,000. Real estate is a great investment for those who have more time than money.

At the end of this chapter, you will find the "Investment Planning Guide," step-by-step charts for allocating any amount of investment capital from $1,000 to $250,000. The "Investment Planning Guide" is a balanced approach to growth, income, tax shelter, and safety, all in one plan which can be easily modified based on your personal financial objectives.

Your objective is to structure your investment plan using a combination of the "10 best investments" to earn over 20% per year. The wealth building power of a 20% return is shown in the "20% Investment Growth Table" (on page 371).

Part A shows how much you will have in 5–20 years with monthly deposits of 10% out of your paycheck.

Part B shows the results with yearly deposits as you would make in an IRA/Keogh account.

Part C shows the results you will achieve with lump sum investments like those in self-directed annuities or an IRA rollover.

No plan will work unless you do. Everything you need in order to profit from investing has been included in the chapters of Part III. From now on, procrastination, not ignorance, is your only enemy.

20% INVESTMENT GROWTH TABLE

Part A

Mthly Deposits	5 Yrs	10 Yrs	15 Yrs	20 Yrs
$ 100	$ 10,000	$ 38,000	$ 114,000	$ 318,000
200	21,000	77,000	228,000	636,000
300	31,000	115,000	342,000	954,000
400	41,000	153,000	456,000	1,272,000
500	52,000	192,000	570,000	1,590,000
1,000	104,000	383,000	1,139,000	3,181,000

Part B

Yrly Deposits	5 Yrs	10 Yrs	15 Yrs	20 Yrs
$ 1,000	$ 9,000	$ 31,000	$ 86,000	$ 224,000
2,000	18,000	62,000	173,000	448,000
3,000	27,000	93,000	259,000	672,000
4,000	36,000	125,000	346,000	896,000
5,000	45,000	156,000	432,000	1,120,000
10,000	89,000	312,000	864,000	2,240,000

Part C

Lump Sum Dep	5 Yrs	10 Yrs	15 Yrs	20 Yrs
$ 10,000	$ 25,000	$ 62,000	$ 154,000	$ 383,000
20,000	50,000	124,000	308,000	767,000
30,000	75,000	186,000	462,000	1,150,000
40,000	100,000	248,000	616,000	1,534,000
50,000	124,000	310,000	770,000	1,917,000
100,000	249,000	619,000	1,541,000	3,834,000

INVESTMENT PLANNING GUIDE
(INVESTMENT CAPITAL = $1,000)

	Amount Invested	New or Borrowed Capital	Invest. Return	Current Income	Deferred Income	Tax Shelter
Asset Management	100	—	10%	10	—	—
Mutual Fund	900	—	20%	180	—	—
Margin Account	—	900	10%[3]	90	—	—
Retirement Program	—	2,000[1]	20%	—	400	2,400
Personal Residence	—	80,000[2]	6%	—	4,800	4,800
TOTALS	1,000	82,900		280	5,200	7,200

One-Year Investment Results

Current Income = $ 280   28%

Deferred Income = $4,800   480%

Total Income = $5,080   508%

Tax Savings[4] = $2,160

TOTAL RETURN $7,240

With $1,000 of your own money and $2,000 borrowed for an IRA plus the purchase of your own home you have created an investment return of $5,080 per year and, including the $2,160 tax savings, a total one-year return of $7,240. Based on $1,000 original investment and the use of borrowed money, your total investment return is 28%. When you include real estate appreciation, your total return is 508%!

Notes:
1. The $2,000 is borrowed money for an IRA or payroll deduction for a company retirement plan.
2. The personal residence down payment and financing is made using a combination of assumable mortgages or borrowed money.
3. The return on the margin account is after interest is deducted.
4. Tax savings based on $7,200 of tax shelter is based on 30% federal and state tax bracket.

INVESTMENT PLANNING GUIDE
(INVESTMENT CAPITAL = $5,000)

	Amount Invested	New or Borrowed Capital	Invest. Return	Current Income	Deferred Income	Tax Shelter
Asset Management	500	—	10%	50	—	—
Mutual Fund	2,000	—	20%	400	—	—
Margin Account	—	2,000	10%[3]	200	—	—
Retirement Program	—	3,000[1]	20%	—	600	3,600
Personal Residence	—	80,000[2]	6%	—	4,800	4,800
Invest. Real Estate	2,500	80,000	6%	—	4,800	7,200
TOTALS	5,000	165,000		650	10,200	15,600

One-Year Investment Results

Current Income = $ 650   13%

Deferred Income = $10,200   204%

Total Income = $10,850   217%

Tax Savings[4] = $ 4,680

TOTAL RETURN $15,530

With $5,000 of your own money and $3,000 borrowed or payroll deducted for your retirement plan, $2,000 from a mutual fund margin account and your own home, you have created an investment return of $10,850 (217%) plus $4,680 in tax savings.

Notes:
1. The $3,000 is borrowed money for an IRA or payroll deduction for a company retirement plan.
2. The personal residence down payment and financing is made using a combination of assumable mortgages or borrowed money.
3. The return on the margin account is after interest is deducted.
4. Tax savings based on $15,600 of tax shelter is based on 30% federal and state tax bracket.

INVESTMENT PLANNING GUIDE
(INVESTMENT CAPITAL = $10,000)

	Amount Invested	New or Borrowed Capital	Invest. Return	Current Income	Deferred Income	Tax Shelter
Asset Management	1,000	—	10%	100	—	—
Mutual Fund	4,000	—	20%	800	—	—
Margin Account	—	4,000	10%[3]	400	—	—
Retirement Program	—	4,000[1]	20%	—	800	4,800
Personal Residence	—	100,000[2]	6%	—	6,000	6,000
Invest. Real Estate	5,000	100,000	6%	—	6,000	9,000
TOTALS	10,000	208,000		1,300	12,800	19,800

One-Year Investment Results

Current Income = $ 1,300   13%

Deferred Income = $12,800   128%

Total Income = $14,100   141%

Tax Savings[4] = $ 5,940

TOTAL RETURN $20,040

With $10,000 of your own money and $4,000 borrowed or payroll deducted for your retirement plan, $4,000 from a mutual fund margin account and your own home, you have created an investment return of $14,100 (141%) plus $5,940 in tax savings.

Notes:
1. The $4,000 is borrowed money for an IRA or payroll deduction for a company retirement plan.
2. The personal residence down payment and financing is made using a combination of assumable mortgages or borrowed money.
3. The return on the margin account is after interest is deducted.
4. Tax savings based on $19,800 of tax shelter is based on 30% federal and state tax bracket.

INVESTMENT PLANNING GUIDE
(INVESTMENT CAPITAL = $25,000)

	Amount Invested	New or Borrowed Capital	Invest. Return	Current Income	Deferred Income	Tax Shelter
Asset Management	1,000	—	10%	100	—	—
Mutual Fund	10,000	—	20%	2,000	—	—
Margin Account	—	10,000	10%[3]	1,000	—	—
Self-Directed Annuity	5,000	—	20%	—	1,000	1,000
Retirement Program	—	7,000[1]	20%	—	1,400	8,400
Discounted Mortg.	4,000	—	30%	800	400	400
Personal Residence	—	150,000[2]	6%	—	6,000	6,000
Invest. Real Estate	5,000	100,000	6%	—	6,000	9,000
TOTALS	25,000	267,000		3,900	14,800	24,800

One-Year Investment Results

Current Income = $ 3,900   16%

Deferred Income = $14,800   59%

Total Income = $18,700   75%

Tax Savings[4] = $ 7,200

TOTAL RETURN $25,900

With $25,000 of your own money, $7,000 payroll deduction for your retirement plan, $10,000 from a mutual fund margin account, your own home and the purchase of $100,000 of investment real estate, you have created an investment return of $18,700, (75%) plus $7,200 in tax savings.

Notes:
1. The $7,000 is borrowed money for an IRA or payroll deduction for a company retirement plan.
2. The personal residence is already owned.
3. The return on the margin account is after interest is deducted.
4. Tax savings based on $24,800 of tax shelter is based on 30% federal and state tax bracket.

INVESTMENT PLANNING GUIDE
(INVESTMENT CAPITAL = $50,000)

	Amount Invested	New or Borrowed Capital	Invest. Return	Current Income	Deferred Income	Tax Shelter
Asset Management	2,000	—	10%	200	—	—
Mutual Fund	15,000	—	20%	3,750	—	—
Margin Account	—	15,000	10%[3]	2,250	—	—
Annuity	10,000	—	20%	—	2,000	2,000
Retirement Program	—	7,000[1]	20%	—	1,400	8,400
Discounted Mortg.	8,000	—	30%	1,600	800	800
Tax Lien						
Certificates	5,000	—	20%	—	1,000	1,000
Personal Residence	—	150,000[2]	6%	—	9,000	9,000
Invest. Real Estate	10,000	150,000	6%	—	9,000	13,500
TOTALS	50,000	322,000		7,800	23,200	34,700

One-Year Investment Results

Current Income = $ 7,800　　16%

Deferred Income = $23,200　　46%

Total Income = $31,000　　62%

Tax Savings[4] = $10,410

TOTAL RETURN　　$41,410

With $50,000 of your own money, $7,000 payroll deduction for your retirement plan, $15,000 from a mutual fund margin account, your own home, and the purchase of $150,000 of investment real estate, you have created an investment return of $31,000, plus $10,410 in tax savings.

Notes:
1. The $7,000 is borrowed money for an IRA or payroll deduction for a company retirement plan.
2. The personal residence is already owned.
3. The return on the margin account is after interest is deducted.
4. Tax savings based on $34,700 of tax shelter is based on 30% federal and state tax bracket.

INVESTMENT PLANNING GUIDE
(INVESTMENT CAPITAL = $100,000)

	Amount Invested	New or Borrowed Capital	Invest. Return	Current Income	Deferred Income	Tax Shelter
Asset Management	3,000	—	10%	300	—	—
Mutual Fund	20,000	—	20%	4,000	—	—
Margin Account	—	20,000	10%[3]	2,000	—	—
Annuity	20,000	—	20%	—	4,000	4,000
Retirement Program	—	7,000[1]	20%	—	1,400	8,400
Discounted Mortg.	22,000	—	30%	4,400	2,200	2,200
Tax Lien Certificates	15,000	—	20%	—	3,000	3,000
Personal Residence	—	200,000[2]	6%	—	12,000	12,000
Ltd. Partnership	20,000	—	14%	1,400	1,400	1,400
TOTALS	100,000	227,000		12,100	24,000	31,000

One-Year Investment Results

Current Income = $12,100   12%

Deferred Income = $24,000   24%

Total Income = $36,100   36%

Tax Savings[4] = $ 9,300

TOTAL RETURN $45,400

Notes:
1. The $7,000 is borrowed money for an IRA or payroll deduction for a company retirement plan.
2. The personal residence is already owned.
3. The return on the margin account is after interest is deducted.
4. Tax savings based on $31,100 of tax shelter is based on 30% federal and state tax bracket.

INVESTMENT PLANNING GUIDE

(INVESTMENT CAPITAL = $250,000)

	Amount Invested	New or Borrowed Capital	Invest. Return	Current Income	Deferred Income	Tax Shelter
Asset Management	5,000	—	10%	500	—	—
Mutual Fund	50,000	—	20%	10,000	—	—
Margin Account	—	50,000	10%[2]	5,000	—	—
Annuity	50,000	—	20%	—	10,000	10,000
Retirement Program	—	30,000[5]	20%	—	6,000	3,600
Discounted Mortg.	50,000	—	30%	10,000	5,000	5,000
Tax Certificates	15,000	—	20%	—	3,000	3,000
Personal Residence	—	300,000[1]	6%	—	18,000	18,000
Business Inv.[4]	25,000	—	20%	—	5,000	10,000
Ltd. Partnership	55,000	—	14%	3,850	3,850	3,850
TOTALS	250,000	380,000		29,350	50,850	85,850

One-Year Investment Results

Current Income = $29,350   12%

Deferred Income = $50,850   20%

Total Income = $80,200   32%

Tax Savings[3] = $25,755

TOTAL RETURN $105,955

Notes:
1. The personal residence is already owned.
2. The return on the margin account is after interest is deducted.
3. Tax savings based on $31,100 of tax shelter is based on 30% federal and state tax bracket.
4. At this level of investment capital, tax shelter and additional income can also be achieved through directly investing in one or more small businesses.
5. The $30,000 represents a Keogh investment assuming you own your own business or profession.

EPILOGUE

*No great thing is created suddenly, anymore than a bunch
of grapes or a fig. If you tell me that you desire a fig, I answer
you that there must be time. Let it first blossom, then bear
fruit, then ripen.*

Epictetus
(c.55–135)

Knowledge eliminates the two undesirable elements of building wealth
—risk and fear. With those out of the way, you become unstoppable.

What is financial success and how do you know when you have it?

Financial success is having the money to do the things you want to
do, when you want to do them, and, most importantly, the attitude to
enjoy them. You must, therefore, determine through your plan and
objectives what financial success means to you.

For some, financial success means having the money to pay the bills
and enough left over for a six-pack and a bag of microwave popcorn.
For a greater number it means living the good life with the right
clothes, cars, perhaps a condominium on the beach, or even travel
to exotic places. It's all available to those who are willing to take
control.

The Constitution guarantees us equality of opportunity, but no one
guarantees equality of results. Results are the product of knowledge
and action and that's what eventually separates financial winners from
losers. Winners are those who see financial opportunities where others
see only problems.

You can build your wealth under any economic conditions including inflation, recession, or even depression. It's what you know and
not what's happening around you that counts. Stop worrying about the
economy, the deficit, and tax laws—they have little to do with your
personal wealth unless fear shifts you into action.

Having a lot of money does not create problems, it solves them. Often

379

on TV talk shows the host will ask me what the downside is to having lots of money. I've never found one.

Money is only green energy—a medium of exchange. It is what money will buy that counts and money buys freedom—the freedom to choose alternatives not available to those without it. If you have money you can choose where and how to live, what kind of car you wish to drive, how often you want to eat out, where you want to spend your next vacation, and when you want to quit working. Without money, the freedom to choose disappears. Your alternatives are often dictated by the thickness of your wallet. Freedom is the reason why any extra time and effort required to build your wealth is worth it.

Wealth building does not require the compromise of your principles. Greed, ruthlessness, conceit, and aggressiveness are not necessary.

You will find these positive traits among most of those with a lot of self-made wealth including:

Compassion	Discipline	Integrity	Decisiveness
Sharing	Caring	Sense of Adventure	Direction

Where do you begin? You already have. Now it's a matter of applying one strategy at a time. By the inch it's a cinch. Strategies don't wear out nor are they used up. Use each strategy again and again until it becomes habit. As you put one strategy into operation choose another and begin stacking them. You will soon be experiencing the momentum principle—producing ten units of results for each unit of effort. Your friends will comment that you have developed the Midas Touch.

Guiding your momentum, and reaching the objectives you have chosen, is one of the most satisfying and exhilarating rewards of life, measurable in terms of:

"Wealth Without Risk"

My best for your success.

Charles J. Givens

APPENDIX I

Fund Family Fact Sheets
Explanation of Terms and Abbreviations Used

FAMILY: The name of the mutual fund family, the company which created and manages the individual funds listed.

FUND NAME: The name of the individual funds that make up the fund family.

TYPE: The two letter code used by the Givens Organization to identify the mutual fund type. The first letter is the major classification.

> S = Stock Mutual Fund
> B = Bond Mutual Fund
> M = Money Market Mutual Fund

The second letter is the sub-classification.

ASSET MIL.: The amount of assets in millions managed by each fund.

DOW SMB: The Dow Jones computer access symbol for those who track mutual funds by computer.

MIN. INVEST.:

INT. The initial minimum investment required to open the account.

ADD. The minimum additional amount which may be added to the account at any time. "0" means that there is no minimum, any amount can be added.

LOADS AND FEES:

IN % The amount of front-end load or commissions deducted from your initial investment. Shown as a percentage.

OUT % The amount of back-end load or commission deducted from any amount you withdraw from your account. Shown as a percentage.

MGT. The percentage deducted from your account each year for management fees.

12B1 The percentage deducted from your account each year supposedly for advertising and promotional expenses of the fund.

SCWB MARG.: Availability of a Charles Schwab margin account (see Chapter 25 "Mutual Fund Margin Accounts").

WITHDRAWAL OPTIONS: The methods which can be used to withdraw the money from your account.

PHONE: Indicates if your money can be withdrawn with a telephone call.

WIRE: Indicates if your money can be wire transferred from your mutual fund account to your bank account. Other than check writing, wire transfer is the quickest way to get access to your money. Check the bottom of the page for minimum required amount for a wire transfer.

CHEK: Indicates if you can write checks on your mutual fund account. Any amount shown is the minimum amount for which a check can be written.

INCOME: Indicates if you can choose to receive monthly checks as income from your mutual fund account. Check the additional Fund Family information at the bottom of the page for the family's minimum investment required in order to receive monthly income checks.

ANNUAL RETURN: Indicates the percentage growth or decline in the value of each mutual fund share for the five years indicated. A dash in place of a number indicates that the fund was not in existence that year.

PHONE SWITCH: Indicates whether you can move your money from one fund to another by calling the mutual fund.

 # SWITCHES PER YEAR: The number of times you may move your money from fund to fund during a 12-month period.

IRA MINIMUM INVEST.: The minimum amount of initial deposit required to open an IRA account in any of the family's funds.

IRA FEE: The amount of the trustee's fee per year for an IRA account.

KEOGH MIN. INVEST. The minimum amount of initial deposit required to open a Keogh account.

MINIMUM WIRE WITHDRAWAL: The minimum amount which can be transferred to your bank account by wire.

MIN. INVEST. FOR MONTHLY INCOME: The minimum initial investment required if you want to receive monthly income checks from the fund.

AMA ADVISORS

Fund Name	Type	Asset Mil	Dow Smb	Min Invest Int	Add	In%	Out%	Mgt	12b-1	Scwb Marg	Phone	Wire	Chek	Income	83	84	85	86	87
Classic Growth	SG	30	PRFNX	300	0	0	0	.75	.5	Yes	Yes	Yes	No	Yes	7.4	5.3	22.9	11.4	−1.7
Global Growth	SG	108	—	300	0	0	0	.85	.5	No	Yes	Yes	No	Yes	—	—	—	—	—
Growth & Inc.	SI	13.3	—	300	0	0	0	.75	.5	No	Yes	Yes	No	Yes	—	—	—	—	—
Income	SI	35	PROTX	300	0	0	0	.75	.5	Yes	Yes	No	No	Yes	8.9	8.3	8.3	12.7	−0.6
Money Fund Port.	MM	218	—	2000	100	0	0	.50	.5	No	Yes	Yes	50	Yes	—	—	—	6.2	6.1
Money Fund Treas.	MG	32	—	2000	100	0	0	.50	0.0	No	Yes	Yes	50	Yes	—	—	—	—	5.6

PHONE SWITCH—All Funds   # SWITCHES/YEAR—Unlimited   IRA MINIMUM INVESTMENT—$300.00   KEOGH MIN. INVEST.—$300.00

MINIMUM WIRE WITHDRAWAL—$1000.00   MIN. INVEST. FOR MONTHLY INCOME—$5000.00 to $10,000.00   IRA FEE—$10.00

AXE-HOUGHTON MGR

Fund Name	Type	Asset Mil	Dow Smb	Min Invest Int	Add	In%	Out%	Mgt	12b-1	Scwb Marg	Phone	Wire	Chek	Income	83	84	85	86	87
Stock Fund	SG	66	AXBTX	1000	0	0	0	.7	.45	Yes	No	No	No	Yes	23.7	−15.3	31.1	10.4	−6.0
Fund B Inc.	SI	159	AXBBX	1000	0	0	0	.6	.45	Yes	No	No	No	Yes	10.9	6.3	32.9	23.1	−3.5
Income Fund Inc.	BL	53	AXBAX	1000	0	0	0	.6	.45	Yes	No	No	No	Yes	7.4	15.3	26.6	15.8	1.8
Money Market	MM	112	—	1000	100	0	0	.5	.25	Yes	No	Yes	5,000	Yes	7.9	9.2	6.8	5.5	6.0

PHONE SWITCH—All Funds   # SWITCHES/YEAR—Unlimited   IRA MINIMUM INVESTMENT—$25.00   KEOGH MIN. INVEST.—$250.00

MINIMUM WIRE WITHDRAWAL—$1000.00   MIN. INVEST. FOR MONTHLY INCOME—$10,000.00   IRA FEE—$10.00

AMERICAN ASSOCIATION OF RETIRED PERSONS (AARP)

Fund Name	Type	Asset Mil	Dow Smb	Min Invest Int	Add	Loads and Fees In%	Out%	Mgt	12b-1	Scwb Marg	Phone	Wire	Chek	Income	83	84	Annual Return 85	86	87
Capital Growth	SG	76	ACGFX	250	0	0	0	.62	0	No	Yes	Yes	No	Yes	—	—	28.8	16.7	.2
Growth & Income	SI	252	AGIFX	250	0	0	0	.49	0	No	Yes	Yes	No	Yes	—	—	30.2	16.6	.8
General Bond	BL	115	AGBFX	250	0	0	0	.49	0	No	Yes	Yes	No	Yes	—	—	15.8	10.7	1.2
Ins. Tax Free Gen.	BX	250	ATTGX	250	0	0	0	.49	0	No	Yes	Yes	No	Yes	—	—	10.2	16.3	-1.5
GNMA & US Treas.	BG	2717	AGNMX	250	0	0	0	.45	0	No	Yes	Yes	No	Yes	—	—	17.9	10.4	2.0
Ins. Tax Free Short	BY	70	AITSX	250	0	0	0	.49	0	No	Yes	Yes	No	Yes	—	—	5.7	7.9	3.3
Money Fund	MM	194	ARPXX	250	0	0	0	.48	0	No	Yes	Yes	100	Yes	—	—	—	6.0	5.4

PHONE SWITCH—All Funds   # SWITCHES/YEAR—4   IRA MINIMUM INVESTMENT—$250.00   KEOGH MIN. INVEST.—$10,000.00   MINIMUM WIRE

WITHDRAWAL—No Min.   MIN. INVEST. FOR MONTHLY INCOME—$10,000.00   IRA FEE—0   KEOGH MIN. INVEST.—$250.00

BABSON FUNDS

Fund Name	Type	Asset Mil	Dow Smb	Min Invest Int	Add	Loads and Fees In%	Out%	Mgt	12b-1	Scwb Marg	Phone	Wire	Chek	Income	83	84	Annual Return 85	86	87
Babson Enterprise	SA	35.7	BABEX	1000	100	0	0	1.50	15	No	No	No	No	Yes	—	-5.0	38.6	9.0	-9.2
Babson Growth	SG	219.6	BABSX	500	50	0	0	.75	15	No	No	No	No	Yes	15.9	0.3	29.6	18.8	2.7
Babson Value	SG	12.3	BVALX	1000	100	0	0	.95	15	No	No	No	No	Yes	—	—	26.5	20.7	3.3
Bab. Tax Free Inc.	BX	20.8	BALTX	1000	100	0	0	.95	0	No	No	No	No	Yes	8.9	9.0	20.4	21.3	-1.9
Bond Trust	BL	64.2	BABIX	500	50	0	0	.75	15	No	No	No	No	Yes	9.5	12.9	20.7	13.8	1.9
Tax Free Inc. Short	BY	16.2	—	1000	100	0	0	.95	0	No	No	No	No	Yes	4.9	8.1	11.1	10.4	3.5
Money Market Prime	MM	55.4	BMMXX	1000	100	0	0	.85	15	No	Yes	Yes	500	Yes	8.7	10.1	7.6	6.1	5.9
Tax Free Inc. MM	MX	10.7	—	1000	100	0	0	.95	0	No	Yes	Yes	500	Yes	5.3	5.3	5.0	4.5	4.1
Money Market Fed	MG	3.7	—	1000	100	0	0	.85	15	No	Yes	Yes	500	Yes	—	—	—	—	5.6

PHONE SWITCH—All Funds   # SWITCHES/YEAR—Unlimited   IRA MINIMUM INVESTMENT—$1,000.00 (Exception Bond Trust & Growth)   IRA FEE—$10.00

KEOGH MIN. INVEST.—$100.00–$1000.00   MINIMUM WIRE WITHDRAWAL—None   IRA MINIMUM INVESTMENT—$1,000.00 (Exception Bond Trust & Growth)   MIN. INVEST. FOR MONTHLY INCOME—$10,000.00

BOSTON CO. ADVISORS

Fund Name	Type	Asset Mil	Dow Smb	Min Invest Int	Min Invest Add	In%	Out%	Mgt	12b-1	Scwb Marg	Phone	Wire	Chek	Income	83	84	85	86	87
Special Growth	SA	30	BOSSX	1000	0	0	0	1.00	.45	No	Yes	Yes	No	Yes	39.6	70.9	34.7	7.6	-3.5
Capital Apprec	SG	433	BCCAX	1000	0	0	0	.75	.45	No	Yes	Yes	No	Yes	24.0	6.9	35.0	22.5	.5
Mass. Tax Free	BY	14	—	1000	0	0	0	.50	0.00	No	Yes	Yes	No	Yes	—	—	—	17.6	-0.9
Tax Free Bond	BY	9	—	1000	0	0	0	.50	0.00	No	Yes	Yes	No	Yes	—	—	—	18.3	2.4
GNMA	BL	14	BGMFK	1000	0	0	0	.65	.45	No	Yes	Yes	No	Yes	—	—	—	—	0.8
Managed Income	BS	51	BOSGY	1000	0	0	0	.60	.45	No	Yes	Yes	No	Yes	6.0	11.8	21.8	15.1	5.7
Cash Management	MM	283	BCAXX	1000	0	0	0	.50	.45	No	Yes	Yes	500	Yes	8.9	10.3	7.9	6.3	6.1
Mass. Tax-Free	MX	148	BCMXX	1000	0	0	0	.50	0.00	No	Yes	Yes	500	Yes	—	5.5	4.9	4.4	4.2
Tax Free Money	MX	26	—	1000	0	0	0	.50	0.00	No	Yes	Yes	500	Yes	—	5.5	4.9	4.1	4.0
Government Money	MG	66	BOGXY	1000	0	0	0	.50	.45	No	Yes	Yes	500	Yes	8.3	9.5	7.2	5.6	5.3

PHONE SWITCH—All Funds   # SWITCHES/YEAR—Unlimited   IRA MINIMUM INVESTMENT—$500.00   KEOGH MIN. INVEST.—$500.00
MINIMUM WIRE WITHDRAWAL—$1000.00   MIN. INVEST. FOR MONTHLY INCOME—$10,000.00   IRA FEE—$10.00

BULL & BEAR GROUP

Fund Name*	Type	Asset Mil	Dow Smb	Min Invest Int	Min Invest Add	In%	Out%	Mgt	12b-1	Scwb Marg	Phone	Wire	Chek	Income	83	84	85	86	87
Special Equity	SA	2	BULHX	1000	100	0	0	1.0	1.0	Yes	Yes	Yes	No	Yes	—	—	—	—	-6.4
Capital Growth	SA	65	BULSX	1000	100	0	0	1.0	1.0	Yes	No	Yes	No	Yes	15.4	-5.0	27.7	3.7	-4.6
Equity Income	SI	13	BULAX	1000	100	0	0	0.6	1.0	Yes	No	Yes	No	Yes	11.9	7.7	25.7	19.3	-4.7
Golconda Inv.	SP	32	BULGX	1000	100	0	0	1.0	1.0	Yes	Yes	Yes	No	Yes	.6	-25.0	2.6	35.0	30.4
High Yield	BL	133	BULHX	1000	100	0	0	0.7	0.5	Yes	Yes	Yes	No	Yes	—	7.8	20.6	6.0	-6.4
Tax Free Inc.	BX	16	BLTFX	1000	100	0	0	0.7	0.5	Yes	Yes	Yes	No	Yes	—	—	22.4	19.7	-.9
US Gov. Guar. Sec	BG	44	BLTFX	1000	100	0	0	0.7	0.5	Yes	Yes	Yes	No	Yes	—	—	—	—	5.4
Dollar Res.	MM	88	BULXX	1000	100	0	0	0.5	0.2	Yes	Yes	Yes	250	Yes	8.6	10.3	7.9	6.3	6.0

PHONE SWITCH—All Funds   # SWITCHES/YEAR—Unlimited   IRA MINIMUM INVESTMENT—$100.00   KEOGH MIN. INVEST.—$100.00
MINIMUM WIRE WITHDRAWAL—$1000.00   MIN. INVEST. FOR MONTHLY INCOME—$10,000.00   IRA FEE—$5.00

* Funds available in most but not all states.

CALVERT GROUP

Fund Name	Type	Asset Mil	Dow Smb	Min Invest		Loads and Fees				Scwb Marg	Withdrawal Options				Annual Return				
				Int	Add	In%	Out%	Mgt	12b-1		Phone	Wire	Chek	Income	83	84	85	86	87
Equity	SG	6	CFEQX	2000	250	0	0	0.7	0.7	Yes	Yes	Yes	No	Yes	9.0	-6.6	21.2	11.5	-8.2
Tax Free Res. Long	BX	82	CTILX	2000	250	0	0	0.6	0.3	No	Yes	Yes	No	Yes	—	7.7	18.8	16.6	7.1
Tax Free Res. Ltd.	BY	148	CTFLX	2000	250	0	0	0.6	0.3	No	Yes	Yes	250	Yes	6.2	7.5	8.5	8.1	3.5
Social Inv. MM	MM	58	CSIXX	1000	250	0	0	0.7	0.2	Yes	Yes	Yes	250	Yes	9.3	10.2	7.8	6.2	5.8
Tax Free MM	MX	729	CTMXX	2000	250	0	0	0.5	0.0	No	Yes	Yes	250	Yes	—	—	—	4.8	4.6

PHONE SWITCH—All Funds   # SWITCHES/YEAR—Unlimited   IRA MINIMUM INVESTMENT—No Minimum   IRA FEE—$10.00
KEOGH MIN. INVEST.—$250.00 in Equity only   MINIMUM WIRE WITHDRAWAL—No Minimum   MIN. INVEST. FOR MONTHLY INCOME—$10,000.00

COLUMBIA FUNDS

Fund Name	Type	Asset Mil	Dow Smb	Min Invest		Loads and Fees				Scwb Marg	Withdrawal Options				Annual Return				
				Int	Add	In%	Out%	Mgt	12b-1		Phone	Wire	Chek	Income	83	84	85	86	87
Special	SA	21	CLSPX	10,000	100	0	2	1.0	.15	Yes	Yes	Yes	No	Yes	—	—	—	15.6	3.0
Growth	SA	194	CLMBX	1000	100	0	0	0.7	.15	Yes	Yes	Yes	No	Yes	21.4	-5.5	32.0	6.9	14.7
Municipal Bond	BX	118	CMBFX	1000	100	—	2	0.5	.15	Yes	Yes	Yes	No	Yes	—	—	19.8	16.8	1.4
Fixed Income Sec.	BL	100	CFISX	1000	100	—	—	0.5	.15	Yes	Yes	Yes	No	Yes	—	12.2	20.2	12.3	.9
US Gov Guar. Sec.	BG	7	CFISX	1000	100	—	—	0.5	.15	Yes	Yes	Yes	No	Yes	—	—	—	—	4.1
Daily Income	MM	450	CDIXX	1000	100	0	0	0.5	.15	Yes	Yes	Yes	500	No	8.5	9.5	7.6	6.2	6.0

PHONE SWITCH—All Funds   # SWITCHES/YEAR—Unlimited   IRA MINIMUM INVESTMENT—$1000.00   IRA FEE—$25.00
KEOGH MIN. INVEST.—$1000.00   MINIMUM WIRE WITHDRAWAL—No Minimum   MIN. INVEST. FOR MONTHLY INCOME—$5000.00

DREYFUS CORP.

Fund Name	Type	Asset Mil	Dow Smb	Min Invest Int	Min Invest Add	In%	Out%	Mgt	12b-1	Scwb Marg	Phone	Wire	Chek	Income	83	84	85	86	87
Strategic Agg.	SA	93	DRCVX	2500	100	0	0	.75	0.2	Yes	No	No	No	Yes	—	—	—	15.7	—
New Leaders	SA	80	DNLBX	2500	100	0	0	.75		Yes	No	No	No	Yes	—	—	—	12.3	-5.0
Growth Opp.	SG	432	DREQX	2500	100	0	0	.75	0.0	Yes	No	No	No	Yes	31.1	-12.1	30.7	15.3	6.8
Third Century	SG	138	DRTHX	2500	100	0	0	.75	0.0	Yes	No	No	No	Yes	20.0	1.1	29.7	4.6	2.5
Fund	SI	2364	DREVX	2500	100	0	0	.65	0.0	Yes	No	No	No	Yes	19.5	3.2	25.2	16.2	8.2
Convertible Sec.	SI	237	DRSPX	2500	100	0	0	.75	0.0	Yes	No	No	No	Yes	20.8	7.4	23.9	25.2	-2.6
Mass TE Bond	BX	78	—	2500	100	0	0	.60	0.0	Yes	Yes	No	No	Yes	—	—	—	17.9	-3.4
NY Tax Exempt	BX	1414	DRNYX	2250	100	0	0	.60	0.0	Yes	Yes	No	No	Yes	—	8.0	20.6	17.1	-2.6
Cal. TE Bond	BX	1121	DLAXX	2500	100	0	0	.50	0.0	Yes	No	Yes	No	Yes	—	5.0	18.8	17.7	-1.7
Insured TE Bond	BX	177	—	2500	100	0	0	.60	0.2	Yes	Yes	Yes	No	Yes	—	—	—	17.0	-1.9
Tax Exempt Bond	BX	3138	DRTAX	2500	100	0	0	.60	0.0	Yes	Yes	Yes	No	Yes	11.5	8.6	19.4	17.3	-1.7
A Bond Plus	BL	239	DRBDX	2500	100	0	0	.65	0.0	Yes	No	Yes	No	Yes	7.6	12.3	23.1	14.0	-1.7
GNMA	BL	1977	DRGMX	2500	100	0	0	.60	0.2	Yes	No	No	No	Yes	—	—	—	9.6	1.8
Pk. Ave NY TE Int.	BY	63	RABFX	2500	100	0	0	.40	0.0	Yes	Yes	Yes	Yes	Yes	—	—	14.9	14.2	—
Int. Tax Exempt	BY	979	DFTEX	2500	100	0	0	.60	0.0	Yes	Yes	No	No	Yes	15.4	7.3	16.1	15.4	1.1
Park Ave TE MM	MX	250	PATXX	2500	100	0	0	.30	0.0	Yes	Yes	Yes	500	No	—	—	4.8	4.8	—
Cal TE Money	MX	156	DLAXX	2500	100	0	0	.50	0.0	Yes	No	Yes	500	Yes	—	—	5.0	4.4	—
Tax Exempt MM	MX	2635	DTEXX	5000	100	0	0	.50	0.0	Yes	Yes	Yes	500	Yes	—	—	—	—	4.1
Pacific Horizon MM	MX	765	PHTXY	1000	100	0	0	.30	0.0	Yes	Yes	Yes	500	Yes	—	5.6	4.5	4.0	—
MM Inst. Gov. Sec.	MG	765	DMMXX	2500	100	0	0	.50	0.0	Yes	Yes	Yes	500	Yes	—	9.9	8.3	6.5	5.9
Pacific Horizon Gov.	MG	1168	PHGXX	1000	100	0	0	.30	0.0	Yes	Yes	Yes	500	Yes	—	—	7.9	6.5	—
Dollar Internat'l	MM	267	—	5000	5000	0	0	.20	0.0	Yes	Yes	Yes	500	No	—	10.7	7.8	6.4	—
Liquid Assets	MM	7379	DLAXX	2500	100	0	0	.50	0.0	Yes	Yes	Yes	500	Yes	—	—	—	6.5	6.2
Pacific Horizon	MM	617	PCMXX	1000	100	0	0	.30	0.0	Yes	Yes	Yes	500	Yes	—	—	—	6.5	—

PHONE SWITCH—All Funds   SWITCHES/YEAR—Unlimited   IRA MINIMUM INVESTMENT—$750.00   KEOGH MIN. INVEST.—$750.00

MINIMUM WIRE WITHDRAWAL—No Minimum   MIN. INVEST. FOR MONTHLY INCOME—$5000.00   IRA FEE—$5.00

FIDELITY

Fund Name	Type	Asset Mil	Dow Smb	Min Int	Invest Add	In%	Out%	Mgt	12b-1	Scwb Marg	Phone	Wire	Chek	Income	83	84	85	86	87
OTC	SA	765	FDCPX	2500	250	3	0	.35	0	Yes	No	No	No	Yes	—	—	69.0	11.4	1.6
Capital APP.	SA	860	FDCAX	2500	250	2	1	.30	0	No	No	No	No	Yes	—	—	—	—	19.3
Growth Co.	SA	145	FDGRX	1000	250	3	0	.30	0	Yes	No	No	No	Yes	—	-5.5	39.8	13.0	-1.7
Magellan	SA	7800	FMAGX	1000	250	3	0	.30	0	Yes	No	No	No	Yes	38.2	2.1	43.1	23.7	0.9
Freedom***	SA	1111	FDFFX	500	250	0	0	.30	0	Yes	No	No	No	No	—	3.3	28.7	14.0	9.3
Value	SA	85	FDVLX	1000	250	0	0	.40	0	Yes	No	No	No	Yes	32.2	-8.7	22.1	14.7	-8.6
Contra Fund	SA	87	FCNTX	1000	250	0	0	.10	0	Yes	No	No	No	Yes	23.2	-8.3	27.0	13.1	-2.0
Trend	SG	601	FTRNX	1000	250	0	0	.10	0	Yes	No	No	No	Yes	26.6	-2.2	28.2	13.3	-4.2
Tr. Port Growth **	SG	48	EQPGX	1000M	none	0	0	.70	0	No	No	Yes	No	Yes	—	7.4	41.5	14.5	6.0
Growth & Income	SI	1118	FCRIX	2500	250	2	0	.20	0	Yes	No	No	No	Yes	22.2	1.2	27.7	15.6	3.3
Fidelity Fund	SI	873	FFIDX	1000	250	0	0	.10	0	Yes	No	No	No	Yes	29.1	10.4	25.0	16.9	-1.6
Equity Inc	SI	3476	FEQIX	1000	250	2	0	.10	0	Yes	No	No	No	Yes	—	—	—	—	—
Real Estate	SI	68	FQDEX	2500	250	2	0	varies	0	Yes	No	No	No	Yes	—	—	—	—	-7.7
Puritan	SI	3958	FPURX	1000	250	0	0	.10	0	Yes	No	No	No	Yes	25.3	10.2	28.5	20.7	-1.9
Balanced	SI	121	FAFTX	2500	250	2	0	.50	0	Yes	No	No	No	Yes	—	—	—	—	1.9
Qualified Div.*	SI	189	FQDFX	50M	none	0	0	varies	0	No	No	Yes	No	No	15.5	20.7	25.7	21.0	-4.9
Convertible Sec.	SI	1	—	2500	250	0	0	.20	0	Yes	No	No	No	Yes	—	—	—	—	-4.9
Tr. Equity Port. **	SI	513	EQPIX	1000M	none	0	0	.50	0	No	No	Yes	No	Yes	—	20.7	25.6	17.4	—
Select Prec. Metals	SP	188	FDMPX	1000	250	2	1	.35	0	Yes	No	No	No	Yes	2.9	-26.4	-10.5	32.8	37.5
Sel. Amer. Gold	SP	69	FSAGX	1000	250	2	1	.35	0	Yes	No	No	No	Yes	—	—	—	18.1	40.5
Sel Energy Serv	SS	112	FSESX	1000	250	2	1	.35	0	Yes	No	No	No	Yes	—	—	—	-15.7	-11.8
Sel Chemicals	SS	39	FSCHX	1000	250	2	1	.35	0	Yes	No	No	No	Yes	—	—	—	26.9	14.8
Sel Tech.	SS	201	FSPTX	1000	250	2	1	.35	0	Yes	No	No	No	Yes	52.4	-16.9	7.4	-7.5	-11.8
Sel. Software	SS	24	FSCSX	1000	250	2	1	.35	0	Yes	No	No	No	Yes	—	—	—	13.9	9.4
Sel. Computers	SS	19	FDCPX	1000	250	2	1	.35	0	Yes	No	No	No	Yes	—	—	—	7.9	-6.4
Sel Electronics	SS	5	FSELX	1000	250	2	1	.35	0	Yes	No	No	No	Yes	—	—	—	-23.9	-13.5
Sel Telecomm	SS	10	FSTCX	1000	250	2	1	.35	0	Yes	No	No	No	Yes	—	—	—	19.8	15.2
Select BioTech	SS	39	FRIOX	1000	250	2	1	.35	0	Yes	No	No	No	Yes	—	—	—	3.5	-3.3
Sel. Defense	SS	7	FSDAX	1000	250	2	1	.35	0	Yes	No	No	No	Yes	—	—	26.4	5.0	-23.2
Sel. Automation	SS	6	FSAVX	1000	250	2	1	.35	0	Yes	No	No	No	Yes	—	—	—	—	—
Health Care Del	SS	229	FHSNX	1000	250	2	1	.35	0	Yes	No	No	No	Yes	—	—	—	—	—
Sel. Healh	SS	2	FSPHX	1000	250	2	1	.35	0	Yes	No	No	No	Yes	14.1	-1.1	59.4	22.0	-0.6

Fund	Type	No.	Ticker	Min	Add			Exp	Load										
Sel. Air Trans	SS	26	FSLAX	1000	250	2	1	.35	0	Yes	No	No	No	Yes	—	—	—	12.8	−20.1
Sel. Trans.	SS	1	FTRAN	1000	250	2	1	.35	0	Yes	No	No	No	Yes	—	—	—	—	—
Sel. Automotive	SS	5	FSAYX	1000	250	2	1	.35	0	Yes	No	No	No	Yes	—	—	—	—	—
Sel. Cap. Goods	SS	3	FCAPX	1000	250	2	1	.35	0	Yes	No	No	No	Yes	—	—	—	—	—
Sel. Ind. Mat.	SS	1	FINDX	1000	250	2	1	.35	0	Yes	No	No	No	Yes	—	—	—	—	—
Sel Paper Forest	SS	59	FSPFX	1000	250	2	1	.35	0	Yes	No	No	No	Yes	—	—	—	—	3.9
Sel. Housing	SS	2	—	1000	250	2	1	.35	0	Yes	No	No	No	Yes	—	—	—	—	—
Sel Food & Agri.	SS	8	FDFAX	1000	250	2	1	.35	0	Yes	No	No	No	Yes	—	—	—	22.5	7.5
Sel Bdcst & Media	SS	12	FRMPX	1000	250	2	1	.35	0	Yes	No	No	No	Yes	—	—	—	—	19.9
Sel Energy	SS	5	FSENX	1000	250	2	1	.35	0	Yes	No	No	No	Yes	20.3	2.4	17.9	5.5	−1.8
Sel Life Ins	SS	1	FSLTX	1000	250	2	1	.35	0	Yes	No	No	No	Yes	—	—	—	−0.5	−21.7
Select Prop-Cas	SS	10	FSPCX	1000	250	2	1	.35	0	Yes	No	No	No	Yes	—	—	—	7.7	−12.2
Sel. Broker	SS	17	FSLBX	1000	250	2	1	.35	0	Yes	No	No	No	Yes	—	—	—	9.5	−36.9
Sel. Financial	SS	92	FIDSX	1000	250	2	1	.35	0	Yes	No	No	No	Yes	37.1	18.0	41.7	15.0	−16.6
Sel. Reg. Banks	SS	3	FSRGX	1000	250	2	1	.35	0	Yes	No	No	No	Yes	—	—	—	—	—
Sel. S&L	SS	26	FSCSX	1000	250	2	1	.35	0	Yes	No	No	No	Yes	—	—	—	27.5	−7.9
Sel. Leisure	SS	94	FDLSX	1000	250	2	1	.35	0	Yes	No	No	No	Yes	—	—	56.5	15.7	5.7
Sel. Rest.	SS	1	FREST	1000	250	2	1	.35	0	Yes	No	No	No	Yes	—	—	—	—	—
Sel. Retail	SS	15	FSRPX	1000	250	2	1	.35	0	Yes	No	No	No	Yes	—	—	—	14.2	−7.4
Sel. Elect. Util.	SS	11	FSEUX	1000	250	2	1	.35	0	Yes	No	No	No	Yes	—	—	—	—	−17.3
Sel. Utilities	SS	211	FSUTX	1000	250	2	1	.35	0	Yes	No	No	No	Yes	20.0	20.9	31.7	24.0	−9.2
Global Bond	BX	—	—	2500	250	0	0	.50	0	Yes	No	Yes	No	Yes	—	—	—	—	19.1
NYTF Yld Muni	BX	354	FTFMX	2500	250	0	0	.40	0	Yes	No	Yes	No	Yes	—	—	20.9	16.8	—
Cal Free HY	BX	579	FCFXX	2500	250	0	0	.45	0	Yes	500	Yes	No	Yes	—	—	16.6	17.5	−3.7
Ltd. Term Muni	BX	578	FLTMX	2500	250	0	0	.15	0	Yes	500	Yes	No	Yes	9.9	9.9	17.3	15.2	1.1
Penn Free Hy Muni	BX	23	FPURX	2500	250	0	0	.10	0	Yes	No	No	No	Yes	—	—	—	—	—
High Income	BX	1671	FAGIX	2500	250	0	0	.55	0	Yes	No	Yes	No	Yes	18.4	10.4	25.6	17.9	0.5
High Yield Mun.	BX	2279	FHIGX	2500	250	0	0	.45	0	Yes	No	Yes	No	Yes	12.5	9.8	21.4	18.9	−3.7
Agg. Tax-Free	BX	4	FATEX	2500	250	0	0	.50	0	Yes	No	Yes	No	Yes	—	—	—	17.4	1.7
Texas Tax-Free	BX	29	FTEXX	2500	250	0	0	.30	0	Yes	500	Yes	Yes	Yes	—	—	—	—	−0.8
Mass Free Muni	BX	724	FDMMX	2500	250	0	0	.45	0	Yes	No	Yes	Yes	Yes	—	8.4	19.6	16.9	−1.5
Minn. Tax Free	BX	93	FDMDX	2500	250	0	0	.45	0	Yes	No	No	Yes	Yes	—	—	—	17.0	−4.1
Mich Tax Free	BX	127	FMHTX	2500	250	0	0	.45	0	Yes	No	Yes	Yes	Yes	—	—	—	18.9	−3.1
Ohio Tax Free	BX	106	FOHFX	2500	250	0	0	.45	0	Yes	No	Yes	Yes	Yes	—	—	—	16.4	−2.4
Munic. Bond	BX	1154	FMBPX	2500	250	0	0	.40	0	Yes	No	Yes	No	Yes	9.2	9.0	20.1	19.5	−1.6

FIDELITY (cont.)

Fund Name	Asset Type	Asset Mil	Dow Smb	Min Invest Int	Min Invest Add	In%	Out%	Mgt	12b-1	Scwb Marg	Phone	Wire	Chek	Income	83	84	85	86	87
NY Tax Free Ins	BX	158	FNTIX	2500	250	0	0	.40	0	Yes	No	Yes	No	Yes	—	—	—	17.4	-3.2
Cal Ins TF	BX	2	FCTFX	2500	250	0	0	.45	0	Yes	No	Yes	500	Yes	—	—	—	—	—
Insured Tax Free	BX	145	FMUIX	2500	250	0	0	.45	0	Yes	No	Yes	No	Yes	—	—	—	18.3	-2.2
Short Term	BS	52	FSHRX	2500	250	0	0	.50	0	No	No	No	No	Yes	—	—	—	—	3.2
Tr. Fixed Tac Port **	BL	446	FFDPX	1000M	none	0	0	.45	0	No	No	Yes	No	Yes	—	—	20.2	14.3	—
GNMA	BG	937	FGMNX	1000	250	0	0	.50	0	Yes	No	Yes	No	Yes	—	—	—	12.7	1.2
Gov. Securities	BG	745	FGOVX	1000	250	0	0	.50	0	No	Yes	Yes	No	Yes	5.8	11.2	17.6	14.7	1.1
Short Term TF	BY	11	FPURX	2500	250	0	0	.50	0	Yes	No	Yes	500	Yes	—	—	—	—	—
Corp. Trust-ARP *	BY	276	FCPTX	50,000	none	0	0	.60	.2	No	No	Yes	No	No	—	—	16.5	6.4	6.7
Flexible Bond	BY	437	FBNDX	2500	250	0	0	.40	0	Yes	No	Yes	No	Yes	6.5	11.7	21.1	13.6	0.1
Mort. Sec.	BY	752	FMSFX	1000	250	0	0	.50	0	Yes	No	Yes	No	Yes	—	—	18.6	10.9	2.7
Thrift Trust	BY	368	FTHRX	1000	250	0	0	.35	0	Yes	No	Yes	500	Yes	9.3	13.4	20.9	13.2	—
Select MM	MM	570	—	1000	250	0	0	.35	0	No	No	Yes	No	Yes	—	—	—	6.4	5.8
Daily Inc Tr	MM	2772	FDTXX	5000	500	0	0	varies	0	No	Yes	Yes	Yes	Yes	9.0	10.2	8.0	6.6	6.2
Cash Reserves	MM	5262	FDRXX	1000	250	0	0	.50	0	No	No	Yes	500	Yes	8.8	10.2	7.9	6.5	6.3
US Gov. Res	MG	728	FGRXX	1000	250	0	0	.48	0	No	No	Yes	500	Yes	8.6	9.8	7.8	6.4	6.0
Mass TF Money	MX	380	FDMXX	2500	500	0	0	.45	0	Yes	Yes	Yes	500	Yes	—	5.2	4.7	4.2	—
NY TF Money	MX	320	—	2500	250	0	0	.40	0	No	Yes	Yes	500	Yes	—	—	—	4.2	3.8
Cal. TF Money	MX	242	FCFSX	2500	250	0	0	.45	0	Yes	Yes	Yes	500	Yes	—	—	—	4.5	4.1
Penn TF Money	MX	17	FPURX	2500	250	0	0	.10	0	No	Yes	Yes	500	Yes	—	—	—	—	—
Tax Exempt Money	MX	3670	FTEXX	5000	250	0	0	.30	0	No	Yes	Yes	500	Yes	5.0	5.8	5.2	4.5	4.3

PHONE SWITCH—All Funds except Tr Fixed IAC Port LT   # SWITCHES/YEAR—Min 4—in most cases Unlimited   IRA MINIMUM INVESTMENT—$500.00

IRA FEE—$10.00   KEOGH MIN. INVEST.—$250.00 (Daily Inc at 500.00)   MINIMUM WIRE WITHDRAWAL—$5000.00   MIN. INVEST. FOR MONTHLY INCOME—$5000.00

* Corporations Only
** Designed for Banks
*** Limited to tax qualified retirement plans and tax-exempt organizations

FINANCIAL PROGRAMS

Fund Name	Type	Asset Mil	Dow Smb	Min Invest Int	Min Invest Add	Loads and Fees In%	Loads and Fees Out%	Loads and Fees Mgt	Loads and Fees 12b-1	Scwb Marg	Withdrawal Options Phone	Withdrawal Options Wire	Withdrawal Options Chek	Withdrawal Options Income	Annual Return 83	Annual Return 84	Annual Return 85	Annual Return 86	Annual Return 87
Dynamics	SA	76	FIDYX	250	50	0	0	.75	0	Yes	No	No	No	No	12.3	-13.8	29.1	6.2	3.9
Industrial Fund	SG	351	FLRFX	250	50	0	0	.75	0	Yes	No	No	No	Yes	14.4	-1.2	28.4	8.2	-0.1
Industrial Inc.	SI	357	FIIIX	250	50	0	0	.75	0	Yes	No	No	No	Yes	23.5	9.7	30.7	14.4	4.9
Strategic Gold	SP	41	FGLDX	250	50	0	0	.75	0	Yes	No	No	No	No	—	—	-4.5	38.7	16.0
Strategic Tech	SS	14	FTCHX	250	50	0	0	.75	0	Yes	No	No	No	No	—	—	27.3	21.9	-5.3
Strategic Health	SS	10	FHLSX	250	50	0	0	.75	0	Yes	No	No	No	No	—	—	31.5	29.5	7.0
Strategic Energy	SS	6	FSTEX	250	50	0	0	.75	0	Yes	No	No	No	No	—	—	13.6	7.2	5.0
Strategic Financial	SS	1	FSBSX	250	50	0	0	.75	0	Yes	No	No	No	No	—	—	—	—	-11.2
Strategic Leisure	SS	2	FLISX	250	50	0	0	.75	0	Yes	No	No	No	No	—	—	32.2	18.8	.7
World of Tech.	SS	8	FPWTX	250	50	0	0	1.00	0	Yes	No	No	No	No	—	—	—	16.5	2.3
Strategic Utilities	SS	18	—	250	50	0	0	.75	0	Yes	No	No	No	No	—	—	—	—	-4.9
Strategic European	SS	8	FEUBX	250	50	0	0	.75	0	Yes	No	No	No	No	—	—	—	—	-4.5
Strategic Pacific	SS	28	FPBSX	250	50	0	0	.75	0	Yes	No	No	No	No	—	—	27.3	71.9	9.8
Bond Sh. US Gov.	BG	8	—	250	50	0	0	.50	0	Yes	No	No	No	No	—	—	—	14.3	-5.1
Bond Select Inc.	BL	20	FBDSX	250	50	0	0	.50	0	Yes	No	No	No	No	5.1	5.2	22.7	18.7	-1.6
Tax Free Inc	BX	103	FTIFX	250	50	0	0	.50	0	Yes	No	No	No	Yes	8.0	9.1	22.9	22.1	-4.0
Bond Sh. High YD	BS	38	FHYPX	250	50	0	0	.50	0	Yes	No	No	No	No	—	—	26.5	14.5	3.5
Daily Inc Shares	MM	213	FBSXX	250	50	0	0	.50	0	Yes	Yes	Yes	500	No	9.1	10.5	7.8	6.2	6.1
Tax Free Money	MX	28	—	250	50	0	0	.50	0	Yes	Yes	Yes	500	Yes	—	5.5	5.5	4.7	3.9

PHONE SWITCH—All Funds   # SWITCHES/YEAR—4   IRA MINIMUM INVESTMENT—$250.00   KEOGH MIN. INVEST.—$50.00

MINIMUM WIRE WITHDRAWAL—$1000.00   MIN. INVEST. FOR MONTHLY INCOME—$10,000.00   IRA FEE—$5.00

FOUNDERS MUTUAL DEPOSITOR CORP.

Fund Name	Type	Asset Mil	Dow Smb	Invest Min Int	Invest Add	In%	Out%	Mgt	12b-1	Scwb Marg	Phone	Wire	Chek	Income	83	84	85	86	87
Frontier	SA	3	—	1000	100	0	0	1.0	.25	Yes	No	No	No	Yes	—	-12.2	15.2	18.9	5.2
Special	SA	67	FRSPX	1000	100	0	0	1.0	0.00	Yes	No	No	No	Yes	23.5	71.1	28.8	19.6	10.2
Growth	SG	68	FRGRX	1000	100	0	0	1.0	0.00	Yes	No	No	No	Yes	19.4	1.8	31.9	17.3	1.9
Blue Chip	SI	174	FRMUX	1000	100	0	0	0.5	.25	Yes	No	No	No	Yes	25.1	11.4	12.7	14.6	1.9
Equity Income	SI	13	FRINX	1000	100	0	0	1.0	.25	Yes	No	No	No	Yes	15.3	—	—	—	—
Gov. Sec. Fund	BG	3	—	1000	100	0	0	0.8	.25	Yes	No	No	No	Yes	—	—	—	—	—
Money Market	MM	37	FMMXX	1000	100	0	0	0.5	0.00	No	No	Yes	500	Yes	8.6	9.9	7.3	6.0	5.9

PHONE SWITCH—All Funds   # SWITCHES/YEAR—Unlimited   IRA MINIMUM INVESTMENT—$500.00   KEOGH MIN. INVEST.—$500.00
MINIMUM WIRE WITHDRAWAL—No Minimum   MIN. INVEST. FOR MONTHLY INCOME—$5000.00   IRA FEE—$10.00

GOV. INV. TRUST

Fund Name	Type	Asset Mil	Dow Smb	Invest Min Int	Invest Add	In%	Out%	Mgt	12b-1	Scwb Marg	Phone	Wire	Chek	Income	83	84	85	86	87
Special Growth	SA	13	GISGX	1000	None	0	0	.75	1.0	No	Yes	Yes	No	Yes	—	-1.3	47.2	15.1	-2.0
Select Growth	SG	3	—	1000	None	0	0	.75	1.0	No	Yes	Yes	No	Yes	—	9.7	32.5	21.2	0.5
Equity Income	SI	2	—	1000	None	0	0	.75	1.0	No	Yes	Yes	No	Yes	—	11.1	25.7	18.5	-4.8
Tax Free High Yd	BX	39	GTFHX	2000	None	0	0	.62	0.0	No	Yes	Yes	Yes	Yes	—	8.0	17.3	19.4	0.2
Inc. Max Inc*	BL	11	GITMX	1000	None	0	0	.62	1.0	No	Yes	Yes	Yes	Yes	—	9.6	22.0	9.1	-2.8
Inc. A Rated	BL	6	—	1000	None	0	0	.62	1.0	No	Yes	Yes	Yes	Yes	—	14.4	25.2	13.0	-1.1
Cash Tr. Reg.	MG	6	—	1000	None	0	0	.50	0.7	No	Yes	Yes	Yes	Yes	—	5.5	—	6.0	-0.5
Tax Free Tr.	MG	20	—	2000	None	0	0	.50	0.7	No	Yes	Yes	Yes	Yes	—	—	5.6	4.3	-0.5
Gov. Inv. Trust	MG	193	GITXX	2000	None	0	0	.50	0.0	No	Yes	Yes	Yes	Yes	8.5	10.0	7.5	6.0	5.9
Cash Tr. Gov MM	MG	4	—	1000	None	0	0	.50	0.7	No	Yes	Yes	Yes	Yes	—	—	—	5.9	—

PHONE SWITCH—All Funds   # SWITCHES/YEAR—Unlimited   IRA MINIMUM INVESTMENT—$500.00   KEOGH MIN. INVEST.—$500.00
MINIMUM WIRE WITHDRAWAL—No Minimum   MIN. INVEST. FOR MONTHLY INCOME—No Minimum   IRA FEE—$12.00
* Invests in Low-Grade Bonds

LEXINGTON MANAGEMENT CORP.

Fund Name	Type	Asset Mil	Dow Smb	Min Int	Invest Add	In%	Out%	Mgt	12b-1	Scwb Marg	Phone	Wire	Chek	Income	83	84	85	86	87
Growth	SA	25	LEGGX	1000	50	0	0	0.75	.25	Yes	No	Yes	No	Yes	9.9	-11.8	26.7	20.6	-0.5
Research	SI	112	LEXRX	1000	50	0	0	0.75	.25	Yes	No	Yes	No	Yes	28.6	-4.1	26.3	20.2	0.1
Goldfund	SP	103	LEXMX	1000	50	0	0	1.00	.25	Yes	No	Yes	No	Yes	-6.6	-24.0	13.0	32.7	46.3
GNMA Inc	BL	107	LENNX	1000	50	0	0	0.60	.25	Yes	No	Yes	No	Yes	7.5	11.8	18.3	11.9	1.6
Cr. Un Gov. Sec*	BL	—	—	100M	100M	0	0	0.00	0.00	No	—	—	—	—	—	—	—	—	—
Money Mkt	MM	197	LMMXX	1000	50	0	0	0.50	.25	No	Yes	Yes	100	Yes	8.9	10.3	8.0	6.3	6.2
Tax Free MF	MX	118	LTFXX	1000	50	0	0	0.50	.25	No	Yes	Yes	100	Yes	5.3	6.0	5.1	4.5	4.2
Gov Sec MM	MG	12	LSGXX	1000	50	0	0	0.50	.25	No	Yes	Yes	100	Yes	8.2	9.7	7.6	6.0	5.8

PHONE SWITCH—All Funds   # SWITCHES/YEAR—7 day hold except for Money Mkt. which is unlimited   IRA MINIMUM INVESTMENT—$250.00
IRA FEE—$5.00   KEOGH MIN. INVEST.—$250.00   MINIMUM WIRE WITHDRAWAL—$1000.00   MIN. INVEST. FOR MONTHLY INCOME—$10,000.00
* Designed for Institutional Investors Only.

MONEY MGMT. ASSOC.

Fund Name	Type	Asset Mil	Dow Smb	Min Int	Invest Add	In%	Out%	Mgt	12b-1	Scwb Marg	Phone	Wire	Chek	Income	83	84	85	86	87
Rushmore Stk Mkt	SG	1	—	2500	0	0	0	.5	0	No	No	No	No	No	—	—	—	8.8	6.2
Rushmore OTC	SG	2	—	2500	0	0	0	.5	0	No	No	No	No	No	—	—	—	17.6	0.6
Fund for TF Inv Lg	BX	10	—	2500	0	0	0	.5	0	No	Yes	Yes	250	No	—	—	—	11.8	0.3
Fund for TF Int.	BY	9	—	2500	0	0	0	.5	0	No	No	No	No	No	—	—	—	12.1	-1.0
Rushmore GNMA	BG	10	—	2500	0	0	0	.5	0	No	No	No	No	No	—	—	—	9.1	—
Rushmore US Gov	BG	1	—	2500	0	0	0	.5	0	No	No	No	No	No	—	—	—	10.5	—
Rushmore MM	MM	37	—	2500	0	0	0	.5	0	No	No	No	Yes	No	—	—	—	6.0	5.8
TF Inv MM	MX	41	FFTXX	2500	0	0	0	.5	0	No	No	No	No	No	—	—	—	4.2	3.8
Gov. Investors	MG	686	FUSXX	2500	0	0	0	.5	0	No	Yes	Yes	250	No	—	—	—	6.0	5.6

PHONE SWITCH—All Except the "Rushmore" Funds   # SWITCHES/YEAR—Unlimited   IRA MINIMUM INVESTMENT—$500.00   IRA FEE—$10.00
KEOGH MIN. INVEST.—$500.00   MINIMUM WIRE WITHDRAWAL—$5000.00   MIN. INVEST. FOR MONTHLY INCOME—Not Available

NEUBERGER & BERMAN MANAGEMENT

Fund Name	Type	Asset Mil	Dow Smb	Invest Min Int	Add	Loads and Fees In%	Out%	Mgt	12b-1	Scwb Marg	Phone	Wire	Chek	Income	83	84	85	86	87
Manhattan	SA	294	CNAMX	500	50	0	0	0.50	0.0	No	No	No	No	Yes	26.6	7.0	37.1	17.0	0.0
Partners	SG	515	PARTX	500	50	0	0	0.65	0.0	No	No	No	No	Yes	19.0	7.6	29.9	17.3	4.3
Guardian Mutual	SI	505	GUARX	500	50	0	0	0.75	0.0	Yes	No	No	No	Yes	25.1	7.3	25.3	11.9	−1.0
Energy	SS	378	ENEGX	500	50	0	0	0.65	0.0	No	No	No	No	Yes	22.2	4.8	22.5	10.5	0.1
Liberty	BL	11	CNALX	500	50	0	0	0.65	0.0	No	No	No	No	Yes	16.6	5.9	21.0	18.2	−4.6
Ltd. Matur.	BS	94	NLMBX	50M	10M	0	0	1.50	0.0	No	Yes	No	No	Yes	—	—	—	—	3.6
Money Mkt	MM	125	NBMXX	5000	250	0	0	1.50	0.0	No	Yes	No	No	Yes	—	—	—	—	5.5
TF Money Fd	MX	206	NBTXX	2000	200	0	0	0.50	0.2	No	Yes	Yes	250	Yes	—	—	5.0	4.3	4.2
Gov Money	MG	143	NBGXX	2000	200	0	0	0.50	0.0	No	Yes	Yes	250	Yes	—	9.5	7.4	5.8	5.2

PHONE SWITCH—All Funds   # SWITCHES/YEAR—Unlimited   IRA MINIMUM INVESTMENT—$250.00   IRA FEE—$9.00
KEOGH MIN. INVEST.—$250.00 except Ltd Matur. at $30,000   MINIMUM WIRE WITHDRAWAL—$1000.00   MIN. INVEST. FOR MONTHLY INCOME—$5000.00 except
Ltd Matur. at $50,000

NEWTON (M&I INV. MGMT. CORP)

Fund Name	Type	Asset Mil	Dow Smb	Invest Min Int	Add	Loads and Fees In%	Out%	Mgt	12b-1	Scwb Marg	Phone	Wire	Chek	Income	83	84	85	86	87
Growth	SG	32	NEWTX	1000	50	0	0	.75	.25	Yes	Yes	No	No	Yes	23.5	−8.2	28.7	9.7	−3.6
Income	BL	13	NWTNX	1000	50	0	0	.75	.25	Yes	Yes	No	No	Yes	11.4	12.1	12.8	9.0	2.5
Money Mkt	MM	46	NMFXX	1000	250	0	0	.75	0.00	No	Yes	Yes	500	Yes	8.5	10.1	7.6	6.7	6.4

PHONE SWITCH—All Funds   # SWITCHES/YEAR—Unlimited   IRA MINIMUM INVESTMENT—$500.00   IRA FEE—$10.00   KEOGH MIN. INVEST.—$500.00
MINIMUM WIRE WITHDRAWAL—$1000.00   MIN. INVEST. FOR MONTHLY INCOME—$10,000.00

SAFECO ASSET MANAGEMENT CO.

Fund Name	Type	Asset Mil	Dow Smb	Min Invest Int	Add	Loads and Fees In%	Out%	Mgt	12b-1	Scwb Marg	Withdrawal Options Phone	Wire	Chek	Income	Annual Return 83	84	85	86	87
Growth	SG	67	SAFGX	1000	100	0	0	.50	0	Yes	No	No	No	Yes	31.6	-7.1	20.5	1.8	7.0
Equity	SE	50	SAFQX	1000	100	0	0	.50	0	Yes	No	No	No	Yes	21.2	3.3	31.9	13.3	-4.8
Income	SI	144	SAFIX	1000	100	0	0	.50	0	Yes	No	No	No	Yes	28.3	9.9	31.6	20.6	-6.0
Cal. TF Inc	BX	32	SFCAX	2500	250	0	0	.55	0	Yes	No	No	No	Yes	—	7.5	21.1	19.8	-2.1
Muni Bond	BX	195	SFCOX	2500	250	0	0	.55	0	Yes	No	No	No	Yes	10.3	10.1	21.6	19.8	0.2
US Gov Sec	BL	17	—	1000	100	0	0	.65	0	No	No	No	No	Yes	—	—	—	—	—
Money Mkt	MM	47	SAFXX	1000	100	0	0	.50	0	No	No	Yes	500	Yes	9.0	10.1	7.8	6.2	6.2
TF Money	MX	17	—	1000	100	0	0	.50	0	No	Yes	Yes	500	Yes	—	—	4.6	4.2	4.2

PHONE SWITCH—All Funds   # SWITCHES/YEAR—Unlimited   IRA MINIMUM INVESTMENT—$250.00   KEOGH MIN. INVEST.—$250.00

MINIMUM WIRE WITHDRAWAL—$5000.00   MIN. INVEST. FOR MONTHLY INCOME—$5000.00   IRA FEE $5.00

SCUDDER

Fund Name	Type	Asset Mil	Dow Smb	Min Invest Int	Min Invest Add	Loads In%	Loads Out%	Loads Mgt	Loads 12b-1	Scwb Marg	Withdrawal Phone	Withdrawal Wire	Withdrawal Chek	Withdrawal Income	83	84	85	86	87
Development	SA	296	SCDVX	1000	0	0	0	1.00	0	Yes	Yes	Yes	No	Yes	18.1	−10.2	19.7	7.8	−1.4
Cap. Growth	SA	442	SCDUX	1000	0	0	0	.65	0	Yes	Yes	Yes	No	Yes	22.4	0.4	36.6	16.6	−0.7
Internat'l	SS	710	SCINX	1000	0	0	0	.75	0	Yes	Yes	Yes	No	Yes	29.1	−0.9	49.8	50.8	0.9
Global	SG	41	—	1000	0	0	0	1.00	0	Yes	Yes	Yes	No	Yes	—	—	—	—	2.9
Growth & Inc	SI	384	SCDGX	1000	0	0	0	.60	0	Yes	Yes	Yes	No	Yes	13.4	−4.5	34.5	17.9	3.5
NYTF	BX	137	SCYTX	1000	0	0	0	.60	0	Yes	Yes	Yes	No	Yes	—	9.2	15.9	14.2	−0.6
Cal TF	BX	175	SCYTX	1000	0	0	0	.60	0	Yes	Yes	Yes	No	Yes	—	7.0	18.3	16.9	−1.7
Managed Mun	BX	664	SCMBX	1000	0	0	0	.60	0	Yes	Yes	Yes	No	Yes	9.1	10.1	17.4	16.8	0.3
Gov. Mort Sec	BL	248	SGMSX	1000	0	0	0	.60	0	No	Yes	Yes	No	Yes	—	—	—	11.2	1.5
Income	BL	248	SCSBX	1000	0	0	0	.60	0	No	Yes	Yes	No	Yes	10.7	12.2	21.7	14.6	.8
Gov. Zero Coupon 2000	BS	1	—	1000	0	0	0	.55	0	No	Yes	Yes	No	No	—	—	—	—	−8.8
Gov. Zero Coupon 1995	BS	1	—	1000	0	0	0	.55	0	No	Yes	Yes	No	No	—	—	—	—	−3.8
Gov. Zero Coupon 1990	BS	1	—	1000	0	0	0	.55	0	No	Yes	Yes	No	No	—	—	—	—	1.4
Target Tax Free 1996	BS	21	—	1000	0	0	0	.60	0	No	Yes	Yes	No	No	—	—	—	15.0	1.1
Target Tax Free 1993	BS	117	STTFX	1000	0	0	0	.60	0	Yes	Yes	Yes	No	No	—	8.2	14.4	12.7	2.6
Target Tax Free 1990	BS	104	STFTX	1000	0	0	0	.60	0	No	Yes	Yes	No	No	—	8.0	11.0	10.0	3.2
Target Tax Free 1987	BS	35	STETX	1000	0	0	0	.60	0	No	Yes	Yes	No	No	—	8.6	7.1	6.1	3.4
Target General 1990	BS	16	—	1000	0	0	0	.65	0	Yes	Yes	Yes	No	No	−0.5	13.0	18.3	12.0	3.1
Target General 1994	BS	8	—	1000	0	0	0	.65	0	No	Yes	Yes	No	No	—	—	21.2	14.7	1.4
Target General 1987	BS	5	—	1000	0	0	0	.65	0	Yes	Yes	Yes	No	No	4.5	10.1	14.3	6.4	5.3
Target US Gov 1990	BS	6	—	1000	0	0	0	.65	0	Yes	Yes	Yes	No	No	−0.9	12.4	16.9	11.9	2.0
Target US Gov 1987	BS	2	—	1000	0	0	0	.65	0	Yes	Yes	Yes	No	No	0.0	12.2	12.8	6.6	4.4
Cash Inv TR	MM	1164	SCTXX	1000	0	0	0	.5	0	No	Yes	Yes	100	Yes	8.4	10.1	7.8	6.5	6.1
Tax Free Money	MT	382	STFXX	1000	0	0	0	0.0	0	No	Yes	Yes	100	Yes	4.5	5.4	4.6	4.3	4.1
Gov Money	MG	140	SCGXX	1000	0	0	0	.5	0	No	Yes	Yes	100	Yes	8.2	9.6	7.3	5.9	5.2

PHONE SWITCH—All Funds # SWITCHES/YEAR—3 IRA MINIMUM INVESTMENT—$240.00 IRA FEE—None KEOGH MIN. INVEST.—$240.00 to $500.00

MINIMUM WIRE WITHDRAWAL—$5000.00 MIN. INVEST. FOR MONTHLY INCOME—$10,000.00

SELECTED FUNDS

Fund Name	Type	Asset Mil	Dow Smb	Min Invest		Loads and Fees				Scwb Marg	Withdrawal Options				Annual Return				
				Int	Add	In%	Out%	Mgt	12b-1		Phone	Wire	Chek	Income	83	84	85	86	87
Special Shares	SG	35	LISSX	1000	100	0	0	.5	1.0	Yes	No	Yes	No	Yes	27.8	-4.6	23.7	7.3	0.4
Amer. Shares	SG	264	LISAX	1000	1000	0	0	.5	1.0	Yes	No	Yes	No	Yes	21.4	14.9	33.3	17.1	0.2
Money Mkt	MM	16	SMMXX	1000	100	0	0	.5	0.0	No	No	Yes	500	Yes	8.4	9.5	7.0	5.7	6.0
Money Mkt Gov	MG	1	—	1000	100	0	0	.5	0.0	No	No	Yes	500	Yes	8.1	9.3	7.0	5.3	6.0

PHONE SWITCH—All Funds   # SWITCHES/YEAR—Unlimited   IRA MINIMUM INVESTMENT—No Minimum   IRA FEE—$10.00
KEOGH MIN. INVEST.—No Minimum   MINIMUM WIRE WITHDRAWAL—$1000.00   MIN. INVEST. FOR MONTHLY INCOME—*
* 10,000 min. for Stocks
* 5,000 min. for Money Market

STEIN, ROE & FARNHAM

Fund Name	Type	Asset Mil	Dow Smb	Min Invest		Loads and Fees				Scwb Marg	Withdrawal Options				Annual Return				
				Int	Add	In%	Out%	Mgt	12b-1		Phone	Wire	Chek	Income	83	84	85	86	87
Special	SA	189	SRSPX	2500	100	0	0	0.75	0	Yes	No	Yes	No	Yes	33.0	-1.0	29.4	14.6	3.5
Universe	SA	46	SRUFX	2500	100	0	0	1.00	0	No	No	Yes	No	Yes	20.4	-18.7	28.3	13.7	-1.6
Discovery	SA	37	SRDFX	2500	100	0	0	1.00	0	No	No	Yes	No	Yes	—	-12.2	45.3	-5.3	-1.3
Farn. Cap. Opp.	SA	171	SRFCX	2500	100	0	0	0.75	0	Yes	No	Yes	No	Yes	12.1	-16.7	24.9	16.7	8.7
Farn. Stock	SA	232	SRFSX	2500	100	0	0	0.50	0	Yes	No	Yes	No	Yes	14.0	-9.7	26.5	16.8	5.2
Prime Eq. Growth	SG	33	—	2500	100	0	0	—	0	No	Yes	Yes	No	Yes	—	—	—	—	
Total Return	SI	140	SRFBX	2500	100	0	0	0.50	0	Yes	No	Yes	No	Yes	13.4	5.1	25.6	16.9	0.3
High Yd Muni.	BX	181	SFMFX	2500	100	0	0	0.50	0	No	No	Yes	No	Yes	—	—	21.0	18.9	-0.9
Inter Muni.	BX	96	SRIMX	2500	100	0	0	0.50	0	No	No	Yes	No	Yes	—	—	—	12.2	1.9
High Yld Bonds	BL	94	SRHBX	2500	100	0	0	0.65	0	No	No	Yes	No	Yes	—	—	—	—	4.2
Managed Bonds	BL	163	SRBFX	2500	100	0	0	0.50	0	No	No	Yes	No	Yes	6.7	11.4	22.6	16.1	0.8
Gov. Plus	BG	24	—	2500	100	0	0	0.60	0	No	No	Yes	No	Yes	—	—	—	—	0.2
Cash Reserves	MM	816	STCXX	2500	100	0	0	0.50	0	No	Yes	Yes	150	Yes	8.7	10.3	7.8	6.3	6.1
Tax Ex. Money	MX	253	STEXX	2500	100	0	0	0.50	0	No	Yes	Yes	150	Yes	—	5.6	4.8	4.2	4.1
Gov. Reserves	MG	36	SGRXX	2500	100	0	0	0.50	0	No	Yes	Yes	50	Yes	8.1	8.7	7.1	5.6	5.3

PHONE SWITCH—All Funds   # SWITCHES/YEAR—4   IRA MINIMUM INVESTMENT—$500.00   IRA FEE—$10.00   KEOGH MIN. INVEST.—$500.00
MINIMUM WIRE WITHDRAWAL—$1000.00   MIN. INVEST. FOR MONTHLY INCOME—$10,000.00

STRONG-CORNELIUSON CAPITAL MGMT.

Fund Name	Type	Asset Mil	Dow Smb	Min Invest Int	Min Invest Add	Loads and Fees In%	Loads and Fees Out%	Loads and Fees Mgt	Loads and Fees 12b-1	Scwb Marg	Withdrawal Phone	Withdrawal Wire	Withdrawal Chek	Withdrawal Income	Return 83	Return 84	Return 85	Return 86	Return 87
Opportunity	SA	43	SOPFX	1000	500	2	0	1.0	0	Yes	No	Yes	No	Yes	—	—	—	59.9	11.8
Total Return	SI	518	STRFX	250	200	1	0	0.8	0	Yes	No	Yes	No	Yes	40.7	10.5	25.4	20.0	6.0
Investment	SI	339	STIFX	250	200	1	0	0.8	0	Yes	No	Yes	No	Yes	44.7	9.7	19.4	17.6	-0.3
Income	SI	119	STACX	1000	200	0	0	0.6	0	Yes	No	Yes	No	Yes	—	—	—	30.0	4.4
Tax Free Inc	BX	2	—	2500	200	0	0	0.6	0	No	No	Yes	No	Yes	—	—	—	—	—
Gov. Sec	BS	1	—	1000	200	0	0	0.6	0	No	No	Yes	No	Yes	—	—	—	—	—
Money	MM	26	—	1000	200	0	0	0.5	0	No	Yes	Yes	500	Yes	—	—	—	6.5	6.3
Tax Free Money	MX	—	—	1000	200	0	0	0.5	0	No	Yes	Yes	500	Yes	—	—	—	—	4.6

PHONE SWITCH—All Funds   # SWITCHES/YEAR—5   IRA MINIMUM INVESTMENT—$250.00   IRA FEE—$10.00   KEOGH MIN. INVEST.—$250.00
MINIMUM WIRE WITHDRAWAL—$2500.00   MIN. INVEST. FOR MONTHLY INCOME—$5000.00

USAA INV. MANAGEMENT

Fund Name	Type	Asset Mil	Dow Smb	Min Invest Int	Min Invest Add	Loads and Fees In%	Loads and Fees Out%	Loads and Fees Mgt	Loads and Fees 12b-1	Scwb Marg	Withdrawal Phone	Withdrawal Wire	Withdrawal Chek	Withdrawal Income	Return 83	Return 84	Return 85	Return 86	Return 87
Mutual Sunbelt	SA	116	USAUX	1000	25	0	0	.50	0	No	Yes	Yes	No	Yes	23.9	-18.1	23.0	5.6	-0.8
Mutual Inc	SI	238	USAIX	1000	25	0	0	.50	0	No	Yes	Yes	No	Yes	10.5	14.0	19.0	12.6	2.6
Cornerstone	SG	49	USCRX	1000	100	0	0	.75	0	No	Yes	Yes	No	Yes	—	—	14.7	40.8	9.0
Mutual Growth	SG	179	USAAX	1000	25	0	0	.50	0	No	Yes	Yes	No	Yes	15.7	-7.5	20.0	10.0	5.6
Gold	SP	35	USAGX	1000	100	0	0	.75	0	No	Yes	Yes	No	Yes	—	—	-20.7	55.6	15.7
Tax Ex Sh. Tm	BY	249	USSTX	3000	100	0	0	.50	0	No	Yes	Yes	250	Yes	6.3	7.6	9.5	8.2	2.4
Tax Ex Int.	BY	337	USATX	3000	100	0	0	.50	0	No	Yes	Yes	No	Yes	19.6	8.8	16.3	13.6	0.9
Tax Ex-HY	BX	901	USTEX	3000	100	0	0	.50	0	No	Yes	Yes	No	Yes	11.4	10.4	19.8	17.3	-3.6
Mutual Money	MM	309	USAXX	1000	25	0	0	.50	0	No	Yes	Yes	250	Yes	8.6	10.4	7.8	6.3	6.3
TE Money Mkt	MX	280	USEXY	10,000	100	0	0	.50	0	No	Yes	Yes	250	Yes	—	—	5.3	4.9	4.5

PHONE SWITCH—All Funds   # SWITCHES/YEAR—Unlimited   IRA MINIMUM INVESTMENT—$250.00   IRA FEE—$10.00
MINIMUM WIRE WITHDRAWAL—$1000.00   MIN. INVEST. FOR MONTHLY INCOME—$10,000.00

T. ROWE PRICE

Fund Name	Type	Asset Mil	Dow Smb	Min Invest Int	Add	Loads and Fees In%	Out%	Mgt	12b-1	Scwb Marg	Withdrawal Options Phone	Wire	Chek	Income	Annual Return 83	84	85	86	87
Cap. Appr	SA	69	PRWCX	1000	1000	0	0	.70	0	No	Yes	No	Yes	No	—	—	—	-0.7	-7.4
New Horizons	SA	1034	PRNHX	1000	100	0	0	.65	0	Yes	Yes	No	Yes	No	19.4	-9.5	24.2	-0.1	-2.1
Internat'l Stk	SS	790	PRITX	1000	100	0	0	.75	0	No	Yes	No	No	No	28.5	-5.8	44.7	61.8	7.9
New Amer	SG	84	PRWAX	1000	100	0	0	.60	0	Yes	Yes	No	Yes	No	—	—	—	14.3	-9.4
New Era	SG	497	PRNEX	1000	100	0	0	.50	0	Yes	Yes	No	Yes	No	25.3	3.3	23.3	16.0	17.7
Growth Stk	SG	1273	PRGFX	1000	100	0	0	.50	0	Yes	Yes	No	Yes	No	11.7	-1.2	35.2	21.8	3.4
Growth Inc	SI	389	PRGIX	1000	100	0	0	.50	0	Yes	Yes	No	Yes	No	32.4	1.8	19.7	8.0	-4.7
Equ. Inc	SI	94	PRFPX	1000	100	0	0	.50	0	Yes	Yes	No	Yes	No	—	—	—	26.7	3.7
Tax Free HY	BX	274	PRFHX	1000	100	0	0	.50	0	No	Yes	Yes	Yes	500	—	—	—	20.4	.02
GNMA	BG	317	PRGMX	1000	100	0	0	.55	0	Yes	Yes	Yes	Yes	No	—	—	—	11.0	0.9
NYTF	BY	64	PRCTX	1000	100	0	0	.55	0	No	Yes	Yes	Yes	No	—	—	—	—	-2.9
CALTF	BY	32	PRKCX	1000	100	0	0	.55	0	No	Yes	Yes	Yes	No	—	—	—	—	-6.7
Tax Free Inc	BY	1474	PRTAZ	1000	100	0	0	.50	0	No	Yes	Yes	Yes	500	7.0	7.1	16.9	19.8	-4.3
High Yield	BL	765	PRHYX	1000	100	0	0	.62	0	Yes	Yes	Yes	Yes	No	—	—	—	14.2	3.0
Int'l Bond	BL	70	RPIBX	1000	100	0	0	.75	0	Yes	Yes	Yes	Yes	No	—	—	—	—	28.1
New Income	BL	945	PRCIX	1000	100	0	0	.50	0	Yes	Yes	Yes	Yes	5000	9.7	10.7	17.6	13.9	2.1
Tax Free Short Int	BS	307	PRFSX	1000	100	0	0	.50	0	Yes	Yes	Yes	Yes	500	—	6.8	11.8	9.7	2.2
Short Term	BS	196	PRWBX	1000	100	0	0	.50	0	No	Yes	Yes	Yes	500	—	—	12.5	8.9	5.2
Prime Reserve	MM	2739	PRRXX	1000	100	0	0	.40	0	No	Yes	Yes	Yes	500	9.0	10.5	8.0	6.4	6.2
US Treas	MG	161	—	1000	100	0	0	.50	0	No	Yes	Yes	Yes	500	8.4	9.5	7.3	5.7	5.3
NYTF Money	MX	13	PTEXX	1000	100	0	0	.45	0	No	Yes	Yes	Yes	500	—	—	—	—	3.7
Cal TF	MX	14	PTEXX	1000	100	0	0	.45	0	No	Yes	Yes	Yes	500	—	—	—	—	4.1
Tax Exempt	MX	1081	PTEXX	1000	100	0	0	.50	0	No	Yes	Yes	Yes	500	5.2	5.9	5.0	4.6	4.3

TWENTIETH CENT.

Fund Name	Type	Asset Mil	Dow Smb	Min Invest Int	Min Invest Add	In%	Out%	Mgt	12b-1	Scwb Marg	Phone	Wire	Chek	Income	83	84	85	86	87
Growth	SA	1231	TWCGX	0	0	0.0	0.0	2	0	No	Yes	Yes	No	Yes	24.4	−11.2	33.9	18.8	13.0
Gift Trust	SA	11	TWGTX	0	0	0.5	0.5	2	0	No	Yes	Yes	No	No	—	−14.3	55.3	28.0	8.7
Select	SA	2393	TWCIX	0	0	0.0	0.0	2	0	No	Yes	Yes	No	Yes	29.9	−7.7	33.8	20.4	5.6
Ultra	SA	247	TWCUX	0	0	0.5	0.0	2	0	No	Yes	Yes	No	Yes	26.3	−19.0	26.2	10.3	6.7
Vista	SA	216	TWCVX	0	0	0.5	0.0	2	0	No	Yes	Yes	No	Yes	—	−16.3	22.5	26.3	6.0
Long Term	BL	11	—	0	0	0.0	0.0	2	0	No	Yes	No	No	Yes	—	—	—	—	7.4
Tax Exempt Int.	BY	9	—	0	0	0.0	0.0	2	0	No	Yes	No	No	No	—	—	—	—	4.8
Tax Exempt Lg Tm	BX	8	—	0	0	0.0	0.0	2	0	No	Yes	No	No	No	—	—	—	—	5.7
US Gov.	BG	356	—	0	0	0.0	0.0	2	0	No	Yes	Yes	No	Yes	6.9	12.2	12.9	9.1	3.8
Cash Reserves	MM	462	TWCXX	0	0	0.0	0.0	0	0	No	Yes	Yes	No	Yes	—	—	—	6.1	5.9

PHONE SWITCH—All except Gift Trust   # SWITCHES/YEAR—12   IRA MINIMUM INVESTMENT—0   KEOGH MIN. INVEST.—0
MINIMUM WIRE WITHDRAWAL—$10.00 Fee   MIN. INVEST. FOR MONTHLY INCOME—$5,000.00   IRA FEE—$10.00

VALUE LINE INC.

Fund Name	Type	Asset Mil	Dow Smb	Min Invest Int	Min Invest Add	In%	Out%	Mgt	12b-1	Scwb Marg	Phone	Wire	Chek	Income	83	84	85	86	87
Lev Growth	SA	282	VAIIX	250	25	0	0	.75	0	Yes	No	No	No	No	8.0	−8.9	27.1	23.0	2.8
Spec Sit.	SA	123	VALSX	250	25	0	0	.75	0	Yes	No	No	No	No	19.3	−25.5	21.1	5.1	−9.3
Fund	SA	205	VLIFX	250	25	0	0	.75	0	Yes	No	No	No	No	−1.3	−15.1	35.6	17.0	5.0
Income	SI	140	VALTX	250	25	0	0	.75	0	Yes	No	No	No	No	6.5	2.6	23.7	15.5	−2.3
Convertible	SI	62	VALLX	1000	250	0	0	.75	0	Yes	No	No	No	No	—	—	—	16.7	−6.1
Tax Ex Hi. Yd	BX	228	VLHXX	1000	250	0	0	.50	0	No	No	No	No	No	—	—	19.8	13.7	0.5
Agg Inc Tr	BL	48	VAGIX	1000	250	0	0	.50	0	No	No	No	No	No	—	—	—	—	−2.0
US Gov Sec	BL	237	VALBX	1000	250	0	0	.50	0	Yes	No	No	500	No	5.8	13.7	21.2	10.7	3.4
Cash	MM	461	VLCXX	1000	100	0	0	.40	0	No	No	Yes	500	No	8.9	10.4	7.9	6.5	6.3
TE MM	MX	37	VLTXX	1000	100	0	0	.50	0	Yes	Yes	Yes	500	No	—	—	4.7	4.3	4.1

PHONE SWITCH—All Funds   # SWITCHES/YEAR—8   IRA MINIMUM INVESTMENT—0   KEOGH MIN. INVEST.—0
MINIMUM WIRE WITHDRAWAL—$1000.00   MIN. INVEST. FOR MONTHLY INCOME—Mo. Inc.: Not Avail   IRA FEE—$10.00

UNITED SERVICES ADVISORS

Fund Name	Type	Asset Mil	Dow Smb	Min Invest		Loads and Fees				Scwb Marg	Withdrawal Options				Annual Return				
				Int	Add	In%	Out%	Mgt	12b-1		Phone	Wire	Chek	Income	83	84	85	86	87
Lo Cap	SA	3	LOCFX	100	50	0	2	.75	0	Yes	No	No	No	Yes	—	—	—	-6.6	-13.2
Growth	SG	8	GRTHX	100	50	0	0	.75	0	Yes	No	No	No	Yes	—	-26.4	21.0	11.5	-11.2
Good/Bad Times	SG	22	GBTFX	100	50	0	0	.75	0	Yes	No	No	No	Yes	11.1	2.7	24.0	11.3	0.6
Income	SI	4	USINX	100	50	0	0	.75	0	Yes	No	No	No	Yes	—	1.3	15.3	5.6	-4.3
Gold Shares	SP	292	USERX	100	50	0	0	.75	0	Yes	No	No	No	Yes	1.0	-29.6	-26.8	37.5	31.6
Prospector*	SP	66	PSPEX	—	—	0	2	—	—	Yes	—	—	—	—	—	36.8	0.0	30.9	25.4
New Prospect.	SP	50	—	100	50	0	2	.75	0	Yes	No	No	No	Yes	—	—	—	38.5	31.1
Tax Free	BX	5	—	100	50	0	0	.75	0	Yes	No	No	No	Yes	—	—	11.3	16.9	-0.2
GNMA	BG	5	—	100	50	0	0	.66	0	Yes	No	No	No	Yes	—	—	—	—	-1.3
Treasury Sec	MG	73	USTXX	100	50	0	0	.50	0	No	Yes	Yes	250	Yes	6.9	9.5	7.2	5.4	5.4

PHONE SWITCH—All Funds   # SWITCHES/YEAR—12   IRA MINIMUM INVESTMENT—None   IRA FEE—$10.00   KEOGH MIN. INVEST.—None
MINIMUM WIRE WITHDRAWAL—No Minimum   MIN. INVEST. FOR MONTHLY INCOME—$5000.00
* Not selling shares.

VANGUARD

Fund Name	Type	Asset Mil	Dow Smb	Min Invest Int	Min Invest Add	Loads In%	Loads Out%	Mgt	12b-1	Scwb Marg	Phone	Wire	Chek	Income	83	84	85	86	87
Naess & Thomas	SA	24	NAESX	3000	100	0	0	.60	0	Yes	Yes	Yes	No	Yes	—	—	—	0.2	-7.0
Explorer*	SA	261	VEXPX	—	—	0	0	.33	0	Yes	Yes	Yes	No	Yes	—	—	—	-8.5	-6.9
Explorer II	SA	77	VEIIX	3000	100	0	0	.45	0	Yes	Yes	No	No	Yes	—	—	—	-7.2	-4.3
WL Morgan	SA	538	VMRGX	1500	100	0	0	.33	0	Yes	Yes	Yes	No	Yes	—	—	—	7.0	5.0
World US	SG	135	WWUSX	1500	100	0	0	.33	0	Yes	Yes	Yes	No	Yes	14.0	1.2	36.6	7.8	-5.4
Index Trust	SI	931	VFINX	1500	100	0	0	6.00	0	Yes	Yes	Yes	No	Yes	21.3	6.2	31.2	17.8	4.7
Windsor*	SI	4565	WWNDX	—	—	0	0	.35	0	Yes	Yes	Yes	No	Yes	30.0	19.5	27.9	20.3	1.2
Windsor II	SI	1235	WWNFX	1500	100	0	0	.35	0	Yes	Yes	Yes	No	Yes	—	—	—	21.5	-2.1
US Trustees	SI	—	VTRSX	25000	100	0	0	.85	0	Yes	Yes	Yes	No	Yes	—	—	—	—	—
Star	SI	567	VGSTX	500	100	0	0	0.00	0	Yes	Yes	Yes	No	Yes	—	—	—	13.8	1.6
World Int.	SI	472	VWIGX	1500	100	0	0	.33	0	Yes	Yes	Yes	No	Yes	43.1	-1.0	55.5	56.7	12.7
Qualified Div I*	SI	157	VQDIX	—	—	0	0	.33	0	Yes	Yes	Yes	No	Yes	32.9	25.2	30.1	21.5	-4.8
Qual. Div II	SI	124	VQIIX	3000	100	0	0	.33	0	Yes	Yes	Yes	No	Yes	7.9	10.4	29.7	24.7	-7.7
Qual. Div III	SI	95	VDPTX	25000	1000	0	0	.20	0	Yes	Yes	Yes	No	Yes	5.5	3.0	11.4	4.2	3.0
Fixed Inc. HI Yd	SI	904	VWEHX	3000	100	0	0	.25	0	Yes	Yes	Yes	250	Yes	—	7.5	22.2	16.9	2.6
Bond Mkt	SI	43	—	3000	100	0	0	varies	0	Yes	Yes	Yes	No	Yes	—	—	—	—	1.5
Fixed Inc GNMA	SI	1864	VFII	3000	100	0	0	.15	0	Yes	Yes	Yes	250	Yes	9.5	1.4	20.7	11.7	2.2
Fixed Inc US Treas.	SI	73	—	3000	100	0	0	varies	0	Yes	Yes	Yes	250	Yes	9.0	—	—	—	2.9
Fixed Inc Sh Term	SI	410	VFSTX	3000	100	0	0	varies	0	Yes	Yes	Yes	250	Yes	—	14	14.9	11.4	4.4
Wellesley Inc.	SI	495	VWINX	1500	100	0	0	.25	0	Yes	Yes	Yes	No	Yes	18.6	16.6	27.4	18.2	-1.9
Wellington	SI	1331	VWELX	1500	100	0	0	.20	0	Yes	Yes	Yes	No	Yes	23.4	10.7	28.4	18.3	2.3
Convertible Sec.	SI	73	VCVSK	3000	100	0	0	.45	0	Yes	Yes	Yes	No	Yes	—	—	—	—	-10.7

Fixed Inc Inv	SI	587	VWESX	3000	100	0	0	.25	0	Yes	Yes	Yes	250	Yes	6.6	14.2	22.0	14.3	0.2
Spec Gold	SP	158	VGPMX	1500	100	0	1	.30	0	Yes	Yes	No	No	Yes	—	—	-5.4	49.7	38.7
Spec Tech	SS	20	VGTCX	1500	100	0	1	.30	0	Yes	Yes	No	No	Yes	—	—	13.9	5.7	-11.9
Spec Health	SS	47	VGHCX	1500	100	0	1	.30	0	Yes	Yes	No	No	Yes	—	—	45.6	21.4	-0.5
Spec Service	SS	23	VGSEX	1500	100	0	1	.30	0	Yes	Yes	No	No	Yes	—	—	43.7	12.7	-13.5
Spec Energy	SS	32	VGENX	1500	100	0	1	.30	0	Yes	Yes	No	No	Yes	—	—	14.4	12.5	6.1
Muni H Yield	BX	654	VWAHX	3000	100	0	0	varies	0	Yes	Yes	Yes	250	Yes	10.3	9.3	21.7	19.7	-1.6
Penn Ins. TF	BX	2003	—	3000	100	0	0	varies	0	Yes	Yes	Yes	250	Yes	—	—	—	—	-1.3
NY Ins TF	BX	77	—	3000	100	0	0	cost	0	Yes	Yes	Yes	250	Yes	—	—	—	—	-3.5
Cal Ins. TF	BX	89	VCITX	3000	1000	0	0	cost	0	Yes	Yes	Yes	No	Yes	—	—	—	—	-3.9
Muni-Lg Tm	BX	523	VWLTX	3000	100	0	0	cost	0	Yes	Yes	Yes	250	Yes	9.4	8.5	20.8	19.4	7.1
Muni Lg Tm Ins.	BX	685	VILDX	3000	100	0	0	cost	0	Yes	Yes	Yes	250	Yes	—	—	19.3	18.6	.1
Muni Inter Tm	BS	762	VWITX	3000	100	0	0	cost	0	Yes	Yes	Yes	250	Yes	6.4	9.5	17.3	15.8	1.6
Muni Short Tm	BS	834	—	3000	100	0	0	cost	0	Yes	Yes	Yes	250	Yes	5.0	6.8	7.0	7.4	4.1
MM Prime	MM	4674	VMMXX	1000	100	0	0	cost	0	No	Yes	Yes	250	Yes	8.9	10.6	8.1	6.0	6.5
MM Insur	MM	113	VMPXX	1000	100	0	0	.90	0	No	Yes	Yes	250	Yes	—	9.8	7.4	6.0	6.0
MM Muni Bond	MX	2065	VMSXX	3000	100	0	0	cost	0	No	Yes	Yes	250	Yes	5.0	6.0	5.2	4.7	4.5

PHONE SWITCH—All Funds except Index Tr, Naess & Thomas, Explorer II & Geminii II   # SWITCHES/YEAR—Unlimited   IRA MINIMUM INVESTMENT—$500.00

IRA FEE—$10.00   KEOGH MIN. INVEST.—$500.00   MINIMUM WIRE WITHDRAWAL—No Minimum   MIN. INVEST. FOR MONTHLY INCOME—$10,000.00

* Closed to New Investors:

1. Should be used by corporations seeking 70% dividend tax exclusion.
2. Star fund holds shares of other Vang. funds which are subject to management fees.

APPENDIX II

Tax Lien Sales

Contact these State and County offices for more information about tax lien certificate and property sales described in Chapter 29.

ALASKA

Contact counties Anchorage and Fairbanks

ARIZONA

State Dept. of Revenue
402 W. Congress Street
TUCSON, AZ 85701
(602)628-5725

ARKANSAS

Property Sales
Commissioner of State Lands
Room 109, State Capital Bldg.
LITTLE ROCK, AR 72116

CALIFORNIA

Property Sales
Kern County Tax Collector's Office
1415 Truxtun Avenue
BAKERSFIELD, CA 93301
(805)861-2601

Tax Collector
PO Box 1438, Room 310
SANTA ANA, CA 92702
(714)385-4837

Tax Collector
225 N. Hill, Room 143C
LOS ANGELES, CA 90012
(213)974-2045

Tax Collector
1600 Pacific Highway Room 162
SAN DIEGO, CA 92101
(619)531-5837

COLORADO

Tax Lien Sales
El Paso County Assessor
27 E. Vermijo Avenue
COLORADO SPRINGS, CO 80903
(303)520-6600

Treasury Division
144 W. Colfax Avenue
DENVER, CO 80202
(303)575-3458

CONNECTICUT

Tax Collector's Office
550 Main
HARTFORD, CT 06103

WASHINGTON, DC

Real Property Tax Office
300 Indiana Avenue, N.W.
WASHINGTON, DC 20001

FLORIDA

Revenue Collector
501 S.E. 6th Street
FT. LAUDERDALE, FL 33301
(305)765-4604

Clerk's Office
330 East Bay Street
JACKSONVILLE, FL 32202
(904)633-6510

Tax Collection Division
101 W. Flagler Street
MIAMI, FL 33130
(305)375-5444

State Dept. of Revenue
1458 U.S. Highway 19 S. Suite 230
CLEARWATER, FL 33546
(813)535-4691

Hillsborough County Tax Collector
Room 190F
TAMPA, FL 33602
(813)272-6070

GEORGIA

Tax Commissioner's Office
120 W. Trinity Place
DECATUR, GA 30030
(404)371-2196

ILLINOIS

Peoria County Clerk Room 109
324 Main Street
PEORIA, Il 61602
(309)672-6059

INDIANA

Lake County Treasurer's Office
11 E. 4th Avenue
GARY, IN 46401
(219)886-3621 ext. 244

IOWA

Polk County Treasurer's Office
2nd Avenue & 111 Court Avenue
DES MOINES, IA 50307
(515)286-3060

KANSAS

County Counsellor
200 E. 7th Room 203
TOPEKA, KS 66603
(913)295-4042

Foreclosure Dept.
Sedgwick County Courthouse
525 N. Main Room 112
WICHITA, KS 67203
(316)268-7482

KENTUCKY

County Courthouse Lien Dept.
PO Box 33033
LOUISVILLE, KY 40232
(502)625-5785

MAINE

Property Tax Office
State Office Bldg. Suite 24
AUGUSTA, ME 04333
(207)289-2011

MARYLAND

Tax Sales Division
200 N. Holiday Street
BALTIMORE, MD 21202

MASSACHUSETTS

Dept. of Revenue
200 Portland Street
BOSTON, MA 02204
(617)727-2300

MICHIGAN

Washtenaw County Treasurer's Tax
Collector's Office
PO Box 8645
ANN ARBOR, MI 48107
(313)994-2520

Genessee County Treasurer's Office
1101 Beach Street
FLINT, MI 48502
(313)257-3054

Treasurer's Office
PO Box Y
GRAND RAPIDS, MI 49501
(616)774-3641

Treasurer's Office
PO Box 215
MASON, MI 48854
(517)676-0251

MINNESOTA

Dept. of Property Taxation
Tax Forfeited Land Unit
A603 Government Center
MINNEAPOLIS, MN 55487

MISSOURI

Property Tax Division
415 E. 12th
KANSAS CITY, MO 64106
(816)881-3232

Tax Collector
940 Boonville
SPRINGFIELD, MO 65802
(417)868-4036

MONTANA

Property Assessment Division
Mitchell Bldg.
616 Helena Avenue
HELENA, MT 59620
(406)444-2981

NEBRASKA

Real Estate Division, Tres. Office
Civic Center
OMAHA, NE 68103
(402)444-7272

NEVADA

Washoe County Tax Collector's
Office
PO Box 11130
RENO, NV 89520
(702)785-5450

NEW JERSEY

Real Estate Division
280 Grove Street
JERSEY CITY, NJ 07301
(201)645-3760

Tax Assessor's Dept.
City Hall
155 Market Street
PATERSON, NJ 47505
(201)881-3484

NEW MEXICO

Taxation & Revenues Dept.
First National Bank Bldg. E.
5301 Central Avenue NE
ALBUQUERQUE, NM 87198
(505)841-8000

NEW YORK

Real Property Taxation
95 Franklin
BUFFALO, NY 14212
(716)846-8333

Real Estate Dept.
City Hall Room 023B
30 Church Street
ROCHESTER, NY 14614
(716)428-6951

Real Property Tax Commission
110 Grove
WHITE PLAINS, NY 10601
(914)682-2337

NORTH CAROLINA

Delinquent Tax Dept.
201 S. Eugene Street
GREENSBORO, NC 27402
(919)373-3852

NORTH DAKOTA
County Attorney's Office
BISMARCK, ND 58501
(701)222-6672

OHIO
Delinquent Taxes—Real Estate
Hamilton County Courthouse
Rm. 126
CINCINNATI, OH 45202
(513)632-8570

County Treasurer
Real Estate Tax Dept.
1219 Ontario Street
CLEVELAND, OH 44113
(215)443-7420

Real Estate Tax Dept.
One Government Center
TOLEDO, OH 43604
(419)245-4305

OREGON
Assessment & Taxation Dept.
Property Tax Division
125 E. 8th Avenue
EUGENE, OR 97401
(503)687-4203

PENNSYLVANIA
Lehigh County Sheriff's Office
PO Box 1548
ALLENTOWN, PA 18105
(215)820-3175

SOUTH DAKOTA
Sheriff's Office
PO Box 186
PIERRE, SD 57501
(605)223-2746

TENNESSEE
Tennessee Dept. of Revenue
Andrew Jackson Bldg.
500 Deaderick Street
NASHVILLE, TN 37242
(615)741-3581

Clerk & Master
Hamilton County Courthouse
Mayfield Annex, 4th Floor
CHATTANOOGA, TN 37402
(615)757-2424

Clerk & Master
Suite 125, City-County Bldg.
400 Main Avenue
KNOXVILLE, TN 37902
(615)521-2555

UTAH
County Treasurer Dept.
Room 105 City & County Bldg.
SALT LAKE CITY, UT 84111
(801)535-7404

VERMONT
Cost Assessment
43 Randall Street
WATERBURY, VT 05676
(802)241-3500

WEST VIRGINIA
State Auditor's Office
State Capital Bldg.
CHARLESTON, WV 25305
(304)348-2262

Tax Lien Information For Various States

See "Tax Lien Sales," page 404 for information on State and County Agencies handling Tax Lien Sales.

ARKANSAS—Public Auction of Tax-Delinquent Properties.

CALIFORNIA—Public Auction of Tax-Delinquent Properties.

SAN DIEGO

To get on Public Tax Sale mailing list send $3.00.
Tax sale brochure mailed four weeks prior to auction.
Oral public auction—no mailed or sealed bids.
Successful bids of $5,000 or less payable at auction.
$5,000 or 10% (whichever is greater) required as downpayment on properties over $5,000
Balance due in 90 days or deposit is forfeited.
Deed conveys title to purchases free of most all liens and mortgages.
Minimum bid is 25% of County Assessor's fair market value.

LOS ANGELES

Public Auction List $12.00 by mail. List includes description, minimum bids.

SANTA ANA

Marshall's Office (714)834-3500; one sale per year of homes.
Trust Deed Service Company (714)385-4837; One or two properties sold per day, residential and commercial.
Bidders must show amount to cover minimum bid and must register.
Bidders card is then issued.
Bids are verbal.
Full price must be paid at auction.
All liens and mortgages other than federal liens are extinguished by asection.
Terms: cash, certified checks, cashier's checks, traveler's checks.
Write or call to be put on mailing list for notification.

BAKERSFIELD

Bidders register on morning of sale.
Maps of property can be purchased from County Assessor (805)861-2311.
Full payment required by cash, cashier's check or certified check.
$1.10 per $1,000 California transfer tax assessed.

COLORADO—Tax Lien Certificates
Taxes are delinquent August 1st.
Delinquent taxes advertised in October in Daily Journal.

Tax lien sale held middle of November in Denver; October in Colorado
   Springs.
Bidding starts at amount of taxes plus interest to date of sale.
If a premium is bid, buyer does not recover premium.
Interest paid to winning bidder is Federal Reserve discount rate plus 9%.
   1987 rate was 15% or 1.25% per month.
Buyers may pay subsequent year's taxes to be included in their original
   certificate at same rate of interest.
If the property has not been redeemed after three years, buyer applies for
   and receives a deed to the property.

CONNECTICUT

HARTFORD
Approximately 100 city-owned properties including vacant land and build-
   ings sold by Request for Proposal.
Bidder submits proposal for use of property, city chooses which proposal to
   accept. Low to moderate income housing proposal has precedence.
Current list available from city.

DISTRICT OF COLUMBIA—Tax Lien Certificates
Properties advertised in *Washington Post* in December.
Tax lien sale starts about 3rd week in January and lasts 6 days.
Sale at Municipal Center, 300 Indiana Ave., NW, room 3106.
Bidders must register prior to sale.
Deposit of $100 or 20% of bid required.
Opening bid is amount of delinquent taxes.
All bidders register and receive bidding card.
Winning bidder has five days to pay balance.
Buyer receives deed if property not redeemed in two years.
All mortgages and liens, other than federal, eliminated.

FLORIDA—Tax Lien Certificates—18% Interest Rate
Opening bid is 18%; subsequent bids, if any, are for lower interest rate.
Auction dates: Some counties once or twice per year on prescribed date,
   others at random.
Sales often conducted over several days due to number of properties.
Life of a tax lien certificate is seven years.
After two years, buyer may force a sale at auction.
Some counties require fees of about $500 to force sale.
Property is then sold at public auction to highest bidder.
Tax lien certificates can be sold to other investors.
Mandatory interest of 5% if property is paid.
10% deposit required to bid, balance due in 48 hours.
Sales are usually in May or June.

GEORGIA—Tax Lien Certificates–10% Interest Rate
Bidding begins at amount of lien and is sold to highest bidder.
Redemption period is 12 months.
Buyer has the right of redemption after 12 months by proper notice to all interested parties.

INDIANA—Public Auction of Tax-Delinquent Properties
Sales advertised in papers; no mailing list.
Dates of sales usually in August or October.
Information available from County Treasurer's Offices.

IOWA—Public Auction of Tax-Delinquent Properties
Sale in June.
Preregistration required.
Verbal and mailed bids acceptable.

KANSAS—Public Auction of Tax-Delinquent Properties
Open auction—no sealed bids.
Minimum bid is unpaid taxes and advertising costs.
Redemption Period—the amount of time the original owner/delinquent tax-payer has to pay the taxes and interest before the property is deeded to the tax lien certificate holder or sold at a public auction.
Buyer—the winning bidder at a tax lien certificate auction or public auction of a property.

KENTUCKY—Tax Lien Certificates—12% Interest
Certificate of delinquency issued to bidders.
Called Tax Bills in Kentucky.
Property goes to auction for open bid.

MAINE—Sale of State-owned Tax-Acquired Properties.

MARYLAND—Tax Lien Certificates—Interest Rate 24%
Baltimore 1987 list was a total of 3000 properties.
Amount paid at time of winning bid is unpaid taxes.
Balance of bid, if any, is paid prior to issuance of deed.
Redemption period is six months.
If not redeemed, buyer files a Bill of Complaint in Equity Court to foreclose and receive possession of property.

MASSACHUSETTS—Sale of Delinquent Tax Properties at Public Auction
Contact treasurer of city or town for dates and procedures for auction.
Minimum bid is amount of unpaid taxes and interest.

MICHIGAN—Tax Lien Certificates—Interest Rate 15% to 50%
Tax certificate sales usually held in May.
Payment due within 48 hours of winning bid.
Sales conducted after taxes delinquent for three years.
Contact county treasurer in each of the 83 counties.
Liens not sold by the county can be purchased at the State Treasurer's office.

If property is not redeemed prior to next annual sales, interest rate goes to 50% retroactive.

Buyer can take title by serving notice to all owners of interest and occupants within five years with a waiting period of six months after notice.

Buyer must make purchases at subsequent tax sales until he has absolute title.

MINNESOTA—Public Auction of Tax-Delinquent Properties

Properties not sold at auction available anytime at appraisal value.

20% down payment at time of sale.

Balance in 5 to 10 annual installments make these properties very attractive.

Sales subject to existing leases.

Title passed after full payment.

MISSOURI—Public Auction of Tax-Delinquent Properties

Properties with taxes delinquent for two years, are sold at public auction.

Minimum bid is unpaid taxes plus advertising costs.

(Note: some counties review price bid through the court. If bid is too low, buyer must increase bid or is refunded money.)

MONTANA—Public Auction of Tax-Delinquent Properties

Sales conducted by County Treasurers.

For a list of County Treasurers write:

Montana Association of Counties

1802 Eleventh Ave.

Helena, MT 59601

(406)442-5209

NEBRASKA—Public Auction of Tax-Delinquent Properties

Minimum bid is the delinquent taxes quoted in the foreclosure action.

Check treasurer's office for total taxes due.

Omaha auction in October.

NEVADA—Public Auction of Tax-Delinquent Properties

Contact County Treasurer.

Notice in paper four weeks prior to sale.

NEW JERSEY—Public Auction of City-Owned Properties

Governing body sets minimum bid.

10% deposit, balance due in ten days.

Properties sold as is.

NEW MEXICO—Public Auction of Tax-Delinquent Properties

Auctions in all counties at courthouse.

For listing of County Clerks' offices for the 31 counties write:

Taxation Department

PO Box 630

Santa Fe, NM 87509

Auctions begin at 10 A.M. and go until all properties are sold.

No set auction schedule. Published in legal papers.

Oral bidding by buyer or his agent.

Sales wipe out all other liens and mortgages except federal.

Minimum bid is delinquent taxes, interest, and penalties.

Personal check with letter of credit from bank accepted.

NEW YORK—Tax Lien Certificates

Sales conducted by county except in Westchester Co., which handles auctions by city.

If property is auctioned, buyer pays 20% at sale with 60 days to pay balance.

Rochester has an attractive Urban Property auction program.

NORTH CAROLINA—Public Auction of Tax-Delinquent Properties

Conducted by counties as often as three to four times per year.

10% deposit required balance in ten days.

Upset bids can be filled by others during ten-day period.

NORTH DAKOTA—Public Auction of Tax-Delinquent Properties

County sets minimum bid.

Oral bids once per year.

Eighty-six properties auctioned in Bismarck in 1987.

OHIO—Public Auction of Tax-Delinquent Properties

Sheriffs sales held every Thursday in Cincinnati, similar in other areas.

Forfeited land sale each June.

10% deposit upon successful bid, 30 days for balance.

Minimum bid is 66% of appraised value.

OREGON—Public Auction of Tax-Delinquent Properties

Most areas have mailing lists you can get on.

Properties first auctioned. Those not sold available for private sale.

Minimum acceptable amount published for each property.

Sealed bids accepted with 10% or $300 maximum deposit.

PENNSYLVANIA—Public Auction of Tax-Delinquent Properties

Mortgage and judgment defaults handled by Sheriff's office.

Tax defaults handled by Tax Claim Bureau.

10% deposit required at sheriff's sale, balance 30 days.

3% poundage and transfer tax required.

Bidding begins at $1.00 above judgment and sheriff's costs.

SOUTH DAKOTA—Tax Lien Certificates

All auctions conducted third Monday in December at each County Treasurer's office.

Properties advertised in county newspapers.

Tax Certificates must be held four years before buyer may start proceedings to acquire a tax deed.

Bids are oral and bidders must be present.

TENNESSEE—Public Auction of Tax-Delinquent Properties

Chattanooga auctions in June, others scheduled as needed.

Sale of properties liened for three years.

Nashville sales two to three times yearly—no specific date.
Announcement in legal and local papers.

UTAH—Public Auction of Tax-Delinquent Properties
Properties subject to a tax lien on January 15th of each year are deemed to
  have been sold to county. County resells in May.
Minimum bid is back taxes penalties, interest, and costs.
No competitive bidding allowed if an owner of record or mortgage holder
  bids.
Bids accepted for a portion of a property.

VERMONT—Public Auction of Tax-Delinquent Properties
Sales conducted by towns and municipalities.

WEST VIRGINIA—Tax Lien Certificates
Yearly in October or November; sheriffs of the 55 counties sell real estate
  with delinquent taxes.
Sales are for prior year's delinquent taxes.
Redemption period is 18 months.
Buyer is liable for subsequent year's taxes.
Buyer can eventually secure a deed from the County Clerk.
State conducts a second sale for properties not sold by original sheriff's sale.

INDEX

Accelerated Cost Recovery System (ACRS), 241
Accidents, and automobile insurance, 47
Account, mutual fund, 301
ACRS. *See* Accelerated Cost Recovery System
Adjustable rate mortgage (ARM), 99, 100, 107
Adjusted gross income (AGI), 132–133
Adviser, to mutual fund, 301
Aggressive growth stock funds, 305, 307, 324
  best performing, 306
AGI. *See* Adjusted gross income
Allowances, nondeductible, 231
  See also Withholding allowances
Alternate MACRS depreciation. *See* Straight-line depreciation
Alternative Minimum Tax (AMT), 252
AMAs. *See* Asset Management Accounts
A. M. Best Rating, 345, 347
American Express, 51, 82, 83, 281, 283
American Stock Exchange, 305
Amortization, negative, 99
Amortized mortgage, 99
AMT. *See* Alternative Minimum Tax
Annually renewable term (ART) insurance, 69, 71–72, 74, 75–77
Annually Renewable Term (ART) Insurance Chart, 71, 72, 74, 75–77
Annuities, 68–69, 177
  rollover to, 73
Annuities, self-directed, 273, 340–352
  advantages of, 368–70

and children, 344–45
choosing, 345–46
and commissions, 341, 343–44, 345–46
and estate, 344
performance of, 261, 375–78
and rollover, 342
Self-Directed Annuities Planning Chart, 343, 345, 346–52
and tax reform, 341–42
and withdrawals, 343, 346
Annuitizing, 342
Anti-theft equipment discount, 47
Appeals and review system, 148
Apple Computer, 223
Appreciables, credit for, 80
Arkansas, 113
ARM. *See* Adjustable rate mortgage
ART insurance. *See* Annually renewable term insurance
Asked price, 301
Asset expensing method, 157
  for automobile deduction, 235–236
  for small business, 239–40, 243
"Asset Management Account Comparison Chart," 284, 285
Asset Management Accounts (AMAs), 280–85, 315
  advantages of, 368, 369
  vs. checking accounts, 282
  and debit card, 283
  interest rates in, 281
  and legal float, 281–82
  performance of, 261, 372–78
  SIPC insurance for, 283
  for small business, 284, 285
  yearly fees for, 283–84
Attitude money, 20% as, 276–77
Attorneys, 358, 360
  for irrevocable trust, 155
Auctions, and tax lien certificates, 362–64